ON CHRISTIAN THEOLOGY

Challenges in Contemporary Theology

Series Editors: Gareth Jones and Lewis Ayres
University of Birmingham and Trinity College, Dublin

Challenges in Contemporary Theology is a series aimed at producing clear orientations in, and research on, areas of 'challenge' in contemporary theology. These carefully co-ordinated books engage traditional theological concerns with mainstreams in modern thought and culture that challenge those concerns. The 'challenges' implied are to be understood in two senses: those presented by society to contemporary theology, and those posed by theology to society.

Already published

These Three Are One
David S. Cunningham

After Writing
Catherine Pickstock

Mystical Theology
Mark A. McIntosh

Engaging Scripture
Stephen E. Fowl

Torture and Eucharist
William T. Cavanaugh

Sexuality and the Christian Body
Eugene F. Rogers, Jr

On Christian Theology
Rowan Williams

Forthcoming

Alien Sex: The Body and Desire in Cinema and Theology
Gerard Loughlin

ON CHRISTIAN THEOLOGY

Rowan Williams

Blackwell
Publishing

BLACKWELL PUBLISHING
350 Main Street, Malden, MA 02148-5020, USA
9600 Garsington Road, Oxford OX4 2DQ, UK
550 Swanston Street, Carlton, Victoria 3053, Australia

First published 2000

13   2007

Library of Congress Cataloging-in-Publication Data

Williams, Rowan, 1950–
    On Christian theology/Rowan Williams.
        p.   cm. – (Challenges in contemporary theology)
    Includes bibliographical references and index.
    1. Theology, Doctrinal. I. Title. II. Series.
    BT75.2.W544 1999
    230–dc21   99–36585
                                                    CIP

ISBN: 978-0-631-21439-7 (hbk.: alk. paper) – ISBN: 978-0-631-21440-3 (pbk.: alk. paper)

A catalogue record for this title is available from the British Library.

Set in 10.5 on 12.5pt Bembo
by Ace Filmsetting Ltd, Frome, Somerset

The publisher's policy is to use permanent paper from mills that operate a sustainable
forestry policy, and which has been manufactured from pulp processed using
acid-free and elementary chlorine-free practices. Furthermore, the publisher ensures
that the text paper and cover board used have met acceptable environmental
accreditation standards.

For further information on
Blackwell Publishing, visit our website:
www.blackwellpublishing.com

For Jane

CONTENTS

ACKNOWLEDGEMENTS

The essays in this volume first appeared as follows:

'Theological Integrity' in *New Blackfriars*, March 1991 (pp. 140–51); also in *Cross Currents*, Fall 1995 (pp. 312–25).

'The Unity of Christian Truth' in *New Blackfriars*, February 1989 (pp. 85–95).

'The Judgement of the World' as 'Postmodern Theology and the Judgment of the World' in *Postmodern Theology. Christian Faith in a Pluralist World*, ed. F. B. Burnham, HarperCollins, San Francisco, 1989 (pp. 92–112).

'The Discipline of Scripture' as 'Der Literalsinn der Heiligen Schrift' in *Evangelische Theologie* 50, 1990 (pp. 55–71) and 'The Literal Sense of Scripture' in *Modern Theology* 7:2, 1991 (pp. 121–34).

'On Being Creatures', the fourth Eric Symes Abbott Memorial Lecture, 1989, printed as a pamphlet for Westminster Abbey.

'Beginning with the Incarnation' as 'The Incarnation as the Basis of Dogma' in *The Religion of the Incarnation. Anglican Essays in Commemoration of Lux Mundi*, ed. Robert Morgan, Bristol Classical Press, 1989 (pp. 85–98).

'The Finality of Christ' in *Christology and Religious Pluralism*, ed. Mary Kelly, the Sisters of Our Lady of Sion, London, (privately published) 1990 (pp. 21–38).

'Word and Spirit' as 'Wort und Geist' in *Das Religiöse Bewusstsein und der Heilige Geist in der Kirche* (*Beiheft zur Ökumenischen Rundschau* 40), ed. Klaus Kremkau, Verlag Otto Lembeck, Frankfurt am Main, 1980 (pp. 77–94).

'Trinity and Revelation' in *Modern Theology* 2:3, 1986 (pp. 197–212).

'Trinity and Ontology' in *Christ, Ethics and Tragedy. Essays in Honour of Donald MacKinnon*, ed. Kenneth Surin, Cambridge University Press, 1989 (pp. 71–92).

'Trinity and Pluralism' in *Christian Uniqueness Reconsidered. The Myth of a Pluralistic Theology of Religions*, ed. Gavin D'Costa, © Orbis Books, Maryknoll, NY, 1990 (pp. 3–15). By permission of Orbis Books.

'Between the Cherubim: the Empty Tomb and the Empty Throne' in *Resurrection Reconsidered*, ed. Gavin D'Costa, Oneworld Publications, Oxford, 1996 (pp. 87–101).

'The Nature of a Sacrament' in *Signs of Faith, Hope and Love. The Christian Sacraments Today*, ed. John Greenhalgh and Elizabeth Russell, London, 1987 (pp. 32–44). By permission of St Mary's, Bourne Street.

'Sacraments of the New Society' in *Christ: The Sacramental Word*, ed. David Brown and Ann Loades, SPCK, London, 1996 (pp. 89–102).

'Incarnation and the Renewal of Community' as 'Incarnation and Social Vision – a New Look at an Old Theme', the Gore Lecture for 1989, in *Theology Wales*, Winter 1998 (pp. 24–40).

'Interiority and Epiphany: a Reading in New Testament Ethics' in *Modern Theology* 13:1 (= *Spirituality and Social Embodiment*, ed. L. Gregory Jones and James J. Buckley, Oxford, 1997) (pp. 29–51); sections 1–3 also as 'Ethik und Rechtfertigung' in *Rechtfertigung und Erfahrung*, ed. M. Beintker, E. Maurer, H. Stoevesandt and H. G. Ulrich, Christian Kaiser Verlag, Gütersloh, 1995 (pp. 311–27).

'Resurrection and Peace' in *Theology*, November 1989 (pp. 481–90); also in *Readings in Modern Theology*, ed. Robin Gill, SPCK, London, 1995 (pp. 306–16).

' "Nobody Knows Who I Am Till the Judgement Morning" ' in *Trevor Huddleston. Essays on his Life and Work*, ed. Deborah Duncan Honoré, Oxford, 1988 (pp. 135–51). By permission of Oxford University Press.

Every effort has been made to trace copyright holders. The author and publishers gratefully acknowledge the copyright holders for permission to reproduce copyright material, and apologize in advance for any inadvertent use of copyright material.

PREFACE

The suggestion that some kind of collection of scattered pieces such as the following might be a good idea came from several friends and former pupils (exasperated by the labours of trawling for obscure journals). I wish to record my great gratitude to them for their interest, their enthusiasm and their role again and again in shaping my thinking. Special thanks to Lewis Ayres, Gareth Jones and Linda Woodhead; and to Alex Wright at Blackwell for his unfailing support and help. Many of these pieces bear the imprint of conversations over many years with Nicholas Lash, John Milbank, Stephen Sykes and Maurice Wiles, all of whom disagree with each other as much as with me on many things, but all of whom have been generous friends in the household of faith. Elisabeth Koenig of the General Theological Seminary, New York, has done sterling work in listing things I have published (and reading them sympathetically), and I hope this book will ease some of her bibliographical struggles. My wife Jane remains my dearest friend and favourite theological interlocutor, constantly challenging and clarifying my thoughts. To her and the children I must say far more than just thanks.

Newport
Feast of St Thomas Aquinas, 1999

PROLOGUE

'What is your methodological starting point?' I remember being thus challenged on the first occasion of my delivering a lecture in a German university. It may be thought by insular souls to be a peculiarly Germanic question; British theologians are a good deal more inclined to begin haphazardly and let the methodology look after itself. But the challenge is a serious and necessary one, and, in introducing these essays, I feel some obligation to sketch a response, even if it is unlikely to be much more satisfactory than the stumbling remarks I recall making to my colleague in Bonn.

I assume that the theologian *is* always beginning in the middle of things. There is a practice of common life and language already there, a practice that defines a specific shared way of interpreting human life as lived in relation to God. The meanings of the word 'God' are to be discovered by watching what this community does – not only when it is consciously reflecting in conceptual ways, but when it is acting, educating or 'inducting', imagining and worshipping. The theologian emerges as a distinct and identifiable figure when these meanings have become entangled with one another, when there is a felt tension between images or practices, when a shape has to be drawn out so that the community's practice can be effectively communicated. But this does not mean that theologians do not exist prior to such moments. A person shaping their life in a specific way, seeking discipline and consistency in relation to God, is theologizing, forming a reflectively consistent speech for God. The believing artist or the liturgist or hymnographer is likewise engaged in a theological task. But it is likely to be only in crisis that people emerge who see their essential job as pushing forward the considerations of coherence and transparency that are already at work in more 'informal' ways. And of course, when this happens, the possibilities of crisis are actually multiplied: when you try to tidy up an unsystematized speech, you are likely to lose a great deal. What the early Church condemned as heresy was commonly a tidy version of its language, in which the losses were adjudged too severe for comfort – or rather (since 'comfort' can't be quite the right word here), in which the losses were adjudged to distort or to limit the range of reference of religious speech. The question would arise of whether the same God was still being spoken of; or whether a new version of the believing community's speech allowed as much to be said as an older version.

In various ways, these are still the issues that surround the proper role of theology in the Church. It may not quite be true that – as some radical contemporary theologians would insist – a real theologian is always a 'heretic' because that is implicit in creative religious thinking; but the risk of conceptual conflict is certainly increased when theology comes to its visible and public expression. This is one reason for the deep suspicion with which churches habitually regard theologians. However, this suspicion overlooks the precon-scious reflection, the ordering of experience, that is constantly going on in the Church, the 'informal' theology of prayer, art and holy action. It's no use pretending that there is a real and recognizable religious practice that does not include this – just as it's no use pretending that there is a reading of the Bible that is free of selection and interpretation. And what is more, from the other end, so to speak, the would-be professional theologian can so understand his or her task as to forget their practical and historical rootedness in the informal theologizing of the community as it develops.

With all this in mind, I propose a typology of theological activity that allows for some clarity about appropriate methods but does not embargo the delivery of believing utterances until the methodology is wholly clear. This typology owes something to Schleiermacher's in *The Christian Faith*, where he distinguishes between the poetic, the rhetorical and the scientific or 'descrip-tively didactic'. I believe we need three such categories; but I think we need to be clearer about their *interaction* than Schleiermacher seems to be, and clearer about denying that they represent an advance towards an ideal form of fully self-conscious reflection. So I shall suggest a threefold division into *celebratory*, *communicative* and *critical* styles.

Theology begins as a *celebratory* phenomenon, an attempt to draw out and display connections of thought and image so as to exhibit the fullest possible range of significance in the language used. It is typically the language of hymnody and preaching, as we hear it in the Church's early centuries – in the Odes of Solomon or the poetry of Ephrem Syrus, in festal homilies and certain kinds of scriptural commentary. But you could equally well identify it in Dante or Langland, in the conventions of Byzantine iconography and of the more intelligent modern choruses. Eastern Orthodox theology still tends to operate in this mode predominantly; but quite a lot of the work of a sophisticated Western theologian such as Hans Urs von Balthasar might be characterized as essentially 'celebratory', in the sense that his intention is less to argue than to evoke a fullness of vision – that 'glory' around which his theology circles so consistently. Not that he fails to argue, or that he gives us nothing but impressionistic sketches; there is an *appropriate* rigour to this enterprise that will be familiar to anyone who knows anything about the composition of poetry or the attempt to find a proper aesthetic congruence in creative work.

The problem comes when that congruence becomes so densely worked that the language is in danger of being sealed in on itself. The cross-referencing of images and patterns, in more and more intricate ways, the displaying of an ever-more complex texture to the language of belief, will risk 'freezing' the reflective process and denying it the possibility of actively illuminating and modifying the concrete historical discourses of its environment, and of being renewed and extended by them. Theology seeks also to persuade or commend, to witness to the gospel's capacity for being at home in more than one cultural environment, and to display enough confidence to believe that this gospel can be rediscovered at the end of a long and exotic detour through strange idioms and structures of thought. This is what I mean by the '*communicative*': a theology experimenting with the rhetoric of its uncommitted environment. Once again, the early Church furnishes examples of this in the colonizing of Stoic and Platonic territory by the Apologists or Clement and Origen; but the same process is at work in 'The Dream of the Rood' in the strange transformation of the crucifixion narrative into the conventions of Teutonic hero-lays; or – most spectacularly – in the scholastic appropriation not only of Aristotle but of Aristotle mediated by Jewish and Muslim commentators. More recently, the use of Marxist categories in liberation theology tells a similar story, as do contemporary essays in the theological reading of feminist theory (Irigaray and Kristeva, as read by a Sarah Coakley or a Graham Ward). The assumption is that this or that intellectual idiom not only offers a way into fruitful conversation with the current environment but also that the unfamiliar idiom may uncover aspects of the deposit of belief hitherto unexamined. In fact, it involves a considerable act of trust in the theological tradition, a confidence that the fundamental categories of belief are robust enough to survive the drastic experience of immersion in other ways of constructing and construing the world.

But there can come a point here where the passage through unfamiliar media of thought provokes a degree of crisis: is what is emerging actually identical or at least continuous with what has been believed and articulated? This is a question that prompts further probing of what the 'fundamental categories' really mean. Is there a stable conceptual area in the discourse of belief that will always remain unaffected by mediation in other idioms? And, if not, what, if any, kind of continuity and coherence belongs to this discourse? This nagging at fundamental meanings is what constitutes a *critical* theology, alert to its own inner tensions or irresolutions. Already in the early Church, we find the apophatic tradition developing alongside the elaborations of doctrinal formulae: Pseudo-Dionysius is careful to deny that, for example, the apparent ascription of number to the divine subsistents places those subsistents in any kind of set of objects. They are neither three nor one 'in our sense of the words'. Negative theology remains one of the most basic forms of critical theology, sometimes doing no more than sounding a warning note against the idea that we could secure a firm grip upon definitions of the divine. But it is probably in the philosophical theology of Western modernity that this element comes into its own – whether through something like Hegel's dissolution and reformation of theological categories, or the relativizing of particular theological formulations in the light of a recognition of religious pluralism (as in the work of John Hick), or in the varieties of postmodern theology lately so abundant, or in the older debates from the 1950s and 1960s about the intelligibility of religious discourse, or in the methodological and typological essays of the Yale school (Hans Frei, George Lindbeck, David Kelsey).

Critical theology (which, as these examples illustrate, may be as easily conservative as revisionist) may move in one of two ultimate directions. The critical impulse may issue in agnosticism, even nihilism; it may issue in the 'atheous' theologies of Don Cupitt or Mark C. Taylor; it may more prosaically at least prompt a fairly thoroughgoing revaluation of dogmatic language (Maurice Wiles or, more radically, Gordon Kaufmann). On the other hand, it may move towards a rediscovery of the celebratory by hinting at the gratuitous mysteriousness of what theology deals with, the sense of a language trying unsuccessfully to keep up with a datum that is in excess of any foresight, any imagined comprehensive structure. And the cycle begins again.

I do not mean to suggest that whole theologies really fall under one or the other style. But the sense of what David Tracy has taught us to call a 'public' in theology unmistakably shapes the priorities and methods of theologians. It is legitimate in the celebratory mode to imagine a believing public and to employ methods of internal elaboration of themes, refinement of imaginative patterns, and so on, without too much attention to 'critical' – category three – issues of conceptual clarity. The communicative style may draw on a less rich native vocabulary than category one makes available, because it assumes a public to whom that vocabulary is basically strange. The critical theologian should not be deflected by considerations of conventional piety from challenging and testing the language of celebration, or even the language of communication when this latter takes for granted a stable and unproblematic native tongue, never unsettled by the enterprise of translation. But to try and arrange these in some kind of hierarchy, to regard one as the true paradigm or the goal to which the others aspire, is a serious misunderstanding of the way in which theology works. It has a mobility to it that involves recognition of the weakness of any one mode in isolation; and it points to an essential restlessness in the enterprise of Christian utterance that reflects the eschatological impulse at its heart, the acknowledgement that the events of Jesus' life and death open up schisms in any kind of language, any attempt to picture the world as immanently orderly or finished.

Some of these sketchy observations are elaborated in what follows. I present this typology of theological voices in part to explain why the 'register' of some of these chapters is a bit unstable in ways which I hope will make sense in the light of this conviction about the mobility of the discourse. There are essays here that I should describe as primarily critical, others that are more biased towards the celebratory, and a few that have elements of the communicative or rhetorical moment. Several, I suspect, may be hard to classify (so they seem to me). And I have deliberately kept in some texts that are without footnotes or other learned apparatus because I believe they crystallize points made or adumbrated in more technical discussions, and thus illustrate a little of the movement from register to register, or public to public, that is part of the experience of many theologians, perhaps especially those, like myself, with responsibilities outside the academy. The danger of self-indulgent rambling is painfully real where there is such a diversity of style or mode or 'voice'; what is always hard is to find the right kind of rigour for each, because it is not the case (as remarked above) that the differences between these styles are differences between careful and carefree (or careless) talking. How far the risk has been avoided in what follows the reader will judge; but I hope the reader will bear in mind an underlying aim in these pages – to *display* modes of arguing and interpreting rather than to advance a single system. If – to anticipate the first chapter – there is such a thing as theological integrity, it is not to be reduced to insistence upon a monolithic and supposedly scientific mode of engagement with the material. Finally, the continuities or unities lie in a more elusive place; something to do with the coherence of a biography. If that implies that incoherence here is also an index of lived incoherence, that is an uncomfortably plausible connection: a reminder of the inescapable place of repentance in all theological speech worth the name.

Part One

DEFINING THE ENTERPRISE

Chapter One

THEOLOGICAL
INTEGRITY

I

What makes us say of any discourse that it has or that it lacks 'integrity'?
Usually we can answer this in terms of whether such a discourse is really
talking about what it *says* it is talking about. This is not necessarily to make
a pronouncement on the integrity or otherwise of this or that speaker, who
may or may not know that the discourse serves a purpose other than what it
professes. It would be quite in order to say – as a Marxist might – that
eighteenth-century aesthetics was an integral part of the ideology of bourgeois cultural dominance, that what determined its judgements and strategies was a particular pattern of economic relations, without thereby saying
that Johnson or Hawksmoor was a liar, or that Bach did not 'mean' it when
he wrote *ad maiorem Dei gloriam* at the head of his compositions. Somebody
perpetuating such an aesthetic today, when we know (according to the
Marxist) so much about its real determinants, would be dishonest: they could
not mean what an eighteenth-century speaker meant because they know
what that speaker (on the charitable interpretation) did not – the objective
direction, the *interest* in fact served by the discourse. The discourse is without integrity because it conceals its true agenda; knowing that concealment
robs us of our innocence, the 'innocence' of the original speaker; for we
know too that speech cannot be content with concealment.

Why is it so important that speech should not conceal its purposes? Discourse that conceals is discourse that (consciously or not) sets out to foreclose the possibility of a genuine response. By operating on two levels, one
acknowledged and one not, it presents to the hearer a set of positions and
arguments other than those that are finally determinative of its working.
Thus the repudiation or refutation of the surface position leaves the body of
the discourse untouched, since it will not engage the essential agenda. A

two-level discourse is one which steps back from the risks of *conversation* – above all from those two essential features of conversation, the recognition of an 'unfinished' quality in what has been said on either side, and the possibility of correction. During the years of the Second Vatican Council, a journalist reporting the views of various members of the British hierarchy on artificial contraception noted that some bishops argued against it by appealing to the supposed feelings of the 'ordinary man' (*sic*) or to the opposition expressed by secular writers such as Orwell; the journalist wryly observed that these points were equally irrelevant to the issue and to what had been going on in the bishops' heads when they made up their minds. This irrelevance is precisely the retreat from conversation implicit in the concealment of purpose.

Such a lack of integrity in speech is manifestly a *political* matter. To make what is said invulnerable by displacing its real subject matter is a strategy for the retention of power. It can operate at either end of the social scale: in the language of those in control, which will be essentially *about* the right to control, and in the language of the powerless in the presence of the powerful, which takes on the images and definitions offered by the latter as the only possible means of access to their world, their resources. Of course, there are times when this becomes a deliberately ironic (and thus subversive) move on the part of the powerless, but it remains, as *discourse,* without integrity: it is still talking *about*, and negotiating its way in, the power relations that prevail, whatever it claims to be saying.

A hasty clarification may be in order. It is important not to see all this in a naively reductionist way, as if what was concretely being said was arbitrary, indifferent, systematically divorced from any sort of truth-telling. Potentially truthful forms of speech can be used as tools of control and can equally be detached from such uses. If it is possible to see and to argue with a real structure of thought in a discourse, this separates it from any crassly ideological bondage. Only if there is no such coherent structure is one dealing with pure ideology (in the sense of a language that is *fundamentally* preoccupied with power and completely successful in concealing this fact). Thus the validity of Marxist argumentation is not to be settled simply by pointing to its ideological use as a tool of this or that Communist bureaucracy; nor that of Freudian theory by pointing to the patterns of economic and professional power in the world of psychoanalytic practice, or the depoliticizing effects of psychoanalytic rhetoric in certain contexts – and so on. Integrity *can* be recovered by such schemata to the extent that they show themselves capable of conversation. To believe otherwise is to hold a philosophically rather crude view of the determination of theories by their deployment.

Having integrity, then, is being able to speak in a way which allows of answers. Honest discourse permits response and continuation; it invites collaboration by showing that it does not claim to be, in and of itself, final. It does not seek to prescribe the tone, the direction, or even the vocabulary of a response. And it does all this by showing in its own working a critical self-perception, displaying the axioms to which it believes itself accountable; that is to say, it makes it clear that it accepts, even within its own terms of reference, that there are ways in which it may be questioned and criticized. It is a skill that may be learned rather than a system to be accepted. It sets out a possible framework for talk and perception, a field for debate, and so a field for its own future transmutations. When it resists debate and transmutation, claiming that it may prescribe exactly what the learning of its skills should lead to, it is open to the suspicion that its workings are no longer answerable to what they claim to answer to: the further determinant has been added of the need to safeguard the power that licenses this kind of talk; and thus integrity disappears.

Religious talk is in an odd position here. On the one hand, it is making claims about the context of the whole moral universe, claims of crucial concern for the right leading of human life; it is thus not likely, *prima facie*, to be content with provisional statements. On the other hand, if it really purports to be about the context of the moral universe, it declares itself to be uniquely 'under judgement', and to be dealing with what supremely *resists* the urge to finish and close what is being said. How is the context of the moral universe to appear in our speech without distortion? If it is represented as something whose operations have been securely or finally charted and whose authority can be straightforwardly invoked by this or that group of speakers, what is in fact happening is that such a discourse is claiming to define 'the moral universe' itself. Yet all speakers speak from a perspective, social and historical, and their words are *part* of the universe they claim to see as a whole. Since that is so, it will be right to suspect that the claim to understand and to speak for the global context of your own speaking is essentially a claim to power and a prohibition of free response and continuation. So it looks as though religious discourse is doomed to continual betrayals of its own integrity, making claims that actually subvert themselves, that cannot but display their own 'ideological' character. To understand what religious language is doing is indeed, in this perspective, to become incapable of believing it. To appeal to a total perspective is to betray the dominative interest at work in what you are saying, for there can be no conversation with a total perspective. And if what cannot be answered (or rather, cannot be conversed with) cannot honestly be said in the first place – because it will be a statement about the speaker's power, not about what the speaker claims to be talking about – it seems as though integrity in religious discourse is unrealizable.

This is very nearly true, and it is essential for anyone wanting to talk theology to know it. If there is a reply to be made (if, that is, this account is not to become itself in turn a totalizing ideological proscription of religious language), it must be in part through a probing of the notions of 'total perspective' and the 'moral universe', and in part through the tracing of how various traditions of religious speech and practice concretely and consciously deal with the central tension.

We swiftly assume that to talk about a 'moral universe' is to be able to set out a system of connections in our behaviour, locating every kind of moral determination in a comprehensive pattern that will show its status and significance. A systematic secular account of this, such as early Freudianism, offers to interpret appearances, to reveal their inner logic, the 'script' they are enacting. Religious accounts, supposedly, relate that interpretation to a context over and above the sum total of worldly interactions: their 'script' is the will of God. But in practice, both secular and religious attempts to speak of a moral universe commonly work as *strategies* for responding consistently and intelligibly to the world's complexity rather than as exhaustive interpretations; which suggests that we can read the religious account as claiming that it is in learning to respond to our ultimate origins and 'calling' that we learn to respond truthfully or adequately to the world. To say that a religious discourse is 'about' the whole moral universe may be simply to say that it offers a sufficient imaginative resource for confronting the entire range of human complexity without evasion or untruthfulness; only when divorced from this context of a kind of imaginative skill does religious discourse fall into the trap of pretending to be a comprehensive system for plotting, connecting, 'fixing' and exhaustively accounting for the range of human behaviour. In other words, religious and theological integrity is possible as and when discourse about God *declines the attempt to take God's point of view* (i.e. a 'total perspective').

But how then does it establish itself as dealing with the wholeness of the moral universe? How does it talk of God as context and origin without slipping into the 'total perspective' mode? Only, I suggest, by showing *in* its workings what is involved in bringing the complexity of its human world to judgement before God; not by seeking to articulate or to complete that judgement. A religious discourse with some chance of being honest will not move too far from the particular, with all its irresolution and resistance to systematizing: it will be trying to give shape to that response to the particular that is least evasive of its solid historical otherness *and* that is also rooted in the conviction that God is to be sought and listened for in all occasions. For the Christian tradition, as for the Jewish, this means that depicting the wholeness or unity of the moral universe, or the world as a moral unity, is bound up with depicting histories of truthful response to the world – a 'wholeness' of perception and action, in which the resourcefulness of the discourse in enabling unillusioned vision is concretely set out. Christian reflection takes as normative a story of response to God in the world and the world in God, the record of Israel and Jesus. In that record, what is shown is the way in which imperfect, distorting responses to God so consistently generate their own re-formation, as they seek to conform to the reality of what it is and was that called them forth, that they finally issue in a response wholly transparent to the reality of the calling; and this culminating response creates a frame of reference, a grammar of human possibilities, believed to be of unrestricted significance, an accessible resource for conversion or transformation in any human circumstance. It generates the willingness to repeat the story to the ends of the earth, as the unifying shape of a life wholly given to God. 'The world as a moral unity' means here 'the world as capable of finding community in the shared likeness of Jesus' response to God'.

The biblical record does not consist only of narrative – or, rather, it is the *kind* of narrative it is (in other words, a story of the re-formation of human responses to God) because it weaves together history and liturgy: the God perceived in the life of Israel is constantly addressed as well as talked *about*. The same interweaving can be observed, more dramatically, in Augustine's *Confessions*, and works in the same way. The language of worship ascribes supreme value, supreme resource or power, to something other than the worshipper, so that liturgy attempts to be a 'giving over' of our words to God (as opposed to speaking in a way that seeks to retain distance or control over what's being spoken of: it is in this sense that good liturgy does what good poetry does). This is not to say that the language of worship itself cannot be starkly and effectively ideological; but where we find a developing and imaginative liturgical idiom operating in a community that is itself constantly re-imagining itself and its past, we may recognize that worship is at some level doing its job. That is what the overall canonical structure of Jewish Scripture puts before the reader; and, insofar as the New Testament portrays the life, death and resurrection of Jesus as something which opens up an unprecedently direct and undistorted language for prayer, praise, 'sacrifice', and so on, it is to be read as reinforcing the same point. The integrity of a community's language about God, the degree to which it escapes its own pressures to power and closure, is tied to the integrity of the language it directs *to* God.

II

Language about God is kept honest in the degree to which it turns on itself in the name of God, and so surrenders itself to God: it is in this way that it becomes possible to see how it is still *God* that is being spoken of, that which makes the human world a moral unity. Speaking of God is speaking to God and opening our speech to God's; and it is speaking *of* those who have spoken to God and who have thus begun to form the human community, the unrestricted fellowship of holiness, that is the only kind of universal meaning possible without the tyranny of a 'total perspective'.

How, then, is our language surrendered, given to God? The first and most obvious category in our language that speaks of this is *repentance*. To admit failure before God is for speech to show the judgement of God – or rather, exposure to the judgement of God – in the simplest of ways. But given this rather banal observation, we can, on the basis of what has so far been said, generalize the point. Religious discourse must articulate and confront its own temptations, its own falsehoods. It is, in other words, essential to theology that theologians become aware of how theology has worked and continues to work in the interests of this or that system of power. To acquire such awareness is neither to dismiss theological utterances clouded with this particular kind of ambiguity as worthless, nor to entertain the fancy that there could be a theological discourse with no trace of 'interest'. Nor is it an undifferentiated repudiation of power as such, but simply the recognition that not all power articulated in theological language attempts either transparency to God's power (God's endless resource and accessibility) or the *giving* of power to those addressed (the resource of God offered for liberation or renewal). Theology has to study its own workings, not in narcissism but in penitence. It is one reason why it is more than ever vital to have what we so often lack at the moment, a theological view of the Church's history. New theologies constructed by what was the invisible underclass of earlier generations (women, the developing world) have plundered the Egyptian storehouses of sociology and psychology, often without discrimination, to identify the interests in which our discourse has worked. This task needs constantly to be renewed in a properly *theological* idiom, if it is not to become a new ideological bondage: the critique thus developed has to be related afresh to the fundamental story of belief, rather than staying at the level of reductionist secular suspicion, however crucial a tool this is in alerting us to the problem.

But there is a further dimension, less obvious but perhaps more practically significant. One of the temptations of theology has been – at least in the modern era – to suppose not so much that there is a normative content for theological utterance, but that there is a normative *style*. This is, of course, a version of discourse about power: in proper reaction to what can look like self-indulgent or uncritical devotional and liturgical language, theologians can fall into the assumption that the mode of critical austerity in their utterances is something to which other people's speech should conform; or else, faced with a plurality of ambiguous utterances, the theologian seeks prescriptively to re- duce the disturbingly wide range of meanings and resonances that exist in the more 'primary' religious talk of story and hymnody. In either case, the theo- logian risks breaking off one of the most crucial conversations he or she is likely to be involved in, conversation with an idiom *deliberately* less controlled, more concerned with evocation and suggestion. The theologian needs to affirm theologically the propriety of different styles, and to maintain exchange and mutual critique between them. The repentance of theological discourse can be shown in the readiness of any particular version of it to put in question not only this or that specific conclusion within its own workings, but the adequacy or appropriateness of its whole idiom. This is again, perhaps, to look to the plurality of style and genre in Scripture as a model of the collaborative enterprise that speaking of God *can* be.

Here we begin to move into a second area of reflection on 'giving our language to God'. Bible and liturgy use the metaphor of the 'sacrifice of praise'; as if the language of ascribing worth, beauty and desirability to God represented some sort of *cost* to us. So it does: praise is nothing if not the struggle to voice how the directedness of my regard depends on, is moulded by, something irreducibly other than itself. It is my speech seeking to trans- mute into its own substance something on whose radical difference that very substance depends; so that it must on no account *absorb* it into itself, as that would be to lose the object's generative power. The transmutation is a re- forming of the language, not the disappearance of the praised object into existing patterns of words, foreordained responses. It is, as David Jones said of all art that is in any sense representation, a 'showing forth under another form'; and for this to be serious, it entails some sense at some stage of loss of control, unclarity of focus. A celebratory work that simply uses a repertoire of stock techniques that direct our attention not to what is being celebrated but to the smooth and finished quality of its own surface is a failure. So with the language of praise for God: it needs to do its proper work, to articulate the sense of answering to a reality not already embedded in the conventions of speech; to show the *novum* of God's action in respect of any pre-existing human idiom.

There are several ways in which this may happen – glossolalia as a language of praise is one clear instance. But in the articulate literature of praise, the evocation and celebration of a natural order that has no immediate 'relevance' to the human is a central aspect of address to God. This is what is at work in certain strands of the Wisdom tradition of Jewish Scripture, and is most sharply and paradoxically expressed in the 'anti-Wisdom' of Job 38–41, in which the inaccessibility of the world's order and the arbitrariness of creation ('God hath deprived her [the ostrich] of wisdom', Job 39.17), the otherness of the material world ('Doth the hawk fly by thy wisdom?', Job 39.26), locates the language of praise in the context of what it cannot absorb or exhaust. The 'irrationality' of the world becomes the raw material for words about God, not as an explanatory device but precisely as a final context.

More specifically, praise in the Judaeo-Christian tradition looks to the saving presence of God, in those events that are understood as forming the particular historical difference of the tradition – the events we call 'revelatory'. The Christian sacrifice of praise is, above all, the Eucharistic recapitulation of Jesus' passion and resurrection, and the act that introduces believers into the whole process of praising God is likewise an enactment of the paschal event. In both these sacraments, words and actions are given over to be moulded to the shape of a movement in history, so that the time in which we speak is taken up in the time of 'God's action'. Here the action of praise necessarily involves evoking a moment of dispossession, of death, in order to bring the *novum* of God into focus: baptism speaks (though conventional Western versions of its symbolism obscure this) of a loss, of a disappearance, of a submerging of identity; the Eucharist – apart from its actual penitential episodes – identifies the worshippers with the unfaithful apostles at table with Jesus, and enacts (again in muted and barely visible form in much of our liturgical practice) a breaking which is seen as signifying the 'cost' to God of our restoration to wholeness, and so, obliquely, the moment of our own loss of God (the loss of a God whose power answers to our perceived needs and definitions).

The praise of God is thus not a matter simply of euphoric fluency; because of its attempt to speak to and of the reality of God and not simply to collapse back upon itself as a mere articulation of religious emotion, it involves 'the labour, the patience and the pain of the negative', a dispossession in respect of what is easily available for religious language. This dispossession is, at its simplest, the suspension of the ordinary categories of 'rational' speech; at a more pervasive level, it is a dispossession of the human mind conceived as central to the order of the world, and a dispossession of the entire identity that exists prior to the paschal drama, the identity that has not seen and named its self-deception and self-destructiveness. In praise, God is truthfully spoken of by learning to speak of the world in a certain way, and of the self in a certain way; by giving over what is said to the pattern of creation and redemption, a pattern moving through loss and disorder to life.

To use a word like 'dispossession' is to evoke the most radical level of prayer, that of simple waiting on God, contemplation. This is a complex area: let me venture some dogmatic assertions. Contemplation in its more intense forms is associated with *apophasis*, the acknowledgement of the inadequacy of any form, verbal, visual or gestural, to picture God definitively, to finish the business of religious speech (the acknowledgement that is at work in praise as well), and the expression of this recognition in silence and attention. Contemplation is a giving place to the prior actuality of God in what is misleadingly called 'passivity': misleadingly, because it is not a matter of suspending all creaturely activity (as if that were possible) in pure attention to the divine void.

The classical literature on this, above all the great Carmelite doctors, but to some extent the early Jesuits as well, envisages a process which *begins* with drastic interruptions of 'ordinary' speech and action, conscious policies of asceticism or detachment, sometimes issuing in what might well have to be called temporary pathological states, periods of suspension of the ordinary habitual workings of mind or body. There is a *strategy* of dispossession, suspicion of our accustomed ways of mastering our environment: a search for prayer beyond deliberate and ordered meditation, the expectation of failure in coping with the 'truths of faith' when trying to use them for the stirring of devotion, essays in physical privation or isolation, scepticism or hostility towards internal and external props of devotion (pious sensations or edifying images). In conjuction with such a strategy, we may of course expect a measure of emotional strain or disturbance, profound and even frightening depressive symptoms. All this is preliminary (most misunderstandings of St John of the Cross arise from a failure to notice this, with the consequent complaint that nature and grace are being set in opposition). The fruition of the process is the discovery that one's selfhood and value simply lie in the abiding faithful presence of God, not in any moral or conceptual performance; which is a radical affirmation of the *goodness* of nature. For St Teresa, this is the discovery of the King in the central chamber of the 'interior castle'; for St John of the Cross, more subtly, it is the simplification of the three 'faculties of the soul', the three components of conscious, intentional life – memory, understanding and will – into the three theological virtues – hope, faith and love.

For both, the state of 'union' to which the entire process moves is one in which 'God' has *ceased* to be the interruption of our earthly action, because the self acts out of an habitual diffused awareness that its centre is God. The self is *fully* conscious (even if only at a rather elusive level) that it is the object of an unchanging creative love, conscious that for it to be itself is for it to be dependent on God's presence at its root or centre. To act from its centre *is* to give God freedom in the world, to do the works of God. The self, we could say, has attained integrity: the inner and the outer are no longer in tension; I act what I am, a creature called to freedom, and leave behind those attempts at self-creation which in fact destroy my freedom. As Teresa puts it, Martha and Mary unite: truthful, active and constructive love issues from and leads into patience and silence, or, better, is constantly *contemporary* with patience and silence.

The work done in the dispossession of Christ's cross is finished only in the communicating to human beings of the divine liberty in their fleshly and historical lives – in the shorthand of doctrinal language, the sharing of Jesus' risen life. The contemplative process is ultimately a reconciliation with, not an alienation from, creatureliness, from the life of the body in time: Teresa considered it one of the marks of the unitive state that one no longer wished for death. Contemplation, in other words, is a deeper appropriation of the vulnerability of the self in the midst of the language and transactions of the world; it identifies the real damaging pathologies of human life, our violent obsessions with privilege, control and achievement, as arising from the re-fusal to know and love oneself as a creature, a body. The contemplative is thus a critic of the ideological distortion of language in two ways: negatively, as exposing some of the sources of our fears and obsessions, positively as looking to a fusion of 'inner' and 'outer', or, rather, a dismantling of that dichotomy as normally understood. The self as liberated from the need to be in control of the transactions in which it is involved does not require the subterfuges of escape from direct conversational speech which constitute the erosion of integrity already described.

III

It would be possible to elaborate the point further, looking at other facets of prayer: thanksgiving involves the recognition of oneself as a recipient of un-planned benefits, intercession acknowledges the reality of the need of others and one's own relative powerlessness in respect of their future; both can speak of that displacement or dispossession of perspective that we have dis-cussed in relation to penitence, praise and contemplation. But this is enough to bring into focus the significance of prayer for an honest theology. Prayer of the kind I have been trying to describe is precisely what *resists* the urge of religious language to claim a total perspective: by articulating its own in-completeness before God, it turns away from any claim to human complete-ness. By 'conversing' with God, it preserves conversation between human speakers.

Religious practice is only preserved in any integrity by seriousness about prayer; and so, if theology is the untangling of the real grammar of religious practice, its subject matter is, humanly and specifically, people who pray. If theology is itself a critical, even a suspicious discipline, it is for this reason. It seeks to make sense of the practice of dispossessed language 'before God'. It thus lives with the constant possibility of its own relativizing, interruption, silencing; it will not regard its conclusions as having authority independently of their relation to the critical, penitent community it seeks to help to be itself.

This has some consequences for the way theology conceives its practice. If theology is understood primarily as a 'science' in the common understand-ing of that term, it will assume that its job is to clarify, perhaps to explain; it will seek to establish procedures for arguing and criteria for conclusions; it will be interested in whether or not there are good reasons for saying this or that. For an empirically based science, the only interruptions that matter are those of new phenomena not catered for in previous schemata. But the history of theology does not look very much like what this account might suggest; and, on the basis of what I have been trying to outline, we should not expect it to. There is a rigour and a discipline appropriate to theology, but it is the rigour of keeping on the watch for our constant tendency to claim the 'total perspective': it is almost a rigour directed *against* the naive scientific model. Theology will probe those aspects of religious practice which pull in the direction of ideological distortion, those things which presuppose that there is a mode of religious utterance wholly beyond the risks of con-versation, a power beyond resistance, a perspective that leaves nothing out. It will challenge the fantasy that such things are available to human beings; but it will also challenge the notion that these are the terms in which *God* is to be imagined.

Even if unanswerable power is denied to men and women, ascribing it to God is still to remain under the spell of the same fantasy and to use the myth of absolute power and final speech against the world of historical learning and communion. Theology can remind the world of religious discourse that it offers not a total meaning but the possibility of a perception simplified and unified in and through the contingencies of human biography: not the conquest but the transformation of *mortal* vision. God is there not to supply what is lacking in mortal knowledge or mortal power, but simply as the source, sustainer and end of our mortality. The hope professed by Christians of immortal life cannot be a hope for a non-mortal way of seeing the world; it is rather the trust that what our mortality teaches us of God opens up the possibility of knowing God or seeing God in ways for which we have, by definition, no useful mortal words.

Theology of this sort nags away at the logic of our generative religious stories and rituals, trying to set out both in its speech *and* in its procedures what the logic entails. It will understand doctrinal definition as the attempt to make sure that we are still speaking of *God* in our narratives, not about the transactions of mythological subjects or about the administration of religious power. Theology of this sort does not bring in alien categories for either the defence or the criticism of doctrinal statements, but is willing to learn from non-theological sources something about the mechanisms of deceit and control in language. It is there to test the truthfulness of religious discourse, its fidelity to itself and its openness to what it says it is about; but it does not do this by trying to test the 'truth' of this or that religious utterance according to some canon of supposedly neutral accuracy. Establishing the truth of a religious claim is a matter of discovering its resource and scope for holding together and making sense of our perceptions and transactions without illusion; and that is a task in which the theologian *as* theologian has a role, but not a uniquely privileged one (as if he or she alone were free enough from the heavy clay of piety to see between the words of believers into the life of God).

Theology needs to make connections, to search out and display unities or analogies (good biblical interpretation has always sought to do this), and – borrowing the phrase from Dietrich Ritschl's *Logic of Theology* (London, 1986), – to 'try with overall outlines' (p. 92). But, as Ritschl immediately goes on to say, it should be abidingly conscious of its peril in this regard. It can draw us away from the particularity of real objects in their actuality – real history, real materiality, real pain, seduced by the promise of explanation, of total perspective; and then it is in need of 'prophetic interruption', the showing of its own powerlessness 'by the suffering of a child, the rehearing of a biblical story, the long-neglected perception of the danger of war in our time' (p. 95). Theology can be no more and no less (and not otherwise) 'systematic' than the processes of faith to which it is answerable, and if it is confident of itself in ways divorced from this, it loses its integrity. It can learn again from its foundational language – or from other discourses struggling with how to speak truthfully of a moral universe. 'To give back to theology a tone and atmosphere worthy of its subject matter, to restore resonance to its speech, without empty piety or archaic biblicism, the qualities of venture, slowness, and strain, which mark Heidegger's procedures are required. It is the opposite qualities of safeness, haste and ease which mark most theological discourse today, and that is a measure of its failure to attain the essential.' So says Joseph O'Leary in *Questioning Back: The Overcoming of Metaphysics in Christian Tradition* (Minneapolis, 1985, p. 33). 'Venture, slowness and strain': but we should not romanticize idle inarticulacy or take refuge in the 'ineffable' quality of our subject matter. Talking theologically, talking of how religion avoids becoming the most dramatically empty and power-obsessed discourse imaginable, is necessary and very difficult. It is out to make the discourse of faith and worship both harder and more authoritative (more transparent to its origin). And to do this it needs to know when it has said what it can say and when it is time to shut up.

At the end of Iris Murdoch's *Henry and Cato*, the enigmatic and clever Brendan, priest and scholar, is on his way to India. He explains to Cato, ex-priest and accidental murderer, the tormented centre of the book's world, why he is going.

'I was getting too addicted to speculation. I sometimes felt that if I could hang on just a little longer I would receive some perfect illumination about everything.'

'Why don't you hang on?'

'Because I know that if it did come it would be an illusion – one of the most, oh, splendid. The original *felix culpa* in thought itself.'

'That sounds like despair.'

'The point is, one will never get to the end of it, never get to the bottom of it, never, never. And that never, never, never is what you must take for your hope and shield and your most glorious promise. Everything that we concoct about God is an illusion.'

'But God is not an illusion?'

' "Whosoever he be of you who forsaketh not all that he hath, he cannot be my disciple." '

'I don't believe you've given up theology at all. Theology is magic. Beware.'

'I know.'

'I must go and catch my train to Leeds.'

Chapter Two

THE UNITY OF
CHRISTIAN TRUTH

Theological pluralism has been pressed upon us with increasing enthusiasm over the past twenty years. It has been seen as the only appropriate response to the cultural fragmentation of our world, and also as the discourse from the first.[1] We have been too easily misled, by a harmonizing biblical exegesis on the one hand, and a Denzinger-based version of doctrinal history on the other, into supposing that the articulation of what is believed by Christians to be true about God and the world naturally falls into a pattern of tidily unified correlations. The pendulum has now swung a fair way towards the opposite pole from this. Contemporary New Testament study insists on the sharp conflicts between different strands of primitive Christian understanding and practice,[2] and doctrinal history is more disposed to emphasize contingent, non-theological factors at work in the definition of 'orthodoxy' at various points, with the half-hidden and disturbing inference to be drawn that there may have been no strictly *theological* criteria immediately available to discriminate among varieties of 'Christianity' (if we can indeed go on using the one simple word . . .).[3]

It is not surprising, then, that in one way or another the question is continually raised of the limits of pluralism – or, rather less starkly, of how pluralism

[1]   See David Tracy, *The Analogical Imagination. Christian Theology and Culture of Pluralism* (London, 1981), pp. 448–9, for an observation on this.
[2]   Raymond Brown's work on the distinctive contours of Johannine Christianity should be mentioned; and for an extreme recent example of the emphasis on the diversities of early Christianities, see Burton Mack, *A Myth of Innocence. Mark and Christian Origins* (Philadelphia, 1988), esp. the first section.
[3]   On the various factors at work in determining early Christian orthodoxy, see E. P. Sanders (ed.), *Jewish and Christian Self-Definition*, vol. I: *The Shaping of Christianity in the Second and Third Centuries* (London, 1980), and the volume of essays in honour of Henry Chadwick edited by R. Williams, *The Making of Orthodoxy* (Cambridge, 1989).

avoids becoming 'repressive tolerance',[4] an intellectually idle and morally frivolous prohibition against raising uncomfortable questions about Christian truth. Pluralism as a strategy *can* (though it need not) collude with privatizing, voluntarist versions of belief ('Well, this is what makes sense to *me*'), and so can look like a betrayal of what most Christians would still see as a central affair in their commitment – the conviction that there is a common hope and a common vocation for human beings, such that the welfare or salvation of one section of humanity cannot be imagined as wholly different from or irrelevant to that of the rest of the race (or the rest of the planet, for that matter).

If we *do* believe that this is built in to the way we talk about salvation, we have a good *prima facie* case for saying that not everything and anything is compatible with Christian theology. This ought to be obvious: if there is nothing Christian theology cannot say, there is no way of using the term 'Christian theology' as an intelligible description. The very potent liberal reluctance to say that something is an inadmissible or incomprehensible move in theological talk has, however, sometimes left an impression that such talk is answerable to nothing but this or that theologian's sense of his or her own inner integrity. We need to say that it is, after all, possible to be a bad, silly, or mistaken theologian. (It is when we know what a mistake is – in *any* sort of discourse – that we know we are responsible to something other than individual taste or will; if you want to know what sort of truth-claims a certain discourse is making, ask what, if anything, it means by a mistake and how it identifies it.) But, given this, how do we articulate limits and criteria? 'Christian truth' is an expression pointing to some integrity and coherence in corporate Christian talk and action; how does this claimed integrity and coherence function critically in the concrete processes of that talk and action?

In his recent book on *The Logic of Theology*,[5] Dietrich Ritschl sets out the two main strategies theology has tended to deploy in answering these questions. We can construct 'monothematic' theologies in which unity (and thus critical self-appropriation) is bound to a single focal theme or doctrinal nexus; or we can attempt to list and summarize the topics which a coherent theology ought to deal with, and to display their interdependence (what Ritschl, following classical European convention, calls the *loci* method – the allocation of a *locus* within an overall classificatory scheme to particular and 'partial' themes).

Thus, on the first approach, theological discourse is answerable to a single

[4] See Tracy, *op. cit.*, p. 449, and the final chapter of his more recent *Plurality and Ambiguity. Hermeneutics, Religion, Hope* (London, 1987).
[5] London, 1986.

point of judgement: for Luther, justification by faith alone, for a modern liberation theologian, the hermeneutical privilege of the poor. Two of the theological giants of the century, Barth and Rahner, can both be seen as, in some sense, 'monothematic' in intent – if not always in practice. For Barth, the sovereign liberty of God manifested in the bare fact that speech about God is made possible and authorized in a Godless world, the world where, by definition, God is not – this is the touchstone of theological integrity, the unifying perception. For Rahner, in sharp contrast, the unifying theme is the preconceptual apprehension, underlying human knowing, of the unlimited field in which that knowing operates; and from this anthropological starting-point, a vision of grace and nature, Christology and ecclesiology unfolds with impressive consistency.

The second approach is that of medieval theology – commentaries on the *Sentences* of Peter Lombard, the great *Summae* of the thirteenth century – and of most theology, Protestant and Catholic, from the sixteenth to the nineteenth century. Because twentieth-century essays in this encyclopaedic mode are far more self-conscious than earlier instances about their methodological options, they stand much closer to the monothematic style. Thus the systematic essays of Tillich, Weber, Macquarrie, and comparable writers, or the ambitious project of Pannenberg, are manifestly controlled by the author's decision to adopt organizing principles over and above – say – the shape of the creeds alone, or the traditional order of dogmatic 'treatises'. What still sets them apart from clearly monothematic treatments is the claim to produce a map of the whole territory, displaying an ordered relation between topics, while at the same time allowing these topics a relative autonomy sufficient to justify their treatment as quasi-independent areas of enquiry within an overarching process of reflection.

Ritschl indicates the serious problems faced by both these accounts. 'Monothematic' theologies are all very well so long as they do not set themselves up as exclusive paradigms. History brings necessary shifts in theological perspective, so that what appears urgent and immediate in one context will recede in another. While there may be no way of articulating a theology wholly concerned with matters of 'lasting importance' alone (a theology free from history), the method of theology requires some means of holding open the wider question of what it is that is more than momentary or 'occasional' in theology, what might connect monothematic visions in a critical and fruitful relation to one another. In other words, and going a little beyond Ritschl's terminology, monothematic theology on its own secures unity only in its own immediate context, so that that unity has to be constructed afresh in a different context: and therefore, paradoxically, this kind of approach leads to a plurality of systems with no principles for relating their organizing perspectives, an untrammelled pluralism. Moreover, the monothematic approach may not only encourage 'the formation of closed systems'[6] in a general way, but foster an irreconcilable and illimitable multiplicity of such systems in competition or hostility.

And as for the project of encyclopaedic doctrinal surveys, this, as Ritschl notes, has two major weaknesses. It distorts biblical and traditional discussions by lifting material from its original context to serve a generalized exposition of some isolated theme; and it seeks an essentially illusory permanence, another closed system, incapable of responding to 'prophetic interruption'.[7] Thus, in its claim to do justice to the wholeness of the Christian heritage, this approach erodes the concreteness of that heritage. To quarry Augustine or Calvin for arguments on specific topics, while amputating the historical and polemical setting of those arguments, is to risk a bland homogenization of the past, indeed a refusal to see it *as* the past; and so, in refusing to acknowledge that there is a genuinely 'occasional' aspect to theology, it condemns itself to an abstract generality far from the actual mode in which the tradition took shape.

But if these two most obviously available ways of articulating the unity of Christian claims will not do, are we doomed to a theological world of private taste and non-communicating options about 'style' – a theological mirror of the cultural situation of our age?[8]

Ritschl points out that there are simple intuitive tests we can perform to find out whether we really believe in such a picture: he invites us[9] to consider what would *stop* us from describing certain statements ('Only morally perfect people can become members of the Church', 'One should kill all severely handicapped newborn children', and so on) as correct or even possible moves in Christian talk – which is essentially a form of the question which I touched on earlier, about what counts as a mistake. The process of answering this question uncovers for us 'regulative statements' or 'implicit axioms'[10] at work in our discourse: what our actual commitments are in the

---

[6] Ibid., p. 111.

[7] Ibid., p. 92.

[8] On the dominance of style in a late capitalist environment, see Bryan Turner, *Religion and Social Theory* (London, 1983).

[9] *Op. cit.*, p. 93.

[10] *Op. cit.*, pp. 108ff. For a general discussion of the notion of an 'implicit axiom' in various kinds of discourse, see Ritschl's essay, 'Die Erfahrung der Wahrheit. Die Steuerung von Denken und Handeln durch Implizite Axiome', *Konzepte, Ökumene, Medizin, Ethik. Gesammelte Aufsätze* (Munich, 1986), pp. 147–66.

process of testing the integrity and intelligibility of our language. This is helpful in reminding us of the practical oddity, if not unintelligibility, of an unqualified pluralism; it leaves open, however, the question of how these axioms may be grasped as composing any sort of unity themselves. It is possible to say – as I think Ritschl implies – that awareness of 'implicit axioms' is a sort of regulative *moment* in theology, which points to a wholeness of perspective in fact unattainable from any historical standpoint. The unity of Christian discourse can only *show itself* in this oblique way, as axioms emerge to light. This seems to me to be quite right as far as it goes; but I think more can be said about what *positively* conditions the search for some articulation of this elusive unity. Ritschl himself turns to this in the second main section of his work; while acknowledging my debt to his discussion, I want to suggest a slightly different way in which the issue might be tackled.

With Ritschl, I believe (as I have already indicated) that 'the conception of the unity of humanity, which has a theological basis, calls for the venture of an overall view'.[11] What I have called 'the conviction that there is a common hope and a common vocation for human beings' is more than just a pious sentiment. To belong to the community of Christian belief at all is to assume that the pattern of relation between persons and between humanity and God which is displayed as gift and possibility in the Church is open to humanity at large, and to act on that assumption in respect both of the internal structures and of the external policy of the Church. Christian belief involves exposure to what the New Testament calls 'the judgement of this world', and its corporate articulation and living out claims to be a mediation of that judgement to the nations, and a mediation also of the hope that lies in and beyond the judgement. In other words, the *fact* of a community committed to mission, to inclusiveness, to calling human persons and society to account, is the source of the question about the unity of Christian truth.

If we were content to say that there is *no* challenge the Christian community may put to secularity or to other purportedly religious discourses, we should be saying that it is possible to imagine irreconcilable human ends and goods, between which there is no communication; and this would very much lessen the pressure to clarify what it is to suppose that Christian truth is 'one'. Likewise, if we were free to say that all or most conceptions of the human vocation developed by earlier Christian generations were *fundamentally* misconceived or superseded, and that we were authorized to re-imagine the shape of Christian humanity from scratch, we should again be

---

[11] *The Logic of Theology*, p. 202. Cf. R. Williams, 'What is Catholic Orthodoxy?' (pp. 11–25 in *Essays Catholic and Radical*, ed. K. Leech and R. Williams, London, 1983), p. 15.

settling for a plurality of contingent projects, radically vulnerable to the distortions of history, with no inherent critical elements to keep them in motion and dialogue: the 'salvation' of the medieval peasant and of the twentieth-century bourgeois would operate in mutually inaccessible frames of reference. There could be no engagement, critical or affirming, between them; only the blanket dismissal modernity is usually happy to pronounce. If this is problematic in the contemporary context, the same holds across the historical divide.

The focal problem here is not simply that this makes it difficult to talk about 'a' Christian community in any more than a rather formal and boring sense, but that it makes it difficult to talk about *God*. If 'God' is a conceptual tool for the supposedly advanced moral consciousness of an age, or if the word designates an object with a history (i.e. a pattern of involvement with uncontrolled contingencies) the problem is substantially reduced; but this simply begs the question of whether this can strictly be called talk about God at all. The meaning of 'God' as displayed in the history of Israel and the Church has to do with the historical realities of transformation or renewal of such scope that they only be ascribed to an agency free from the conditions of historical contingency, and one that challenges rather than endorses what claims to be the heights of moral and spiritual attainment. And it is out of this meaning of 'God' that there gradually develops the fully articulated doctrine of God characteristic of patristic and medieval theology: the unconditioned act of self-diffusion and self-sharing upon which all things depend – with the important corollary that this act is 'simple', it is what it is without the admixture of elements or constraints from beyond itself, and so is entirely at one with itself, consistent and faithful.

You do not have to hold this view in its full-blown and explicit form for the underlying picture of God involved to pose questions about the unity of religious discourse in a tradition. If there is one God, the acts of that God should, *prima facie*, be consistent; the community established by the divine action should have some unifying points of reference; and reflective speech of that community should in some way articulate the divine consistency, or, at the very least, be able to deal with and contain what seems to make for fragmentation. Thus the canon of Hebrew Scripture can itself be read both as an effort to articulate the deepening sense of the oneness of God's act (Deutero-Isaiah's brilliant fusion of creation mythology with the Exodus tradition and the experience of return from exile is probably the most striking instance) and as the perception of that oneness in and through the *overcoming* of the dramatic ruptures in Israel's history – the beginning and the end of the monarchy, the schism between the kingdoms, the destruction of the first temple, the exile. The unity of God's action, of the community itself and of the community's speech, has to be constructed in the reworking of narrative, law and 'prophecy', the interweaving of new layers;[12] and this labour is enabled by that fundamental self-interpretation without which the community of Israel would not exist, the conviction of an origin in the *call* of God, undetermined by any worldly factors, and a constitution by the covenanted promise of God.

Precisely this is what is at work also in the relation of the New Testament writings to this canon. The activity of God in Jesus is linked up with the unity of creation, covenant, exodus and restoration: what *is* and is *done* in Jesus is assimilated to these acts.[13] Consequently, the unity of the Christian *ekklesia* with Israel must be affirmed; and, at the same time, some account must be given of why the manifest and bitter separation between Church and synagogue, and the manifest rejection of Jesus by those to whom the interpretation of Israel's tradition formally belonged, did not constitute a fragmenting of the unity of God's act. What is clear in the New Testament is not that there can be a single systematic resolution to all this, but that these issues have a necessarily high priority, given the sort of thing the Church is and the sort of thing its talking about God is. And if the New Testament is less a set of theological conclusions than a set of generative models for how to do Christian thinking,[14] our own consideration of how we should speak of the unity of doctrinal language must be shaped by the methods displayed in these writings.

In old and New Testaments alike, unity is evidently articulated through *analogy*: diverse events, persons, patterns of behaviour are reconstructed in writing and in the editing processes of canonical formation[15] so as to manifest a shared form, a family resemblance. This works in a particularly interesting way when Christian writers claim for their own the heroes of the Jewish scriptures, so that these figures become resources for the self-understanding

---

[12]   See the excellent study of canonical formation and its significance by James A. Sanders, *Torah and Canon* (Philadelphia, 1972).

[13]   Apart from the way in which language appropriated to the Torah as the principle of creation is used of Jesus in some strands of the New Testament (notably the beginning of Colossians), there has been some speculation about whether the symbolic significance of the *Aqedah*, the 'sacrifice' of Isaac, related in rabbinic traditions to creation and Exodus, was early transferred to the death of Jesus. See R. Williams, *Eucharistic Sacrifice. The Roots of a Metaphor* (Nottingham, 1983), for a brief introduction to this question.

[14]   See n. 13 above.

[15]   J. A. Sanders, *op. cit.*; and, for a wider discussion of the varieties of 'canonical criticism', James Barr, *Holy Scripture: Canon, Authority, Criticism* (Oxford, 1983).

of the ordinary Christian convert. What is – or should be – happening in the life of the believer is given graspable shape by referring it to the story of Abraham, as in Romans. Hebrews gives us a long catalogue of Jewish saints re-imagined as paradigms of the 'hope for things unseen', the venturing beyond the easy and familiar, that is being enjoined upon the letter's recipients. To put it as simply as possible: the *roles* Christians can take on are the roles created and enacted by the fathers of Jewish faith.[16] A central aspect of establishing the unity of the God of the covenant and the God of Jesus is establishing the continuity, the analogical relation, between the role that a Christian may stand in before the God of Jesus and the role of an Abraham or Moses before the God of Israel: this life *now* can have *that* kind of structure. Indeed, the very identifying of a present community's relation to God in virtue of its faithfulness to Jesus as a 'covenant' licenses the filling-out of this general analogical move by applying it to individuals in both covenantal orders. And this construction by analogy of a community's relation to God is a process already at work in the Jewish scriptures – in the Law's various levels of redaction, in which the present community under instruction is imagined as Israel in the desert, in the literary reappropriation of archaic prophetic idiom,[17] in the effective assimilation of Babylonian to Egyptian captivity – so that Jewish scripture's *method* is itself an analogue for what is being done in the New Testament.

If, in the Bible, the unity of Jewish and of Christian discourse is understood as required by a commitment to the unity of God, and if the unity of God is in turn understood and articulated in terms of the unity or continuity of the possible forms that human life, individual or corporate, may take before God, we have a possible lead in considering the problem of the unity of our discourse today. Rush Rhees wrote that 'The question whether we are still talking about God now, or whether we are really worshipping God now, cannot be settled by referring to any object'.[18] How, then, is it settled? On the evidence of Jewish and Christian scripture, it is settled by considering the compatibility and coherence of the roles made available, the patterns of life opened up in the speech that witnesses to the foundational events of the Jewish and Christian communities. 'Is it the same God?' is a question not

---

[16]   On the appropriating of roles, see A. C. Thiselton, 'Knowledge, Myth and Corporate Memory' (pp. 45–78 in *Believing in the Church. The Corporate Nature of Faith*: the Report of the Church of England Doctrine Commission, London, 1981), pp. 65–6.

[17]   See John Barton, *Oracles of God* (London, 1986), on this interpretation of the 'classical' prophetic literature.

[18]   Rush Rhees, *Without Answers* (London, 1969), p. 131.

to be answered apart from the question, 'Is it the same hope?' or 'Is it the same pattern of holy life?'.

If this is right, what most significantly threatens unity is the existence of incompatible models of Christian (or Jewish) humanity. This may take the form already mentioned, of assuming that my salvation can go forward in a way that does not affect and is not affected by the question of salvation's accessibility for some other person or group: the refusal to see what is so central to Paul's vision of the *ekklesia* – the recognition that I do not go to heaven except in relation to those I serve and am served by in the Body of Christ, that what is given to me or to us is given for the whole. When forms of Christian discourse can be identified as systematically ignoring or trivializing this – especially, in our age, by racial or sexual exclusivity – they must be seen as fragmenting the perception of God's unity. But awareness of this distortion or fragmentation can also encourage us to look with anachronistic severity at some past styles of Christian sanctity; a commitment to the unity of God's action should at least give us reason to spend time asking what points of 'analogy' may exist with what we take for granted as the pattern of holiness now – and how our present accounts of it may be questionable and partial.[19]

In other words, the search for a *theological* unity in what we say involves a high degree of sustained conversation with the history of Christian ethics and spirituality (in its full historical complexity and ambiguity) – with the history of how the vocation of human beings is imagined by Christians. And in reading the texts of faith in the context of the sacramental action of the community, we are reminded of what is, in fact, a significant aspect of all reading of texts: we are not the first or the only readers. We read *as* we perform identifiably similar actions to those performed by other readers, re-presenting a single story which is believed to be the point of focus for all our analogies – what interprets and is interpreted by the life of the new community, and thus connects 'new' and 'old' worlds. What makes the process of the Christian analogizing of sanctity possible at all is the unifying 'form' of Jesus' life, death and resurrection seen as the point upon which the analogical lines of Hebrew narrative converge.

Why not, then, simply answer the question about unity by saying this? By saying that Christian truth is unified by its reference to the one figure of Jesus Christ? Formally, this would be true enough; but it would tell us too little. As it stands, it would run two different sorts of risk. It could reduce the

---

[19]   In this respect, of course, the project of theological analogy exercised on the narratives of Christian life is as much a matter of mutual critical address as any other variety of hermeneutics.

range of Christian ethics and spirituality to a mechanical obedience or to imitation of Jesus of Nazareth as a clearly identifiable and characterizable historical figure; or else, if it took with appropriate seriousness the challenges to this picture from historical and literary criticism of the gospels, it would evacuate the idea of 'reference' to Jesus of nearly all positive agreed content.

The Christological issues here are of great complexity, but it ought to be clear that the options of an historical exemplar and an historical cypher should not exhaust the range of possibilities. I would prefer to say that the figure of Christ acts as a unifying point precisely in and through an attention to the varieties of Christian humanity. Being the Church at all takes it for granted that there is a history of corporate belief which witnesses to the action of the one God; and the events around Jesus, especially the cross and resurrection, are the hinge connecting one part of this story (the covenant with Israel) with another (us). How this connection is made without appearing to rob Israel as it now exists of its history is a question of some obvious gravity, which needs a lot more reflection. But from the standpoint of the Church we can at least say that the events around Jesus make possible those new modes of human being spoken of, symbolized and enacted in the Church, and the appropriation and transformation of Jewish paradigms in a radically different context. To explore the continuities of Christian patterns of holiness is to explore the *effect* of Jesus, living, dying and rising; and it is inevitable that the tradition about Jesus is re-read and re-worked so that it will make sense of these lived patterns as they evolve. We constantly return to imagine the life of Jesus in a way that will help us to understand how it sets up a continuous pattern of human living before God. Who Jesus is must be (and can only be) grasped in the light of what Christian humanity is; but that Christian humanity is centrally characterized by the acknowledgement of dependence on a gift realized in the history of Jesus. It refuses to claim the right of self-definition or self-constitution.

Thus we become able to say what is, theologically speaking, at work in Jesus by tracing the continuities of Christian holiness, not simply in comparative biography, but in what Christian language in and out of worship offers as possibilities for the shaping of a life Godward: in more conventional theological language, we identify what is to be a child of God, given a share in the liberty of God, and identify in Jesus the formal, the material and the efficient cause of there being such a pattern in human lives. This is not to suppose that theological considerations can provide us with bits of otherwise inaccessible biographical information; since the embodiment of divine sonship is not a *feature* of the life of Jesus among others, an additional piece of straightforwardly verifiable fact about this human being's human life, the confession of Jesus as incarnate Son of God does not *of itself* specify any particular bio-graphical facts.[20] Yet equally this does not leave us to construct unchecked mythical fantasies: the bare facts of Jesus' Jewishness, his perceived role as a prophet, and the nature of his death set boundaries to what can be said of him – as they also set boundaries to what can be said about Christian human-ity.

The knowledge of Jesus' identity as 'Son' or 'Word' in history is not something to be read off from a supposedly neutral record, nor, on the other hand, is it some kind of abstract projection of transcendental significance on to an historical void. It is realized in the process by which the memory of Jesus and the humanity of the Church give shape and definition to each other, so that the 'memory' of Jesus is never simply the recollection of a distant individual, and the 'humanity' of the Church is never simply an opti-mistic moral project. This definitive interaction, which is what sacraments and the reading of scripture are supposed to be about, is the context in which we speak of the agency of the one God as witness and interpreter, as the Holy Spirit. And it is worth recalling Vladimir Lossky's account of the Spirit as that which realizes in the endless diversity of human lives the set of renewed human possibilities opened up by the work of Christ.[21]

The unity of Christian truth is perceivable to the extent that we can per-ceive a unity in Christian holiness, the unity anchored in the form of Christ, in the enfleshment of God's eternal act of complete response to the complete self-gift we call 'God the Father'. The limits of Christian truth are perceiv-able as we engage in the hard work of spelling out the human meanings, the hopes and possibilities, carried in this or that theological utterance. Be-fore applying either the test of consistency with a 'monothematic' principle or the test of immediate conceptual compatibility with an encyclopaedic or systematic exposition, we should ask whether a Christian utterance does or does not conserve the possibility of the kind of analogy I have been sketch-ing: does it presuppose and serve the conviction that the lives of men and women are open to the horizons indicated by those models of 'Christian

---

[20]   I take this to be the force of Eamon Duffy's remark that 'the divinity of Jesus is not a "fact" about him', in 'The Philosophers and the China Shop', *New Blackfriars*, October 1988, p. 449; and I am not quite clear why Professor Dummett ('What Chance of Ecumenism?' *New Blackfriars*, December 1988, pp. 541–2) takes this so much *in malam partem*. The whole point of Chalcedonian Christology as developed in the doctrinal tradition seems to be the denial that divinity is a characterization among others of the human nature of Jesus, either an additional feature or a substitute for some human lack.

[21]   Vladimir Lossky, *The Mystical Theology of the Eastern Church* (London and Cambridge, 1957), ch. 8, esp. pp. 166–7.

humanity' which the Church's history has developed around the focal sign of Jesus' living and dying? Does it – to recall the terminology used earlier – continue to offer intelligible roles for the living out of new creation? Does it conserve a hope for shared, unrestricted human renewal/liberation/salvation?

If we come at the question of theological unity from this perspective, a number of further implications appear. First of all, we can come to recognize both of the methods described by Ritschl as possible *styles* of theologizing, while denying that either has any final privilege over the other, or over any other: there are internal pressures in theological language urging it to organize itself around this or that theme, or to display its overall conceptual and systematic shape, but this does not mean that theology *must* decide on every occasion to be monothematically or systematically determined (if it were otherwise, the greater part of the history of theology would be ruled out of order).[22]

Second, we are or should be kept attentive to the location of theology in the Church, understood as a community whose corporate activity seeks and hopes to be taken up in God's activity as characterized in the foundational record of Israel and Jesus – i.e. understood not merely as a cultic institution, though it is worship and reflective prayer that witness to and deepen the immersion of human acting in God's.

And third: when theological unity or coherence looks most threatened, the problem is likely to be an underlying anxiety or confusion about the characterization of God's activity – and thus about the nature of holiness. Such confusion is caused by uncertainty about how to read the Bible in a post-critical age, by intensified awareness of challenges to the Christian model from other persuasive accounts of human wholeness, by the sense of a lack of focus or integrity in how the Church as an institution behaves – in short, by all kinds of factors endemic in the situation of the Church at the present time.

Attempts to speak of the unity of Christian discourse which ignore these factors will fail to address the central issue. The vision of unity in our context, and perhaps in every Christian context, is more likely to emerge by way of a newly critical and constructive reading of scripture – the revived 'analogical' skills of a base community, the profound hermeneutic of parable, much discussed in the USA in recent years, the whole process of

[22] Ch. 16 of Nicholas Lash's *Easter in Ordinary. Reflections on Human Experience and the Knowing of God* (London, 1988) has some salutary things to say about the necessary co-existence of plurality in theological idiom and integrity in witness (see p. 266 in particular).

claiming the Bible as a *source* of critique. And it is also more likely to emerge by way of the demanding and sometimes alarming conversations that must be pursued in our society about what human beings and societies may hope for; and by candid engagement with the Church's liability to treat its unity as an end in itself not much related to its honesty. All the time, though, we must remember that none of this makes any sense without some confidence in the possibility of the reality of our own transformation in Christ, the confidence that can be nurtured only by the disciplines of praise and of silence.

Chapter Three

THE JUDGEMENT OF
THE WORLD

In the nineteenth century, Kierkegaard retold the story of Abraham and Isaac with shattering effect; several generations have grown up spiritually and intellectually in the shadow of this retelling in terms of the 'suspension of ethics', the realm of risk and terror beyond morality. More recently, Jung in his *Answer to Job* reworked the scriptural text into an extraordinary new mythological shape: the blind God of the natural and primal order looks with envy at the creature who has the self-awareness to challenge him; the conflict between Job and his maker shows why that maker himself must at last identify himself with human suffering, must become Jesus Christ. Only as human is God self-aware; only as human is God fully God, the active and transfiguring archetype of the human itself.

What is going on here? Should we call these enterprises translations of the world's experience into biblical categories, or the opposite? It is because I find I am not at all clear about the answer to this that I want to put some questions to the project so persuasively outlined by Professor Lindbeck in his book, *The Nature of Doctrine*, [. . .] the project of inserting the human story into the world of scripture: 'Intratextual theology redescribes reality within the scriptural framework rather than translating scripture into extrascriptural categories.'[1] I have no doubt at all of the need to revive and preserve a scriptural imagination capable of deploying decisive and classical narratives in the interpretation of the human world – nor any doubt of the present weakening of such an imagination in our culture. But I am both interested and perturbed by the *territorial* cast of the imagery used here – of a 'framework' within whose boundaries things - persons? – are to be 'inserted'. Is this in fact how a scripturally informed imagination works? I believe that the

[1]   George A. Lindbeck, *The Nature of Doctrine: Religion and Theology in a Postliberal Age* (Philadelphia: Westminster Press, 1984), p. 118.

reality is more complex, and that it sits less easily with the picture Professor Lindbeck has outlined of a church heavily committed to the refinement and deepening of a scriptural speech and culture *within* its own territory.

What I shall be proposing is that we may have misunderstood the alternatives before us. The 'world of scripture', so far from being a clear and readily definable territory, is an *historical* world in which meanings are discovered and recovered in action and encounter. To challenge the Church to immerse itself in its 'text' is to encourage it to engage with a history of such actions and encounters; and in the era after the disappearance of a unitary Christian world-view, this is to engage with those appropriations of biblical narrative on the frontiers of the Church and beyond represented by figures such as Kierkegaard and Jung.[2] If, as has sometimes been said, the Bible is itself a history of the *re*-reading of texts, our reading of it should not be so different. What we are dealing with is a text that has generated an enormous family of contrapuntal elaborations, variations, even inversions – rather like the simple theme given to Bach by Frederick the Great, that forms the core of *The Art of Fugue*. When we have listened to the whole of that extraordinary work, we cannot simply hear the original notes picked out by the King of Prussia as if nothing has happened. We can't avoid saying now: '*This* can be the source of *that*' – and that is a fact of some importance about the simple base motif.

The Church may be committed to interpreting the world in terms of its own foundational narratives; but the very act of interpreting affects the narratives as well as the world, for good and ill, and it is not restricted to what we usually think of as the theological mainstream. Something happens to the Exodus story as it is absorbed into the black slave culture of America. Something still more unsettling happens to Abraham and Isaac when they have passed through Kierkegaard's hands – or the hands of the agnostic Wilfred Owen, writing in the First World War of how the old man refused to hear the angel 'and slew his son, And half the seed of Europe, one by one'. Where are we to locate this kind of reflection? It is not purely intratextual, conducted in terms fixed by the primal narrative, nor is it in any very helpful sense a 'liberal' translation into an extraneous frame of reference. It is, much more, a generative moment in which there may be a *discovery* of what the

---

[2] On Abraham and Isaac, it is also worth looking at Eric Auerbach, *Mimesis. The Representation of Reality in Western Literature* (Princeton: Princeton University Press, 1953), ch. 1, especially pp. 8–11, where Auerbach suggests how this and kindred narratives help to construct the notion of character as it typically works in Western culture. This again is an instance of our being returned to the scriptural text afresh by its own legacy as appropriated outside the theological community.

primal text may become (and so of what it *is*) as well as a discovery of the world. Owen's savage transformation of Abraham's sacrifice points up what we might miss in Genesis: the final drawing back from slaughter is an act of obedience as great as or greater than the first decision to sacrifice Isaac. It also points up the impotence of the narrative in a world that has lost the means to forgo its pride. Not sacrificing Isaac is a necessary humiliation; the righteous old men of Europe in 1914 are strangers to such a possibility. This is indeed a discovery of scripture and world, and of the gulf between them; and it is now – or should be – part of what the Church reads in Genesis 22. It will have found out *what it is itself saying*, in absorbing this scriptural exegesis from its own margins. And part of my thesis is that the interpretation of the world 'within the scriptural framework' is intrinsic to the *Church's* critical self-discovery. In judging the world, by its confrontation of the world with its own dramatic script, the Church also judges itself: in attempting to show the world a critical truth, it shows itself to itself as Church also. All of which means that we are dealing not with the 'insertion' of definable blocks of material into a well-mapped territory where homes may be found for them, but with *events* of re-telling or re-working traditional narrative patterns in specific human interactions; an activity in which the Christian community is itself enlarged in understanding and even in some sense evangelized. Its integrity is bound up in encounters of this kind, and so in the unavoidable elements of exploratory fluidity and provisionality that enter into these encounters. At any point in its history, the Church needs both the confidence that it has a gospel to preach, and the ability to see that it cannot readily specify in advance how it will find words for preaching in particular new circumstances.

Words like 'preaching' and 'interpretation' have come to sound rather weak; or, at least, they do not very fully characterize the enterprise to which the Church is committed. The Church exists for the sake of the kingdom of God; it is 'engaged in the same business as its Lord: that of opening the world to its horizon, to its destiny as God's Kingdom'.[3] This means that it is essentially missionary in its nature, seeking to transform the human world by communicating to it in word and act a truthfulness that exposes the deepest human fears and evasions and makes possible the kind of human existence that can pass beyond these fears to a new liberty. The Church, in claiming to exist for the sake of opening the world to the fuller life in which God can be

[3] *For the Sake of the Kingdom: God's Church and the New Creation*, the report of the Inter-Anglican Theological and Doctrinal Commission (Cincinnati: published for the Anglican Consultative Council by Forward Movement Publications, 1986), p. 23.

discerned as the controlling meaning of things, claims to have something to contribute to all human cultures, all human essays in the construction of meaning. What is contributed is not easily summed up; but it is at least a Christian participation in the whole business of constructing meanings, the business of art and politics in the widest senses of those words and at most the invitation to a new self-identification, a new self-description, in the categories of Christian prayer and sacrament. Ideally, the Christian sharing in the enterprise of art or politics is working towards the point where these new self-descriptions can be seen as possible and intelligible.

As already intimated, this work involves a passing of judgement; and here we encounter some serious difficulties. In the classical Christian story as presented in John's gospel, judgement is not effected by uttering words of condemnation but by a quite complex process of interaction. The works and words of Jesus demand choice for or against him; they force to the light hidden directions and dispositions that would otherwise never come to view, and thus make the conflicts of goals and interests between people a *public* affair. The inner rejection of one's own identity as God's creature and the object of God's love, the violence done to human truth *within* the self, becomes visible and utterable in the form of complicity in rejecting Jesus.[4] The inner readiness to come to judgement and to recognize the possibility of truth and meaning becomes visible and utterable in the form of discipleship, abiding in the community created by God's love. The dramatic event of Jesus' interaction with his people – set out in a series of ritual, quasi-legal disputations – is an event of judgement in that it gives the persons involved definitions, roles to adopt, points on which to stand and speak.[5] They are invited to 'create' themselves in finding a place within this drama – an improvisation in the theatre workshop, but one that purports to be about a comprehensive truth affecting one's identity and future. As John hints (for instance in chapter 3), and as Paul more vividly and clearly sees (as in Romans 11), this is far more than a simple separation of the already godly from the already damned: the scope of Jesus' work is the *world* - so, we must

---

[4]   See, e.g., Sebastian Moore, *The Crucified is No Stranger* (New York: Seabury Press, 1977), as well as later works by the same author, for a fuller account of such a theological option.

[5]   On the trial motif in scripture generally and in the New Testament in particular, see Ulrich Simon, 'The Transcendence of Law', *Theology* 73 (1970), 166–8, and Anthony Harvey, *Jesus on Trial. A Study in the Fourth Gospel* (London: SPCK, 1976). On the wider issue of self-identification or self-discovery through a dramatic process (to which I shall be returning later), see, above all, Hans Urs von Balthasar, '*Theodramatik*', *Prolegomena* vol. 1 (Einsiedeln: Johannes, 1973), particularly Part 2; discussed briefly in Rowan Williams, 'Balthasar and Rahner', *The Analogy of Beauty*, ed. John Riches (Edinburgh: T. & T. Clark, 1986), pp. 11–34, 26–7.

assume, the declaration of a newly discovered identity in encounter with Jesus represents a *change* for at least some. You may recognize your complicity in the rejection of Jesus and at the same time accept the possibility of a different role offered by the continuing merciful presence of God in the post-Easter Jesus. In Paul's terms, all may find themselves both prisoners of disobedience and recipients of grace (Romans 11.32).

The Gospel, then, is what enables this dual self-discovery in women and men; and as Matthew 25 suggests, it may prove difficult to give any general account of what a converting event may be, because neither the rejection of Jesus nor the receiving of his grace may readily be identifiable as such. Proclaiming the Gospel may have much to do with the struggle to make explicit what is at stake in particular human decisions or policies, individual and collective, and in this sense bring in the event of judgement, the revaluation of identities. I think this is rather different from what Professor Lindbeck suggests is the goal of Christian theology – 'to discern those possibilities in current situations that can and should be cultivated as anticipations or preparations for the hoped for future, the coming kingdom'.[6] I am wholly in sympathy with his challenges to the 'liberal' assumption that this is to be achieved by adjusting theology to current fashion, and what I have already said accords in important respects with his call for discernment on the basis of criteria drawn from the specifically Christian narrative ('an intratextually derived eschatology').[7] But I want, in contrast to argue that such discernment is not easily intelligible when divorced from the language of a transformative judgement, enacted in particular *events,* that is the central theme of so many of our foundational texts. In short, I don't think that Christian and theological discernment can ever be wholly 'contemplative' and 'noninterventionist'; I believe it is more importantly exercised in the discernment of what contemporary conflicts are actually *about* and in the effort both to clarify this and to decide where the Christian should find his or her identity in a conflict. The Christian is involved in seeking conversion – the bringing to judgement of contemporary struggles, and the appropriation of some new dimension of the transforming summons of Christ in his or her own life.

Here we come up against the most central issue in the whole of this discussion. How are we to speak of judgement in a fragmented culture? The language of judgement presupposes recognition and communication, the possibility of shared points of reference. To pass judgement is to propose and

---

[6]   Lindbeck, *The Nature of Doctrine*, p. 125.
[7]   Ibid., p. 126.

in certain circumstances (the law court) to effect a definitive 'placing' of who or what it is that is being judged: it affects attitudes towards the object of judgement, it influences the decisions and priorities of others, it shapes what can be 'claimed' by or for the object. All this applies equally to legal, artistic, and moral judgement: none of these makes sense as anything other than a public affair. To put it at its weakest: what would be *meant* by saying, 'I think (judge) that the *St Matthew Passion* is the greatest achievement of European music, but I don't care whether it's ever performed again'? Judgements take for granted a real or possible community of speaking and responding persons, and a history of concrete decisions and acts.

Hence, in a radically pluralist society, the society as such increasingly withdraws from judgement. It will contain groups who continue to believe that judgement is possible or imperative, but the social system overall sees its job as securing a pragmatic minimum of peaceful co-existence between groups, by a variety of managerial skills and economic adjustments. 'Late capitalist societies are neither coherent nor integrated around a system of common values',[8] according to the sociologist Bryan Turner, who goes on to argue that such coherence and stability as there is are secured by a mixture of diverse factors – the apparatus of modern administration itself, the neutralizing of genuine political dissent, the system of palliative welfare benefits, the reduction of the franchise to an almost passive formality, and the social dependency induced by the nature of economic and employment relations in a technologically advanced multinational economy.[9] Societies that are able to control their populations in such ways do not need the legitimization of 'values'; they do not need myth or religion or morality. To put it in other terms, they can evade the question of why *this* social order should be respected, preserved or defended, because they are not threatened, practically speaking, by their inability to answer it: they have sufficient resources, administratively and technically, to guarantee survival for the foreseeable future. If the price of survival is high (permanent large-scale unemployment, the erosion of public health care or state education, the creation of what has come to be called an 'underclass'), it is still manageable, because the damaging results of the system have the effect of moving the disadvantaged further away from the processes of public decision making.

Societies like this (like the UK and USA under their present governments) have no problem in tolerating a 'chaos of personal life-styles' in practice, even where there may be varieties of public rhetoric that commend

[8]   Bryan Turner, *Religion and Social Theory* (London: Heinemann, 1983), p. 197.
[9]   Ibid., pp. 197–8; cf. 240–1.

some lifestyles more than others.[10] In the context of these societies, indeed, *style* is everything: with massive commercial support, cultural options – even when their roots are in would-be dissident groupings – are developed and presented as consumer goods. Religious belief is no exception, whether this process of consumerization appears in the naked crudity of fundamentalist broadcasting or in the subtler ways in which secular media dictate the tone and the agenda of the behaviour and utterances of religious leaders; and religious commitment is reduced to a private matter of style, unconnected with the nature of a person's membership in his or her society. Public life continues, whatever style we adopt. And concern with style notoriously detracts from seriousness about what is to be said (a point noted long ago by Augustine and others[11]): a recent series in the London *Guardian*[12] about postmodernism in the arts noted with anxiety the rising popularity of pastiche and pseudo-traditionalism alongside anarchic and parodic idioms, a kind of new baroque – two sides of the same coin.

There remains, of course, a nostalgia for 'values', which the Church should beware of exploiting. The diffuse discontent that consumer pluralism can engender (although it largely contains and even utilizes it) yields itself readily to any program that dresses itself persuasively enough in moral rhetoric; but this is something essentially unrelated to how priorities are fixed in government (as recent British and American policies make depressingly clear). The Church misconceives its missionary task if it simply latches on to this kind of window dressing and echoes the individualistic and facile language of moral retrenchment that often accompanies a further intensification of administrative control and the attrition of participatory politics. To put it in language lately made familiar by Richard Neuhaus, there may be a 'naked public square', but, before the churches rush into it, they have to ask whether the space opened up is genuinely a *public* one, or is simply the void defined by a system that can carry on perfectly well in the short term with this nakedness.[13]

My worry with Professor Lindbeck's proposal is that it might end up encouraging the continuance of this situation. In *The Nature of Doctrine*, he identifies with admirable precision the danger of reducing faith to a commodity marketed to atomistic selves in a hopelessly fragmented culture, and goes on to defend the idea that a unified future world rescued from the

---

[10] Ibid., p. 241.
[11] It forms the central theme of Augustine's *De doctrina christiana*, Book 4.
[12] 1–3 December 1986.
[13] Turner, *Religion and Social Theory*, p. 246.

acids of modernity would be more likely to be fostered by 'communal enclaves', concerned with socialization and mutual support rather than with 'individual rights and entitlements', as opposed to religious traditions that eagerly abandon their distinctiveness in favour of a liberal syncretism.[14] This may be so; but unless these 'enclaves' are also concerned quite explicitly with the problem of restoring an authentically public discourse in their cultural setting, they will simply collude with the dominant consumer pluralism and condemn themselves to be trivialized into stylistic preferences once more. The communal enclave, if it is not to be a ghetto, must make certain claims on the possibility of a global community, and act accordingly.

Naturally, this raises for many the spectre of theocratic totalitarianism. But such an anxiety, though quite proper in itself, is not necessitated by these 'claims on . . . a global community', for a number of reasons. First of all, theocracy assumes that there can be an end to dialogue and discovery; that believers would have the right (if they had the power) to outlaw unbelief. It assumes that there could be a situation in which believers in effect had nothing to learn, and therefore that the corporate conversion of the Church could be over and done with. Second, following from this, theocracy assumes an end to history. The powerful suggestions of Barth and von Balthasar[15] about history between the resurrection and the second coming as the gift of a time of repentance and growth are set aside; instead of God alone determining the end of the times of repentance, the Church seeks to foreclose the eschaton. Third, most obviously, theocracy reflects a misunderstanding of the hope for God's kingdom, a fusion of divine and earthly sovereignty in a way quite foreign to the language and practice of Jesus. Theocracy, the administration by Christians of a monolithic society in which all distinction between sin and crime is eroded, is neither a practical nor a theologically defensible goal.

The Christian claim, then, is bound *always* to be something evolving and acquiring definition in the conversations of history: it offers a direction for historical construction of human meaning, but it does not offer to end history. Like the humane Trotskyism of Raymond Williams, it envisages a 'long revolution', at best an asymptotic approach to a condition that history is itself (by definition) incapable of realizing – a perfect communality of language and action free from the distortions imposed on understanding by

---

[14]   Lindbeck, *The Nature of Doctrine*, pp. 126–7.
[15]   See Barth's *Church Dogmatics* II.2, and Balthasar's *Theology of History* (London/New York: Sheed and Ward, 1963) and *A Theological Anthropology* (New York: Sheed and Ward, 1968).

the clash of group interests and the self-defence of the powerful.[16] The Christian may have no clearer a picture than anyone else of what this would look like, but can at least contribute specific perceptions of what holds back the coming of such a world, and specific possibilities of transforming acts and decisions – conversion in the broad sense already outlined, or what Dietrich Ritschl in his superb new book on *The Logic of Theology* calls the work of the 'therapeutic spirit' in the creative renewal of persons and communities.[17]

Christians in general and theologians in particular are thus going to be involved as best they can in those enterprises in their culture that seek to create or recover a sense of shared discourse and common purpose in human society. This can mean various things. The most obvious is some sort of critical identification with whatever political groupings speak for a serious and humane resistance to consumer pluralism and the administered society. These days, such groupings are less likely than ever to be found within historic mainstream political parties, though there are some countries happily, where moral imagination has not been so completely privatized. For many, it has been ecological issues, feminism, civil rights and 'peace' networks that have provided a new political language and a sense of the urgency and possibility of human unity. All of these are themselves in constant danger of being marginalized, and all have their fringes of mere style, apolitical and exclusivist posturing. The task of keeping them related to what remains of a democratic public process, to the parties that people actually vote for, is a hard and thankless one: if my suggestions are right, it may well be a major task for the informed Christian. But I have in mind also the work of those artists who have a commitment to the future of language and imagination: here too the Christian's business is engagement and solidarity, a willingness to listen and respond. The English playwright Howard Barker argues in the *Guardian* (10 February 1986) for the necessity of a revival of tragedy, in order to break through the false collectivism of 'populist' theatre (typified by the musical) and put people back in touch with the isolation of their own pain – a paradoxical move towards the *authentically* public by way of intensifying the personal. In Britain the television dramas of Alan Bleasdale and Dennis Potter have perhaps most vividly exemplified such a move. Can the Christian, in whatever way, help to nurture both the production and the

---

[16]   Any echoes of Habermas's notion of the 'ideal speech situation' are deliberate. On this concept, see John Thompson's excellent introduction to Habermas's thought in *Critical Hermeneutics. A Study in the Thought of Paul Ricoeur and Jürgen Habermas* (Cambridge (UK): Cambridge University Press, 1981), especially pp. 92–4.

[17]   Dietrich Ritschl, *The Logic of Theology* (London: SCM, 1986), p. 240; cf. pp. 231, 275–7.

reception of these statements? For many people, these are thresholds – perhaps more – of judgement, of 'therapeutic transformation'.[18] And, in a very different way, contemporary scientific and medical practice reflects the struggle between mechanistic, dominating, administrative patterns and a relatively new, tentative, not always very coherent concern for unity and interdependence. Here is a further field for learning and for solidarity.

The late Cornelius Ernst, OP, in a seminally important essay on 'Theological Methodology', argued that the meaning of the world in Christ could only be articulated in a continuing search for a 'total human culture, the progressive discovery of a single human identity in Christ'.[19] The form of this search was quite simply any and every process of human self-definition in response to mass culture, the threat of a 'totalizing' society of technological manipulation and control. 'There is at least a single discernible adversary.' If the essence of the Church is missionary, this is precisely the search and the struggle to which the Church is committed. Professor Lindbeck suggests that those who give primacy to the question of how the Gospel is preached in a post-Christian environment 'regularly become liberal foundationalists', preoccupied with *translating* the Gospel into alien terms, or at least redefining it in response to secular questions.[20] I am not so sure. For one thing, as I have argued, preaching is not something extraneous to the identity and integrity of the Church; we are not allowed to sidestep the question. But equally, it is not clear that the only alternative to intensive in-house catechesis is translation into a foreign language in a way that sacrifices the distinctiveness of the Gospel. I don't see Cornelius Ernst as a 'liberal foundationalist': he is, I think, suggesting not a search for *words* equivalent to our traditional terms (so that we presuppose a more neutral or abstract content), but a search for what recognizably – however imperfectly – shares in the same project that the Gospel defines. Can we so *rediscover* our own foundational story in the acts and hopes of others that we ourselves are re-converted and are also able to bring those acts and hopes in relation with Christ for their fulfilment by the re-creating grace of God?

This is certainly a potentially riskier task than simple translation either into or out of traditional Christian and scriptural terms. The Christian engaged at the frontier with politics, art or science will frequently find that he or she *will not know what to say*. There can be a real sense of loss in respect to traditional

[18] Ibid., p. 231.
[19] Cornelius Ernst, 'Theological Methodology', *Multiple Echo*, ed. Fergus Kerr and Timothy Radcliffe (London: Darton, Longman & Todd, 1975), p. 85.
[20] Lindbeck, *The Nature of Doctrine*, p. 132.

formulae – not because they are being translated, but because they are being tested: we are discovering whether there is any sense in which the other languages we are working with can be at home with our theology. I'd agree entirely, by the way, with Professor Lindbeck that a deeper catechesis in that theology and its images is indispensable, but I think it is so because of the testing it will endure in the process of 'playing away from home', conversing with its potential allies. And to take an obvious political example – if the most plausible allies in a situation are people with similarly global commitments, the encounter is loaded with the possibilities of tragic conflict. If the most plausible ally in the Philippines or Chile or South Africa is a Marxist, the Christian may be tested to the uttermost (not every Christian with Marxist or socialist sympathies shares the optimism of many liberation theologians). The Christian woman actively involved in feminism will record the same kind of tension. The paradox of our situation often seems to be that the struggle for Christian integrity in preaching leads us close to those who least tolerate some aspects of that preaching.

The difficulty appears equally in the consequent need to know when to be silent, when to wait. This account of the Christian mission is not a recipe for talkative and confident activism; it requires something like a contemplative attention to the unfamiliar – a negative capability – a reluctance at least to force the language and behaviour of others into Christian categories prematurely, remembering that our understanding of those categories themselves is still growing and changing. The premature and facile use of Christian interpretative categories in fact invites judgement of another kind. My title is deliberately ambiguous: the Church judges the world; but it also hears God's judgement on itself in the judgement passed upon it by the world. 'The burden of proof lies on believers and the life they lead', writes Ritschl, pointing out the way in which, when transformation becomes no more than an inflated metaphor, the language of new creation is projected more and more towards the future: present conversion becomes accordingly unreal – verbal or figuratively only.[21] Preaching cannot be heard.

But the judgement of the world can cut more deeply. The weightiest criticisms of Christian speech and practice amount to this: that Christian language actually fails to transform the world's meaning because it neglects or trivializes or evades aspects of the human. It is notoriously awkward about sexuality; it risks being unserious about death when it speaks too glibly and confidently about eternal life; it can disguise the abiding reality of unhealed and meaningless suffering. So it is that some of those most serious about the

---

[21] Ritschl, *The Logic of Theology*, p. 237.

renewal of a moral discourse reject formal Christian commitment as something that would weaken or corrupt their imagination.[22] It may equally be
that a Church failing to understand that the political realm is a place of
spiritual decision, a place where souls are made and lost, forfeits the authority
to use certain of its familiar concepts or images in the public arena. Bonhoeffer,
in his justly famous meditation for his godson's baptism in May of 1944,
speaks powerfully of this loss of authority: 'Our church, which has been
fighting in these years only for its self-preservation, as though that were an
end in itself, is incapable of taking the word or reconciliation and redemption to mankind and the world. Our earlier words are therefore bound to
lose their force and cease.'[23] This is emphatically not a 'liberal' observation or
a demand for better translations into modish secularity, but a sober recognition that, in the world as it is, the right to be heard speaking about God must
be earned. The Christian is at once possessed by an authoritative urgency
to communicate the good news, and constrained by the awareness of how
easily the words of proclamation become godless, powerless to transform.
The urgency must often be channelled into listening and waiting, and into
the expansion of the Christian imagination itself into something that can
cope with the seriousness of the world. It is certainly true that, for any of this
to be possible, here must be a real immersion in the Christian tradition itself,
and to this extent Professor Lindbeck's programme is rightly directed. But if
I were devising schemes of Christian education, I should be inclined to set
such immersion side by side with an exposure to political and cultural issues
that might help to focus doctrinal language in a new way: only so, I believe,
can a theological formation be an induction into *judgement* – hearing it as
well as mediating it.

In the same meditation for his godson, Bonhoeffer makes one of his celebrated references to the need for a non-religious language in which to
proclaim the Gospel; 'so to utter the word of God that the world will be
changed and renewed by it.'[24] This will not be a conscious modernizing or

---

[22]   Angela Tilby (who has for some years done much to deepen the seriousness of religious
broadcasting in the UK) writes in an essay entitled 'Spirit of the Age. A reflection on ten years
of theology, television, mad vicars and magazines' (*Christian* vol. 5, no. 3 [1980]): 'I am disturbed to discover that the playwright Dennis Potter who has through this decade been in-
tensely aware of the pain and ambiguity of our condition feels he *cannot* enter the community
of formal Christian believing because he believes the jollity, the triviality and the half-truths
masking suffering would deprive him of his power to write' (p. 12).
[23]   Dietrich Bonhoeffer, *Letters and Papers from Prison* (enlarged edition) (London: SCM, 1971),
p. 300.
[24]   Ibid.

secularizing of the terminology of dogma and liturgy; it is certainly not something that can be planned. It will be like Jesus' own language (and practice, we must assume) in that it effects the presence of God's peace with his creatures, and so, as Bonhoeffer says in a later letter (July 1944), it exposes the actual godlessness of the world.[25] It is non-religious in the sense that it is not primarily concerned with securing a space within the world for a particular specialist discourse. Whether or not it uses the word 'God', it effects faith, conversion, hope. Bonhoeffer's paradigm (as the July letter explains) is the encounters in the gospels between Jesus and those he calls or heals: these are events in which people are concretely drawn into a share in the vulnerability of God, into a new kind of life and a new identity. They do not receive an additional item called faith; their ordinary existence is not re-organized, found wanting in specific respects and supplemented: it is transfigured as a whole.

Bonhoeffer might equally well have pointed to the parables of Jesus. These are not religious stories or expositions of a tradition, but crystallizations of how people decide for or against self-destruction, for or against newness of life, acceptance, relatedness. Repeatedly, as the kingdom of God is spoken of, Jesus simply presents a situation, a short narrative: like *this*, he says. The riddle of the parables, the fact that they are seen as hopelessly enigmatic by friends and enemies, lies in making the connection with one's own transformation – that is, encountering God in the parable, receiving that therapy of the spirit that Dietrich Ritschl writes of, becoming open in a certain way. This, of course, is why the Christian does not repeat the gospel parables in isolation. Only as the parables of *Jesus* can they be properly heard. They are part of a life – a language and practice that culminate in events through which a decisive new being emerges, a new community, a new human identity. The parables have their sense *within* the larger parable that is the life, death and resurrection of Jesus: in relation to this man, the transformation or conversion or therapy which the parables narrate becomes concretely possible. Through the community destroyed in betrayal and desertion at the cross, and re-created at Easter, the possibility of such relation is still open. But if this is the context in which the enigmatic and secular parables ultimately make sense, it is no less true that the events opening the door of the kingdom of God only make sense because they are events concerning a man who had told parables, and enacted them. First we are accustomed to the *pattern* of challenge and transformation, the loss

---

[25] Ibid., p. 362.

and recovery of self that is involved in hearing a parable. (Think of King David listening to Nathan; forgetting himself so far as to be shocked into recognizing himself.) Only then can we see the loss and recovery of God himself in cross and resurrection as the opening to us of comprehensive change and healing, and see the way in which the meanings of love lie beyond the capacity of human beings for virtue, religion and faithfulness, and survive all loss that can be imagined.

The transfiguring of the world in Christ can seem partial or marginal if we have not learned, by speaking and hearing parables, a willingness to lose the identities and perceptions we make for ourselves: all good stories change us if we hear them attentively; the most serious stories change us radically. That is why tragedy is important, especially in a culture of false communality. And if we can accept a very general definition of parable as a narrative both dealing with and requiring 'conversion', radical loss and radical novelty, it may not be too far-fetched to say that the task of theology is the exploration of parable, and so of conversion. The skills for this may be, and should be, learned largely from scripture; yet – as was suggested at the beginning of this chapter – such learning must include those transformations of scriptural narrative that restore to us or open to us the depth of what the narrative deals with, even when these versions do not belong in a mainstream of exegesis. This is perhaps the place to mention the importance of contemporary feminist exegesis as an example of disturbing scriptural reading which forces on us the 'conversion' of seeing how our own words and stories may carry sin or violence in their telling, even as they provide the resource for overcoming that sin and violence. The centre may be localizable, but the boundaries are not clear. Theology should be equipping us for the recognition of and response to the parabolic in the world – all that resists the control of capital and administration and hints at or struggles to a true sharing of human understanding, in art, science and politics. It should also equip us to speak and act parabolically as Christians, to construct in our imagining and our acting 'texts' about conversion – not translations of doctrine into digestible forms, but effective images of a new world like the parables of Christ. Part of the power of T. S. Eliot's *Four Quartets* is its extraordinary reticence about recognizable Christian language. And the force of the witness of the L'Arche communities is in what they are, collaborations of those we call handicapped and those we call normal, not in the theological articulation that may (and must) be given. *This* is what is involved in speaking parabolically, and it is action nourished by the theological grasp of what the life and death of Jesus are, by scripture and the wrestle with dogmatic and devotional tradition; but not confined by it.

Such formation in our tradition goes with and presses us further into the disciplines of listening – to our own untheologized memories and context, the particularity of where we are, and to the efforts at meaning of the rest of the human race. Good doctrine teaches silence, watchfulness, and the expectation of the Spirit's drastic appearance in judgement, recognition, conversion, for us and for the whole world.

Chapter Four

THE DISCIPLINE OF SCRIPTURE

I

In recent years, British and American theology has shown a good deal of interest in reclaiming the insights of 'pre-critical' exegesis, and in challenging what has been seen as the unproductive dominance of scholarly concern with original forms of a scriptural text, with questions about the community background of this or that strand of tradition, or with the redactional concerns of an editor or a series of editors. In short, there has been a widespread dissatisfaction with all the modern conventions of textual study – source, from and redaction criticism – and a reaction towards alternative modes of reading. We have seen pleas for a return to allegory,[1] a sophisticated deployment of modern literary theory to question any remaining obsession with authorial intentions,[2] and the various forms of canonical criticism,[3] insisting that we read scriptural texts in the context of their present and deliberate positioning in relation to each other as constituting a *single* book, settled once and for all in a community's history.[4] With all this in mind, though, it has become difficult to see how what is also a central aspect of traditional and

[1] See ch. 5 of *Discerning the Mystery*, Andrew Louth (Oxford, 1983).
[2] The work of Dan Via and J. D. Crossan in the USA should be mentioned; on this area, see ch. 7 of *Biblical Interpretation*, Robert Morgan with John Barton (Oxford, 1988). A very critical account may be found in Lynn M. Polland, *Literary Criticism and Biblical Hermeneutics: A Critique of Formalist Approaches* (Scholars Press, 1985).
[3] Brevard Childs, *Introduction to the Old Testament as Scripture* (London, 1979), is a significant text, but should not be taken as representative of all forms of 'canonical criticism'. Equally important and rather different is *Torah and Canon*, James A. Sanders (Philadelphia, 1970 and 1972).
[4] On the difficulties in this approach, *Holy Scripture: Canon, Authority, Criticism*, James Barr (Oxford, 1983), remains by far the finest study.

'pre-critical' hermeneutics, the belief in the primacy of the 'literal' sense of Scripture,[5] can now be understood. If we have become suspicious of a hermeneutic that looks for authorial meanings and treats them as normative, if – in literary theory in general – we have been taught a certain uneasiness about the whole notion of normative meaning, how are we to talk about a 'primary' or authoritative level of reading that is bound to history, in the way traditional exegesis conceived the *sensus litteralis* to be?

One way of seeing how the relation between literal and non-literal senses of Scripture has been worked out in doctrinal history is to see it as a tension between what I shall call 'diachronic' and 'synchronic' styles of reading. I can read a text in a more or less 'dramatic' way, by following it through in a single time-continuum, reading it as a sequence of changes, a pattern of transformations; or I can read it as a 'field' of linguistic material, of signs that refer backwards and forwards to each other in a system of interaction more like the surface of a picture than a performance of drama or music. There is a reading – we could say – where the unity of what is read is worked out in time, and a reading where the unity is worked out in something more like space. The former, the diachronic reading, is not by any means a naive strategy: it can operate at several different levels. I may begin by simply following the movement of the text as it stands; but that will alert me to deeper movements or rhythms within it, relations between whole blocks of material, all the ways in which a text can display subversions and tensions within its own progression – the ways in which it can put itself in question. I may become aware of a 'strategy' in the text itself; and that awareness may compel a recognition of the narrative context of the act of writing, of the world of the writer and of his or her goals as they are enacted in the text. If diachronic reading is a reading which can show me something of a text's intentionality (in the widest sense – its internal direction and its consciously envisaged audience), it will put to me questions about the writer's world, questions about history, even if only the history of the process of composing. And such questions are not necessarily a way of disregarding the specificity of the writing as it presents itself, to the extent that they genuinely arise from the act of reading with attention and patience.

To take an example: T. S. Eliot's *Four Quartets* can be read most simply as a sequence of more or less interrelated meditations on time and eternity, or on the presence of meaning within the apparent blind contingency of the

---

[5] First unambiguously defended by Thomas Aquinas, especially in *Summa Theologiae,* I.l.ix and x. The discussion in *Sacra Doctrina. Reason and Revelation in Aquinas,* P. E. Persson (London, 1957), especially pp. 47–70, is still a good introduction.

world. Closer reading, however, brings to light contradictions and cross-currents: one section will be seen as making a proposal that will be under-mined or rejected, or at least forced into a new light, by a subsequent development; a good second reading will display the movement of earlier stages in a significantly different light from that in which they were first understood. We learn to see ironies or even falsities not visible in our initial movement through the text. In Eliot's own words, there is a 'new and shock-ing valuation' within the movement of the poems.[6] The whole work ap-pears as an exercise in the conscious putting into question of the poet's own symbolic idiom; and we grasp this more adequately insofar as we are aware of the pull towards symbolist self-reference, a self-contained world of poetic discourse, in the rest of Eliot's work up to the time of the *Quartets*, and aware too of the poetic voices – Dante, Baudelaire, Mallarmé, Yeats – that were for Eliot both a formative influence and a seduction, a danger. Eliot's quarrel with his own preferred poetic voice is part of a larger world of relat-ing and conflicting poetic idioms.

To say, as I should want to claim, that all this belongs with a 'literal' reading of the text may seem an odd use of the term; but all the levels of reading I have described are unified by the fact that they are generated out of the experience of reading the text 'diachronically', as a movement in time. One level of movement appears as reflecting or opening the door to an-other, and the reading never wholly escapes from the primary fact that the reader has *taken time*[7] in following the progression of the text as it stands. A mature reading capable of discerning at an early stage meanings which in fact depend upon later moments remains in this sense diachronic, because the *possibility* of such a reading would still be consciously dependent upon the prior fact of a *lectio continua* in which the reader had to experience the tem-poral formation and emergence of meanings. It is, of course, possible to do what some critics of the *Quartets* have done,[8] and regard each section, even

---

[6]   *East Coker* 86–7; and cf. Ronald Bush, *T. S. Eliot. A Study in Character and Style* (Oxford, 1983), ch. 11, on the centrality of this strategy in the *Quartets* as a whole.

[7]   Nelson Goodman argues, in 'Twisted Tales; or, Story, Study, and Symphony', *On Narra-tive*, ed. W. J. T. Mitchell (Chicago, 1981), pp. 99–115, that 'in a narrative neither the telling nor what is explicitly told need take time' (pp. 110–11), on the basis of the possibilities of 'organizing' a story on a pictorial surface, and doing so according to a variety of principles by no means self-evident to the 'reader'. This is an important and subtle essay; but I still don't see how the organizing of a story can do other than presuppose *sequence* and invite sequential response – which is what I understand as 'taking time'. Cf. the article referred to in n. 25 on the whole notion of taking time as a category of interpretation.

[8]   A dramatic example is *Word Unheard: A Guide through Eliot's Four Quartets*, Harry Blamires (London, 1969). Religious interpreters seem especially prone to this disastrous method.

each line, as enunciating a single vision, identical from beginning to end of
the sequence, so that early lines are made to bear a freight of deliberate
positive meaning in a quite undialectical way. This may or may not be a
fruitful reading (I find it for the most part decidedly *not*); but it should at least
be clear that it could not exist at all without the experience of first working
through the whole complex over time, with all that implies of provisionality
and 're-visioning'. Thus, to attend to a 'literal' sense in this sort of context is
to insist upon there being some controlling force in the fact that meaning
comes to light in a process of learning to perceive; it is to challenge the idea
that there could be an adequate reading of the text which ignored the time
of the text itself, its own movement, with the time of the writer and the
writer's world opened up to us through the movement of the text. It is to
protest against any reading which elided or softened or simply ignored the
tensions realized and worked through in the time of the text, its movement
as something that bear continuous reading. Concern with the literal, the
diachronic, is a way of resisting the premature unities and harmonies of a
non-literal reading (whether allegorical, existentialist, structuralist or decon-
structionist), in which the time that matters is only the present of the reader
faced with the 'spatial' expanse of a text cut off from its own inner processes
and the history of its production.

Something like this seems to be at work in Thomas Aquinas' insistence on
the priority of the literal sense.[9] He takes the literal sense to be that which
refers to the intention of the author – who, in the case of Scripture, is God;
and this intention is primarily manifest in events, not in the text itself, for
God can communicate through the material processes of the world's history,
while human beings can only organize words to convey their meanings.
What Scripture has to tell us can be apprehended only through awareness of
a reference to the lives and actions of 'those persons through whom God's
revelation reaches us';[10] the narrative of Scripture displays the 'authority' of
these figures, their status as enacting or communicating the purposes of God,
and that authority is the basis of the normative significance of 'Scripture or
teaching' (*sacra scriptura vel doctrina*). All readings of Scripture are finally
answerable to this, so that nothing in *doctrina* can be established solely on the
basis of a non-literal reading.[11] As Thomas makes clear,[12] the literal sense is

[9]   *Illa ergo prima significatio, qua voces significant res, pertinet ad primum sensum, qui est sensus
historicus, vel litteralis*; *STh* I.l.x.c.
[10] *Singularia traduntur in sacra doctrina . . . ad declarandam auctoritatem vivorum per quos and nos
revelatio divina processit*; ibid., ii ad 2.
[11] Ibid., ix ad 2.
[12] Ibid., x ad 3.

not dependent on a belief that all scriptural propositions uncomplicatedly depict real states of affairs detail by detail; it can and does include metaphor within the literary movement that leads us into the movement of God within the time of human biography. In this way, Thomas sketches an understanding of the literal that allows for a plurality of *genres* within it; it is the failure to see and to develop this insight that has led to those narrow and sterile definitions of the literal sense against which recent hermeneutics has so sharply reacted.

Paradoxically, it was the development of a more sophisticated literary hermeneutic, by way of historical and comparative criticism, that led to the effective redefinition – and the disastrous shrinkage – of the literal sense that we associate with fundamentalism.[13] Correctly identifying 'literal' with 'historical', in sound traditional fashion, fundamentalism assumed that 'historical' could be applied only to a univocally descriptive and exact representation of particular sequences of 'fact'. Against the potential totalitarianism of this, and the equally stagnant prospects of a formal and archaeological historical criticism, the retrieval of non-literal or 'pre-critical' modes is entirely intelligible. But this in its turn has its dangers. Of the problems of post-structuralist exegesis I shall say more shortly; but at least some forms of 'canonical' criticism risk just that elision of *conflict* that has characterized other styles of non-literal exegesis. An uncritical canonical criticism threatens to prohibit or ignore any questions about meaning that arise from the refusal to take the homogeneity of the canon for granted. If this reaction against the literal were to prevail, it would point either to a new totalitarianism of canonical context, understood without reference to history, or to an *arbitrary* pluralism, in which the idea of a given textual content capable of effectively challenging or changing the reader would be hard to sustain.[14] To guard intelligently against this, we need to re-examine and re-state the case for the primacy of the literal; this essay is an attempt to begin that task.

II

It is in fact very difficult to make sense of the idea of a total triumph for synchronic, non-literal or 'spatial' reading. 'We love stories because our lives

---

[13] For illuminating discussion of how fundamentalism represents a narrowing of 'traditional' categories of exegesis, see especially ch. 9 of *Fundamentalism*, James Barr (London, 1977).

[14] Barr, *Holy Scripture*, ch. 4 (especially p. 95) and the postscript, pp. 130–71, is one of the most thorough and insightful critiques of Childs' views on the canon as the norm of criticism; cf. p. 67, 'canons do not give us hermeneutical guidance'.

are stories' says one recent contributor to this discussion;[15] that is to say that we are aware in our own lives of the process of learning and producing meanings, and naturally look, in our reading, for comparable processes of production. The meanings in our reading are like the meanings in the rest of our experience, they are to be discovered, unfolded: the reading of narrative in particular has an open future and a gradually accumulating past. So long as our humanity remains unintelligible except as a life of material change, irreversible movement, it is unlikely – to say the least – that we could establish non-diachronic modes of reading as primary. It is quite true that works which set out to operate in a linear temporal mode of the simplest kind escape from this constraint in all kinds of ways;[16] but I have already suggested that this, so far from leading us directly to synchronic interpretation, has the effect of opening us up to more than one 'time' in the text, more than one story. We can and we must read the cross-currents and subversions in a text, but we do not thereby escape the 'literal'. We are still concerned with how meanings grow and are produced; the text is not allowed to slip into timelessness.

This is only a brief hint of how the pressure towards abandoning normativity in literary theory comes up against the problem of human materiality (the point is familiar enough that both structuralist and post-structuralist theories of interpretation are pervasively idealist). But the question has a much sharper focus for Christian theology. Christian language takes it for granted, in several different ways, that meanings are learned and produced, not given in iconic, ahistorical form. It grows out of a particular set of communal and individual histories, and its images and idioms are fundamentally shaped by this fact. And, in working through concepts like penitence, conversion and hope, in its commitment to the freedom of God and God's grace to draw historical realities into a future as yet undetermined, it resists the notion that the understanding of faith can be only a *moment* of interpretative perception with its own synchronic integrity and completeness, as opposed to a process with strong elements of risk and provisionality.

[15] Sallie TeSelle, *Speaking in Parables. A Study in Metaphor and Theology* (Philadelphia, 1975), p. 138.

[16] Frank Kermode, 'Secrets and Narrative Sequence', *On Narrative* (pp. 79–97), pp. 80–4: note particularly, on p. 83, 'Whatever the comforts of sequence, connexity (I agree that we cannot do without them), it cannot be argued that the text which exhibits them will do nothing but contribute to them'; and, on p. 97, 'It seems that a god and a devil write simultaneously, another *dédoublement* if you like, and one that, somehow, the good reader must emulate; for if he does not he will, by concurring in the illusions of limit and authority, deny the god (the hidden god of secrets) his due.'

Consequently, Christian interpretation is unavoidably engaged in 'dramatic' modes of reading: we are invited to identify ourselves in the story being contemplated, to re-appropriate who we are now, and who we shall or can be, in terms of the story. *Its* movements, transactions, transformations, become *ours*; we take responsibility for this or that position within the narrative. This has some affinity with what exegetical tradition has called 'moral' interpretation, in that the text is read as something requiring change in the reader, change of a kind depicted in the text itself; but whereas moral exegesis could easily become a matter simply of accumulating *exempla*, icons of behaviour, so to speak, a 'dramatic' reading means that our appropriation of the story is not a static relation of confrontation with images of virtue or vice, finished pictures of a quality once and for all achieved and so no longer taking time, but an active working through of the story's movement in our own time. In fact, it may be misleading to speak here of 'story' in too simple a way. The same 'dramatic' process is no less at work in the proper reading of an *argument*: the epistles of Paul require dramatic exegesis, require to be read in a 'time' of statement and counter-statement, movement and counter-movement. To abstract from this – as in the often disastrous history of the readings of Romans 9–11, for instance – is to make the text serve other purposes than its own process, its own production of meaning; it is, once again, to look for premature harmonies.

'Dramatic' reading, then, belongs with the literal sense as I have been trying to define it. It assumes that the diachronic is a central element in the working of Christian text and interpretation, and also – very importantly – that the time of the text is recognizably continuous with my time. The movements, transactions and transformations of the text are not different in kind from the movement of my own experience, from how I tell my own story. Hence, of course, the significance in all this of the parabolic mode of Jesus' teaching: the story *moves* in recognizable ways, sufficiently recognizable to invite the hearer's or reader's identification. But, remembering that the movement of the text may open up the further movement of the writer's own argument with him – or herself, and the writer's engagement with a complex memory, individual and corporate, a world, we may also find ourselves invited to re-appropriate ourselves in terms of that world also, as it shows itself in the text. The weary discussion of problems of cultural relativism in hermeneutics may be moved on a little if we are able to allow that the capacity to *follow* a narrative or argumentative movement in an ancient or difficult text must radically qualify any extreme claims for untranslatability or even uninterpretability; but that is a question in need of more discussion than can be offered here.

III

If it is correct to see the 'dramatic' mode of exegesis as part of what the *sensus litteralis* in its diachronic character includes, there is clearly a sense in which literal reading involves public *performance*[17] – a tangible 'taking of time' now for the presentation of the time of the text. Thus the use of a scriptural lectionary bound to the festal cycle (annual, biennial or triennial) is a major mediation of the literal sense. And at certain seasons, above all the paschal celebration, this is intensified in a way very evidently designed to bring our time and the time of the canonical narrative together. The liturgy of Holy Week involves a thoroughly diachronic reading, in which the congregation has to take on a succession of roles – the city that welcomes Jesus on Palm Sunday, the city that rejects Jesus on Good Friday, the apostles receiving the ministry of Jesus at the Last Supper (in the footwashing ceremony of Maundy Thursday), watching with Jesus in Gethsemane, deserting Jesus at his arrest; the redeemed Israel following the pillar of fire through the night at the Easter Vigil. It is comparable to and as complex as the enactment of the Exodus in the Passover ritual; and it is, of course, the underpinning for the great dramatic 'readings' of Bach's Passions. It insists upon our reading the text of the story of redemption with some sense of the provisional and contingent in its unfolding (as if we did not know the end); only when the movement has been lived and worked through can we say, with the risen Jesus of the Emmaus story, 'It was necessary . . .'.[18]

This reading does not simply rest upon the devotional urge to represent the facts of Jesus' fleshly life so as to stir particular feelings in response, and so is not vulnerable to the problems about the exact historicity of the narrative raised by critical scholarship. Indeed, the uncovering by such scholarship of the distinct interests at work in the diverse strands of the passion story can enhance the diachronic nature of the reading by offering different traject-ories through the same fundamental movement (something already obscurely recognized in the fact that, historically, the Holy Week liturgy enjoined the reading of all four gospel accounts of the passion), and suggesting a dia-chronic movement *between* these versions themselves, one narrative responding

---

[17]   I owe this notion above all to the essay by Nicholas Lash, 'Performing the Scriptures', in his *Theology on the Way to Emmaus* (London, 1986), pp. 37–46.
[18]   See 'The Emmaus Story: Necessity and Freedom', by Timothy Radcliffe, *New Blackfriars* 64 (1983), pp. 483–93, for a fine exposition of how this is articulated in the Easter narrative of Luke 24.13–35.

to another – a point I shall return to later. Equally, however, we are not to suppose that we have to do here with a mythical time (Eliade's *in illo tempore*), whose duration is only a pattern of formal interaction between points in a structure without wider context: this story *can* be generalized into an archetypal and iconic pattern, but, for the necessary grasp, the necessary following of the narrative demanded by a good first reading, we need to know who Jews and Romans are, and what is the nature of the texts (of prophecy) that make up the historical frame of reference of the New Testament text as it unfolds. The telling of this story is quite overtly a 'conversation' with realities that the surface of the narrative does not itself explicate or display – the world of prophetic expectation, the stories and hopes of a broader religious tradition. These are quite simple and contingent points at which it calls for *location* in its world, since its own frame of reference has the incompleteness characteristic of all genuinely historical discourse, discourse aware of the time of its world. 'The world of the text' is an important concept as we attempt to see just how a text does establish its range or frame of reference, establishes the conditions for its own meaningfulness; but of course no text, not even the most hermetically symbolist, creates an exhaustive account of these conditions. And – in the case of canonical narratives like the passion stories, or canonical arguments like the Pauline epistles – we are dealing with texts that emerge in communities which are in any case acutely aware of working against the background of a past which they must reckon with and make sense of.

Here we are brought back to the point that our diachronic reading assumes a continuity between the time(s) of the text and what we recognize as movement and production in our own lives. We are *able* to make time now for the performance of canonical narrative and argument because it is the kind of thing that takes time in our own 'narrative'; and we are *able* to enter the time of the canonical text because we see it as a possible movement or process for the kind of beings we are. *Analogy* is fundamental to literal reading – an *analogia durationis* if you want a spurious technical term: the interpretative confidence that this text can be *followed* on my terms as reader. This is what is presupposed in some concluding remarks of Werner Jeanrond's fine study, *Text und Interpretation als Kategorien theologischen Denkens*:[19]

> Theologie kann sich also nicht allein darin erschöpfen, die Technik des Verstehens von alten Texten oder die historisch-kritische Erhebung von Textursprüngen zu diskutieren. Theologie muss vielmehr aufgrund solcher

---

[19]   Tübingen, 1986.

Vorarbeiten auch mit den Texten selbst im Gespräch kommen, d.h. mit dem, was die Texte darstellen. Die Texte der christlichen Tradition weisen gleichzeitig vor und zurück, Sie verweisen auf ihre Zeit, ihre individuellen Umstände und durch diese konkrete Situationen hindurch auf unsere Seit mit ihren konkreten Gegebenheiten. Und gerade weil sie immer noch verweisen können, nennen wir sie 'klassisch'.

All I should wish to add to this lucid summary is that the idea of a movement between two concrete situations, the location of the text and the location of the reader, depends on the mediation of a text which enacts the producing of a meaning in such a way that it is open to its own situation, its own production, and offers an analogical bridgehead to the world in which the reader experiences the production of meaning. It depends, that is to say, on a text that can be read diachronically in the first instance.

IV

Jeanrond notes [20] that fruitful interpretation acknowledges and works with radical differences in human experience; and if the preceding discussion is on the right lines, 'literal' exegesis has a particularly strong stake in the realities of *conflict*. The movement of our canonical texts is frequently a quite explicit response to or rebuttal of some other position *within* the same canonical framework; the world it opens to us is one of uneasy relationships and discontinuities. The meaning of one portion of scriptural text is constructed in opposition to another. To read literally, diachronically, is here to read the movement of the text in relation to the movement of conflict or resistance in the world *of* (in) the text and the world from which the text is produced; and at this point the opposition between literal reading and the harmonies of certain non-literal readings is most marked.

The clearest, almost paradigmatic, case in Christian Scripture is the relation between the writings of 'old' and 'new' covenants. To read the New Testament with any understanding at all is to see it as in part an attempt to claim and re-order the existing texts and traditions of a community from which the producers of these new texts seek to distance themselves even as they seek to present themselves as its true heirs.[21] But within both Old and New Testa-

---

[20] p. 150.
[21] The sense in which it is and is not accurate to describe the New Testament as a gloss on the Old is well summarized in Barr, *Holy Scripture*, p. 69–70.

ments the same pattern is visible. There are conflicting 'bids' to define the community and order its history. The various distinct strata of the Pentateuchal documents may speak only of a contingent accumulation of traditions, but the relation of the Chronicler to the Deuteronomic historian is more complex: judgements of persons and actions are at times more evidently in tension. Indeed, the Chronicler might in some ways be seen as already smoothing out the 'diachronic' theology of the Deuteronomist, who is genuinely concerned with the interaction between the purposes of God and the contingencies and betrayals of Israel's history. The Chronicler's David and Solomon are already close to being icons; neutral or favourable assessments of monarchs like Uzziah and Joash in Kings are revised in the light of how the priestly ideology of the Chronicler's day defined piety; and so forth. Sharper conflict still is evident in the near-certain contemporaneity of Ruth and Jonah with the reforms of Ezra: Ruth not only tells the story of a 'mixed marriage' such as the policy of Ezra and Nehemiah disallowed, it also presents this disreputable event as a crucial moment in the working out of the covenant, since David is presented as Ruth's descendant; while Jonah wittily contrasts the disobedience and stubbornness of a Hebrew prophet of impeccable credentials with the ready obedience of everyone and everything else, from the natural order itself to the most ruthless and savage of Israel's enemies, who respond promptly and generously to the summons to repentance. In both Ruth and Jonah, the integrity of the covenant, which Ezra's circle seek to preserve by an enforcement of 'purity', separateness, is made to rest primarily on God's single-minded will to show mercy and to raise up new things, rather than on a narrow interpretation of human single-mindedness. Yet Ezra is not written out of the story as a whole: without that zeal for renewal, the very sense of the covenanted identity of God's people, symbolized in the rebuilt Temple, would be eroded, and the history of divine faithfulness that is taken for granted in Ruth and Jonah would be in danger of oblivion.[22]

The New Testament also exhibits similar signs of rival 'bids for definition'. The familiar tension between the Letter of James and the central tenets of Pauline soteriology is only the most dramatic instance. Some scholars read the Johannine corpus as presupposing a church with no visible structured ministry; so that it may be in part directed against communities (post-Pauline and Matthean, for instance) that have institutional forms of leadership.[23]

---

[22] See Sanders, *Torah and Canon*,[2] pp. 111–12, for comments on Ruth.
[23] The various works of Raymond Brown form the classical statement of this case; see especially *The Community of the Beloved Disciple* (London, 1979) and *The Churches the Apostles Left Behind* (London, 1984).

This is speculative; but we can at least register the unquestionable fact that diverse texts emerge from different sorts of community in the New Testament era. And the existence of four versions of the fundamental story of Jesus, three (at least) very closely related to each other, reflects not only the fact of pluralism, but the fact of engagement *between* theologies: the story is rewritten in the conviction that previous tellings are unbalanced or inadequate; yet the rewriting has the same risk and provisionality. Matthew only 'corrects' Mark at the cost of fresh imbalances and narrowings of focus,[24] so that, as in the liturgy of the Christian year, they must be constantly re-read in counterpoint with each other. There is no resting-place among or between the gospels: their own independent ways of taking time over the story of Jesus reveal something of the time of early communities in animated and often critical dialogue, and oblige us to take time not only in the reading of one sequence but in the 'cross-referenced' reading that observes the time in which their differences are produced.

I have argued elsewhere[25] that to speak of the 'inner life' of a product or a person is to presuppose its capacity to make us 'take time' with it or them; otherwise we are likely to fall captive to the mythology of an essential core of truth from which accidental material and external forms may be stripped away. What I am suggesting here is that it is 'diachronic' reading of Scripture that gives us the 'interiority' of the text, and that this interiority is not a point of hidden clarity and security but a complex of interwoven processes: a production of meaning in the only mode available for material and temporal creatures. Synchronic reading of whatever kind relies on that suspicion of 'surface' phenomena that can make interpretation a systematic exercise in losing or ignoring the object, seeking the 'spirit' through the *absence* of the 'letter'.

But if diachronic reading is the most attentive to the real plurality – discord as well as polyphony – in the material text and its material world, how does it construct any viable sense of *unity* in the text? The answer to this question must be in terms of the fact that 'Scripture' (Jewish as well as Christian) comes to exist as such in a community that says and does identifiable

---

[24] Vigorously argued by J. L. Houlden, *Backward into Light: The Passion and Resurrection of Jesus According to Matthew and Mark* (London, 1987); and for a still more hostile and 'suspicious' reading of Mark itself, Burton Mack, *A Myth of Innocence, Mark and Christian Origins* (Philadelphia, 1988) should be consulted.

[25] Rowan Williams, 'The Suspicion of Suspicion', in *The Grammar of the Heart. New Essays in Moral Philosophy and Theology*, ed. Richard Bell (San Francisco, 1988), pp. 36–53, especially the concluding section (pp. 48–51).

and distinctive things; that has some means of articulating a particular identity. The unity of Scripture has to do with how it becomes part of this articulation, how it establishes itself as a point of reference (a *canon*) for a community with a definite and perceptible historical unity. Its unifying themes are established according to what is understood as unifying the community. This is *not* to reduce its unity to something decided upon by the community to suit whatever happen to be its priorities; it is to say that if the community finds its focus in this or that set of narratives and practices, finds that *these* articulate what the community holds itself answerable to, then what authoritatively matters in the text, and so in some sense organizes the text for a reader in this corporate context, is what grounds or explicates these identifying features.

To put this in a rather different way: Scripture, with all its discord and polyphony, is the canonical text of a community in which there are limits to pluralism. The history of Scripture, internal and contextual, for all its stresses and cross-currents, is being read as the production of the meaning of a corporate symbolic life that has some unity and integrity. We simply do not *know* of historic Christian communities that do not introduce people into their structures by a ritual of identification with the death and resurrection of Jesus, or that do not corporately proclaim that death and resurrection in 'ministries of word and sacrament'. The unities and thus the limits of what it makes Christian sense to say are bound to the question of what – or who – the Church *intends to make present*, as the authoritative point of judgement and the resource for action in hope, in its corporate action, that action which is specific to it as Church. And Scripture is read, then, with that question in mind: how – without gross distortion and selectivity, 'synchronic' reconciliations – are we to 'follow' the history of Scripture so that the authoritative centrality of the narratives presupposed in baptism and eucharist appears? It is because – as we have seen – these narratives have their life in the time of the whole canonical ensemble that we cannot simply make them general and abstract symbols, or simply scour the text for iconic types. The scriptural *history* has to be told, has to be followed diachronically or literally, *as it leads to* Christ and the cross of Christ. A reading of Scripture that takes place in faith cannot avoid Luther's hermeneutical axiom, *crux probat omnia;* without it, the whole idea of a distinctive community of faith, a new creation, a community to whom something specific has happened, is necessarily eroded.

Part of the importance of this lies in the analogical principle sketched earlier. We recognize the duration of the text as familiar: *our* time is like this. But reading Scripture in faith is reading it as moving towards or around a unifying narrative moment, the story of the work of Jesus: *how* it does so,

how we are to carry through such a reading in points of detail, is constantly
elusive; we know only that, as a matter of fact, the movement that is portrayed by the texts of Scripture had produced the identifiable and distinctive
meanings of the Church. Its conflicts are the process that produces a symbolic and communicative whole, and our theological exegesis, our prepara-
tion for the preaching of the text, is the continuing struggle to display how
this might be so. But if we consider our time to be analogous to that of
Scripture and its world, then our diachronic reading becomes something
that speaks of hope. Our time – perhaps more than earlier Christian ages, or
more self-consciously than earlier Christian ages – is characterized by profound conflict in many areas as to what is authentically Christian – conflicts
over areas of sexual and personal ethics (especially, in the West at present,
the admissibility in the Church of overt homosexual partnerships), over economic and public matters (the Church's relation to capitalism), and over the
major issues of war and defence (the legitimacy of the nuclear deterrent).
Honesty compels the admission that none of these questions is likely to be
'settled' in the foreseeable future, certainly not by appeal to what is commonly taken to be the 'literal sense of Scripture' (i.e. particular clusters of
quotations). Yet peaceful co-existence in an undemanding pluralism is an
inadequate response when the matters at issue seem to relate to basic questions about how the gospel can be heard in the struggles of contemporary
social existence.[26] There is a case for protest, even for 'confessional' separation over some issues. But what the foregoing analysis of 'literal' meaning
may suggest is that the existence of conflict and even conscientious division
may be not a sign of eschatological polarization but a necessary part of that
movement of the story of God's people and their language towards the one
focus of Christ crucified and risen that is the movement of Scripture. There
can be an exacting patience in the debates of Christians; the confidence (if
that is the right word) that it is *worth* struggling for the life of the Church in
and through the awkwardness of dissidence and conscientious protest imposes the discipline of 'staying with' the public life and liturgy of the tradition, rather than seeking the shortest solution of a newly constructed
community of the perfect. Even a 'confessing' Church, that is to say, bears
the burdens of historical guilt and the risks of failure, and confesses also its
solidarity with the weakness or sinfulness of the whole historical community
(including its own current opponents) by continuing to place itself under the

---

[26] See, for example, Dietrich Ritschl, *The Logic of Theology* (London, 1986), especially sections IF, IID and IIIA, for reflections relating to this issue; also Rowan Williams, 'The Unity
of Christian Truth' [above, ch. 2].

same judgement of baptism, preaching and Eucharist. To bear with the embarrassing past and present of the Church in this way, even from a stance of protest or a pleading for new directions and commitments, is precisely, I suggest, to have learned what the 'literal' reading of Scripture has to teach – that the unity of Christ, unity in the Easter mystery, is learned or produced only in *this* kind of history, the history of counter-claims and debate.

The temptation is to understand this as a sub-Hegelian affirmation of unity through dialectic; but this is not what is being claimed. The future held for us in Jesus Christ is not produced by a single traceable dialectic (we might adapt St Ambrose's dictum, *non in dialectica complacuit Deo servare populum suum!*); nor does it even follow the unilinear materialist version of the same pattern propounded by Marxism. Christ is 'produced' by the history of the covenant people in a way that is both continuous with, even internal to, the history of its conflicts, yet, as the focal point for the unity of a new people with a new history, he is also for the believer a gratuitous and unpredictable moment in the whole process. This double perception is one way of stating the basic Christological duality behind the classical formula of Chalcedon. And because we assume the analogy between our time and the narrative time of Scripture, and Scriptural time moves toward the specific time of renewal and liberation in Jesus, we in our own conflicts can maintain hope. We are not spared the cost of conflict or promised a final theological resolution; rather we are assured of the possibility of 're-producing' the meaning that is Christ crucified and risen, through our commitment to an unavoidably divided Church – not by the effort to reconcile at all costs, but by carrying the burdens of conflict in the face of that unifying judgement bodied forth in preaching and sacrament. In that openness to the plain historical *difficulty* of belonging to the Church, we open ourselves to the gift of Christ.

In the light of all this, we might try re-conceiving the literal sense of Scripture as an *eschatological* sense. To read diachronically the history that we call a history of *salvation* is to 'read' our own time in the believing community (and so too the time of our world) as capable of being integrated into such a history, in a future we cannot but call God's because we have no secure human way of planning it or thematizing it. In other words, so far from the literal or historical sense being a resource of problem-solving clarity, as it might appear to be for the fundamentalist, an area of simple truthfulness over against the dangerously sophisticated pluralism of a disobedient Church, it may rather encourage us to take historical responsibility for arguing and exploring how the gospel is going to be heard in our day. It can do this because it shows us a history (inside and outside the text) of real and harsh divisions that is both taken up and 'overtaken' by grace. It suggests that what matters is not our ability to finish our business or to secure consensus, as if Christ would be 'audible' only in this mode, but our readiness to decide, to take sides, as adult persons, and to live with the consequence and cost of that within the disciplines we share with other Christians of openness to the judgement of the Easter mystery. These disciplines we share with both past and present, with those near and distant, those we agree with and those we resist, those who are congenial and those who are not. And the common discipline above all of reading Scripture in the public, sacramental worship of the Church, reading 'diachronically' and 'analogically' in the sense I have tried to outline here, should stand as a foundation for hope and hold before us a model of faith.

Part Two

THE ACT OF GOD

Chapter Five

ON BEING CREATURES

I

Christian reflection on creation has been a bit of a Cinderella in twentieth-century theology – at least until the last few years, when a variety of pressures has brought it very much to the fore. New developments in cosmology have aroused some – rather confused – theological interest, on the one hand; and the daily increasing gravity of our environmental crisis has sharpened our concern to relate human interests and needs to the balance of the entire system of the world, on the other – so that we have begun to ask what it might mean to see the *unity* of our humanness with a material world both ordered and limited. Both these developments have very naturally prompted the raising of questions connected with the doctrine of creation. Less directly, pressure has come from certain feminist quarters: has not a redemption-oriented Christian theology functioned as an expression of the male urge to shake off the threatening and humiliating ties that bind spirit to body, to the earth, the cycle of reproduction, woman imaged as the sign of fallenness, of unspiritual nature? Hence the emergence of an interest in 'creation–centred spirituality', which 'begins . . . with the theme of original blessing rather than original sin'.[1] Its characteristic language is one of trust in the material order of the world, the rejection of nature-spirit dualism and indeed of the creator-creation divide, in a certain sense: the key term is 'panentheism', designating the way in which all beings have their life in God, in a simple, 'synchronous', interwoven pattern, a timeless moment which breaks in on our awareness as and when we see the transparency of beings to (God's) Being. This perception of the world becomes the founda-

---

[1] Matthew Fox on 'Creation-Centred Spirituality' in Gordon Wakefield's *Dictionary of Christian Spirituality* (London, 1983), p. 99.

tion for a spirituality that is prophetically critical of our exploitative distance from our world, and generative of a universal compassion working towards justice. It is 'the spiritual tradition that is the most Jewish, the most biblical, the most prophetic and the most like the kind Jesus of Nazareth preached and lived'[2], and it has, according to Matthew Fox, been largely forgotten in Western Christendom in recent centuries.

However, despite this rather naive appeal to the obvious superiority of a 'biblical' spirituality, it is clear that Fox is putting some very grave questions to the whole of the classical Christian account of creation, biblical and post-biblical. It is not a simple matter of reclaiming one bit of Christian tradition to set against another. The problems are forcefully set out in Rosemary Ruether's *Sexism and God-Talk: Towards a Feminist Theology*,[3] which contains an intriguing discussion of the possible agenda underlying the Hebrew myth of creation in its distinctness from Babylonian and Canaanite thought-forms. For the latter, 'creation is a movement of self-regulation *within* a single continuum, 'the matrix of chaos-cosmos'; for the Hebrews, the creator is more like an artisan working on material *outside* his own nature, by what appears as 'a combination of male seminal and cultural power (word-act) that shapes it "from above" '[4]. There is a correlation between cosmic order and moral righteousness: submission to the 'cultural' power of God – the power of God to name, define, locate things – will guarantee the world's harmony. This is already a step towards the more drastic hierarchicalism and alienation of the Greek model of the world's making, where human consciousness (implicitly male) is recognized as akin to the primary agency of God as mind, and foreign to the realm of matter. For Ruether, a theology of the creative matrix must be constructed; not in terms of the static immanence of Babylonian myth, but by understanding that history is *not* the liberation of spirit from nature. 'Feminist theology needs to affirm the God of Exodus, of liberation and new being, but as rooted in the foundations of being rather than as its antithesis.'[5] Instead of a view that privileges historical action as heroic rupture, breaking away from the natural and timeless, a kind of imitation of the primordial rupture between nothing and something which is the authoritative word of creation, we must develop a model of the divine as what encompasses and pervades the system of the universe, the ultimate

---

[2] Matthew Fox, *Breakthrough. Meister Eckhart's Creation Spirituality in New Translation* (New York, 1980). p. 4.
[3] Boston, 1983.
[4] Ibid., p. 77.
[5] Ibid., p. 71.

resourcefulness that enables the system (including our historical action) constantly to recover balance and harmony.[6] This also has the effect[7] of challenging traditional accounts of eschatology: if there is no single, 'linear' story of God's liberative action (a story bound to give unique power and definitional force to the human group that appropriates it), there is no movement to a last end, a millennium – only a confidence that, within the divine matrix, nothing is ultimately lost

Many of these themes are echoed in the more recent work of Sallie McFague, *Models of God: Theology for an Ecological Nuclear Age*.[8] Here again we find the suggestion that the classical view of creation sees it as an exercise of 'cultural' power, the giving of form to the (external) formless. This aesthetic view, God as artist, implies a certain detachment in God's *judgement* of the world: 'An artist, upon completing a work, makes a judgment whether it is good or bad; the judgment is an aesthetic one based on critical standards.'[9] These standards are, McFague suggests 'neutral', not intrinsic to the person of the artist, in sharp contrast to the standards by which a parent judges a child; and it is this latter parental image of 'production' which we ought to be developing as a theological tool, since it allows a far more central importance to the idea of continuity between creator and creation, the bonds of kinship. Despite the problems of putting them together in a logical unity, the images of God as bringing creation to birth and of the world as God's body[10] have a real affinity. God's 'interests', if we can speak in such terms, are bound up with the world's; so that there can be no temptation to model one's behaviour on a God utterly without any investment in the life of creation, as if the best form of life were one which repudiated involvement in or dependency upon the material world.[11] God as maker of what is decisively not God is a dangerous notion, insofar as it generates and legitimates monarchical control over the world, dualistic contempt for the world and the exaltation of abstract 'spirit' – all the pathologies which, for McFague, afflict the culture of the present age, with its crises of international and environmental security.

There are several points of strain, if not contradiction, in all this. It is not at all clear how far for McFague 'Hebrew' thought (whatever exactly this is) escapes the charge of monarchical distortion simply by having a robust doc-

6   Ibid., pp. 85–92, 214–34.
7   Ibid., ch. 10, esp. pp. 250–8.
8   Philadelphia and London, 1987.
9   Ibid., p. 111.
10   Ibid., pp. 69–78.
11   Ibid., pp. 112; cf. pp. 72–4.

trine of covenant;[12] Ruether's critique cuts a good deal deeper than McFague allows on the question of pervasive patriarchialism in Jewish scripture. And the metaphor of the world as God's body – rather more carefully and comprehensively handled by Grace Jantzen – seems, paradoxically, to require a disturbingly stark dualism: we are *not* our bodies, after all, especially when those bodies are 'sick, maimed, ageing, enslaved, or dying';[13] and if we are in the long run somehow not identical with our bodies, it is theologically safe to think of the world as God's body. We are not committed to seeing God's identity as dependent upon the material world;[14] God is in some sense free of any particular body or even the sum total of bodies, as we cannot wholly be. God could in principle form another 'body' to express the divine life, and we do not have that sort of freedom. Yet there is an analogy in the kind of relation we have to our bodies: 'God relates sympathetically to the world, just as we relate sympathetically to our bodies.'[15] This is baffling: 'sympathy' is surely the last thing I can feel for my body since it is my body that feels. If sympathy is the capacity to recognize with moral concern the kinship between another's situation and my own, I could only 'sympathize with my body if 'I' were a kind of parallel being with a different history of sensations. The suspicion grows that the 'God's body' image can only work by trading on precisely the residual dualism that is elsewhere under attack, and by evading some plain and uncomfortable philosophical questions. The results, I think, are far more morally and spiritually worrying than anything the artistic analogy can produce; and McFague's treatment of this latter is again rather puzzling. Does any artist judge her works by these supposedly 'neutral' criteria? Isn't it rather that an artist 'judges' (the wrong word, anyway) the thing made by its own integrity and coherence, an integrity rooted in the artist's own sense of being-in-the-world? And it is perfectly possible to understand one's artistic failure as a moral and personal matter. Anyone disposed to think Sallie McFague right about artists might do worse than read Geoffrey Hill's essay on 'Poetry as "Menace" and "Atonement"'.[16]

There is some fundamental muddle here about the kind of difference we can and should speak of in relation to God and God's world. Both McFague and Ruether, the latter with more sharpness of focus, see the crises of the age

[12]   Ibid., p. 110.
[13]   Ibid., n. 14 on p. 201, referring to John Cobb's essay, 'Feminism and Process Thought' in Sheila Greave Daveney (ed.), *Feminism and Process Thought* (New York, 1981).
[14]   Ibid., pp. 71–2.
[15]   Ibid., p. 73.
[16]   *The Lords of Limit. Essays on Literature and Ideas* (London, 1984).

as rooted, to a very significant extent, in the twin problems of dualism and hierarchy; and they are entirely right to point to elements in the rhetoric and the narrative of much of traditional Christianity which display in strikingly clear form the disastrous possibilities of a certain kind of God–world differentiation, especially when coupled with a parallel spirit–nature disjunction. But neither writer spends long in trying to understand what exactly the doctrine of creation out of nothing actually means in the hands of those who have most carefully dealt with it, and what its implications might be for understanding or imagining ourselves as creatures. The weight of modern objection to what is thought to be the classical doctrine is, at the very least, a witness to the truth that no amount of theological refinement can, of itself, prevent the slide into destructive and sterile patterns of thought that license diseased or oppressive patterns of action and relation. But this means that the answer to the problem is not solely the generation of a new idiom (especially one which is confessedly full of conceptual strains), but should involve a hard look at what the original doctrine's logic is meant to state and safeguard – whether or not we finally decide to go on giving it the privilege it has had in the past. That is the task this lecture attempts to begin.

II

The belief that God created the world out of nothing was unquestionably a *distinctive* Jewish and Christian view in the late antique world. Other accounts of creation may ascribe to God the initiative in setting things in motion or imposing order on passive matter; but the notion of an absolute origin is not to be found with anything like comparable clarity outside the Judaeo-Christian environment. There is a growing trend, of course, towards the view finally expressed in the great Plotinus' work, the source of Neoplatonism, that the entire complex world of things that can be known and talked about depends on or flows out of a simple, wholly unified primary reality, the One; but it would be odd to describe this as an *action* in the way 'creating' seems to be an action. Although it would take too long to discuss here the probable origins of the idea of creation from nothing, it is significant that such language seems to have emerged into full prominence around the time of Israel's return from Babylonian exile (above all in the 'Second Isaiah', Is. 40–55). This deliverance, decisive and unexpected, is like a second Exodus; and the Exodus in turn comes to be seen as a sort of recapitulation of creation. Out of a situation where there is no identity, where there are no names, only the anonymity of slavery or the powerlessness of the ghetto, God makes a human community, calls it *by name* (a recurrent motif in Is. 40–55), gives it or restores to it a territory. Nothing makes God do this except God's own free promise; from human chaos God makes human community. But this act is not a *process* by which shape is imposed on chaos: it is a summons, a call which establishes the very possibility of an answer. It is a short step to the conclusion that God's relation to the whole world is like this: not a struggle with pre-existing disorder that is then moulded into shape, but a pure summons. 'My hand laid the foundation of the earth, and my right hand spread out the heavens; when I call to them, they stand forth together' (Is. 48.13). In the Exodus, God can be said to fight against the 'chaos' of Pharaoh's tyranny and to bring Israel out of the sea as the Babylonian gods brought the world out of watery chaos; but no literal battle is fought, and what exists after was simply not there before. More and more, creation is seen as performed by the free utterance of God alone; the imagery of moulding something out of something else recedes.

What is left is not even the 'cultural' activity described by Ruether: God does not impose a definition but creates an identity. Prior to God's word, there is nothing to impose *on*. This has some interesting implications. It means that creation is *no sort of process*; it is not a change. Aquinas expressed with complete clarity what Isaiah's words ultimately entail when he said that 'creation' simply points you to existing reality in relation to a creator.[17] It does not indicate some enormous event which would explain everything that came later; as Aquinas realized, the doctrine is equally compatible with thinking the universe had an identifiable beginning and thinking it exists eternally. It simply tells you that the entire situation of the universe, at any given moment, exists as a real situation because of God's reality being, as it were, turned away from God to generate what is not God. And this is not an explanation (because the existence of the world is not a puzzling fact, as opposed to other, straightforward facts; it is all the facts there are), but a statement that everything depends on the action of God.[18]

The point for our purposes is that it makes perfect sense, in such a perspective, to say that creation is not an exercise of divine *power*, odd though that certainly sounds. Power is exercised *by* x *over* y; but creation is not power, because it is not exercised *on* anything. We might, of course, want to say that creation presupposes a divine potentiality, or resourcefulness, or abundance of active life; and 'power' can sometimes be used in those senses.

---

[17] *De potentia* III.3.
[18] All this is very helpfully discussed in Gareth Moore's recent book on *Believing in God* (Edinburgh, 1988), esp. pp. 267–82.

But what creation emphatically isn't is any kind of imposition or manipulation: it is not God imposing on us divinely willed roles rather than the ones we 'naturally' might have, or defining us out of our own systems into God's. Creation affirms that to be here at all, to be a part of this natural order and to be the sort of thing capable of being named – or of having a role – is 'of God'; it *is* because God wants it so. And this implies that the Promethean myth of humanity struggling against God for its welfare and interests makes no sense: to be a creature cannot be to be a victim of an alien force (colonized by an alien 'culture'). Conversely, the overcoming of 'nature' as a proper goal for spirituality is highly problematic: we need a very careful theory of how nature is distorted or obscured before this language is remotely possible; an account, in effect, of how we mistake the unnatural for the natural.

Creation in the classical sense does not therefore involve some uncritical idea of God's 'monarchy'. The absolute freedom ascribed to God in creation means that God *cannot* make a reality that then needs to be actively governed, subdued, bent to the divine purpose away from its natural course. If God creates freely, God does not need the power of a sovereign; what is, is from God. God's sovereign purpose *is* what the world is becoming. This may throw some light on a further cluster of controversial issues to do with creation's absolute dependence on God – in the terms of classical theology, the fact that there is no 'real relation' between the world and God. The objection is quite often made that a relationship of unilateral dependence is incompatible with anything we could mean by love. Relations that we call 'loving' are *mutually* constructive; they are not all gift on one side and all receiving on the other. Such a pattern would mean that one party could never 'grow up' to the status of a giver, but would always be looking to have her or his needs met by the other – an infantile perspective; while the person who is defined as a 'giver' only is one we look on with some suspicion, asking what is being blocked or denied by the refusal or inability to receive. In short, if our relation to the creator is one of unconditional dependence, it looks as though both God and (rational) creatures are locked into a pattern which in the human context we should regard as diseased.

Dependence in human affairs is one of the most complex of subjects. We are afraid of it – both because of the diseased relationships that go with unbalanced dependence and, more deeply, because of the strong attraction of the human psyche towards the 'illusion of omnipotence', or at least the illusion of being an individual, self-regulating system. We have, in other words, both good and bad reasons for fearing dependence, and it is not always easy to distinguish between them. Ernest Becker's brilliant work, *The*

Denial of Death,[19] speaks of our sense of ourselves as individuals as a 'vital lie'; to emerge as agents at all, so as to negotiate our position in a highly danger-ous environment, we must believe in the possibility of 'equanimity' – bal-ance and control. Yet to achieve the sense of this possibility, we require support from outside ourselves, from resources of symbolic power. Our prob-lem is thus the overcoming of dependence *by* dependence: 'We enter sym-biotic relationships in order to get the security we need, in order to get relief from our anxieties . . . but these relationships also bind us, they enslave us even further because they support the lie we have fashioned.'[20] To shore up our sense of independence, we intensify our dependence on those external factors which assure us of worth or meaning, while denying more and more stridently that we are involved in dependence at all. The *necessary* illusion of individuality thus condemns us to tragic compulsion, a diet of spiritual salt water. Any kind of health in this situation requires a twofold honesty: the recognition of the inevitability of dependence (since we are *not* self-regulat-ing systems) and the recognition of the fundamental need to imagine one-self, nonetheless, as a true agent, not confined by dependence (in other words, a suspicion of whatever looks like a path of limitless dependence). We are in the almost intolerable position of needing to be educated to fear what we cannot but need.

However: if our fundamental need is for what enables us to stand over against our environment as agents, it should be clear that to recognize hon-estly the character of *that* need is to take a first step away from the compul-sive search for 'piecemeal' securities, the shoring-up of identity by exploiting *specific* facets of the very environment which threatens to swallow the self; it might be possible, in the light of such a recognition, to distinguish the single underlying need for the sense of being an agent from any and every object-specific need, so as to learn some freedom from the pressure of object-specific needs. If I know that I *cannot* secure my sense of myself as agent by an ever-expanding exploitation of limited object needs, I shall at least avoid the appalling trap depicted by Becker – the evacuation of my selfhood by the pursuit of the self's security.

'Limitless dependence', in the sense of accumulating dependent relation-ships to things, persons, institutions, is something quite other than the *funda-mental* dependence we cannot avoid, dependence on whatever it is that enables our sense of being an agent, a giver. And perhaps it is how we conceive that primary dependence that determines how vulnerable or how destructive our

[19] New York and London, 1973.
[20] Ibid., p. 56.

'illusion' of agency is – how much of an 'illusion' in the ordinary sense of the word rather than the subtler Freudian sense of a belief constructed to meet or cope with the demands of what lies beyond the psyche. Sebastian Moore, in *The Inner Loneliness*, identifies our need to imagine ourselves as agents or givers as a need to know we exist *for another*. This is a crucial insight: it implies that to imagine ourselves as agents by imagining ourselves as self-regulating individuals is to misconceive our fundamental need, which is for identity in relation, conversation, mutual recognition. We can imagine ourselves as self-regulating entities, but can only make sense of – let alone *value* or *love* – what is thus imagined by adopting the standpoint of another: by presupposing relation. We cannot, as it were, get behind this and conceive a human identity that is primitively and only an object to itself. To think ourselves as agents or subjects is to think of ourselves as addressed or contemplated: 'my self-awareness is something I am showing you, and your self-awareness is something you are showing me'.[21] There is no self-awareness outside the commerce of agents and speakers. When I *think* I am imagining myself 'for myself', I am actually taking up the position of someone who looks at or speaks to me; and I couldn't do this if I did not know what it is to be looked at or spoken to.

Knowing this is knowing that the 'illusion' of being a personal centre is one that is not, after all, created by the solitary ego struggling for a *modus vivendi* (as Becker might seem to suggest), but is the tissue of the language-shaped world into which we are born; something without which we could not speak to – and so could not *see* – each other *as* other. Yet the awareness of my location within this world carries with it a realization of the impossibility, for *any* inhabitant of the world, of being a pure source of meaning for other inhabitants of the world: all receive before they give, and give only as a response to their receiving. If my identity is given by the 'conversation' I enter at birth, that conversation is in turn a *generated* as well as a generating context. Nothing in the world is absolutely and unilaterally gift; and this can mean a certain persisting instability or insecurity in the tissue of our world. My meaning is given by the context I depend on; but so are other things – notably the oppressive cultural definitions that Ruether points to. The commerce in which we establish our identities is risky because we are also becoming the raw material of other identities: as in Hegel's famous metaphor of the lord and the serf, there is the possibility of becoming instrumental to the self-formation of another person or group in a way which finally does

---

[21] Moore, *The Inner Loneliness* (London, 1982), p. 9.

not allow me to be seen as an agent and a giver. Even if I recognize the basic character of my need, that will not save me from falling victim to the rapacity of another who still conceives the human task as the exploitation of an environment to confirm the illusion of individuality. What offers to give me meaning and security also threatens to lay unacceptable claim upon me. So, when I have made the breakthrough into acknowledging the impossibility of creating an independent self out of my own will, when I have grasped that my being as agent depends on my receiving first, my being there, spoken to, acted on, I can still not be assured of my liberty to act or give because of the risk that I will be conscripted into the project of another. The fundamental need remains, to a greater or lesser degree, open, unmet. If I know that no human dependence can serve here, only two options remain: the constantly fearful and cautious negotiation of my identity, building up what is constructive in my relation to my environment, and vigilantly looking out for the danger represented by the 'cultural' power of others; or an act of trust in my right or capacity to act and give.

The doctrine of creation in its classical form is the religious ground for such an act of trust. To say, 'I exist (along with the whole of my environment) at God's will, I am unconditionally dependent upon God' means – at least – the following things. My existence in the world, *including* my need to imagine this as personal, active and giving, is 'of God'; my search for an identity is something rooted in God's freedom, which grounds the sheer thereness of the shared world I stand in. And to see that is *already* to have the need answered: my needful searching is part of what God gratuitously brings to be. The secret of understanding our createdness is that it makes both sense and nonsense of the 'search for identity': it justifies our need (i.e. it displays it as something other than a neutral fact) and it answers it. Before we are looked at, spoken to, acted on, we *are*, because of the look, the word, the act of God. God alone (as supremely free of the world) can bring a hearer into being by speaking, by uttering (making external 'outering') what the life of God is, in a creative summons. We shall be returning to think further about the implications of this a little later.

We are here, then, we are real, because of God's 'word'; our reality is not and cannot be either earned by us or eroded by others. And to say that we are unilaterally dependent on God is to recognize that God alone is *beyond* the precarious exchanges of creatures who need affirmation. With God alone, I am dealing with what does not need to construct or negotiate an identity, what is free to be itself without the process of struggle. Properly understood, this is the most liberating affirmation we could ever hear. God does not and cannot lay claim upon me so as to 'become' God; what I am cannot be made functional for God's being; I can never be defined by the job of meeting God's needs. This is why I suggested earlier that our understanding of what was involved in depending on God might be helped by the recognition that creation is not an exercise of power by *x* over *y*. We do what we ought to do as creatures *not* when we attempt to resign from nature by treating 'God' as a successful rival for our attention or devotion over against the things and persons of the world, but by our being-in-the-world. This most certainly does not mean (as some of the more philistine advocates of 'secular' theories used to suggest) that reference to God becomes superfluous. On the contrary; on this analysis, we learn being-in-the-world precisely by learning that there is in the world no absolute and independent 'giver', no final source of naming, of identity, not I nor any other individual, nor any corporate identity. We become able to see all attempts *in* the world at providing definitions for other persons and groups as attempts to escape the world; only one 'power' is entirely gift, entirely directed away from its needs (for it has none), and all other powers need to be unmasked or demythologized. The creator's power-as-resource cannot be invoked to legitimize earthly power. Here there is only what I have called the 'negotiation' of needs, the patterns of giving and receiving, speaking and hearing – stripped of violence-inducing anxiety when they rest on the knowledge that the entire process is rooted in God's free utterance.

Moore's *Inner Loneliness* provides some further clues as to what might be involved in conceiving a God beyond need. I need a sense of active identity, which depends on being there *for* another; and clearly the optional form of being there for another is to be the object of another's love, the cause of joy in them: 'at root, self-love and self-gift are one . . . self-love flowers in self-giving, flowers *as* self giving'[22] – or, as I'd prefer to say, self-love *presupposes* self-giving. I can't love myself without being a loved object, which means being, in some measure, given into another's hands, another's life. To say that God is without need is to say that God's identity does not *wait upon* being an object for what is not God. God, it seems, 'needs' only God. Yet there is a world, there *is* what is not God, something for which God is. As creatures, existing because of the utterance of God, we know that God desires to be God *for* what is not God – desires the pleasure or flourishing of what is not God. This desire is *groundless*, in the sense that nothing other than God causes it, and that it cannot be a device to assist God in being God, but it is not *arbitrary*, because there is no extraneous or random element within God's being as God. What God utters (as suggested earlier) is God: the

---

[22] Ibid., p. 24.

summons to the world to be, and to find its fruition in being in the presence of God, sets 'outside' God the kind of life that is God's. So if God's act of creation gratuitously establishes God as the one who is supremely there *for* the world, it seems we must say that God is already one whose being is a 'being for', whose joy is eternally in the joy of another; and since God, as we have said, does not 'wait upon' becoming an object to another, we are led to think of God's own self as eternal identity in otherness, a self-affirming in giving away. 'Love in God does not *result* but *originates* . . . because God is God, the absolutely original, the absolutely originating, an eternal process of self-affirming in self-love.'[23]

There is a kind of closing of the circle here: what begins in the recognition of God's liberty in the saving interruption of history of the world, and leads to the vision of God as that upon which all things depend, ends in affirming the changeless consistency of God as love – saving interruption anchored (to borrow Ruether's words) in 'the foundations of being'; the absolute difference between God and the world presupposed by the doctrine of creation from nothing becomes also a way of asserting the *continuity* between the being of God and the act of creation as the utterance and 'overflow' of the divine life. Belief in creation from nothing is one reflective path towards understanding God as trinity; and belief in God as trinity, *intrinsic* self-love and self-gift, establishes that creation, while not 'needed' by God, is wholly in accord with the divine being as being-for-another. To put it provocatively: God creates 'in God's interest' (there could be no other motive for divine action); but that 'interest' is not the building-up of the divine life, which simply is what is is, but its giving away. For God to act for God's sake *is* for God to act for our sake.[24]

Jacques Pohier's remarkable and haunting book, *God in Fragments*,[25] brilliantly sets this out under the rubric, 'God does not want to be Everything'.[26] Pohier recalls Aquinas' startling *denial* that we ought to love things or persons as a means of loving God or as leading us to God: we should love them for their 'autonomy and consistency', for what the free love of God has made them. 'God is the reason for loving, he is not the sole object of love':[27] it is God who makes it possible to love things and persons for what they are (because to believe in a free creator is to believe that nothing in the world

[23] Ibid., p. 108.
[24] Cf. ibid., p. 25.
[25] London, 1985.
[26] Ibid., pp. 266ff.
[27] Ibid., p. 268.

can enslave us by being 'God' for us). But what is more, to treat God as 'Everything', as the immediate totality of meaning for each and every subject in the world, is to misunderstand the nature of our unconditional dependence on God. God establishes the worth, the legitimacy, the right to be there, of what is in the world, and in that sense gives meaning; but precisely what God does *not* do is to intrude into the integrity of this or that aspect of being in the world as a justification or explanation for specific events. If the explanation of every event, every determination of being, every phenomenon or decision were simply and directly God, then the life of creation would not be genuinely other than God. God grounds the reality and, in the theological sense, the goodness of the world's life, but does not answer specific 'Why?' questions. To think otherwise, Pohier suggests,[28] is for us actually to *reduce* God to ourselves, to define God as the answer, not to our 'need' for reality or identity, but our needs for control and for a world we can chart in relation to the centrality of ourselves – 'and in consequence prevent him from being himself, being God, being other, being for us the life that he wants to be'.[29] If we need God simply in order to understand and accept our very reality, then our relation to God in particular circumstances will *not* be one of need in the ordinary sense, a desperate effort to make God supply this or that desired gratification, physical, intellectual or spiritual. We should instead be capable of receiving God as pure gift, unexpected good news – as the absolutely uncontainable, the irreducibly different; as *God*.

III

It is, then, a doctrine of creation, properly understood, that grounds both our contemplation and our action. Pohier's insight means that we properly relate to God in gratitude and in silence: before God, we can only celebrate the fact that we *are*, and are free to be *human* with God for God and because of God; and wait without clear prediction or absolute conceptual security for the further perception of and delight in God's being God. Before the literally inconceivable fact of the divine difference and the divine liberty, we have no words except thanksgiving that, because God's life *is what it is*, we are. 'We give thanks to Thee for Thy great glory.' The contemplation of God, which is among other things the struggle to become the kind of person who can without fear be open to the divine activity, would not be possible

[28] Ibid., pp. 303–4.
[29] Ibid., p. 304.

if God were seen as an agent exercising power over others, bending them to the divine will. Contemplative prayer classically finds its focus in the awareness of God at the centre of the praying person's being – God as that by which I am myself – and, simultaneously, God at the centre of the whole world's being: a solidarity in creatureliness. It is the great specific against the myth of self-creation and isolated self-regulation. St John of the Cross speaks[30] of the vision of God in the state of union as a vision of the creator, and thus of the beauty which each creature has of itself from God, as well as 'the wise, ordered, gracious and loving mutual correspondence' among creatures. To see God is to find place *in* this 'correspondence'. Contemplation, then, cannot properly be a prostration before a power outside us; it is a being present to ourselves *in* our world with acceptance and trust. Hence – though this would need longer to elaborate – the importance of attention to the praying *body*; the contemplative significance of taking time to *sense* ourselves in prayer, to perceive patiently what and where we materially are.

But to open myself to the divine action is to seek to discover that act which is wholly and purely the movement of a generosity that finds joy in being for the other. There is no 'private' or individual goal possible: our prayer is supposed to deliver us from what gets in the way of our immersion in and continuity with the act of God, what blocks our own happiness in each other. That human life which we believe to have been uniquely open to the divine act, the life of Jesus is a life given to the creation of a people for God, a community without limit; and it is by this life that we begin to orient ourselves at all towards the creator in the first place. Our openness to God is our readiness for the action of a generosity creative of community to be 'enacted' in us – our readiness, therefore to challenge and resist the making or remaking of exclusions and inequalities in creation. The discovery of solidarity in creatureliness has obvious consequences, which hardly need spelling out, for our sense of responsibility in the material world; it puts at once into question the model of unilateral mastery over the world. And if we can grasp this, we can also understand, perhaps, how bizarre a distortion it has been to think that the human spirit 'imitates' God by exploitative mastery. The creative life, death and resurrection of Jesus manifests a creator who works in, not against, our limits, our mortality: the creator who, as the one who calls being forth from nothing, gives without dominating.

We shall also know something about resistance to contemporary lies concerning the possibilities of corporate security in our world. Both the rhetoric and the practice of our defence policies often seem to offend against the

---

[30] Spiritual Canticle B xxxix. 11.

acknowledgement of creatureliness – in two respects, at least. First, there is the offence against any notion of 'creaturely solidarity' implied by the threat not only to obliterate large numbers of the human race (all weaponry is in that sense a threat to our *common* sense of creatureliness) but to unleash what is acknowledged to be an uncontrollable and incalculable process of devastation in our material environment, an uncontainable injury to the ecology of the planet. Second, there is the extent to which our deterrent policies have become bound to a particular kind of technological confidence: somewhere in the not-too-distant future, it might be possible to construct a defensive or aggressive military system which will provide a *final* security against attack, a final defence against the pressure of the 'other'. If I may repeat some words written in 1987 about the problems posed by the Strategic Defence Initiative, the Christian is bound to ask, 'How far is the search for impregnability a withdrawal from the risks of conflict and change? a longing to block out the possibility of political repentance, drastic social criticism and reconstruction?'[31]

These references to our ecological and political infantilism should be a reminder that a 'creation-oriented' theology and spirituality cannot – *pace* Matthew Fox – afford to replace the concept of original sin with 'original blessing', if that means ignoring our deeply rooted aversion to our own creatureliness. At every turn we encounter this protest: in the kind of radically subjectivist theology that makes the abstract ego the legislator of spiritual identity and reduces the creator to a tool in this system; in the kind of religious and political fundamentalism that pins the human value of a person or a community to the injunctions of an extraneous defining and dominating power; in the world of personal relations, when people invest themselves totally in another person, not in covenanted and reciprocal loyalty, but in a desperate need for the other to provide a completeness of truth and meaning for them; and, as we have seen, in the obsessive games of national security and technological short cuts to gratification. Being a creature is in danger of becoming a lost art. My argument in this chapter has been that we are badly in need, not so much of a re-working of the doctrine of creation designed to eliminate what some have seen as the morally or spiritually damaging effects of believing God to be absolutely prior to and other than the world, as of a retrieval of the radical implications of such a belief for an understanding of our liberty before God. The critique provided by feminist theologies such as those of Ruether and McFague, and the attempt to

---

[31] *Star Wars: Safeguard or Threat? A Christian Perspective* (CANA Occasional Papers no. 1, Evesham, 1987), p. 6.

conceive a non-dualistic or 'panentheist' spirituality in the work of writers
like Fox, have a considerable importance in alerting us to the distortions to
which the classical doctrine has fallen victim – God as monarch, God as
imposing alien meanings, God as supremely successful manipulator of a cosmic 'environment'. But the simple, undialectical affirmation of God's identity with the cosmic continuum (an uncritical maternal image to replace an
uncritical patriarchal image?) will not serve – as I think Ruether and McFague
are themselves aware. Authentic difference, a being-with, not simply a
being-in, difference that is grounded in the eternal being-with of God as
trinity, is something which sets us free to be human – *distinctively* human, yet
human in co-operation with others and with an entire world of differences.
To know that our humanness is not functional to any purpose *imposed* from
beyond is to know also the folly and blasphemy of treating portions of the
human race as functional for the lives of other human beings (which is why
this perspective ultimately *reinforces* a serious feminist critique, as well as having some implications about economics and race); and to know the equal
folly and blasphemy of interpreting all creation in terms of its usefulness to
transient human needs. Being creatures is learning humility, not as submission to an alien will, but as the acceptance of limit and death; *for* that acceptance, with all that it means in terms of our moral imagination and action, we
are equipped by learning through the grace of Christ and the concrete fellowship of the Spirit, that God is 'the desire by which all live,'[32] the *creator*. In
Anita Mason's superb novel, *The Illusionist,*[33] Peter's vision in Acts 10 is
movingly re-worked as a perception of the 'unimaginable order' and union
in all things: the passage ends with words which may stand as a summary for
much of this lecture. ' "I am the Giver", said the voice. "Trust me".'[34]

[32] Moore, *The Inner Loneliness*, p. 117.
[33] London, 1983.
[34] Ibid., p. 137.

Chapter Six

BEGINNING WITH THE INCARNATION

For R. C. Moberly, writing in *Lux Mundi* in 1889 on 'The Incarnation as the Basis of Dogma', the question of the legitimacy of dogmatic statement is, ultimately, a question about whether or not the Church is committed to making truth-claims about its Lord. 'Is it true that he was very God? It is either true or false . . . If it is not absolutely true, it is absolutely false' (p. 237).[1] 'For the dogmatic position of the Church and her Creeds, we claim that it is the true and simple expression upon earth of the highest truth that is, or can be, known' (p. 260). Such truth is not discovered merely by attending to the profundity of the heart's affections; it asks to be tried at the bar of reason. It is established by processes familiar to the exact sciences, and rests its case firmly on historical evidence – though we should beware of supposing that such 'proof' or 'evidence' speaks to some abstract logical intelligence. 'That intelligence, as adequately trained to apprehend and give judgment upon religious evidence, is in some respects other, and more, than that intelligence which can deal with evidence into which no element of spiritual consciousness enters' (p. 232). This, however, is said from the perspective of a mature faith; in the first instance we must appeal more partially to the open ground of history – above all, to claims and counter-claims about the resurrection (pp. 234–5). The settling of questions to do with this history is where dogma begins; and it is necessary if faith is not to be irrational. Faith in Jesus Christ is empty if it is incapable of answering the question of *whom* it believes in (pp. 243–4), and any definite answer, 'Arian' no less than 'Catholic', is *dogmatic*.

Moberly – rather like that very different writer, Bonhoeffer – is plainly

---

[1] *Lux Mundi. A Series of Studies in the Religion of the Incarnation*, ed. Charles Gore (London, 1889); page references here are to the fifth edition of 1890.

not concerned with the 'How?' of the Incarnation;[2] indeed he does not, at any point in his essay, begin to explain what this term means to him beyond the assertion that Christ is *verus Deus* and *verus homo*. He has no *theory* of the Incarnation, simply the conviction that the Church must be able to give a response it holds to be true to the question, 'Who is it that is the object of your faith?' The facts of the Church's history forbid an answer to this simply in terms of pointing to a man called Jesus of Nazareth; one way or another, we have to deal with what the human story of this figure means – what is the identity of Jesus in the framework of a reality whose whole structure is held to be significant? Where does he belong in a story of the world as coming from God and relating to God? My sympathies are with Moberly (though not without qualification); and what I propose to attempt here is a re-working of the idea that dogma reflects a commitment to truth that grows out of a particular set of historical relationships, at whose centre lies the narrative of Jesus – not a theoretical construct, but the abiding stimulus to certain kinds of theoretical question. And unless one believes that questions about theory are necessarily idle and abstract, such issues will be closely bound up with what the Church thinks it is, and is doing and hoping.

The trouble is that Moberly himself gives way to a certain abstractness when he discusses the way in which Christian commitment to Jesus actually takes shape. We are told that the dogmatic definitions of the early centuries added nothing to the already existing faith of Catholic Christianity except a new facility in 'distinctions and comparisons . . . definitions and measurements' (p. 239). But what is elided here is the specific nature and origin of that faith within a frame of reference some way removed from Chalcedon; and if that *is* elided, we shall misunderstand at least some of what Chalcedon is itself about. The confession of Jesus as Lord and Anointed in the New Testament is intelligible chiefly against the background of Israel's hope for final restoration, as we are regularly reminded by New Testament scholars: Jesus of Nazareth proclaims and anticipates this restoration, and, in the resurrection appearances, which in some way establish a definite community and tradition around him, he is shown as having achieved this restoration of God's people. He it is, then, who both during and after the days of his flesh determines entry into and membership of the people of God. He is the assayer, the judge; when the renewal that has begun in his resurrection comes to its consummation, it is he who will preside over the tribunal to which the nations must answer for their impenitence. It is in this sense that the resur-

---

[2] Dietrich Bonhoeffer, *Christology* (London, 1966), pp. 29–37 especially on the difference between 'How?' and 'Who?' as Christological questions.

rection 'designates' him as Lord, King, God's son; and in at least one strand of the New Testament, it can also be said that he has received this authority because he is a human being (Jn 5.27), a judge who knows the human heart as no other heavenly or eschatological figure could, and who, perhaps, also represents the plain human suffering and witness of God's chosen against the monstrous beasts of idolatry and oppression – though it is debatable how far Jn 5.27 deliberately alludes to this Danielic theme.[3]

The judge to whom all shall answer, who is also 'son of man': the Christological paradox begins here. But the point I hope to draw out is the significance of *judgement* in this primordial cluster of responses to the story of Jesus. All – the disciples, the people of Israel and their rulers, Herod, Pilate and the Kings of the nations (Acts 4.27–8) – are to stand before the crucified prophet to know their fate, to know where they belong in the new dispensation; or, as the fourth evangelist would more profoundly see it, to discover what is *true* of them, what they have made themselves to be. The finality of Jesus' authority is simply this, that all must ultimately come to *this* light and this presence for their final place or destiny to be made known. To some extent, the preaching of Jesus as Lord is a kind of parabolic drama: this is what has happened, and you must discover where you stand as you discover your response to this. Nathan's 'You are the man' is obliquely echoed in the apostolic kerygma in the early chapters of Acts – 'This Jesus, whom *you* crucified . . .' – just as much as in the more sophisticated invitation of the fourth gospel to come into the light so as to find whether your works are worked in God. It is not only in the Johannine context that the proclaiming of Jesus amounts to a summons to an unprecedented moral and spiritual nakedness in which the truth is given shape.

Dogma about Christ, and the concern for telling the truth about Christ, stems from this primitive sense of a truth being told about *us* as human beings implicated in a network of violence and denial. It is a truth believed not simply because of a contingent set of experiences triggered off by the remarkable insights of a human being, but because the proclamation of Jesus invites into active commitment to a concrete community in which liberation from the dominance of violence and denial is the mainspring of work and hope, sustained by the conviction that Jesus' invitation into God's people continues to be renewed beyond his death; so that nothing can

---

[3] Among Johannine commentators, Hoskyns and Barrett are disposed to see a reference to Daniel; Bultmann is not. Bultmann and Barrett are also cautious about taking 'son of man' here as having any reference to Jesus' human condition, despite the oddity of the lack of an article in the phrase.

remove the authority of that invitation, and thus the authority of the one who invites. As risen from the dead, he is established as the one from whom we may learn where we stand in respect of the reality of God. If the telling of Christ's life, death and rising does not put to us that kind of question and offer us that kind of discovery, the 'dogma' surrounding the story will have failed to do its job. Or, to put it more polemically, the dogma will be misunderstood to the extend that it has ceased to connect with any awareness of a new identity and a new historical humanity formed in confrontation with the story of Jesus.

We should recast Moberly's title. It is not 'the Incarnation' that is the basis of dogma, but judgement and conversion worked out through encounter with the telling of Jesus' story – because 'the Incarnation' in itself is in danger of being just a rather baroque formulation relating to the origin of Jesus' 'earthly' career. Recent theological controversy has amply shown the ease with which the doctrine of incarnation is confused with the question of the mechanics of Jesus' conception. There is no sense in thinking that we can talk about the Incarnation without talking of the whole course of Jesus' life, the whole historical identity of Jesus, including the ways it is received or rejected by those with whom he comes into contact. I take it that part of the force of the doctrine of the hypostatic union is precisely to deny that 'incarnation' is an isolable event in or prior to the biography of Jesus, and that 'divinity' is some *element* in that life; but that is a larger question. A phrase like 'The Incarnation as the Basis of Dogma' begs a fundamental question by assuming that the fact of God's taking human flesh is the fundamental theological datum, intelligible (at some level) in abstraction from the realities of truthfulness and finality, encounter and judgement, in the presence of the entirety of Jesus' story, which I have been trying to characterize as the source of the pressure towards dogmatic utterance. That the language of God's taking flesh remains a crucial part of the exposition of the judgement of Jesus' history needs to be argued, and argued with conscious attention to the particularity of the 'flesh' involved – which does not mean a wistful searching for the pre-dogmatic Jesus of history (another abstraction, insofar as it suggests a picture of Jesus which is nobody's in particular), but a grasp of how *this* story begins to speak of the decisive work of God in its specific historical setting.

If this approach is defensible, Moberly is right to see dogma as representing the Christian concern with truth; but this concern is less to do with rationality or comprehensive elucidation, more involved with the need to preserve the possibility of the kind of encounter with the truth-telling Christ that stands at the source of the Church's identity. This is, in Moberly's terms,

the truth appropriate to the 'intelligence trained to apprehend and give judgement upon religious evidence'; but it assumes that being religious in a
Christian way is irretrievably bound up with the themes of judgement and
repentance – or, to put it less negatively, with conversion and transformation. There is a basic 'shape' to being Christian, determined by the fact that
its identifying narrative is one of *peripeteia*, reversal and renewal. If the paschal story is, as a matter of bare fact, the bedrock of Christian self-identification, that which is drawn upon to explain what the whole project is about,
there is no escaping the pattern there defined of loss and recovery. Faith
begins in a death: the literal death of Jesus for sedition and/or blasphemy,
which is also the 'death' of the bonds between him and his followers, and the
'death' of whatever hope or faith had become possible in his presence prior
to Good Friday; so that what becomes possible in his renewed presence after
Good Friday has the character of a wholly creative, *ex nihilo*, summons to or
enabling of, hope and trust and action. To say this, I should add, doesn't
commit us to speculation about the psychology of the Eleven on Good
Friday or Easter Eve: it merely recognizes that the New Testament narrative
presents us with *Christian* faith as that which the resurrection creates, in that
all the discernible strands of the gospel tradition insist upon the dissolution of
the apostolic band before the crucifixion, and preserve the tradition of
Peter's betrayal. Thus Easter faith is what there is beyond that faith and hope
that exists prior to or apart from the cross of Jesus; what there is left after the
judgement implied by the cross upon human imagining of the work of God
aside from the *ex nihilo* gift of the risen Christ. In the face of the cross, there
is a revelation of a fundamental lack of reality in our faith and hope, and we
are left with no firm place to stand. The 'shape' of Christian faith is the
anchoring of our confidence beyond what we do or possess, in the reality of
a God who freely gives to those needy enough to ask; a life lived 'away' from
a centre in our own innate resourcefulness or meaningfulness, and so a life
equipped for question and provisionality in respect of all our moral or spiritual achievement: a life of *repentance in hope*.

Nothing is more promising and nothing more difficult. That the Church
repeatedly seeks to secure a faith that is not vulnerable to judgement and to
put cross and conversion behind it is manifest in every century of Christian
history. But in so doing, it cuts itself off from the gift that lies beyond the
void of the cross, and imprisons itself in the kind of self-understanding it can
master or control. In such a perspective, the question about dogma becomes
a question about how the Church retains a faithful sense of the accessibility
of God's promises; though the (obvious) paradox is that dogma has so often
been understood as precisely the sign of the Church's command of the data

of revelation, the sign of something being 'done with' and settled rather than of a challenge left open. Because of this misperception of the function of dogma, the Church's dogmatic activity, its attempts to structure its public and common language in such a way that the possibilities of judgement and renewal are not buried, must constantly be chastened by the awareness that it so acts in order to give place to the freedom of God – the freedom of God from the Church's sense of itself and its power, and thus the freedom of God to renew and absolve. This is why dogmatic language becomes empty and even destructive of faith when it is isolated from a lively and converting worship and a spirituality that is not afraid of silence and powerlessness. The more God becomes functional to the legitimizing either of ecclesiastical order or of private religiosities, the easier it is to talk of God; the easier it is to talk of God, the less such talk gives place to the freedom of God. And that suggests that there is an aspect of dogmatic utterance that has to do with making it *harder* to talk about God.

'Do you mean', the sceptic may impatiently say, 'that the complexities or apparent contradictions of traditional dogmatic formulations are simply there as deliberate insults to the intellect, a deliberate muddying of the waters? Because if so, that seems at best a rationalization of endemic conceptual muddle, and at worst mystification.' But the difficulty I am here thinking of is not that of the conceptual structure of creeds and definitions, but rather the way in which a dogmatic tradition sets before us, when working as it ought, large and strange images ('regeneration', 'sin', 'beatitude', or, for that matter, 'incarnation') that indicate a wider world of understanding than mere functionalism and subjectivism about religious language allow for. And this holds even if there remain elements in such a tradition that we can't make sense of: we have to ask how far our conception of religious seriousness can be broadened by living with other models and idioms. Above all, though, it is important to learn the degree to which we do not yet understand even words that are familiar to us. Bonhoeffer's famous and unheeded remark in 1944 has to be recalled: that we talk all too glibly of redemption and regeneration when the life of the Christian community manifests a radical unawareness of what such words mean. And to recover what they mean, we may need to make them strange, to cease to take them for granted, so that we can ask, 'Why should such words ever come to be? and why should they plausibly claim to be concrete good news?' Bonhoeffer's attack on the jargon of 'religion' is far from being a liberal reformist proposal that hard words be made easy or strange words familiar; he is concerned that the real moral and spiritual strangeness – and thus the judgement – of the gospel should again become audible. If we should now learn a greater reticence in talking fluently about 'incarnation' and 'atonement', it is because they have become the familiar words of professional religious talkers. They no longer bring the Church to judgement, and so no longer do the job of dogma. They have become simply ideology, in the most malign sense.[4] And, of course, 'conversion' and 'judgement' are easily conscripted for the same ends, if the theologian is interested primarily in a truth-telling that is confined to systematic explanation and comprehensive conceptualities.

So part of the theologian's task in the Church may be to urge that we stand aside from some of the words we think we know, so that we may see better what our language is *for* – keeping open the door to the promises of God. The question 'Do you believe in "the Incarnation"?' is a quite futile one in itself unless it has something to do with the serious question 'How do you proclaim, and how do you hear proclaimed, the judgement of Christ?' Anglican theology, with its long-standing enthusiasm about the incarnational principle, has often risked blurring the outline of this second question, because the *image* of incarnation, the fusion of heaven and earth, the spiritualizing of matter, has proved so wonderfully resourceful a tool for making sense of a sacramental community with a social conscience and a cultural homeland. This is not wholly mistaken; but the slippage into ideology is perilously close, to the extend that such theology can lose sight of that element underlying the history of incarnational definition that is to do with the radical testing of human 'sense' before the tribunal of Jesus, which is the tribunal of the last days. As Don Cupitt warned, in a provocative essay some years ago, the doctrine of the Incarnation may be a device for uniting what needs to be kept in 'abrupt juxtaposition' and 'ironic contrast'.[5]

When the Church seeks to make definitions – whether in conciliar formulae or in terms and expressions (like 'beatitude' and 'regeneration') canonized implicitly by ages of use and official endorsement in worship and discipline – it is at least recognizing what I have elsewhere described as the 'responsible' character of its faith,[6] its nature as 'answering' to a gift and a

---

[4]   On the complex relation between theological definition and ideology, see Nicholas Lash, 'Ideology, Metaphor and Analogy', in *The Philosophical Frontiers of Christian Theology*, ed. Brian Hebblethwaite and Stewart Sutherland (Cambridge, 1982), pp. 68–94, and Rowan Williams, 'What is Catholic Orthodoxy?' in *Essays Catholic and Radical*, ed. Kenneth Leech and Rowan Williams (London, 1983), pp. 11–25, especially pp. 12–15.
[5]   Don Cupitt, 'The Christ of Christendom', in *The Myth of God Incarnate*, ed. John Hick (London, 1977), pp. 133–47, especially p. 140.
[6]   James Atkinson and Rowan Williams, 'On Doing Theology', in *Stepping Stones. Joint Essays on Anglican Catholic and Evangelical Unity*, ed. Christina Baxter (London, 1987), pp. 1–20, especially pp. 1–4.

pressure beyond its own life at any one moment or in any one place. If it lacked the confidence, the sense of *authorization*, to do this, it would lack that sense of a distinctive identity rooted in a distinctive call, that grounds its being. It would not see itself as a community existing by gift and grace, entrusted with a mission for whose fulfilment it is answerable. 'The Lord did not set his love upon you, nor choose you, because ye were more in number than any people . . . But because the Lord loved you . . . hath the Lord brought you out' (Dt 7.7–8). The theologian's task is to remind the Church both of this fundamental motive and motif in dogma, *and* of that concurrent and inevitable temptation to treat dogma as a solution, a closure. In this, the theologian will share the concern of those who want the Church's liturgy properly to open up a congregation to wonder and newness of life, and will also understand the reticence of the contemplative. The theologian, in fact, can help avert that fatal divorce I mentioned earlier between dogma and worship – not by a piously uncritical defence of dogmatic formulae on the grounds of liturgical use or adherence by holy people, but in helping to articulate the critical dimension of worship itself. It is not a theologian's business first and foremost to defend this or that dogmatic formula, but to keep alive the impulse that animates such formulae – the need to keep the Church attentive to the judgement it faces, and the mission committed to it. If the theologian is engaged in the critique of certain traditional formulae, or the Bonhoefferian bracketing out of familiar jargon, this should arise not from the anxious attempt to clarify according to canons of general rationality (though these canons are not irrelevant; there is such a thing as recognizable nonsense and slipshod argument in theology), but rather from a concern that the question of the gospel is in danger of no longer being put in this or that piece of dogmatic speech. Bultmann's point stands: we need always to ask whether we have rightly understood where the offence, the *skandalon*, of the gospel *now* lies, and to beware of thinking that this offence is identical merely with the contingent strangeness of an unfamiliar cultural idiom.[7]

It may also be part of the theologian's job to offer examples of 'good practice'. I want to turn now to a specific case in which 'dogma', the Church

---

[7] See Bultmann's contributions to *Kerygma and Myth* I, ed. H. W. Bartsch (London, 1953), and his response to Karl Jaspers in *Kerygma and Myth* II, ed. H. W. Bartsch (London, 1962) ('The Case for Demythologizing', pp. 181–94): 'The purpose of demythologizing is not to make religion more acceptable to modern man by trimming the traditional Biblical texts, but to make clear to modern man what the Christian faith is . . . the *skandalon* is peculiarly disturbing to man in general, not only to modern man.' Thus the task is 'clearing away the false stumbling blocks created for modern man by the fact that his world-view is determined by science' (*Kerygma and Myth* II, pp. 182–3).

and the theologian interact in something of the way I have been sketching in general terms. One of the few occasions in the twentieth century when a church has consciously volunteered a definition of its own limits is the celebrated Barmen Declaration of the Confessing Church in 1934.[8] This is, I suggest, a 'dogmatic' act in just the sense I have tried to explain – an acknowledgement of the gospel of Jesus Christ as a call to judgement. And it certainly illustrates the essentially Christological character of dogma (though it does not speak of 'the Incarnation' in particular), in its repudiation of any 'other source of its proclamation, apart from and besides this one Word of God' (art. 1), and in its insistence that the gospel cannot be put at the service of either ecclesiastical or secular projects that have not passed under the judgement of the one Word (arts 3 and 6). Yet Barmen itself has proved problematic in more recent years. It is, notoriously, silent on the Jewish question, even though this, as it affected the Church, was so significant a part of Barmen's agenda; it appears to block out any serious interaction on the part of theology and preaching with other faiths and cultures; its reserve in the face of the messianic claims of the Nazi state could be generalized into political pessimism or indifferentism; and its rhetoric has been seen as patriarchally authoritarian. All these reservations reflect ways in which Barmen has actually been used in the post-war German churches: the 'dogma' of a liberating allegiance to Jesus Christ alone has become the ideology of a religious status quo, and 'it is understandable that its critics should regard it as a product of "false consciousness", an elitist document concerned about the privileged position of the church but not about the persecution of the Jews and other minorities'.[9] Thus the suspicion of dogma as a tool of control and defence *against* judgement is raised; do we then repudiate the statement, or indeed the *possibility* of any such statement?

The South African theologian John de Gruchy, whom I have just quoted on the criticisms made of Barmen, argues that the denial of Barmen would be a grave error, because it would ignore the central theological motivation of the Declaration, and, more significantly, would ignore *what Barmen makes possible* in the hands of a theologian and preacher who is both wholly com-

---

[8] Text in A. C. Cochrane, *The Church's Confession under Hitler* (Philadelphia, 1962), pp. 238–42. and J. W. de Gruchy, *Bonhoeffer and South Africa* (Grand Rapids/Exeter, 1984), pp. 146–50.

[9] De Gruchy, *op. cit.*, p. 127. On the use of Barmen in post-war German discussion, see Barth's remarks in 'An Outing to the Bruderholz', *Fragments Grave and Gay* (London, 1971), pp. 71–94, especially 71–81, and also the abundant material on the early debate about atomic weapons in the German churches in *Theologische Existenz Heute*, 1958 and 1959, especially nos 64 and 70.

mitted to Barmen's side of the struggle, *and* fully aware of the ambivalence of dogmatic statement. Bonhoeffer remained committed to Barmen, despite his growing awareness of the compromised situation even of the Confessing Church, and of the sufferings of the Reich's victims in all sorts of ways of which Barmen was unaware; and despite that sensitivity to the potential emptiness of religious terminology that found such powerful expression in his prison letters. What matters is not that Barmen turned out to be the orthodoxy of people who, for all their courage, had the limitations of their class and profession, but that a church gathering believed itself empowered to act in such a way as to refuse a particular kind of idolatry, a particular evasion of the judgement of Christ. As Barth insisted, Barmen's affirmations and denials alike are a word for a particular crisis, and outside that context they are not simply to be uncritically repeated. But this does not mean that they have only antiquarian interest: if we want, in another context, to identify with Barmen's refusals, we may also need to 'liberate' its affirmations from the past, and set them to work in other ways, aware of the post-history of Barmen — what it made possible, beyond the limitations of those who actually drew it up.

De Gruchy writes that, properly understood, 'Barmen's insistence upon the Lordship of Christ is not inimical to our contemporary concern for the liberation of the oppressed, or to dialogue with other faiths and the doing of theology in diverse cultural contexts'. He elaborates this further:

> For Gentile Christians, the fact that Jesus the *Jew* is Lord should mean a total openness towards and solidarity with the Jewish brothers and sisters of Jesus. For Christians the fact that Jesus is *Lord* should mean a rejection of all ideologies that dehumanize or destroy any sister or brother of Jesus, whether Jew or Arab, black or white. For Christians the fact that Jesus is Lord must mean that he is also *Liberator*, and this requires commitment to his liberating Word and deed . . . For Christians the fact that Jesus is Lord means *freedom* for the church to be the church in the world and not the captive of any ideology . . . But this freedom has a particular form (*Gestalt*) because the fact that *Jesus* is Lord means that lordship can be exercised only in service, self-emptying, suffering, and costly discipleship.[10]

In this passage, de Gruchy demonstrates precisely what the theologian's job is in relation to the Church's public taking of positions. 'Dogma' is tested and interpreted in the light of the question 'How does the Church become

[10]   De Gruchy, *op. cit.*, pp. 128–9.

free to hear and to do the Word of God, free to be its distinctive self?' It is assumed that somewhere in the Church's struggle for self-definition there is a genuine concern to find what it is that keeps it faithful to itself and its Lord (though the seriousness of that concern needs constant testing), so that it is possible to think through the language of dogmatic utterance in such a way as to renew that fidelity, not in bland repetition or in sceptical hostility, but with a sense of an answerability to the judgement of Christ that is shared between the theologian and the dogmatic text. There is a particular kind of hermeneutical charity appropriate here, an assumption that dogmatic utterance is grounded in some sort of concern for the liberty of the gospel, so that there is something to look for. A past dogmatic definition may not necessarily be where we must now begin; but that does not mean we are absolved from the attempt to 'locate' it in the task of witnessing to the basic nature of faith. To repudiate or ignore it would be – as de Gruchy suggests in the case of Barmen – to lose a possible resource for effective proclamation now, as well as to lose sight of the kind of conflict that draws out specific dogmatic pronouncements.

But if it is, as I have argued throughout this essay, the judgement of Christ, our 'dramatic' being caught up into the paschal parable, brought to nothing and brought to life, that is the true basis of dogma, what specifically should we say about those historic formulations of Nicaea and Chalcedon that constitute the heartland of incarnational dogma? Do they have a specially protected status because they articulate the conditions for all other theological definition – so that Moberly is correct after all? I suspect that something like this may be true, but find Moberly's expression of it unhelpfully positivistic. His robust 'true or false?' in respect of *verus Deus, verus homo* short-circuits the details of doctrinal discussion in a way which I think many a patristic writer would have found alarming. More to the point, it needs to be emphasized that it is harder than Moberly makes it sound to find a single brief formulation that intelligibly expresses *the* doctrine of the Incarnation. We do not find in the early Church debates over the truth or falsity of a phrase like *verus Deus, verus homo* in isolation, but a number of conflicts turning upon and issuing in a set of liturgical and disciplinary conventions, decisions about what may and may not publicly be said in the Church's name about Jesus Christ. If we try to work these into a single coherent theory, we invite trouble; and in fact every reasonably sophisticated Christology in the history of Christian doctrine has in practice exercised great flexibility as to the status and 'register' of agreed formulae. To ascribe the name 'Jesus Christ' to the pre-existent Word, *sans phrase* is theologically problematic for the strictest Chalcedonian, yet it is a form of words enjoined in the texts of Nicaea and Chalcedon; all serious patristic and medieval exegesis of Chalcedon took it for granted that this was not a strict and literal usage from which deductions could be drawn. In other words, discussion of the classical formulae has normally, in the history of doctrine, worked with what the formulae have made possible rather than with a notion that they have closed the debate for ever. In effect it has been the negative and regulative aspects of patristic dogma that have been most faithfully observed, while the meaning of phrases like *verus Deus, verus homo* has been the subject of careful and context-sensitive discussion.

As a matter of plain syntax, the novel dogmatic expressions of Nicaea and Chalcedon were elaborations of an introductory 'We believe in one Lord, Jesus Christ'; as in the very different case of Barmen, we are dealing with the implications of commitment to Christ as Lord. But that does not mean that it is a matter of pure indifference how *et in unum dominum* is to be elaborated, or that this elaboration claims only a regulative force. At the very least, the extension of the simple statement of belief in one Lord raises the question of what things are or are not consistent with this confession – in Christian language, Christian practice, and the life of humanity at large. If the confession of Lordship has its roots, as I have argued, in the imagery of the apocalyptic tribunal, if it sets before us, narratively and liturgically, a set of transactions in which we are invited to find our role and our truth, if it is inseparable from the belief that the community has a distinctive *Gestalt* and a distinctive human hope to offer, we have some resources for dealing with the question of what is and is not consistent, and thus with what is or is not a fruitful elaboration of the basic confession. It will not do, clearly, to think of Jesus as one in whom fleshly vulnerability is merely adjectival to an inner supranatural power and identity: he is vulnerable, says the story, in spirit and flesh to the ways in which human beings like you and me betray and kill each other in spirit and flesh. And we may again recall Jn 5.27: here alone is the judge who sees the human heart 'from within', and whose authority and commission depend upon how he lives through the dependence and risk of mortality. Equally, though, it is not enough to say that here is a man who by exemplary achievement manifested a fresh possibility of living. This ignores the crisis and failure of the cross, and the divine reversal of human judgement at Easter; and, in setting before us an exemplary achievement, it fails to break through the imprisoning cycle of struggle, error and guilt from which we need release, absolution, a righting of the past as well as a project for the future. It does not free us to receive renewal of life as sheer gift. Are we to say that Jesus is a man transparent in an exemplary but intermittent fashion to the communication of God's grace? But how then are we to avoid saying that God's self-communication depends on the intermittent receptivity of Jesus – his 'good moments' –

so that this appears only another version of the exemplary achievement model? Or is his significance in the bare fact that he stands at the origin of a new style of experiencing God? If so, what matters is what is being transacted in our interior lives, the religiousness that we find important and interesting; there is nothing perceptible beyond our interiority to which we are answerable. Do any of these options, in short, articulate what it is to be drawn into cross and resurrection and to find there (the Barthian echoes are unavoidable) at once a decisive No and an everlasting Yes to our selves?

The plausibility of these options may be argued, and I have done no more than set them out schematically, so as to indicate where they may become problematic in trying to do justice to a faith which struggles to see the entire human identity of Jesus as divine gift. If these options are indeed as vulnerable as I have suggested, what is left? The story of Jesus is not one of a miraculous suspension and interruption of the human world, nor is it a story of human moral and spiritual heroism; it involves us in a self-declaration and a self-discovery. To be judged by the proclamation of Jesus in his ministry, death and resurrection is to find oneself in a particular human relation – parables judge us effectively because they are about relations,[11] and their judgement invites a changing of relations. And it is to cross a boundary that effort, will, imagination and achievement cannot cross, into new life. 'He stands on the boundary of my existence, beyond my existence, but still for me. This expresses the fact that I am separated from the "I" that I should be by a boundary which I am unable to cross. This boundary lies between me and myself. I am judged in my encounter with this boundary. At this place I cannot stand alone. Here Christ stands, in the centre, between me and myself, between the old existence and the new.'[12] For Bonhoeffer, this mapping of the 'geography' of the encounter with Jesus is part of dealing with the question 'Who?' which he believes to be the only legitimate theological question to put to Jesus. It is the nature of this encounter in the preaching of the gospel that prompts Christology to forswear the solutions both of a 'gnostic' supernaturalism and of the teacher–pupil, hero–emulator scheme. And when we have said that, when we have come to the point of seeing Jesus at the frontier of our existence and understanding in the way Bonhoeffer proposes, we have come to the point at which the Chalcedonian problematic still faces us. How shall we speak of Jesus in a

---

[11] See, e.g., Sallie McFague, *Metaphorical Theology. Models of God in Religious Language* (Philadelphia and London, 1982), pp. 42–54, especially 53; although I have some reservations about the characterization of classical Christology in this section, it expresses much of what I regard as crucial for Christological method.

[12] Bonhoeffer, *Christology*, p. 61.

way that is faithful to the fact that it is *human* existence in which he meets us
and to the character of what we meet as judgement and gift? The Chalcedonian
question will not go away just because we find the terms of its resolution
difficult or indigestible We have here the kernel of the problem of dogma: it
is not a natural starting-point for theological enquiry today, and Moberly's
blunt confidence in our ability to treat it as straightforward propositional truth
is rather rare; yet we must continue to ask how such language was seen to
serve the imperative of the gospel, and what sorts of developments in our
theological thinking it makes possible. We must ask whether, given the terms
of the historic debates, we should be any the better for this particular determination not having been made. If we want to be faithful to the fundamental
impulse of dogmatic speech, we may well, I believe, have to say that the
classical dogmatic tradition has served to keep the essential questions alive.
What would have happened to the Church had other styles prevailed – an
Arian or a Nestorian theology – is not possible to know; what is important is
that, to some degree at least, the Church's reasons for making the declarations
it did have a discernible interest in preserving the scope and comprehensiveness of the work and presence of Christ, against ways of talking that were
(rightly or wrongly) seen as limiting or compromising the creative radicality
of the person of Jesus, and his authority to renew the nature of men and
women in the material and historical world.

I have proposed as a refinement of Moberly's title something like 'Conversion and Judgement as the Basis of Dogma', since I cannot see the full
weight of the doctrine that God united a human individual decisively and
wholly to the divine life as intelligible outside this context. The language of
incarnation is a secondary move in this theological discourse – precarious,
yet unavoidable as one central way of doing justice to what Christian conversion means; a dogmatic utterance without which it is significantly harder
to witness clearly to the *freedom* of the Church to hear and to preach the
gospel. But as itself the *basis* of dogma – ?

> Like rafts down a river, like a convoy of barges,
> The centuries will float to me out of the darkness.
> And I shall judge them.[13]

That is the beginning – and the end – of dogma.

---

[13] Boris Pasternak, *Doctor Zhivago* (London, 1961), p. 539 (from Zhivago's poem, 'Gethsemane',
pp. 537–9).

Chapter Seven

THE FINALITY OF
CHRIST

What do we expect Christ to do? When we speak of Christ's finality, universality or universal significance, what relation are we taking for granted between Christ and the systems (including religious systems) of human meaning? I put the question in this form because Cornelius Ernst's formulation of the problem of grace and nature and God and creation in terms of God as 'Meaning of meaning'[1] has long struck me as helpful. Jesus Christ, Ernst proposes, is the substantive meaning of God for human beings and human beings for God (and so too, presumably, for each other); or, in other words, Jesus is God's participation in and ordering of the systems of human communication that constitute the unity, the possibilities of relation, the 'sense' of human existence in the world, and is also our participation in the 'communication' and relatedness that is the creative life of God. If it is only the life of God (however understood) that finally secures the possibility of a human community that is more than merely tribal, if God is what makes sense of the hope for unlimited projects of communication, sharing of experience and understanding,[2] then the Christian claim is that this sense is, practically and historically, given in Jesus. It is in active relation with him that the possibility of human community begins to become actual; through the embodied Word of God that human beings find a language for their common humanity.

---

[1] Cornelius Ernst, *Multiple Echo. Explorations in Theology*, ed. Fergus Kerr and Timothy Radcliffe (London, 1979), p. 85.
[2] Cf. Helmut Peukert, *Science, Action and Fundamental Theology. Toward a Theology of Communicative Action* (Cambridge, MA, and London, 1986), for an account of the theological enterprise in terms of a theory for the actions of unconditional human solidarity demanded by the very movement of consciousness itself. Peukert is the most systematic theological interpreter of Jürgen Habermas, and his theology is open to the same criticisms as Habermas's social theory; but it stands as an exceptionally thorough attempt to see how the insight that God is the condition of human community might be developed.

Ernst goes on to distinguish this 'substantive' meaning from 'ontological' meaning – the thematizing of how the substantive significance of Christ works, and what are the conditions for it in the structure of reality; and this, he says, is what we can only search for, without expecting a systematic answer, an answer that could have a structure 'in a single mind'.[3] The ontological meaning would only show itself in the reality of a single – or, better, a freely communicating – human culture, in which the diversity of human experience and human struggle would seem to be 'at home' with, focused on, the identity of Jesus. Our task, then, is not to construct premature meta-theories of religion, but to explore how the identity of Jesus can in practice open and sustain converse with human schemes of meaning and draw them actively towards the reality of human community.

This account – if I read it correctly – suggests that there are two ways of taking the assertion that Jesus is the meaning of human meanings and thus two ways of theologizing about his 'universality'. The first is to move immediately to the 'ontological' level, either by developing a metaphysic of the 'cosmic Christ', or more disreputably, I think, by trying to construct the system of spiritual knowledge of which Christ is the (or a) 'symbol'. Both these strategies assume that it is possible and proper to try and articulate a comprehensive account of religious meaning that somehow contains other meanings – the cosmic Christ who is the source and the goal of all religious or creative or 'spiritual' enterprise, and who is at work unacknowledged in all such enterprise, or else the scheme of values symbolized by the narrative of Christ, but separable from that narrative. The second option, however, is to say that the identity of Jesus must engage with the worlds of human meaning for them to be meaningful in any other than 'tribal', limited contexts: the meaning of Jesus is not the container of all other meanings but their test, judgement and catalyst. Jesus does not have to mean everything; his 'universal significance' is a universally crucial question rather than a comprehensive ontological schema. We may still want to confess that in Christ 'all things cohere', but it is possible to understand this as saying not that 'in Christ all meanings are contained' but that 'on Christ's judgement all histories converge'. And, as Ernst insists, what that convergence will look like is not something that can be theorized in advance. A finished account of Christ as containing all meanings would make Christology non-eschatological. What we have to do is to discover how our commitment to the question Jesus poses may make itself audible and intelligible beyond the bounds of the Christian institution.

[3] Ernst, *op. cit.*, pp. 85–6.

In common, I think, with some others, I am trying to escape from the textbook options prescribed for inter-faith dialogue – exclusivism, inclusivism and pluralism, as they are normally characterized.[4] 'All human meaning is to be found explicitly and solely in the person and work of Jesus'; 'All human meaning is to be found ontologically in the Logos and virtually in Jesus'; 'Human meaning is accessible through a multitude of equally valid but culturally incommensurable symbol systems, among which the story of Jesus has its place' – all of these are inadequate to the concrete task of dialogue. The first rules it out in principle, the second makes a bid for ownership of all that is tolerable and recognizable in other traditions, the third allows no more than unquestioning co-existence. If we are to recognize the real otherness of other faiths, and their integrity as systems – and the possibility, therefore, of surprise and of conflict as well as of discovery and self-questioning – we need some further means of reflecting on what we, as Christian believers, bring as our foundational commitment. And what I am suggesting is that we resist the temptation to look for a Christian system that will deal with our perplexities here. We must rather ask about the nature of our foundational 'myths', not as our theological possessions and legitimations, but as our agenda, and try to see what is being said here about the meaning of God and the world for each other, so as to understand what might be involved in claiming that this is what enables other schemes of meaning to become part of a properly and unrestrictedly human discourse.

What then does our foundational myth say? First of all, and very importantly, it locates Jesus, as the focus of faith, within a very specific context of ethnic, religious and political history: the title 'Christ' is the almost indecipherable archaeological trace of his involvement in the story of Israel. We are told that Jesus was God's response to the hope of Israel for restoration and deliverance, but that those (Jewish and Gentile) who were in practical political terms responsible for the maintenance and security of the people of Israel found this 'fulfilment' both unrecognizable as such and profoundly menacing. In crucifying Jesus, the elders of Israel and the 'kings of the Gentiles' effectively extinguish Israel's hope; that hope is a reality only for those who, in the light of God's vindication of the crucified Jesus, have recognized him as God's answer to and consummation of the history and aspiration of Israel, and who are now themselves, therefore, an 'Israel', a people in whose common life the purpose of God for God's human creation is manifest.

On the face of it, this lends itself to the kind of interpretation that makes the whole subject so fraught with moral danger: a religious tradition (Judaism)

---

[4] See, for a lucid summary, Gavin d'Costa, *Theology and Religious Pluralism* (Oxford, 1986).

becomes involved in betrayal and untruthfulness and is supplanted by another (Christianity) which is possessed of the true heritage of the parent
tradition and more. This is the reading, already clearly discernible in the
New Testament, that has prevailed in most of Christian history. It has the
advantage of a certain dramatic simplicity, and the disadvantage (to put it
mildly) of legitimizing the crudest form of the 'Christ as container of all
meanings' theology, and also identifying the 'meaning' articulated in the
Christian institution with this fullness of meaning in Christ.

But the story is in fact more complex, even in the New Testament. First
of all, it is essential to realize that 'Judaism' as a 'religion' is a construct of
later ages, as much a fiction in the first century of the Christian era as 'Hin-
duism' is today. This is not merely to say that there was no normative Judaism
at this time, but that the very concept of a religion is anachronistic here – a
unified system of beliefs and rituals with its own frame of reference over
against other forms of thinking and behaving.[5] And only slowly – and in
some respects fortuitously – did Christianity come to be the first such phenomenon, the first 'religion', in cultural history. We are not, then, dealing
with a collision of systems, or even with the supersession of one system by
another, but with an episode in the political history of a religious people, a
people, that is, whose corporate life significantly involves some shared myths,
texts and rituals, not necessarily consistent or systematized, but loosely
intermeshed, sometimes in conflict. What Christian believers seem to have
claimed at first was something like this: the people of Israel were being summoned to a more intense unity or consistency than hitherto; the logic of
their past was pressing them towards a decision for certain practices and
priorities as against others in order for them to retain and manifest the identity God fundamentally purposed for them, and this decision was bound up
with the mission of Jesus of Nazareth. As Rosemary Ruether points out,
there is nothing formally unique about this: not only is it a familiar prophetic
theme, it is central to what the Deuteronomist and the Ezrahite Chronicler
see as the recurrent shape of Israelite history, a steady purging away of those
practices that do not bespeak the absolute fidelity of God and the people.

However, the eschatological concerns of the age reinforced the sense that

---

[5]   On the question of 'Judaism' at this period, see Jacob Neusner, Williams S. Green and
Ernest Frerichs, eds, *Judaisms and Their Messiahs at the Turn of the Christian Era* (Cambridge,
1987); and on the general question of 'a' religion in the first Christian century, there are some
reflections in Rowan Williams, 'Does it Make Sense to Speak of Pre-Nicene Orthodoxy?' in
R. Williams, ed., *The Making of Orthodoxy: Essays in Honour of Henry Chadwick* (Cambridge,
1989), pp. 1–23.

this decision was a final crisis prior to a major divine intervention to rectify the world's situation; hence the claim that the movements of Israel's hope and Israel's history converged on the figure of Jesus to such an extent that to decide for his 'claim' on Israel's identity was to decide for the 'true' Israel first summoned into being by God in exodus and covenant. Jesus' position *vis-à-vis* Israel moves closer towards that of the divine initiator, the course of the primal liberation and promise, the maker of the people as a people. Thus the Jesus we meet in the gospels calls twelve to be with him as judges of the tribes, assumes a certain (rather ill-defined) liberty in regard to some aspects of the Torah, and dies at the time of the Passover festival, declaring the existence of a new covenant sealed in his blood. What of this can be confidently affirmed to be true of the 'Jesus of history' is unclear, and actually immaterial for our present purposes; we are simply trying to find a characterization of the narrative core of early Christian language. But the implication of this is that rejection of Jesus' claim, Jesus' bid to redefine Israel, is a rejection of Israel's authentic identity. In the retrospectic views of Christian believers after 70 CE, and in the context of deepening conflict in Diaspora synagogues, not only the priestly class but the pietist lay teachers (Pharisees) and, ultimately, the whole people are seen as involved in this rejection, and the image of a 'new' Israel replacing the 'old' begins to take root. What had been Israel itself became a unified system of a new kind, responding to political collapse as it might (according to Christian apologists) have responded to Jesus – by making decisions about a coherent pattern of covenant faithfulness; and so the convention is fixed of Christian–Jewish relations as a rivalry between two comparable systems.

Somewhere, elusively, in this is that deeper and more unsettling point that might take us a bit beyond the clichés of inter-faith dialogue. Our story is about a community (not a race or a 'religion', but a particular historical unit determined by particular systems of power) unable to make a decisive act of faithfulness to its own original nature and calling because its history has not only preserved but also obscured that distinctive sense of identity and mission. Its hopes and desires have become sufficiently unclear for there to be no means of recognizing what it would be for them to be fulfilled. In the language of Amos, the desired Day of the Lord has come and is darkness and not light. The question posed by the narrative is: 'What if the desire to see God were fulfilled, and its fulfillment went unnoticed or unrecognized? What would it be in the history of "religious" words and customs that would render them incapable of equipping their users to see what they purported to be about?' Relating this to the theme with which we began, we could recast the question as: 'What is it that makes religious meanings self-enclosed, self-

referential, self-justifying?' Part of the answer suggested by the story is that
communities of religious meaning do not live in a timeless world of ideas or
vision; they have political and structural histories, and their self-identification in relation to the sacred is invariably bound up with ways in which
power and control are exercised. It is an illusion to suppose that there could
be a decisive disentangling of these elements; but it is important to be able to
ask for a justification of existing power patterns in relation to the primitive
sense of what the community is for. There were Jews in Jesus' day who
refused to participate in the sacrifices in the Temple because of their belief
that the priesthood was hopelessly corrupted by its recent political history;
and it may be that Jesus' cleansing of the Temple reflects a similar belief that
the sacrificial system should be in abeyance until the purification of Israel
was completed. But whether this is so or not, the distancing of the question
of Israel's identity from the policies and concerns of the sacerdotal governing
class is an unmistakable feature of what Jesus was remembered as proclaiming. It is not that a scheme of ideas called 'Judaism' rejects Jesus, or that an
undifferentiated body of adherents to this religion turn their backs on him;
there is a mortal conflict between Jesus' claim on Israel's identity, and the
way that identity is sustained by the rulers of Israel at that specific moment.[6]

How shall religious language and action free itself from ideology (in the
malign sense of that word)?[7] Forget for a moment the categories of 'Judaism'
and 'Christianity', and consider simply the contour of what I have called the
foundational myth of the God whose people are so determined that they
have become unable to recognize God's presence. For such a myth to work
it requires both the background tradition of a God who has some distinctive
purpose for the chosen people, and the specific story of a decisive presence
and fulfillment, a concrete embodiment of the values and desires of God's
people which is also an embodying of God's will and agency, being the
enactment of what God desires in the world. The particular question of
Christian belief cannot be put without the categories of election on the one
hand and incarnation (in a fairly fluid sense) on the other. The challenge
posed by Israel's existence is to do with understanding God strictly in terms
of God's relation to a people summoned to manifest what human life looks
like when systematically and unprotectedly exposed to the pressure of that
initiative power that lies behind all contingent events and agencies, and

---

[6]   See e.g. B. F. Meyer, *The Aims of Jesus* (London, 1979) and N. T. Wright, 'Jesus, Israel and
the Cross', *SBL Seminar Papers 1985*, ed. K. H. Richards (Scholars' Press, 1985).
[7]   Cf. Peukert, *op. cit.*, pp. 199–201, on the critique of ideology in twentieth century social
and psychological theory.

understanding that the effect of that pressure is *tsedaqah* and *shalom*, equitable and healing relations. Accordingly, the Christian refinement to the question is to do with understanding the risk of treating this justice and peace as a privileged possession of one sector of humanity to be protected by political negotiation and cultic mystification. In announcing a 'reassembling' of Israel around the figure rejected by politics and cult, Christian language proposes that the community of religious meaning becomes accessible to all as and when it is free to accept God's re-calling and reconstruction of itself – when, in other words, it is prepared to lose the God who is 'our' God, and who is protected as such by institutional safeguards.

Timothy Radcliffe has pointed out[8] that this pattern of deepening corporate identity through historical-political loss is itself already present in the story of Israel; and he suggests that the way Christianity brings this story to crisis and transformation or re-direction is in demonstrating that 'the vocation of Israel was to become truly the people of God in ceasing to be a people at all'.[9] Yet we are already here plunged into the moral ambiguities of Christianity's relation to Jewish history. What Christian theology has characteristically done is to undermine the legitimacy of Israel's claim to be a people, not in the light of a vision of universal community, but in making a counter-claim to be a 'peculiar people', possessed of unique and exclusive access to the purpose of God. 'Incarnation' has become the ground of final validation for the rights and authority of the new community; rather than serving as itself a sign of the dangers of religious self-enclosure and claims to final legitimacy, it has been domesticated into the community's system of control.[10] It has become ideological. The Christ whose death and resurrection belong within the dialectic of a negation and an affirmation of the calling of Israel[11] is made the undialectical and almost dehistoricized focus of a new and different Israel. Insofar as the Church has not ceased to be a people, with the institutional and political defences appropriate to a people, it has no right to question Israel's continuing existence as a people, as 'Judaism'. The vocation of the Jewish people remains – manifesting a shape of corporate

---

[8] 'The Old Testament as Word of God: Canon and Identity', *New Blackfriars*, vol. 61, no. 721 (1980), pp. 266–75.

[9] Ibid., p. 274.

[10] In other words, the Church reproduces exactly the ideological distortion that may attach to the idea of an exclusive people. See the remarks of Thomas Merton, *Conjectures of a Guilty Bystander* (London, 1968), pp. 119–21, on how the consciousness of Germanic Christianity in the Middle Ages became more anti-Semitic in proportion as it became more 'Judaic' in its self-understanding (Judaic in the sense of an 'Old Testament' interest in war and cult).

[11] The theme of the consistently misunderstood argument of Paul in Rom. 9–11.

human life under the pressure of a faithful creator; the argument for its particularism and exclusivity is the same as ever, that only through this particularly is a fleshly and concrete manifestation of God's will possible. Christianity's story of Jesus highlights the ambiguous and provisional nature of this argument, and so seeks to push the reality of an integrated human community beyond the confines of a people; but it has commonly offered only an ersatz universality, a large-scale tribalism with Christ as source and guarantor of the authoritative and comprehensive system of meaning purveyed by the Church. It has failed to see what lies in its own theology: the conflict, the destructive conflict, between God and our efforts to articulate the pressure of God upon us and to encode and transmit through time that articulation.

'At the heart of the Christian mystery is the full emptiness, the divine absence enacted and disclosed in the life, death and resurrection of Jesus Christ';[12] thus Gerard Loughlin, in a recent critical essay on John Hick's paradigm for the relation of world religions. Loughlin's point is that Hick's account removes or trivializes this specific and radical Christian starting-point: it is paradoxically only through the narrative of a critical fulfilment and embodiment or enactment of God within the world of a religious community that we can lay hold on the idea of a global testing of our religious words and desires, as historical religious behaviour is confronted by the historical enactment of God's presence, by the eschatological. To theologize about the Incarnation, then, may be something other than a search for ways of demonstrating the comprehensive meaningfulness of Jesus (and thus, normally, of the Church's language); it can be, more demandingly, the effort to preserve the edge of conflict between ideology and honest discourse about God. It can thus be the charter for the task of Christian self-criticism, and for that spirituality of negation and absence, 'luminous darkness', that has continued, despite everything, to work with Christianity as a counter to its institutional confidence. The Church, in one sense, runs a greater risk than Israel, in that its institutional life is committed to the preservation, by word and sacrament, of its own questionability, and the ambiguity of all systematized schemes of religious meaning, all attempts at finished religious ontologies. And because of this, it is not free to claim finality for itself; there are things it does not say, meaning it does not carry. In particular, in relation to the Jewish people, it should have learned by now how such a claim serves the most unreconstructed and murderous ideological purposes. 'When things were going well for the "new Israel", when the "people of God" felt strong,

---

[12]   Gerard Loughlin, 'Noumenon and Phenomenon', *Religious Studies* 23 (1988), pp. 493–508.

antisemitism flourished, drawing its confidence from the security of hardened dogmatic positions.'[13]

This quotation is from Dorothee Sölle's important, difficult, and (in the English-speaking world) largely neglected work, *Christ the Representative*, where Sölle suggests that the significance of the idea of a Messiah who has come is that he 'enables non-Jews to become Jews; that is to say, he enables them to live in postponement'.[14] Christ is our representative here in the sense that he realizes and holds open for us the future we have yet to grow into, occupying the 'place' we cannot yet occupy, the place of responsibility for God's action in the world. Judaism, which constantly lives in 'postponement', may risk (according to Gershom Scholem, quoted here by Sölle) despairing of any real accomplishment in history, of devaluing its own commitments by rendering them perennially distant from the historical world. Once again, the distinction is being drawn between the transformative nature of what Jesus has done and the Church's claim to finality – a finality which, though claimed on behalf of Jesus, is in fact a statement about the Church's own aspirations. The true Church, in contrast, is a community enabled to live in provisionality without apathy or resignation: 'where the Church really exists, God is assured of what is still future'.[15] The Church is what, so to speak, promises the world to God, because the world's future is already represented by Christ. However, what is being said about the Church's relation to the Jewish people is not wholly clear: the acceptance of Scholem's characterization seems dangerously near to just that abstract and unhistorical religious construct that has long bedevilled Christian polemical accounts of Jewishness.[16] If Christ 'enables non-Jews to become Jews', does this mean that he also enables Jews to become Jews? Sölle comes close to suggesting this, and what I have been arguing so far in this paper would support some such idea. But I think it is more useful to develop this point in relation not to an essence of messianic Jewishness but to the specific politicizations of Jewishness at specific moments of history. Thus the crucified Jesus puts God's question to the various styles of political defence of Jewishness in the first century of the Christian era; reflecting once again Rosemary Ruether's essay – the anti-

---

[13]   Dorothee Sölle, *Christ the Representative. An Essay in Theology after the Death of God* (London, 1967), p. 109; cf. n. 10 above.

[14]   Ibid., p. 111.

[15]   Ibid., p. 112.

[16]   For criticism, see Neusner, Green and Frerichs, *op. cit.*, especially Williams S. Green, 'Introduction: Messiah in Judaism; Rethinking the Question', pp. 1–13.

messianism, the reversed image of messianism, displayed in the story of Jesus can be part of a contemporary critique of the ersatz messianism of the modern state of Israel.

But how very hard it is to say this with any Christian integrity! Between the first century and the last few decades, the idea of Christianity proffering to Judaism the crucified Christ as a challenge to ideology would have been at best an ironic joke, at worst a moral nonsense. The Church has not been conspicuous for living in provisionality. The continuing existence of the Jewish people has indeed been theologized as a sign of the Church's historical incompleteness (not all Christian theology has explicitly denied the right of Israel to exist), but the record of open anti-Semitism has shown how Christians have felt the urge to finalize their history and seal off the new people of God from the uncertainties of a history which still contained those who 'refused' the gospel. This century has shown what it means for these chiliastic fantasies to be acted out by a state that (as Barth and Bonhoeffer so well understood) was effectively a parodic Church, a purified community of the last days. The eschatological tribalism of the third Reich was a mirror held up to Christian ideology; the Reich's assault on the Jewish people in the urge to bring a kind of finality into history has rightly become for us the paradigm of ideological violence. And from this, some Christians at least have learned to re-read their foundational story as one about ideological violence, and to see Christ as standing in judgement on ecclesial tribalism – which is to say that Jesus has been re-imagined through the medium of the Jewish experience. That is what, in our time, has given flesh to the conflict between God and the human construction of 'definitive meanings'; as if the form of Christ had for us been defined over against the Church by the victims of the Shoah. Christ may indeed speak for the authentic vocation of God's people, to show the pressure of God's reality in the shape of a corporate human life of justice and hopefulness; but the Jewish people, as victims of Christian and post-Christian ideological closure, speak for Christ to Christians in the name of God who is not a Christian, reminding Christians of their 'Jewish' vocation to embody that community of Justice between human beings that is God's purpose.

We could go on tracing the relation between the Church and the Jewish people in its dialectical complexity, but enough has been said to indicate what I think is the basic theological point. There is no settling of the debate: Israel's resistance to absorption by the Church is a refusal to grant that the meanings of Israel are contained and subsumed in the Christian institution, and that refusal is essential for the truthfulness and faithfulness of the Church,

tempted as it is to claim a distorted kind of finality.[17] But the Church's proclamation that Jesus is the embodiment of God's speech and purpose, both
within and against the empirical political history of Israel, puts the counter-
question about the health and faithfulness of the chosen people, setting forth
Jesus as a sign of the eschatological breaking of the boundaries of a people to
create a new world for God. To go on being a Christian is to be committed
to that particular breaking through and that particular hope.

I have spent some time exploring the nature – as I see it – of the Jewish-
Christian tension because I want to suggest that it offers a possible key for
wider reflection on Christology and the inter-faith encounter. Christianity
does not make full sense in its own terms without the belief that the trial and
execution of Jesus are the focal moment of God's own 'controversy' (*rib* in
the Hebrew of the OT)[18] with the chosen people, that the summons of Jesus
is the creative utterance of God in respect of the people. In other words,
Christianity cannot set out its distinctive proposal with full seriousness in the
absence of some account of the 'embodying' or incarnation of God in Christ;
and, as I have tried to indicate, both the significance and the difficulty of
speaking about this derive from the context of a particular religio-political
history. It is unhelpful to treat it as a specific case of a general mythological
pattern of divine embodiment, in abstraction from the call-and-response,
promise-and-fulfilment grammar of Jewishness. To ask, with John Hick in a
celebrated essay,[19] whether Jesus might not have been conscripted into an
avatar pattern if the gospel had travelled as far eastwards as it did westwards is
to miss the point: the 'divinity' of Jesus becomes a theological possibility and
eventually a theological necessity precisely because of his relation to the
institutionalized religious meanings of Israel (this sets the agenda even for the
developments of more obviously Hellenistic speculations such as Logos
theology), and insofar as the background of Israel remained part of the story
of Jesus, this story would generate its own myth and dogma, rather than
simply being absorbed into another mythology.

But this is to say that belief in Christ as the definitive and critical embodiment of God in Israel's history does not allow any easy transition to speaking

[17]   Although Simone Weil was at times fiercely and indeed violently and unjustly critical of
her own Jewish heritage, her refusal of baptism on the grounds of the Church's claims to
pronounce on the standing of individuals before God has about it something of this same
vocation to protest at the Church's distorted versions of God's election and grace.
[18]   See Ulrich Simon, 'The Transcendence of Law', *Theology* 73, (1970), pp. 166–8, for some
profound reflection on the theme of God's controversy with the people.
[19]   'Jesus and the World Religions', John Hick, ed., *The Myth of God Incarnate* (London,
1977), pp. 167–85, p. 176.

of Christ as the 'fulfilment' of all religious traditions; in fact, it makes far
more difficult the idea that Christ contains, even potentially, all systems of
religious meaning, let alone that the Christian Church is the final and definitive arbiter of all true insight in these matters. The history of Jesus enacts a
judgement on tribalized and self-protecting religion, on the confusion between faith and ideology; it is a history of God with us insofar as it declares
that there is liberty to act, to heal and to create community 'outside the
gates' of religious practice that has become oppressive or exclusive – God's
liberty. But that liberty becomes transforming for human beings and human
communities in their readiness for dispossession, for the loss of the God who
is defined as belonging to us and our interests; in passing through that dispossession, religious speech moves some little way closer to being a speech that
human beings as human beings may share.[20] To be a Christian is to claim that
the Jewish story with its interruption and repristination in Jesus is the most
comprehensive working-out of this moment of dispossession – a religious
tradition generating its own near-negation, holding in precarious juxtaposition the faithfulness of God and the alienness and freedom of God. That is
nothing if not a debatable claim. The systematic self-dissolution of Buddhist
language in some of its forms can make a powerful counter-claim to be
comprehensively critical, which could be answered only by moving the debate to the ground of the relative importance of conceptions of historical
growth or hope. A Christian would, presumably, argue that a scheme setting
these aside would miss one of the essential elements in an overall dialectic of
presence and absence, and so would be less comprehensive; the Buddhist
would respond that such a perspective is already coloured by the very story
whose claims are in dispute . . . But if inter-faith encounter is more than a
programme for avoiding disagreement, such debate is inevitable and fruitful.
And if we need to be concerned to state what the Christian question or
challenge is to other faiths, we need to be more alert in hearing the corresponding questions addressed to us – the crucial Buddhist challenge about
the effects of believing in the solidity of an ego bound up in appetite, spiritual as well as physical, for example, or the Muslim anxiety about the fragmentation of religious language without an essentially unitary concept of
God and God's will.

'The resurrection of Jesus Christ and the Pentecost of his Spirit do not

[20]   This I take to be the force of Dietrich Bonhoeffer's meditations on 'religionless' Christianity – not a plea for the secular reduction of faith, but a vision of the language of faith enlarging
itself to become the language of that unrestricted human community spoken of at the beginning of this chapter.

mean that Jesus Christ is henceforward the answer to everything . . . They indicate that God bears witness that the question raised by Jesus Christ is the one by which God manifests himself . . . God does not show himself in Jesus Christ as being the totality of meaning. Jesus Christ does not manifest himself as being the totality of meaning. When they believe that this is nevertheless the case, Christians prevent meaning being found in the manifestation of God in Jesus Christ, which is not a manifestation of the significance of omnipotence. One could say, in a rough paraphrase of St. Paul: We do not have omnipotence of meaning; we do not proclaim to you the totality of meaning; we have nothing to proclaim but Jesus dead and risen; we have only this news which has no value as a response to everything or as the totality of meaning, but has value in itself.'[21] Pohier's words eloquently sum up a great deal of what I have been trying to say; for him, the central and perhaps (paradoxically) 'universal' meaning of Christ is in Christ's revelation, over against all religious totalities of interpretation, of a God who is authentically creator of a world because this God does not wish to be everything.[22] Earlier in the same book, Pohier asks: 'is it not in Jesus Christ himself that we shall find the most effective pointers towards establishing a distance between Jesus Christ and an inadequate absolutisation of Jesus Christ?'[23] For Pohier, the belief that Jesus is indeed the Word made flesh[24] is what keeps at bay the seductions of 'totalized' meaning: only this can plainly show us a God who is intelligibly other than the world, who therefore does not control how the divine is to be met by means of a single set of revealed schemata. Jesus 'uniquely' reveals the God whose nature is not to make the claim of unique revelation as total and authoritative meaning.

This does seem to break through, to some extent, the options of exclusivism, inclusivism and pluralism. Jesus is not dehistoricized or absolutized as an icon of significance, but neither is he depicted as the teacher of one among several possible ways of salvation. He is presented as the revelation of God: as God's question, no more, no less. Being a Christian is being held to that question in such a way that the world of religious discourse in general may hear it. There are certain echoes here of the Barthian opposition between God and religion, but the crucial difference is in how we conceive of the God who questions religion (and thus in the spirituality appropriate to such a God): Barth's God is quintessentially the God who is totality of meaning, and whose

---

[21]   Jacques Pohier, *God – in Fragments* (London, 1985), p. 294.
[22]   The title of Pohier's Section III is 'God is God, so God is not everything'.
[23]   Ibid., p. 59.
[24]   Ibid., p. 50.

will as creator 'not to be everything' is systematically obscured by the theologian's insistence on the emptiness of all created speech and science.[25] But the cross of Jesus is stranger even than the Barthian might suggest: God's difference is beyond all the words and institutions in which it is (inevitably) articulated, and through which it may be turned into a means of control.

In the cathedral at Cologne hangs a large crucifix of the tenth century, commissioned by Archbishop Gero some time between 971 and 976. It shows the dead Christ: a figure of extraordinary stillness, the curve and sag of the heavy corpse as powerful, simple and smooth as the movement of a tree, the eyes closed, the face turned down and away. It is as unlike the great baroque crucifixes as could be. It makes no appeal to facile emotion, exerts no pressure, no blackmail; there is no crown, and the palms are spread flatly on the wood, no fingers joined in blessing. Nothing is explained. It is a plain fact in wood. 'We have the news which has no value as a response to everything.' We have the news of the death of God in the world of religious meanings, which is also the news of the life of God, who does not, after all, live in religious meanings – or rather, God can only live in the grammar of religious talk when that talk expresses God's freedom from it. We have something to say to human religiousness (our own included), but we are not in the business of winning arguments for good and all. What the world, religious and secular, does with the news of Jesus crucified and risen is beyond our control, and if it were otherwise we should have lost what our own 'news' is news of.

---

[25]   This is (deliberately) to overstate the matter: at most, it might legitimately be argued to hold for the Barth of the first volume of the *Church Dogmatics*. For further discussion, see the essays by the present writer and Dr R. H. Roberts in S. W. Sykes, ed., *Karl Barth. Studies of His Theological Method* (Oxford, 1979).

Chapter Eight

WORD AND SPIRIT

Many writers have remarked a certain poverty in theological reflection on the Holy Spirit in Western Christianity over the last decades. Despite the enormous proliferation of literature concerned with the charismatic movement in recent years,[1] and despite the appearance of a number of more substantial essays in English on the Spirit,[2] it is hard not to feel that a certain unease persists. It is an unease reflected very clearly in the fact that more than one recent writer in the Anglican tradition seems to settle for a virtual binitarianism, a trinity of two persons (agents) and a force, or quality, or 'mode of presence'.[3] Looking further afield, it is notable that several of the greatest contemporary theologians on the Continent of Europe share something of this malaise. Barth's doctrine of the Spirit is, notoriously, one of the least developed areas of his system;[4] and this weakness is, if anything, accentuated in the work of perhaps his most distinguished pupil, Eberhard Jüngel.[5] In Roman Catholic theology, neither Rahner nor Küng has provided an

---

[1] See especially *Charismatic Renewal*, ed. E. D. O'Connor (London: SPCK, 1978); *New Heaven? New Earth?*, S. Tugwell and others (London: DLT, 1976); *A Charismatic Theology*, H. Mühlen (London: Burns and Oates, 1978).

[2] Including J. V. Taylor, *The Go-Between God* (London: SCM, 1972); C. F. D. Moule, *The Holy Spirit* (London: Mowbrays, 1978); A. M. Ramsey, *Holy Spirit* (London: SPCK, 1977).

[3] Austin Farrer, *Saving Belief* (London: Hodder, 1964), pp. 128–9; C. F. D. Moule, *op. cit.*, pp. 50–1. Cf. B. M. G. Reardon, commenting on a paper by H. Cunliffe-Jones in *Theology* (June 1972), pp. 298–301.

[4] Though, of course, a pneumatology would have formed part of the completed *Dogmatics*. In addition to the discussion in *Church Dogmatics* I.1.12, see also IV.2.67 and 68, and IV.3, 72 and 73, especially the exposition in 68.2 of the idea of the Spirit as God making himself 'the basis of our love' (IV.2, trans. G. W. Bromiley; Edinburgh, 1968, pp. 757–9, 778–9, etc.).

[5] The subject is scarcely mentioned in *Gottes Sein ist im Werden* (Tübingen, 1964), though it merits a brief section in *Gott als Geheimnis der Welt* (Tübingen, 1977, pp. 512–14, 531–4).

independent treatise on pneumatology, and their respective essays in theo-logical synthesis[6] contain only the most cursory treatment of the subject. Schillebeeckx's fine essay in Christology[7] touches the theology of the Spirit only tangentially.

One could go on quoting such instances (and it needs also to be said that there are some very notable exceptions, in the Protestant and Catholic worlds: the two intriguing and challenging figures of Jürgen Moltmann[8] and Hans Urs von Balthasar[9] stand out here), but it would not be particularly useful. What we need to be asking is why there should be such an awkwardness in this area. One fairly obvious answer might be that, in the present theological climate as seldom before, all the pressures are towards the concrete, the worldly – towards Christology, in fact. For those like Moltmann and Schillebeeckx who are profoundly engaged in dialogue with the Frankfurt School, Christology becomes, above all, the vehicle for coping with the most tor-menting questions of our age about the *humanum* – what is it to be a human being after the Holocaust (or after Vietnam or Rwanda)? The rejection and death of Jesus is in a sense the only *possible* theological datum now: to avoid Christology is to avoid the human question of how to talk of God in the shadow of hell. From this perspective (though Moltmann himself does not draw any such simple conclusion), pneumatology can very easily look both evasive and triumphalist: harsh remarks have sometimes been made (not entirely justly) about the emergence of vigorous charismatic groups in situations of acute social conflict (Latin America, Southern Africa) as a re-directing of frustrated energies unable to manage the realities of secular con-frontation. Christology has a priority simply because there the question of God and the human is most directly raised. Pneumatology can be seen as raising only the question of God and certain limited kinds of human experi-ence. A very acute observer of Roman Catholic pentecostalism in America wrote (several decades ago, surprisingly):

> We have seen too often how 'religion' can become no more than an intellec-tual failure of nerve. How 'God' can become an emotional uplift for the 'gaps' in our lives. How 'Spirit' can become an unexamined blanket-word to cover

---

[6] *Foundations of Christian Faith* (London: DLT, 1978); *On Being a Christian* (London: Collins, 1977). Cf. Küng's *Existiert Gott?* (Munich, 1978), pp. 760–7.
[7] *Jesus. An Experiment in Christology* (London: Collins, 1978; see pp. 644–7, 660–1).
[8] See especially *The Church in the Power of the Spirit* (London: SCM, 1977).
[9] See *On Prayer* (London: Geoffrey Chapman, 1961, and SPCK, 1973), pp. 55–67, 150–4; *Herrlichkeit. Eine Theologische Ästhetik*, III.2. Teil II (Einsiedeln, 1969), section II, *passim*.

a whole range of rich but too-fleeting experiences which may or may not be real (that is, true). For the perhaps unpleasant fact remains that no alert contemporary Westerner can really turn his back on science, on criticism, on *theoria* (in a word, on differentiated consciousness) even in his articulation of his 'moral', and 'Christian' life. More accurately, he can do so only at the price (too often and too willingly paid, I fear) of having that life, at first ecstatic, dissolve into the adventitiousness of a 'religious' atmosphere or a 'leisure' moment or harden into the brittleness of an ideology.[10]

Large questions here, needing very careful discussion. The implication is that what this writer calls 'Spirit-theologies' are in danger of trivializing the whole of theological anthropology: they have little or nothing to say to the *humanum* as such. And this is a very good reason for approaching the theology of the Spirit with reserve and caution. But it should also make us reflect how very odd it is that it should be possible so to separate Christology and pneumatology that the former is thought to be in itself an adequate response to the anthropological question while the latter has little bearing. It is an oddity pointed out very persistently by theologians of the Eastern Orthodox tradition,[11] for whom Western trinitarian theology is rendered hopelessly asymmetrical and 'Christomonist' by the *filioque*. And it suggests that our problem really lies at a deeper level.

What I should like to explore in this paper is the thesis that theologies of Spirit have generally suffered as a result of the predominance of one kind of trinitarian model in the formative ages of Christian reflection, a model which is constantly being questioned by a rather elusive alternative. This alternative is, in fact, the presupposition of a great deal of Christian language and practice, but is less easily manageable at the theoretical level. I should want to argue further that the first model pressed to its logical conclusion is potentially destructive of any kind of trinitarian theology;[12] and this is not an issue which all would find desirable. How far it is possible to give *systematic* shape to the 'alternative' remains to be seen.

---

[10] D. Tracy in *God, Jesus, Spirit*, ed. D. Callahan (New York: Herder, 1969), p. 328.

[11] See, for example, Vladimir Lossky, *The Mystical Theology of the Eastern Church* (London and Cambridge, 1957), chs 3, 8 and 9, and *In the Image and Likeness of God* (New York: St Vladimir's Seminary Press, 1974), ch. 4.

[12] That is to say, that it leads either to a dyad of Father and Word (as sometimes in Barth and his followers) or to a dyad of transcendent God and immanent Spirit (as in G. W. H. Lampe's recent – and deeply impressive – *God as Spirit*, OUP, 1977).

I

The model of which I am speaking is roughly this: God communicates or 'interprets' himself to the world by the mediation of Word and Spirit. The problem to which trinitarian theology is the answer is the problem of revelation: how is God heard or seen to be present to the human world? This seems to me to be a perfectly proper question to ask, and it is clearly important that it was being asked with some seriousness in pre-Christian Judaism, as well as in the Hellenic world.[13] But the difficulties which arise in the early Church show very clearly the problem of fitting together the threefold formulae of the NT and liturgical practice with a basically *twofold* cosmological-revelatory theological picture. The tension has very frequently been noted and discussed,[14] but there a few points which I should like to underline anew. First of all, the model takes it for granted that the two primary terms are 'God' and 'the world': the revealing or mediating reality, the 'bridge-concept,'[15] must occupy a space *between* these terms. Secondly, the mediator is posited to answer the question of how *God* comes to *the world*; that is, the line runs from God 'downwards'. So that, thirdly, the relation between mediator and God is obscure and difficult to state: we do not know what sort of line runs from world *to* God through the mediator. In short, one of the difficulties in all this is that the understanding of God as such is not affected by the 'bridge-concept': the latter is instrumental to solving a problem which has two *clear* starting-points.

Furthermore, it is evident that this scheme strictly requires one mediator only. If we are to speak of a third divine hypostasis at all, Spirit as well as Logos, there is an immediate awkwardness. Second-century Christian writers in this tradition produce a wide and ingenious assortment of solutions, occasionally foreshadowing with remarkable accuracy some of the suggestions of more recent theologians. Thus Hermas cuts the Gordian knot by a straightforward assimilation of Logos and Spirit: the eternal and pre-existent Spirit chooses to dwell in flesh; and as a result of the co-operation of

---

[13]   The question is most interestingly discussed in J. Bowker's *The Religious Imagination and the Sense of God* (OUP, 1978). On the background in Hellenistic Jewish 'Wisdom' speculation, see, e.g., M. Hengel, *Judaism and Hellenism* (London: SCM, 1974), vol. 1, pp. 153–75. I must also mention a still unpublished paper by Professor J. C. O'Neill of Westminster College, Cambridge, on 'The Trinity in the New Testament and Before'.

[14]   See, for example, chapters IV and V of J. N. D. Kelly, *Early Christian Doctrines* (London: A. and C. Black, 5th edn 1977).

[15]   A term favoured by Professor Lampe in *God as Spirit*.

the 'flesh' with the Spirit, it is taken up to God as Son, becoming a 'fellow-councillor' of God.[16] Exactly what status 'the Son' has in this passage and whether he is in any sense pre-existent is not at all clear; what is plain is that the Spirit is the cosmological mediator *par excellence*. Later, we find the *Son* as 'fellow-councillor' in the act of creation itself.[17] Obscure as this is, it does appear that we here have to do with a basically binitarian structure, in which the eternal Son is strictly the same as the Holy Spirit, but the assumption of Jesus into the heavenly realm adds some kind of 'third term' to the divine council. Whatever the correct interpretation,[18] this popular and widely diffused work illustrates quite clearly the degree to which a not very sophisticated theological mind of the second century could take it for granted that the structure of the divine economy was God 'plus' a mediator: how exactly Spirit and Son are to be accounted for separately does not trouble the author.

It does, however, trouble some more acute minds of the period – though still not very much. The relation of Father and Son, or God and his Word, is not problematic: it occupies a central place in all the Apologists, as in Hippolytus. But here the Spirit tends to be introduced as an awkward afterthought. Justin's first Apology offers a notorious instance,[19] where the 'prophetic Spirit' is mentioned as an object of worship after Father, Son, and *angels*. Although 'the Spirit of prophecy' plays a very important part in Justin's argument, his discussion of types of prophecy[20] leaves a very unclear picture: by the Spirit, prophets are enabled to speak in the person of Father or Son. Spirit is what mediates the utterance of one or other of the divine persons to us; but what he or it is in relation to those persons is left vague. Despite this, Justin provides quite clear evidence for baptism in the threefold name,[21] and appeals to Plato for confirmation of a divine triad.[22] That the three-term formula is uncontroverted is quite plain, but there is, understandably, no serious attempt to harmonize this with the cosmological scheme of God and Word – understandably, because there is, at this date, no sense of a tension. Spirit is the divine afflatus in the prophets, but, as such, cannot be clearly distinguished from the Word.[23] It is impossible wholly to systematize Justin's thought on this matter, but there is at least a strong sense that at one level the Spirit can be to the Son what the

---

[16] Hermas, *Sim.* V.vi.
[17] Ibid., *Sim.* IX.xii.
[18] The Vatican MS of Hermas actually has the gloss 'the Son is the Spirit' in *Sim.* V.v.
[19] I *Apol.* vi.
[20] Ibid., xxxvi–xxxix.
[21] Ibid., lxi.
[22] Ibid., lx.
[23] Ibid., xxxvi.

Son is to the Father (though the Spirit can also give utterance to the Father's speech directly). If the Spirit is to have any rationally worked-out place here, it must be, somehow, between the Word and the universe.

Athenagoras' view of the Spirit is more nuanced, but little more consistent or clear.[24] In two places in the *Supplicatio*, he calls the Spirit *aporroia*, 'effulgence',[25] which on its own suggests something a little like Justin's view (especially as here also it is connected with prophecy):[26] the Spirit is a beam of light from the sun, or from a fire, controlling the utterances of prophets, holding creation in being.[27] But it is united to Father and Son,[28] and instructs us about Father and Son and the nature of their oneness;[29] though whether it is to be taken as the principle of their unity, as one passage might suggest,[30] is much more debatable. Evidently, Athenagoras is wholeheartedly committed to the doctrine of a divine triad, in which 'Spirit' is, among other things, the provider of information about the relationship between Father and Son or Word; the common 'agency' of the two persons, perhaps. This is interesting and valuable, but still fairly clearly within the bounds of a controlling interest in the cosmological mediation of the Logos. How the creative activity of Logos and the sustaining activity of Spirit are related is not explored (and this question is made more complicated by the suggestion[31] that the angels are charged with the 'ordering' of the world). In short, the problem of the *rationale* of there being a Spirit at all is still unclear. What does it or he do that the Logos does not? The hint at an answer which Athenagoras suggests is that he clarifies the way in which Father and Word belong to each other; and we might see here a hint of the Johannine notion of the Spirit as interpreter of Jesus' union with the Father.[32] But the sonship of *Jesus* (in the sense in which this idea was important for John or Paul) is not a theme in which any of the Apologists show much interest.

---

[24]   Despite a valiant attempt by Dr L. W. Barnard to assimilate it to later orthodoxy, in his monograph *Athenagoras. A Study in Second-Century Apologetic* (Paris: Beauchesne, 1972), pp. 105–11.

[25]   *Suppl.* 10 and 24.

[26]   Ibid., 10; cf. 7 and 9.

[27]   Ibid., 6.

[28]   Ibid., 10, 12, 24.

[29]   Ibid., 12.

[30]   Ibid., 10. Barnard takes it in this sense (as does Crehan's translation for *Ancient Christian Writers*), though older commentators and translators treat *pneuma* here (I think, more plausibly) as being non-specific – 'power of spirit', not 'of *the* Spirit'.

[31]   Ibid., 10.

[32]   As in Jn 16.12–15.

There may be a clearer sense of it in Hippolytus. The section dealing with the trinity in *Contra Noetum*[33] is of considerable interest on this matter: here the Spirit is portrayed as *sunetizon*, the one who 'harmonizes' Father and Son, brings them together in understanding, in the act of command and obedience.[34] In the Spirit the Father's command and the Son's obedience flow into unity. To know Father or Son independently of the Spirit is not knowledge of the true God: even the apostles' knowledge of the earthly Jesus is imperfect because the Spirit has not yet been given.[35] There is still, however, an uneasiness about the precise status of the Spirit *vis-à-vis* Father and Son. The Trinity consists of two persons and an *oikonomia*, a 'dispensation' of grace and 'symphonic accord', which is Spirit;[36] and historians of dogma have remarked on the asymmetrical character this gives to the trinitarian relationship. Yet here is at least some idea that knowledge of God is knowledge of the relation of Son to Father in loving obedience, and that it is accessible only by a sharing in whatever it is that unites Father and Son. This is a marked and important break with the relentlessly 'linear' view of other theologians of the age – the conceptually somewhat confused mediation of Logos and Spirit instructing about and leading to the transcendent deity of the Father, or uniting to effect the Father's will in creation. Irenaeus' celebrated metaphor of Son and Spirit as the Father's 'two hands' in creation[37] is one of the clearest instances of the latter; and his assimilation of Son and Spirit to 'Word' and 'Wisdom' respectively[38] reflects the inevitable looseness of cosmological images as applied in trinitarian thinking. Yet he, like Hippolytus, can also suggest a picture more akin to that of Pauline theology. There is no other divine Spirit than that which cries 'Abba'; it is this Spirit of sonship by which we grow in the divine likeness,[39] and the gift of Spirit to the prophets is one way in which God prepares human beings for communion with himself.[40] Irenaeus' vivid and fresh soteriology avoids the somewhat mechanical scheme of the Spirit simply 'giving information' about the Word, reflecting or transmitting the

---

[33] 14.1–16.7.

[34] Ibid., 14.5.

[35] Ibid., 14.6.

[36] Ibid., 14.2–4.

[37] *Adv. Haer.* IV, praef. 3, xiv. 1 (in the Armenian), xxxiv. 1; V.v. 1, vi. 1, xxviii. 3; cf. *Apod.* 10, on Word and Spirit as the two angelic powers in the sanctuary. *Apod.* 5 distinguishes their roles as the production respectively of matter and of form.

[38] *Adv. Haer.* IV.xix. 1.

[39] *Apod.* 5; cf. *Apod.* 42 on the gift of the Spirit in baptism.

[40] *Adv. Haer.* IV.xxv. 2.

Word;[41] and his relative independence of philosophical models prevents the cosmological concern becoming too dominant. He and Hippolytus represent a significant step away from the embarrassed abstractness of the Apologists; but they equally illustrate just how elusive alternative structures may prove to be.

The images of derivation beloved of Tertullian in his writings on this subject tend only to confirm what I have called the 'linear' presuppositions of second-century trinitarian thought. The relation of Father, Son, and Spirit is sequential: the relation of Father to Son and Son to Spirit is a series of three *cohaerentes alterum ex altero*.[42] And in *Adversus Praxean* 8, we find the familiar set of images – root and plant, spring and river, sun and ray for Father and Son, with the Spirit as fruit of the plant, brook from the river, *apex* (point of focus) of the sun's ray: the trinity is *a patre decurrens*. And of course, the very simplicity of these images, with their clear location of Spirit between Word and creation, in fact militates against any real substantive distinction for the role of the Spirit. There are passages in Tertullian[43] where Christ is identified with God's Spirit (e.g., as inspirer of the prophets). Any distinction is 'internal', functional: *spiritus substantia est sermonis et sermo operatio spiritus, et duo unum sunt*.[44] Presumably this means something like: '"Spirit" is what gives substantial presence to the word, while "word" is the name we give to Spirit in action.' Hence it is not difficult to see how Tertullian in his Montanist days can come to envisage the Spirit as continuing the work of Christ in a very straightforwardly chronological fashion, supplementing and completing Christ's teaching in the necessarily more severe dispensation appropriate to Christian maturity.[45] Even in the very early *De praescriptione*,[46] he refers to the Spirit as *vicaria vis*, again (it seems) adopting an extremely simple reading of the Johannine material on the Paraclete to suggest that the Spirit directly continues what Christ has initiated in the way of instruction or illumination.

Despite what has frequently been said of Tertullian as the one who gave exact verbal form to what was to become classical trinitarian doctrine, it is clear that he continues to operate well within the categories of the Apologists. His view of the Spirit is conditioned, as theirs is, by the problem of bridging a gap between God and creation: and, like them, he finds a prob-

---

[41]   Though such a model is not wholly absent; see, e.g., *Apod.* 7, and perhaps *Adv. Haer.* xiv.1, if the Latin is to be followed.

[42]   *Adv. Praxean*, 25.

[43]   Collected by H. Bettenson, *The Early Christian Fathers* (OUP, 1956), pp. 179–80.

[44]   *Adv. Praxean*, 26.

[45]   *De monog.* 2, 14; *De virg. vel.* 1.

[46]   13.

lem in conceiving any *structural* necessity for a second mediatorial presence
except as some kind of continuator of the Logos' revealing activity. Origen
offers a similar scheme;[47] and it is a pupil of Origen's, Gregory Thaumaturgus,
who first clearly articulates the idea of the Spirit as *eikōn* of the Son, as the
Son is of the Father,[48] an idea which was to enjoy considerable currency in
later debates.[49] It is a logical outcome of the general tendency of the tradition
we have been considering: the trinity is a *sequence* of divine persons, succes-
sively revealed in a kind of hierarchically ordered illumination. The Spirit is
'nearest' to us; the Father, in whom resides the divine 'monarchy', the 'fount
of godhead', is furthest from us. Growth in the knowledge of God is a
penetration from forecourt to inner chamber.

II

I do not intend to argue that all this is an invalid or useless way of talking
about God. The purpose of this long discussion of primitive trinitarian discourse has been to demonstrate the results in trinitarian theology of the
dominance of an uncomplicated and readily available religious conceptual
structure. 'God and his mediating agencies' is a model fairly conventional in
the Jewish and Hellenistic worlds alike, as has already been remarked. It can
appear most neatly and economically as 'God and his Logos', or in a more
diffused form in some sort of doctrine of graded emanations or of divine
'powers' being distributed within creation.[50] The only structure which is
satisfactorily triadic appears on the scene rather late in the day, in Plotinus's
threefold cosmic process, and this – for various reasons – is taken up only
very cautiously by Christian theologians. Otherwise, there is a real and evident difficulty in providing a rationale for *three* hypostases, no more and no
less. Professor R. P. C. Hanson, in a sharp critique of Orthodox and Greek
patristic pneumatology, asks; 'Why do we need two images, two revealers?
Why should there not be an infinite series of images or revealers if there are
to be more than one?'[51] But there seem to me to be weaknesses of a more

---

[47]   See *In Joh.* 2.2.16; 6; 10.73–78.
[48]   In *Ekthesis tēs pisteōs*, PG 10, 985A.
[49]   See e.g. Athanasius, *Ad Serap.* 1.24 (PG 26, 588B); and it appears in Damascene, *De fide
orth.* 1.13 (PG 94, 856B).
[50]   A commonplace of late classical eclectic philosophy; see, for example, Pseudo-Aristotle,
De mundo, 6.397b.17–20.
[51]   *The Attractiveness of God* (London: SPCK, 1973), p. 134.

than merely logical kind here: if we conceive the Spirit and the Word as illuminators, transmitters of saving knowledge, we are in danger of driving a wedge between the idea of 'Spirit' and the 'spirituality' of Christian people. If the Spirit simply instructs and guides, leads toward the Logos, it is less easy to talk about 'Spirit' as the constitutive reality or quality of Christian existence – Spirit as received in baptism, as invoked in liturgy, received and invoked not simply to instruct or inform but to *transform*. If the phrase 'in the Spirit' is reduced to designating simply the prophet who is receiving extraordinary communications of divine truth, the Pauline emphasis on the Spirit of sonship is seriously obscured. If the Spirit's role is to conduct us to the 'advanced class' where the Logos presides, Christian maturity 'in the Spirit' becomes a rather aridly intellectualist notion. In short, if the role of Spirit is *communication*, in a narrowly 'linear' sense, whether by ecstatic vision or noetic purity, an impoverished and abstract concept of the actual texture of Christian life and experience is likely to result.

I emphasize this point because at least some of our present difficulties about the doctrine of the Holy Spirit seem to rest upon one or other of these models of communication. Some varieties of 'charismatic' theology clearly operate with a doctrine of the Spirit whose focus is communication through prophecy and ecstatic utterance.[52] And – at the opposite extreme – the theology of Professor Geoffrey Lampe, one of the most distinguished exponents of a 'Spirit-centred' dogmatics,[53] rests upon the conviction that 'Spirit' is the term which may and should be used to cover *all* the ways in which God communicates himself to creatures; so that the 'pre-existent' and eternal Christ is in no sense an independent hypostasis, but only a strongly hypostatized metaphor for Spirit. Logos, in fact, is swallowed up in Pneuma, in a fashion a little reminiscent of Hermas. Once again, the general question here is one concerning the bridge between the world and the transcendent God; and for Professor Lampe, the superfluous term is the Word, conceived as eternally distinct from Spirit. God interprets himself through Spirit: Jesus as supremely the recipient and transmitter of grace, the paradigm of 'graced' relationship with God as Father (and Professor Lampe is very far from being arid or intellectualist here), is himself a source of grace because of his consistent 'transparency' to Spirit.

But of course it is not only a reduction of Word to Spirit that we have seen in contemporary dogmatics. It is at least possible to read Barth's early reflections on the Spirit, especially in I.1 and 2 of the *Church Dogmatics*, as a

---

[52]   I am assuming that glossolalia is to be regarded not only as a means of praising God but also as a medium of prophecy.
[53]   *God as Spirit*, 1977.

partial reduction of Spirit to Word. The Spirit is 'the subjective side in the event of revelation',[54] God in us receiving the Word which we cannot receive in our own right, 'the reality in which [God] makes Himself sure of us'.[55] It is indeed the Spirit of adoption, constituting us children of God,[56] and Barth's exegesis of the relevant Pauline and Johannine passages is superb. And the Spirit is 'the act of communion' between Father and Son, the gift given between them.[57] However, the whole discussion is conducted with reference to the problem of *revelation*: how do human beings come to hear the Word? The lengthy treatment in 1.2, 16 of the Spirit as 'subjective reality' and 'subjective possibility' of revelation is couched mostly in terms of the impossibility of there being any immanent or worldly or human ground for the hearing of the Word: 'subjective revelation', the hearing of the Word by this or that person, occurs only on the basis of 'objective revelation', the truth that there is an eternal Word, and an eternal witness to that Word.[58] The Spirit teaches us that 'we are not only approached' by the Word, but taken into Him, that He 'abides with us, and so becomes ours and we His'.[59] 'He is simply the Teacher of the Word';[60] strictly speaking, the 'subjective possibility of revelation' is not the Spirit as such, but the Spirit as making the Word present.[61] By the work of the Spirit, human beings come to recognize the Word as unavoidably 'master',[62] to recognize authority, command, the claim to obedience, to give our responsibility into the hands of the Word and be formed by Him, through the activity of the Spirit.

It seems, then, that for Barth Spirit is what closes the hermeneutical circle. The Word's interpretation of God the Father is interpreted in and to us by the Spirit, since we have no immanent possibility of interpreting any more than of hearing the Word. And what the Spirit realizes in us is our status as God's children, those who belong to God because their sin has been borne by Christ: in the Spirit, we are 'placed with' the Son in his cross and resurrection. We become free for God, *capaces Dei*, in and only in this 'form' of Christ's death.[63] We can interpret ourselves as God's, as belonging in God's

---

[54] *Church Dogmatics* I.1 (2nd edn, trans. G. W. Bromiley; Edinburgh, 1975), p. 449.
[55] Ibid., p. 454.
[56] Ibid., pp. 457–9.
[57] Ibid., p. 470.
[58] I.2 (Edinburgh, 1956), p. 239.
[59] Ibid., p. 242.
[60] Ibid., p. 244.
[61] Ibid., p. 249 (compare the discussion of the *filioque* in I.1, pp. 477–87).
[62] Ibid., pp. 265ff., 269–79, *passim*.
[63] I.1, p. 458.

realm or sharing in the fruits of God's work, only because of the Spirit. Here indeed we are 'made sure' of God because he makes sure of us.

I have attempted elsewhere[64] to discuss what seem to me to be some of the weaknesses of a scheme based so exclusively upon 'interpretation'. There is the familiar risk of turning sin into ignorance (though Barth generally avoids anything so crude); and, more significantly perhaps, there is the identification of the 'saved' condition as 'taking cognizance' of an existing state of affairs. The element of call is muted, the place of Christian *praxis* (as opposed to witness alone) is not clear. Barth, earlier in I. 1, describes the three modes of God's trinitarian being as 'form', 'freedom', and 'historicity':[65] it is the Spirit who constituted revelation as historical, capable of being responded to by individuals in specific contexts.[66] But the sense here given to 'historical' is very obscure, since it appears to have little to do with the actual continuing 'construction' of a human reality. In fact, we return again to our earlier point about the more obvious attractions of Christology for those at all seriously engaged with the *humanum*. Pneumatology looks uncomfortably like an exercise designed simply to explain how we know what Christ does (granted that we do not know it simply by historical inspection or by subjective intuition): the Spirit is the seal of epistemological security, and Barth is perhaps nearer here to the theology of the Apologists than he might have cared to admit.

And yet the notion of Spirit as 'historicity' is tantalizing and deeply suggestive. What I hope to do in the remainder of this essay is to suggest how such a conception might be developed, with reference to the more subtle and elusive models of the divine Spirit in the New Testament. Part of our current *impasse* has to do with the fact that much pneumatology is cast in what might loosely be called a Lukan mould: the Spirit as continuator of Christ's work, filling a space left by Christ's exaltation, manifest in the conviction of extraordinary experiences.[67] It is an idea still well within the horizons of classical and intertestamental Judaism: in the last days, the visible workings of God return to the world, in miracle and prophecy, and this is the outpouring of Spirit. It has been pointed out[68] that the Spirit in the Acts

[64] In an essay contributed to *Karl Barth. Studies in His Theological Method*, ed. S. W. Sykes (OUP, 1980).

[65] I.1 section 8.2; see esp. pp. 315–33.

[66] Ibid., p. 330.

[67] See, e.g., E. Trocmé, 'Le Saint-Esprit et l'Eglise d'après le livre des Actes', in *L'Esprit Saint et l'Eglise. Actes du symposium organisé par l'Académie Internationale des Sciences Religieuses* (Paris: Fayard, 1969), especially the discussion on pp. 40–1. Also J. D. G. Dunn, *Jesus and the Spirit*, (London: SCM, 1977), ch. VII.

[68] See, e.g., E. Haenchen's *The Acts of the Apostles* (Oxford: Blackwell, 1971), pp. 92–3, 95.

of the Apostles occasionally seems to have the role of the *bath qōl* in later Judaism. And Luke is seldom so far from Paul as in his conception of Spirit. If we turn to the Pauline literature, it rapidly becomes clear that the eschatological character of the Spirit's presence, still firmly asserted, has nothing *intrinsically* to do with extraordinary charismata. The central eschatological reality is identification by grace with the obedience of God's Son, through which human beings are set 'on the far side' of judgement and condemnation; so that the Spirit's eschatological character is inseparable from the condition of life lived 'in Christ'. Thus the presence of the Spirit can be associated with 'freedom' (as in II Cor. 3.17–18), the freedom from imperfect and alienating mediation between God and human beings, and of course, with adoptive sonship (Rom. 8.14–17, Gal. 4.6–7), the condition of maturity, the end of servitude, sharing in the quality of Christ's own life, in the tension between suffering and glorification. Emphasis upon the gifts of the Spirit, which are both 'charismatic' and more prosaic (see, notably, I Cor. 12.28–30, where gifts of administration and glossolalia are juxtaposed), is balanced by emphasis upon *life* in the Spirit, with its moral and relational 'fruits' (Gal. 5.22–23). The Spirit is no longer specified by, and thus potentially limited to, the extraordinary and episodic.

At first glance, the Johannine concept of the Paraclete can appear rather as a reflection of Luke's view of Spirit – the substitute mediator and continuator of Christ's work. However, the differences are clear on closer examination; and not the least important of these is the firm and consistent application (in Jn 14–16) of straightforwardly personal language to the Paraclete conceived as, in some sense, 'over against' Jesus and the Father. If Luke invariably sees Spirit as acting 'in a straight line', so to speak, from God and Jesus towards the human world, John sees the Paraclete as active in and with the disciples, moving them towards Father and Son, as well as acting simply *upon* them. The agency of the Paraclete is understood in terms of distance and response rather than simple identification with the agency of Father and Word; it cannot readily be seen in any kind of 'animistic' perspective, or even as a species of *bath qōl* intervention. It is nowhere associated with the extraordinary: the event within the Church's life with which 'holy spirit' is linked is simply the forgiveness of sins (20.23). The test for the Spirit's presence (compare I Cor. 12.3) is the confession of Christ's coming in flesh (I Jn 4.2; cf. 5.6–9). 'The Spirit is the witness, because the Spirit is the truth' (I Jn 5.7): the Paraclete is the spirit of truth, re-presenting the judging and convicting truth of Christ's own presence (Jn 16.7–15), 'glorifying' Christ by his witness.

The parallels between Pauline and Johannine conceptions are fairly clear.

For both, the Spirit is associated with the character of Christian existence as such, creating in the human subject response to, and *conformation* to, the Son. The Spirit' witness is not a pointing to the Son outside the human world, it is precisely the formation of 'Son-like' life in the human world; it is the continuing state of sharing in the mutuality of Father and Son; it is forgiven or justified life. It is also the assurance of the fact that mediation between God and the human is done away: the veil is lifted, truth stands in the midst of us. The distance between God and the world is transcended, so that the relation of slave to master is no longer the appropriate mode for the human apprehension of God. And if all this is, in whatever sense, the work of Spirit, it is clear that the association of Spirit exclusively or chiefly with the more dramatic charismata is a misunderstanding.

It is easy to see why the 'Lukan' model is at first more influential, why the idea of Spirit as substitute or secondary mediator is more readily grasped and developed in the early Church. The association of Spirit with 'adoption' in a very general way is indeed more elusive than its association with clearly defined phenomena, or with the transmission of knowledge of the Logos. The Pauline and Johannine alternative is not easily accommodated in the language of 'interpretation', or even of 'witness' in a simple sense: if the Spirit interprets anything, it is neither Father nor Word, but (as Hippolytus implies) the relation of Father and Son; and he interprets it by re-creating, *translating* it, in the medium of human existence. This is not simply to assimilate the Pauline–Johannine pneumatology to the later model of Spirit as *nexus amoris* in the Trinity; it is to recognize (what many patristic writers were slow to recognize) that the meaning of 'holy spirit' for the Christian cannot be divorced from the vision of Jesus' relation to his Father and all that flows from it. Nor can it be divorced, as Paul so frequently makes plain, from the vision of Christ risen, the Christian conviction that 'Jesus' relation to his Father' is not a contingent fact belonging to the human past alone. For John, the Spirit is not given before the passion and resurrection, because Jesus is not yet decisively 'with' his Father once more, not yet 'glorified' (Jn 7.39). The Jesus who, as risen and exalted, is at the Father's right hand becomes the one who sends the Spirit into the hearts of believers: the Spirit in turn enacts in us the union of Jesus with the Father.

However, if the notions of 'adoption' and 'union' are not to be reduced again simply to the dimensions of limited 'religious experience', they need careful examination. And here Barth's all-too-brief discussion[69] of the crucial New Testament passages provides an indispensable starting-point. As he

---

[69]   *Church Dogmatics* I.1, pp. 458–9.

indicates, it is significant that the word *Abba* occurs on the lips of Jesus only in Gethsemane (Mk 14.36): thus, to cry '*Abba*' with Jesus in the Spirit is not only to put on Christ's sonship but also to recognize that 'This child, sinful man, can meet this Father, the holy God, as a child meets its father, only where the only-begotten Son of God has borne and borne away his sin'.[70] It is the cry from the midst of temptation and despair (Barth quotes Luther's magnificent comments on Gal. 4.6 to illustrate this), the human confession of dependence upon the saving grace of Christ. We can cry '*Abba*' because Jesus so cried in his suffering for us.

Barth, however, does not exhaust the significance of this occurrence of the term; for the cry of '*Abba*' in Gethsemane is surely part of a wider sense of the way in which Jesus' own sonship is inseparable from conflict, decision and suffering, from the cross. The paradox is that it is precisely Jesus' intimacy with the will of his Father that presses him towards the dereliction, the 'Godlessness', of the cross. To be 'Son of God' in the world of violence *is* to be the crucified victim; the sonship of Jesus is in no sense a 'cushion' between him and the felt absence of God in the world. To do the Father's will in the world is to refuse the authority of 'the kings of the Gentiles', and this leads inexorably to the impotence of suffering; and the Father cannot 'rescue' Jesus from outside because that would be the victory of coercion. We do not need (I believe) to talk, as Moltmann seems to wish to do,[71] of the Father's desertion or even annihilation of the Son: Dorothee Sölle's protest about 'theological sadism'[72] is valid and right here. We need rather to see the Father's weakness and powerlessness as the inevitable and necessary corollary of the Son's powerlessness in a world of corrupt and enslaving power. Father and Son are not to be set against each other at Calvary: the God who 'abandons' is the God of Caiaphas, the God whose relation to the world is that of master to slave. But Jesus is not slave but child, and *eldest* child, and adult 'child', and his Father is not the castrating despot of infantile nightmare. 'God' vanishes on the cross: Father and Son remain, in the shared, consubstantial weakness of their compassion. And the Father will raise the Son in the power of Spirit.

To speak of adoptive relation, then, is, in the light of the cross of Jesus, to accept the death of the distant and alien father-God,[73] to accept what might

---

[70] Ibid., p. 458.
[71] *The Crucified God* (London: SCM, 1974), especially pp. 145–53, 240–7.
[72] *Suffering* (London: DLT, 1975), pp. 22–8, especially pp. 26–7.
[73] On this, see Paul Ricoeur's remarkable paper, 'La paternité: du fantasme au symbole', in *L'Analyse du langage théologique: le nom de Dieu*, E. Castelli and others (Paris: Aubier, 1969), especially pp. 239–42.

be called the poverty of the Father. The relation of adoption is a fact, a dimension of reality, not a solution or a promise of easy deliverance. Hence it is possible to see the logic of Paul's conclusion in Rom. 8, that to share Christ's relation to the Father is to share his sufferings, and to understand how II Cor. can juxtapose the condition of freedom and 'unveiled' vision with the experiences of humiliation, pain, frustration, and so forth (II Cor. 6). The God who, as 'omnipotent Father' in the Freudian sense, can intervene to save and console from without, is illusory, a mask of God: his is a nature incompatible with the conviction that in Christ the veil is taken away. Another paradox (and one not, I think, alien to Luther's thought): that it is the God whose working is evident or simple to us that is the God whose face is veiled; the God who is Father and son in the passion and resurrection is the God whose glory has been uncovered for us, whose face we see directly. 'Union' with him involves just this acknowledgement of an experienced *absence* of manifest power.

This may illuminate the tension in Christian spirituality between action and contemplation. The absence of God's manifest power is bound up (as in Gethsemane) with a decision *for* powerlessness, *against* the domination of the world by manipulation or fantasy. It is a decision for reality, for the acceptance of constraint and limit in the human world. But it is still a *decision*: that is to say, it is meant to determine, to create, a course of action, to engage with the constraint of reality, to shape within its boundaries one form of life rather than another. It is not a decision for passivity or disengagement, but a decision to live with and within the potentially hurtful and destructive bounds of the world, a decision not to escape. But because this is an option for *response* and not manipulation, it incorporates the dimension of contemplative receptivity. If the sonship of Jesus means the poverty and vulnerability of Jesus in the world, it is indeed both active and contemplative, both the taking of responsibility for one's place in the world and the refusal to interpret and enact this as coercive power. The modern apostles of non-violence are right to deny that non-violence implies indifference or passivity.[74] And we may look also to Péguy's celebrated affirmation of the continuity between *mystique* and *politique*.[75]

How are we to relate all this to the theology of the Spirit? It does at least suggest a way in which pneumatology might be reconnected with central

---

[74]   P. Régamey's work on *Non-violence and the Christian Conscience* (London: DLT, 1966) is worth mentioning in this connection.
[75]   For an excellent exposition, see ch. 5 of Alan Ecclestone's study of Péguy, *A Staircase for Silence* (London: DLT, 1977).

Christological issues so as to bear more directly on the *humanum*; and it also points to the possibility of restating the classical argument that rests the claim for the Spirit's divinity upon his share in the work of salvation or divinization.[76] In this perspective, to see the Spirit in second-century style as a secondary mediator makes no sense: the work of Spirit, like the Son's work, is bound up precisely with the *loss* of mediatorial concepts designed to explain how the transcendent God (who is *elsewhere*) can be communicated *here*. The pivotal image of Jesus as Son radically changes the simple schema of God-and-the-world. Second-century theology is a witness to the extreme difficulty of assimilating such a shift, and it is not until the post-Nicene period that some of the necessary major reconstructions of language about God begin, slowly and awkwardly, to occur. We are, of course, ourselves part of that post-Nicene period. The notion of Spirit as simply 'communicator' accordingly recedes; and with it the idea that the work of Spirit is typically to be seen in clear and dramatic cases of 'communication' (prophetic ecstasy). The Spirit's 'completion' of Christ's work is no longer to be seen epistemologically, as a supplement or extension to the teaching of Christ, or even as that which makes it possible to hear and receive the Word. It is, rather, a completion in terms of liberation and transformation: it is *gift*, renewal and life. It is not possible to speak of Spirit in abstraction from the Christian form of life as a whole: Spirit is 'specified' not with reference to any kind of episodic experience but in relation to the human identity of the Christian. The question 'Where, or what, is Holy Spirit?' is not answered (as it might be by Luke) by pointing to prophecy and 'charismata' and saying, 'Spirit is the agency productive of phenomena like this'.

How then is it answered? Perhaps not at all. The theological quest which is preoccupied with identifying the *distinctive* quality or work of the Spirit has so often, as Hanson points out,[77] produced only the most sterile abstractions. And there is at least in eastern Christian thought[78] a sense that the 'face' of the Holy Spirit is not there for us to see. If what we are speaking of is the agency which draws us to the Father by constituting us children, we are evidently speaking of an agency not simply identical with 'Father' or 'Son', or with a sum or amalgam of the two. That perhaps is obvious, or even trivial, but it may be that no more can be said of the Spirit's distinctive-

---

[76]   See, e.g., Basil's *De Spiritu Sancto*, PG 32, *passim*.

[77]   *Op. cit.*, pp. 131–4.

[78]   See, e.g., Lossky's *Mystical Theology of the Eastern Church*, pp. 161–2. (referring to Gregory Nazianzen's Fifth Theological Oration, PG 36, 161–4) and 172–3.

ness. The grammar of our talk about the Holy Spirit is not that proper to 'God' as source, ground, terminus of vision and prayer, and so forth, nor that proper to 'God' as the disturbing presence of grace and vulnerability within the world of human relationships as a particular focal story. It is the grammar of 'spirituality' in the fullest sense of that emasculated word, the grammar of the interplay in the human self between the given and the future, between reality as it is and the truth which encompasses it; between Good Friday and Easter. If there can be any sense in which 'Spirit' is a bridge-concept, its work is not to bridge the gap between God and the world or even between the Word and the human soul, but to span the unimaginably greater gulf between suffering and hope, and to do so by creating that form of human subjectivity capable of confronting suffering without illusion but also without despair.

Spirit is the pressure upon us towards Christ's relation with the Father, towards the self secure enough in its rootedness and acceptance in the 'Father', in the source and ground of all, to be 'child', to live vulnerably, as a sign of grace and forgiveness, to decide for the cross of powerlessness.[79] The sign of Spirit is the existence of Christlikeness (being God's child) in the world. And the connection of Spirit with ecclesiology belongs here. We are so used to the rhetoric of the Church as the 'Spirit-filled community' that we have frequently lost a sense of the Church as sign of the Spirit rather than its domicile. The Church signifies (means, points to) the humanity that could be, that could exist in this tension between security and powerlessness, so that it is indeed in one sense *the* place where Spirit is seen. It is 'seen' in prayer and sacrament; that is to say, prayer and sacrament (and I include the reading and preaching of scripture under this head) *name* and interpret the deepest direction and growth of human life as being *in* Christ and *towards* the Father. Baptism and the Eucharist are both sacraments of the inseparability and the tension of suffering and hope. The Byzantine stress on the invocation of the Spirit to consecrate the eucharistic elements – and with them the whole body of believers – vividly points this up:[80] Spirit is active where broken flesh and shed blood become the sign and promise of human wholeness and union with the Father.

Perhaps, too, it is not irrelevant to suggest that some of those experiences associated in the Catholic mystical tradition with maturity in the life of prayer

[79] See Schillebeeckx, *op. cit.*, section III, chs 2 and 3; and compare the treatment of 'critical theology' in the same author's earlier essay, *The Understanding of Faith* (London: Sheed and Ward, 1974), ch. 7, sections II and III.
[80] See, for example, P. Evdokimov, *L'Orthodoxie* (Neuchâtel: Delachaux et Niestlé, 1965), pp. 249–51.

have the same 'signifying' quality.[81] The 'night of faith', the dissolution of tangible mental and emotional securities, in the ascent of contemplative prayer is, for a writer like John of the Cross, part of the way of *illumination*, and a necessary stage before union. Here again, Spirit, the illuminative action of God, can appear where suffering and promise coincide, where death and Godlessness are interpreted in terms of sonship. The relation of this to the early Luther's theology, indeed to the tension between faith and experience which characterizes so much in the Lutheran tradition, may be worth further exploration.[82]

To talk about an entry into the 'Age of the Spirit' is usually nonsense, and often dangerous nonsense. But there may, nonetheless, be aspects of the contemporary consciousness of Western humanity (and I am not equipped to speculate beyond the limits of the West) peculiarly attuned to some such theology of Spirit as I have tried to outline. There are culturally irreversible processes which have indeed obliged us to question certain models of the transcendent in a way which makes concepts of Word and Spirit as 'mediators' very hard to sustain. We can recognize perhaps more clearly the disturbing confusion of theological language in the New Testament under the pressure of the figure of the crucified Messiah: we can accept more readily the breaking of certain kinds of sacral barrier, so that 'Spirit' ceases to be confined to the extraordinary but becomes a qualification of Christian human being. Above all, a theology of Spirit as belonging in the ambience of mortality and secularity, the powerlessness of the cross, refuses to take us away from the *humanum* in its most problematic aspects. Spirit may be a mode of interpreting the world's Godlessness to the world, it is Spirit which takes us out of infantile transcendentalism, uncriticized theism, into the faith of Jesus crucified. The face of Spirit is – as Vladimir Lossky memorably expressed it[83] – the assembly of redeemed human faces in their infinite diversity. Human persons grown to the fullness of their *particular* identities, but sharing in the common divine gift of reconciled life in faith, these are the Spirit's manifestation. The Son is manifest in a single, paradigmatic figure, the Spirit is manifest in the 'translatability' of that into the contingent

---

[81] Simon Tugwell, in his book *Did You Receive the Spirit?* (London: DLT, 1972), ch. 10, argues that 'charismatic' prayer and the experiences traditionally associated with the entry into contemplative prayer should be seen as parallel ways of 'discovering' the Spirit. This may be a *little* oversimplified, but it is valuable and suggestive.

[82] I have attempted to discuss this, though only very sketchily, in *The Wound of Knowledge. Christian Spirituality from the New Testament to St John of the Cross* (London: DLT, 1979), chs 7 and 8.

[83] *Op. cit.*, p. 173.

diversity of history. Freedom in the Spirit is uncircumscribed; and yet it always has the shape of Jesus the Son – another way of expressing Paul's paradoxes of law and liberty. It is Spirit who leads us to 'Godlessness' in order to bring out of us the cry of '*Abba*'; who emancipates us from God to bring us to the trinity.

Regressive spiritualities are those which seek to restrict the Spirit again to a mediatorial or an episodically inspirational role. They represent the struggle to retain uncriticized theism as one element in some sort of composite religious scheme (Word and Spirit *added* to the Father), and to avoid the critical experience of Godlessness. They will run the risk of making Spirit a refuge from the critical rather than a pressure towards the critical. This essay has been in part an attempt to set out what is involved in some classical and modern theologies of Spirit as interpreter of the Word or agency of inspiration and to question the adequacy of such models for a critical theology. I have, however, no single accessible model to put in their place. The very term 'Spirit' is, as has often been pointed out,[84] a weak and unspecific word, lending itself to much confusion; and this may be taken to underline what I have already called the elusiveness of our subject. Since this is an elusiveness and an unclarity more pervasively present in the NT writings than in some of the more conceptually satisfying schemes of later dogmatics, I do not think we need be unduly disturbed. And after all, if Christian theology is done in the community which lives in Spirit, the problem is no more and no less than the impossibility of seeing one's own face.[85] It may be – as so often in contemporary dogmatics – that we can utter only negations with any confidence. I have not intended to denigrate the charismatic movement and the theologies associated with it: I *have* attempted to question the highly assertive mode of some of these theologies and the (as it appears to me) restrictive assumptions underlying them, the dangers of operating unawares with an only partially Christianized view of transcendence and of divine agency. Yet here again we are brought up against the diversity and unclarity of our NT material: the charismatic may well object to the characteristic preferring of Paul over Luke in most post-Reformation theology. I am painfully aware that this essay has failed to engage directly with this hermeneutical question; but I hope what I have written may suggest some affinities

---

[84]   By Aquinas, for instance, in *Summa Theologiae* I.xxxvi.1, and II.IIae.xiv.1.

[85]   And is parallel to the problem of honest theological talk about the resurrection. I am deeply grateful to David Jenkins for illuminating comments on this question; and see his paper, 'The Anguish of Man, the Praise of God and the Repentance of the Church', in *Study Encounter*, vol. X, no. 4 (1974) (available from the publications office of the WCC).

with the hermeneutic expressed by Luther in the words *crux probat omnia*. As we observed at the beginning of this chapter, there is a suspicion of pneumatology as something tempted to bypass the cross – not least the cross of twentieth-century experience, religious and secular; here at least our negation can be confident. But a great deal of thinking has still to be done if we are to rescue the theology of Spirit from religiosity and set it to work in the shadow of the contemporary crucifixions of God and the human.

Part Three

THE GRAMMAR OF GOD

Chapter Nine

TRINITY AND REVELATION

I

In spite of everything, we go on saying 'God'. And, since 'God' is not the name of any particular thing available for inspection, it seems that we must as believers assume that we talk about God on the basis of 'revelation' – of what has been shown to us by God's will and action. If the word occurs in our speech and is not obviously vacuous, we are driven to conclude that we are – so to speak – *authorized* to use it. Yet this idea of being 'authorized' to speak of God is fraught with risk, and has frequently been put to deeply corrupt use. If revelation is seen as the delivery of non-worldly truth to human beings in pretty well unambiguous terms, discourse about God cannot be said to have roots in the ordinary events on which we depend for the 'authorizing' of our usual speech. It is possible to see the Incarnation itself simply as a sophisticated technique for ensuring that such non-worldly truth is accurately communicated: that God became human was a regrettable necessity which we may safely ignore after we have reached a certain stage of theological expertise.

Theology, in short, is perennially liable to be seduced by the prospect of bypassing the question of how it *learns* its own language. We can only talk intelligently about 'authorization' if we attend to this question; otherwise, authorization simply becomes an appeal to unchallengeable authority, and theological language is thought of as essentially heteronomous, determined from an elusive 'elsewhere'. This is true not only of the kind of propositional account of revelation which very few contemporary theologians would accept, but which was once characteristic of wide areas of Protestant and Catholic theology alike; it is also (paradoxically) true of a liberal theology which appeals to some isolable core of encounter, unmediated awareness of the transcendent, buried beneath the accidental forms of historical givenness, a trans-cultural, pre-linguistic, inter-religious phenomenon. This may not result in quite the same intellectual totalitarianism as the 'propositional' approach; yet it still operates with a model of truth as something ultimately separable in our minds from the dialectical process of its historical reflection and appropriation. The impatience of some modern Anglo-Saxon theologians with the dogmatic tradition sometimes seems in part an impatience with debate, conflict, ambivalence, polysemy, paradox. And this is at heart an impatience with learning, and with learning about our learning.[1]

The danger of glib talk about 'authorization' and the authority linked with it is of theologizing what is 'given' as if the given represented the finished, the fixed. A metaphysical theism which ignores the Kantian challenge and discards its own negative, critical and self-subverting correctives awards itself a privileged – and ultimately insupportable – position within human language.[2] A Christology whose concerns are circumscribed by a preoccupation with the model of *Christus Consummator* will risk becoming a merely theoretical or ideological reconciliation of human conflict,[3] locating, once again, a centre of achieved, privileged, non-ambiguous language and practice in the midst of a fragmented reality – an area of heteronomy, occupied by those whose task is defined as applying or bestowing what they possess, transmitting the fruits of this 'achieved' status to those who do not possess it. The notion of faith as a healing or life-giving *project*, a proposal made in hope, looking towards a future of shared life and shared struggle, is liable to recede in such a perspective. 'Learning about learning' is learning how we develop meaningful constructs out of historical process and decision: in other words, it is (or can be) equally a learning about *doing*. To begin from a sense of achievedness, consummation, inevitably pushes such learning into the background; and thus it undermines its own claim to be able to speak with authority to an experience of conflict and fragmentation, to the historical aspiration and work of men and women.

The uncomfortable question with which we are left is: 'How do we speak

[1] I am – manifestly – indebted to various treatments of some of these themes by Donald MacKinnon. See, for example, his remarks on 'dialogue' (*Explorations in Theology*; London: SCM, 1979, pp. 161–5): to attend to the process of discovering truth in 'dialogue' is to attend to the inexorability of fact, to avoid the facile theoretical resolutions of a total intellectual structure. It is an attention built into the very claims of 'realism'.

[2] Hence the force of, e.g., Don Cupitt's critique of 'metaphysical theism'; though his own resolutely apophatic proposal may be no less vulnerable to a charge of premature closure. Cf. the exchange between us in *Modern Theology* 1 (Oct. 1984).

[3] *Christus Redemptor et Consummator* is the title of F. Olofsson's comprehensive study of B. P. Westcott's theology (Uppsala, 1979), a study very sensitive to the risks of incarnationally oriented theology lacking a serious engagement with the *theologia crucis*, though only hinting at the political and social ambiguity of such an approach.

of revelation or authorization without taking the obvious ideological short-cut?' Barth attempts, in the early volumes of his *Church Dogmatics*, to sketch a model of revelation which, because it never permits the revealed Word to be a human possession, avoids at first sight the danger of confusing author-ization with ecclesiastical, or even scriptural, authority in the narrow sense. And he is careful to guard against the suggestion of a crude heteronomy.[4] Yet precisely because of the absolute isolation of the revelatory event from any historical condition (it occurs *in*, but not *as part* of history), the question of 'learning about learning' is again circumvented. Revelation interrupts the uncertainties of history with a summons to absolute knowledge, God's know-ledge of and interpretation of himself.

How else, then, do we speak of revelation? The point of introducing the notion at all seems to be to give some ground for the sense in our religious and theological language that the initiative does not ultimately lie with us; before we speak, we are addressed or called. Paul Ricoeur, in an important essay on the hermeneutics of the idea of revelation,[5] has attempted to link the concept with a project for a 'poetics', which will spell out the way in which a poetic text, by offering a frame of linguistic reference other than the normal descriptive/referential function of language, 'restores to us that par-ticipation-in or belonging-to an order of things which precedes our capacity to oppose ourselves to things taken as objects opposed to a subject'.[6] The truth with which the poetic text is concerned is not verification, but mani-festation.[7] That is to say that the text displays or even embodies the reality with which it is concerned simply by witness or 'testimony' (to use Ricoeur's favoured word).[8] It displays a 'possible world', a reality in which my human reality can also find itself: and in inviting me into its world, the text breaks open and extends my own possibilities.[9] All this, Ricoeur suggests, points to poetry as exercising a *revelatory* function – or, to rephrase this in the terms

---

[4] On the question of 'theonomy' as the foundation of authentic *autonomy* see *Church Dogmat-ics* II.2, pp. 177–81, 184.

[5] 'Toward a Hermeneutic of the Idea of Revelation', *Essays on Biblical Interpretation*, ed. with an introduction by L. S. Mudge (London, 1980), pp. 73–118.

[6] Ibid., p. 101.

[7] Ibid., p. 102.

[8] Cf., in the same collection. 'The Hermeneutics of Testimony', pp. 119–54: 'testimony' relates to the particularities of events, not to supposed common essences, and so calls forth an act, an event, in the interpreter. Thus a 'hermeneutic of testimony' is opposed to the aspiration to absolute knowledge – knowledge which is nobody's in particular. The parallels with MacKinnon are clear.

[9] Cf. R. Williams, 'Poetic and Religious Imagination', *Theology*, May 1977 (pp. 178–87), pp. 185–6.

proposed at the beginning of this paragraph, it manifests an initiative that is not ours in inviting us to a world we did not make. This function is a challenge to the naive aspiration of human consciousness to autonomy ('the pretension of consciousness to constitute itself'[10]); yet it does not impose a simple heteronomy instead, it does not insist that meaning is delivered to us from a normative 'elsewhere'.

Revelation, on such an account, is essentially to do with what is *generative* in our experience – events or transactions in our language that break existing frames of reference and initiate new possibilities of life. Returning to some earlier remarks, we could say that revelation decisively advances or extends debate, extends rather than limits the range of ambiguity and conflict in language. It poses fresh questions rather than answering old ones. And to recognize a text, a tradition or an event as revelatory is to witness to its generative power. It is to speak from the standpoint of a new form of life and understanding whose roots can be traced to the initiating phenomenon. And we might add that – as an obvious corollary – when there is no longer a felt need to use the category of revelation, this can be attributed to an atrophying of the sense of belonging in a *new* world. Put in directly religious terms, it is the withering of anything that might be called an experience of grace, and a loss of confidence in the human worthwhileness or hopefulness of life in grace.

Thus 'revelation' is a concept which emerges from a questioning attention to our present life in the light of a particular past – a past seen as 'generative'. In terms of the scriptural history of Israel, the events of the Exodus were revelatory insofar as they were generative of the community of Israel itself; and Torah was revelatory because it was what specified the form of life of that community. In an exhaustive study,[11] Norman Gottwald has argued that if we are attempting to isolate an 'Old Testament doctrine of God', the only serious way in which this can be done is by attention to the social structures of Israel: the distinctiveness of YHWH does not lie in any theological attribute peculiar to him, but in the simple fact that he is the God of a people who live 'thus-and-not-otherwise' – the sort of God who can be the God of *this* community with its particular, socially distinctive features. For Gottwald, the salient features are the anti-authoritarian elements in Israel;[12] so that it

---

[10] Ricoeur, *op. cit.*, p. 109.

[11] *The Tribes of Yahweh. A Sociology of the Religion of Liberated Israel 1250–1050 B.C.E.* (London: SCM, 1979).

[12] E.g. 'Yahweh's uniqueness lay in the fact that "he" was the symbol of a single-minded pursuit of an egalitarian tribal social system' (p. 693). This is, of course, intended as a sociological and historical observation, not intended to foreclose any further discussion of the ontological status of such a symbol, or to suggest that YHWH is a mere 'projection'.

should be possible to say of Israel's God that he cannot be the God of un-critical and authoritarian societies. But the main point is that Gottwald points us towards a concept of revelation dovetailing with Ricoeur's: the 'revela-tion' of YHWH occurs as part of the process whereby a community takes cognizance of its own distinctive identity. It constitutes a concept of God for itself by asking what it is that constitutes *itself*. To be able to answer the question about our roots, our context, what it is that has formed us, is at least to begin to deal with the question of the meaning of 'God'.

So it is right to say (with R. L. Hart, in his immensely important, if her-metic, essay on revelation[13]) that revelation is bound up with memory and yet not simply specified by reference to a sealed-off past occurrence. ' "Rev-elation" embraces (a) that which incites the hermeneutical spiral and also (b) this "that which" taken into human understanding, the movement of the hermeneutical spiral itself'[14] – or, in the terms I have already used, 'revela-tion' includes, necessarily, 'learning about learning'. Any theology of revela-tion is committed to attending to event and interpretation together, to the generative point and to the debate generated. And, if this is a correct analy-sis, the model of revelation as a straightforward 'lifting of a veil' by divine agency has to be treated with caution. 'Revelation' is certainly more than a mythologically slanted metaphor for the emergence of striking new ideas: the whole of our discussion so far presupposes that the language of revelation is used to express the sense of an initiative that does not lie with us and to challenge the myth of the self-constitution of consciousness. But the lan-guage of veil-lifting assumes a kind of passivity on the part of the finite consciousness which abstracts entirely from the issue of the newness of the form of life which first prompts the question about revelation. 'Is this event revelation?' is only a question that can be asked on the basis of the wider question: 'If we live like this, has revelation occurred?' And the problem of how to distinguish true from false 'revelations' can only be resolved in such a wider perspective – as Catholic theology has always recognized where alleged visions or locutions are concerned.[15]

---

[13] *Unfinished Man and the Imagination. Toward an Ontology and a Rhetoric of Revelation* (New York, 1968), especially pp. 83–105.

[14] Ibid., p. 99.

[15] A good discussion in Karl Rahner, *Visions and Prophecies* (London, 1963). I am grateful to Mr Rex Tomlinson for directing my attention to this work.

II

Turning now more specifically to the matter of biblical revelation: we have noted already how it is possible to see the revelatory character of Torah as having to do with its constituting of a distinctive social organism; how is this to be applied to the New Testament, to the revelatory character of the life, death and resurrection of Jesus? The 'generative' event is one which breaks open and extends possible ways of being human. Torah is experienced as a new and distinctive definition of a human community; and if the pattern proposed is right, the same must be true of Jesus of Nazareth. His revelatory significance is apprehended by way of what it means to belong to the community whose character and limits he defines – not simply as 'founder' but as present head and partner in dialogue and relation. A detailed consideration of this would require a sustained analysis of the language of the whole New Testament (and probably the Apostolic Fathers also): in the limited compass of this paper, I can only sketch some possibilities for further discussion. Thus, for example: to belong to a community associated with or defined by Jesus is to use certain kinds of language about resurrection – a fairly basic distinctive theme. It is also to be engaged in a startlingly vehement and bitter debate about Israel and the Law, especially (in Paul's churches at least) about circumcision. It is to treat 'Father' as a normal and indeed normative address to the God of Israel. And it is to be involved in active commendation of Jesus as a determinative focus of commitment for – in principle – any human being: to speak of him as the 'judge' of all. In terms of the actual social life of Christian groups, it is to be preoccupied with issues about the equality and complementarity of 'ministerial' gifts, about the relative standing of rich and poor, about the legitimate place (or lack of it) of marriage and sexuality, about degrees of contact with the 'non-believing' world and right and wrong responses to its contempt or hostility.[16]

Jesus is the 'Lord' of communities with these concerns; and so we may begin to answer our question by analysing these or other features of the communities' life as consequences of acknowledging Jesus as Lord. If the early communities exhibit a profound puzzlement about their boundaries, about issues of purity and separation (virginity, abstinence from idol-meats, circumcision), this assuredly reflects the memory of the Church's Lord as a

---

[16] Much illumination is to be gained from Wayne A. Meeks, *The First Urban Christians. The Social World of the Apostle Paul* (Yale University Press, 1983), especially ch. 3, 'The Formation of the Ekklesia'.

man who, in his own words and actions, generated immense confusion on this subject, sharply challenging the available models of distinctiveness and 'cleanliness'.[17] If the communities are concerned about what it means to call God 'Father', this concern is rooted once again in the language and experience of the Church's Lord: to be under Christ's Lordship is to recognize his name for God as defining your relation to the same God, to recognize Jesus' 'Abba' as the decisive interpretation of your own prayer. It is important to grasp that early Christianity was, as much as anything else, the discovery of fresh modes of prayer; and the connection with Jesus' own prayer is swiftly and authoritatively made. And if the early communities are committed to proclaiming and spreading the record of Jesus as 'good news', it is because Jesus' constant proclamation of the impending Kingdom is of more than merely local relevance: judgement is to be enacted upon all, and there is no theological excuse for restricting the offer of a grace which will carry men and women through this judgement (because God is a God of mercy, an 'Abba', and because there are no clear social, ethnic or ritual prescriptions limiting the possible scope of the redeemed community).

So the Church takes cognizance of itself as a community which is open to all, which addresses God in total intimacy and trust, and which engages in mission. As such, it becomes aware of itself as '*not*-Israel', and equally as *not* a cult among cults: its vision is global. It becomes aware of a fresh and distinctive style of human existence, and begins both to tell the story of Jesus so as to show the 'generative' quality of his life, and to celebrate his present Lordship in exploratory and variegated hymnic images. And the more a sense of *universal* mission, universal significance, develops in the Church's self-understanding, the more imperative does it become to attribute universal significance to the generative event of Jesus, and to celebrate it in appropriately cosmic terms. The most far-reaching and imaginatively brilliant synthesis of recollection and celebration is, of course, the Fourth Gospel; but the treatments of resurrection and exaltation in Matthew and Luke present a parallel development. In the resurrection of his crucified flesh, Jesus is freed from local and temporal limitation (yet without losing his historical identity) to send his messengers into all the world.[18]

Putting the point another way: the Christian community has a focus for its identity in Jesus, yet the 'limits' set by Jesus are as wide as the human race itself. The Christian 'community' is potentially the whole world: Jesus offers

---

[17]   Ibid., pp. 103, 153–4; cf. John Riches, *Jesus and the Transformation of Judaism* (London: DLT, 1980), especially chs 6 and 8.
[18]   Mt. 28.16–20, Lk 24.46–49, Acts 1.8.

new possibilities for the form of human life as such, not merely for a particular group to find an identity. In his faithful and obedient relation to the Father, Jesus sketches a new and comprehensive vocation for human beings. So to come to be 'in Christ', to belong with Jesus, involves a far-reaching reconstruction of one's humanity: a liberation from servile, distorted, destructive patterns in the past, a liberation from anxious dread of God's judgement, a new identity in a community of reciprocal love and complementary service, whose potential horizons are universal. It is not surprising that the language of 'new creation' should be employed,[19] nor that a parallelism with Adam, the beginner of the old humanity, should evolve,[20] nor even (if certain modern exegetes are correct) that Jesus should be seen as 'functionally' equivalent to the Torah.[21] And from there it is not too long a step to the final stage of this process, whereby the significance of Jesus is understood as parallel to the significance of the act of creation itself: 'In the beginning was the Word . . .'

This is to say of Jesus that the 'generative' character of his story is as radical as the generative significance of our language about the world's source and context, God. In the familiar Pauline phrase, his is now 'a name above every other name'. The experienced reconstruction of human possibility spills over into the reconstruction of discourse about God: if new humanity, then a new God. The revelatory nature of the life, death and resurrection of Jesus is manifest in this 'initiation of debate' at an unprecedentedly comprehensive level. The potential strain upon our normal framework of talk about God, the degree of possible ambiguity and conflict, is unique. Jesus is God's 'revelation' in a decisive sense not because he makes a dimly apprehended God clear to us, but because he challenges and queries an unusually clear sense of God (as the giver of Torah to Israel): not because he makes things plainer – on the 'veil-lifting' model of revelation – but because he makes things darker. And yet Paul can triumphantly use the language of theophany, glory and unveiling to describe the work of Jesus:[22] like John, he sees what has happened, however disorienting and confusing, as the generation of a less illusion-ridden or fantasy-ridden theism. Jesus represents the *immediacy* of divine presence and creativity in the world, and thus the overthrow of our conceptual idols. 'We are in him who is true, in his Son Jesus Christ. This is the true God and eternal life. Little children, keep yourselves from idols.'[23]

---

[19]   II Cor. 5.17.
[20]   Rom. 5.12–19, I Cor. 15.21–22, 45–49.
[21]   As perhaps in Col. 1.15–17.
[22]   II Cor. 3 and 4.
[23]   I Jn 5.21.

Thus the claim that Jesus of Nazareth 'reveals' God (more specifically, the God of Israel) is a statement affirming that what is thought to be character-istic of God alone – radical 'generative power', global creativity, the capacity to constitute the limits of human existence, and so forth – has been experi-enced in connection with the life and death of a human being; that direct and immediate knowledge of God is to be had definitively in the leading of a life governed by the memory and the presence of Jesus. The drastic liberty or creativity which we call 'God's' because it cannot be contained in lan-guage descriptive of the 'contents of the world' is reflected, echoed, embod-ied – incarnated – in what Jesus is experienced as affecting. Jesus' reconstruction of humanity, liberating men and women from the dominance of past pat-terns, is Godlike. Using the traditional dogmatic language, we could say that 'grace', or 'the forgiveness of sins', or 'justification' is seen as a comprehen-sive enough transaction to be called creative and divine: if creation is to be saved from its diseases and restored to wholeness and integrity, the restoring agency must be level with, comparable to, the creative itself.

This at once poses a problem: we have said that we call radical creativity God's because it cannot be contained in 'worldly' language; yet Jesus as a human being *is* containable in worldly language, he belongs in the same network of historical contingencies as we ourselves do. And even more ob-viously, the mediation of his grace in the believing community operates within that finite network. The notion of radical divine initiative is a regu-lative idea, 'holding the ring' for our variegated apprehensions of generative power: must it not, therefore, be a concept of a different order from any-thing we can use in respect of any human event? All events in the world are *generated*, even if in important respect they are also generative; while God is not generated, but purely generative. It is precisely this problem that pro-duced the long-drawn out dogmatic crisis of the fourth century[24] in the Christian Church (though the issue was less about the 'generatedness' of the human Jesus than about the derivative status of the heavenly Logos). And in response to this crisis, the anti-Arian wing of the Church gradually devel-oped its insistence that a distinction could properly be drawn between being 'derived' or dependent and being created (i.e. being contingent and mut-able): the Godhead of Jesus is unquestionably the former; but this does not

---

[24] As to whether the Son, being *begotten* (*gennētos*), can rightly be said to share the same absolute and self-sufficient (*agenētos*) nature as the Father, who is both unbegotten (*agennētos*, from *gennaō*) and self-sufficient (*agenētos*, from *ginomai*). The answer of developed orthodoxy is that the *life* of the Father and Son is equally *agenētos*, but it is a life they share precisely in their mutual relation – i.e. neither is *agenētos* qua person, but only by nature.

simply reduce what is at work in his history to a level inferior to that of the creator.

Does this help? It allows us to say that radical liberty and creativity is not such a simple, univocally applicable concept as might be supposed: there is a proper liberty generated out of dependence, a proper creativity which is *responsive* rather than simply initiatory. Absolute creativity is *not* a part of the world; but it is possible to imagine a creativity of comparable generality in its effect which nevertheless arises as response to, or reflection of, that prior 'absolute' creativity. What needs to be said of Jesus is that his power to re-mould the image of human being, his liberty in re-constituting the boundaries of human vocation and identity, is not limited by the history of which he is the inheritor or the society of which he is a member. Without ceasing to *be* an inheritor of that history and a member of that society, he acknowledges as his 'limit' only the will of the God he calls Father: his liberty is itself a function of his obedience. So Jesus shares the creativity of God, yet not as a 'second God', a separate *individual*:[25] he is God *as* dependent – for whom the metaphors of Word, Image, Son are appropriate.

What I am suggesting is a tentative sketch of what might be meant by ascribing 'divinity' to Jesus without simply walking into the logical absurdity of saying that Jesus 'is' the creator of the world, *tout court*. It may be worth noting that the tradition of classical trinitarian theology has been far from indifferent to these issues: Aquinas makes it plain that the second person of the Trinity is 'apt' to be incarnate (as the Father is not) because he is both image of the Father and exemplar of the creation; and also because, as Son, he is eternally what we are called to be. Our salvation is in becoming adoptive children of God, and it is proper that this should be realized through the mediation of the God who is already and for ever 'Son', God as eternal issue or response.[26]

If we then go on to ask about the divinity of the agency which perpetually renews the experience of grace and re-creation in the believing community, yet which is not straightforwardly identical either with the absolute creativity which is the source and context of all things, or with the historical event generating the reconstruction of the human world, similar points emerge. Radical generative power is ascribed to the life of Jesus, but it is also ascribable to those events in which, through the ages, the community learns and

---

[25]   This answers the Arian criticism that Alexandrian episcopal orthodoxy involved belief in two rival first principles. See, e.g., the letter of Eusebius of Nicomedia to Paulinus of Tyre, in Theodoret, *Historia ecclesiastica* 1.6 (ed. Parmentier; Leipzig, 1911, pp. 27–8).

[26]   See, e.g., *Summa Theologiae* III.iii.8.

re-learns to interpret itself by means of Jesus (and nothing else and nothing less). Once again, we have to do with a derived or responsive creativity: it is the same radical renewing energy as is encountered in the event of Jesus, which is in turn continuous with the absolute generative power which founds the world. It is not reducible to a human recollecting of Jesus; it is rather the process of continuing participation in the foundational event – the forming of Christ in the corporate and individual life of believers. It is on this basis that we speak of the rite of initiation into the believing community both as an 'immersion' in the death and resurrection of Jesus – a being engulfed in that paradigm – and as a receiving of God as 'Spirit' – a perilously vague term, as theologians have long recognized,[27] but a useful cipher for that mode of creative presence and action which cannot simply be identified with 'the Father' and 'the Son'. So, as with the Son, we do not say that the process of re-presentation and re-apprehension of Jesus in the Church *is* straight-forwardly the ultimate *initiating* source of divine life; but the creative grace which is enacted in Jesus is the same creative grace enacted between human beings in the Church, in the 'fellowship of the Holy Spirit'. The Spirit is Jesus' Spirit and therefore God's Spirit: it is what God gives in Jesus, and that gift is always and invariably the breaking of bondage and the dawn of hope.

In the events of Jesus and the Spirit-in-the-Church,[28] incarnation and Pentecost, creative and generative power is shown in the form of *grace*. That is, creativity is seen to be exercised in terms of compassionate acceptance, the refusal of condemnation, the assurance of an abiding relationship of heal-ing love. God is glorified as Lord of creation by the act which brings unpredicted and unprecedented fulfilment to his creatures. And so it is through what we learn to say of Son and Spirit that we can interpret the abstract notion of 'absolute creativity' as the absolute gratuity of love, rather than the exercise of simple untrammelled power for its own sake. If creativity, radical newness, appears decisively in the human world as grace, the final ground of creativity is, at the very least, not alien to love, to mercy and gift. 'The Father' loves and does not negate, frustrate or destroy. 'The Father himself loves you, because you have loved me and have believed that I came from the Father.'[29] Initially, the notion of radical creativity renders problematic

---

[27] See, e.g., Augustine, *De trinitate* V.xi.12: *potest appellari trinitas et spiritus et sanctus.*

[28] Cf. Rahner's account of the 'modalities of divine self-communication' in *The Trinity* (Lon-don, 1970), especially pp. 82–99. But I am extremely uneasy with the distinction drawn be-tween communication as 'history' and communication as 'spirit', as this threatens to confine the Spirit to a rather abstractly conceived absolute future rather than identifying Spirit in the concrete life, work, prayer and conflict of the community.

[29] Jn 16.27.

any account of truly generative occurrence within the world; but a fuller understanding of what this generative power in the world actually *consists* in, as grace and absolution or renewal, does at least render the idea of creativity, and thus the idea of 'God' itself, more than a contentless postulate. None of this finally resolves the basic difficulty of spelling out the nature of the continuity between absolute and derivative; but for a Christian committed to some kind of talk about God as a 'gracious' or 'loving' or even 'personal' God, only a trinitarian account of God seems able to safeguard theology against agnosticism and formalism.

III

Hart proposed that 'revelation' be taken to include both the event generating a hermeneutical enterprise and 'the movement of the hermeneutical spiral itself'. What I have so far suggested is that the Christian doctrine of God as Trinity permits us to see 'revelation' occurring in this way – through Son and Spirit together – and to see the structure of revelation itself as in a manner corresponding to God's own being. In fact, this last statement brings us back to something very close to Barth's insistence that the doctrine is simply an exegesis of the statement that 'God reveals himself'.[30] However, for Barth revelation is fundamentally the impartation of God's self-knowledge: we participate by revelation in this ultimate epistemological security. If we come at revelation from the more modest – if finally more demanding – position of Ricoeur's 'hermeneutics of testimony', the correspondence between the hermeneutical process and the divine act is of another kind. Revelation, from this perspective, is nothing to do with absolute knowledge. It both is and is not completed, 'over'; *what* we are interpreting is unquestionably this historical narrative and not another; we are not waiting for a more comprehensive or adequate story, because precisely of the comprehensiveness of the questioning provoked by this story. Yet this is not to say that there is an end to questioning or unclarity. The claims of our foundational story to universal relevance and significance mean that is must constantly be *shown* to be 'at home' with all the varying enterprises of giving meaning to the human condition. Thus the 'hermeneutical spiral' never reaches a plateau. For the event of Christ to be authentically revelatory, it must be capable of both 'fitting' and 'extending' any human circumstance;

---

[30]   *Church Dogmatics* 1.1 section 8; for a fuller discussion, see R. Williams, 'Barth on the Triune God', in *Karl Barth. Studies of his Theological Method*, ed. S. W. Sykes (Oxford, 1979).

it must be re-presentable, and the form and character of its re-presentation are not necessarily describable in advance. The work continues, for the theologian and the Church at large, of discerning and naming the Christ-like events of liberation and humanization in the world *as* Christ-like, and, at the level of action, expressing this hermeneutical engagement in terms of concrete practical solidarity. And this unending re-discovery of Christ or re-presentation of Christ, the revelatory aspect of the 'hermeneutical spiral', is, in Trinitarian perspective, what we mean by the illuminating or transforming operation of the Spirit. 'He will take what is mine and give it to you.'[31]

We also noted in the previous section that the generative significance of Jesus was 'learned' in the early communities in connection with the problems which they faced in grasping their distinctive identity as communities over against Judaism and the world of Hellenistic cults – problems to do with limits, relations to the 'outside' and mutual relations within the group. In recognizing these problems as *theological*, the Church admitted that the task of relating its present social reality to the events of Jesus' life, death and resurrection was basic to its self-understanding. To ask questions (of the kind arising at Corinth) about gifts of ministry and their interrelation was to ask what the fact of being in a community acknowledging Jesus as Lord *meant* in the organizing of life together. The 'lordship' of Jesus generates a communal life increasingly distinct from other contemporary options: the asking of fundamental theological questions represents the Church's movement from relatively unreflective to self-aware allegiance to Jesus. His lordship has to be theologized in gospel and worship, and the way in which he 'specifies' the new humanity has to be explored and articulated. This is how, over the protracted period during which the New Testament was composed, the Spirit may be said to have prompted the confession 'Jesus is Lord', in ever-greater richness and inclusiveness of meaning – the Spirit at work in the community's puzzlement at its own existence and character.

If this is how the initial Christological confession comes to be made, how the comprehensive generative significance of Jesus is first learned, then the conclusion seems clear enough that the constant re-learning of Jesus' significance has to do with an honest awareness of the strain and conflict presently experienced in the Church. Problems such as the ordination of women, the revision of the liturgy, the place and function of episcopacy, baptismal policy in secularized areas, and so on, are essential stages in the 'hermeneutical spiral' whereby the significance of Jesus, the *divinity* (the decisive generative quality) of Jesus, is recovered. Thus, for example: if I belong to a congregation which

---

[31] Jn 16.15.

(in the person of its priest – which itself begs a question) operates what is sometimes called an 'indiscriminate' baptismal policy, my puzzlement may be to do with how a symbol of commitment (immersion, initiation) has become divorced from its natural function in relation to a visible and continuous belonging to a particular group. If I belong to a congregation which baptizes selectively, my puzzlement will be over the way in which a symbol of acceptance (adoption, incorporation) is seen to operate as a symbol of exclusion, stipulating conditions to be satisfied before acceptance is possible. Either case may generate puzzlement at what the Church is meant to *be*. Both ought therefore to provoke some interrogation of the basic Christian confession: what does commitment to Christ involve us in? Are we more concerned to see our mission as implying prophetic demand, a summons to 'own' one's faith in public risk and visible involvement? Or are we concerned with mission as gratuitous affirmation of wounded, frustrated or marginalized people – the risk being, so to say, God's rather than ours? Both queries lead us to a fresh engagement with the events which have in the first place created a community *in which such questions are worth asking*; both will attempt to relate the seriousness or worthwhileness of the questions to what is understood of the foundational event of creative compassion in Jesus of Nazareth; both will regenerate our understanding of Jesus' lordship. And if there is not one answer to the question which can be established to everyone's satisfaction, if the debate cannot be arrested, that matters far less than the fact of a shared acknowledgement of the worthwhileness of the question and of the mode – which might be called 'trustful interrogation' – in which it is explored.

So my thesis is that any such puzzlement over 'what the Church is meant to be' *is* the revelatory operation of God as 'Spirit' insofar as it keeps the Church engaged in the exploration of what its foundational events signify. To identify Word and Spirit as simply two stages of a single process of divine communication[32] somewhat misses the point of the necessary distinction between the event that defines the field and the terms of the interpretative enterprise, and the enterprise itself. The renewed human possibility of liberty or creative responsibility generated in Jesus is concretely and particularly generated in this or that aspect of the community's life, in all those things that provoke fresh engagement with Jesus. And this includes not only the 'public' questions and conflicts I have mentioned, but also the less easily discussed conflicts of spirituality, the appropriation of traditions of understanding and structures of practice in prayer. It may be indeed that conflicts

---

[32] See G. W. H. Lampe's subtle and nuanced argument for the fundamental identity of Christ and Spirit in chs 3 and 4 of his classic study *God as Spirit* (Oxford, 1977).

of this sort provoke the most serious Christological questionings of all: Hans Urs von Balthasar's profound and even harrowing treatment of the themes of Christ's dereliction and descent into Hell are inextricably connected with his sensitivity to the cost and pain of Christian contemplation.[33] And, in a rather different vein, what Simone Weil has to say about the person and work of Christ is organically related to her understanding of the conflict between the order of necessity and the order of compassion as she experienced it in her own life (both 'public' and 'interior' – there being no facile separation of these realms for her.)[34]

If, then, we follow something like Ricoeur's analysis of revelation, a statement like 'God reveals himself' will mean that God invites us into his 'world': new life is manifested historically, in event, speech, and memory restoring to us a 'participation-in or belonging-to an order of things which precedes our capacity to oppose ourselves to things taken as objects opposed to a subject'.[35] And in this case, the 'order of things' in question is the primary order of all things, the creative liberty of God. Further, because that liberty is both freely shown and freely given to us, it is manifested as inseparable from care, love, grace: creativity is gift and nurture, not abstract power and capacity-to-effect. If creativity is revealed in this way, as *call*, invitation, then it is essentially self-diffusing or self-sharing. For us to share *in* it therefore means that we are called to share it: our participation in God's liberty is necessarily a participation in the act of *making* free. And as God is present in the basic event of our liberation in Jesus, so he is present in the Church as it struggles to make men and women free and to understand more deeply the shape and the nature of the liberty it is there to generate. 'God reveals himself' means that the meaning of the word 'God' establishes itself among us as the loving and nurturing advent of *newness* in human life – grace, forgiveness, empowerment to be the agents of forgiveness and liberation. This advent has its centre, its normative focus, in the record of Jesus; it occurs among us now as the re-presentation of Jesus through the Spirit; and it rests upon and gives content to the fundamental regulative notion of initiative, creative or generative power, potentiality, that is not circumscribed by the conditions of the empirical world – the *arché* of the Father, the ultimate source.

---

[33] A summary of these themes can be found in *On Prayer* (trans. A. V. Littledale; 2nd edn, London: SPCK, 1973), Part II, chs 2 and 3.

[34] See (out of an enormous range of possible examples) the reflections on incarnation and cross in the *Notebooks*, vol. 2, pp. 345, 414–17 (trans. A. Wills; London: RKP, 1956), or the section on 'The Cross' in *Gravity and Grace* (London: RKP, 1952), pp. 79–83.

[35] Ricoeur, *op. cit.*, p. 101.

With such a scheme, we are indeed compelled to a 'negative' theology in the traditional sense: not a theology of agnosticism, not merely a system of transcendental postulates, but a theology consistently aware of its locations within the 'hermeneutical spiral', the appropriation in concrete circumstances, in debate and conflict, of the founding events of faith. It is 'negative' because obliged to be not only critical of the Church's language and practice but also self-critical, suspicious of its recurring temptation to theoretical resolution and conceptual neatness. It is 'negative' because it recognizes the way in which 'God' is specified in the flux of interpretation and action in the community's life – not in the definition of a concept, certainly not in speculation about what kind of an individual might possess an assortment of very unusual metaphysical characteristics. St Thomas (basing himself on a long tradition of reflection in Greek and Latin theology) asserted that *Deus* was the name of an *operatio*:[36] and that elegantly sums up the nature of the theological problem. Talking about an 'activity' flowing from, between, within, three termini does not easily lend itself to conceptual tidiness. Understanding God as Trinity is participating in the advent of grace and freedom; *theological* understanding is the conscious and articulate effort to sustain the critical and dialectical aspect of this participation – keeping Word and Spirit in touch with each other, so to speak. Which means that the theologian's involvement in the more basic understanding, in the events of grace, is taken for granted. Nicholas Lash, writing of Newman's discussion of the royal, priestly and prophetic (theological) offices in the Church, reminds us that the theologian's critical task must not isolate him or her from the other two dimensions of Christian living: 'For the theologian to discharge his responsibilities within the community, he must experience the tensions between the spontaneity of faith, the pragmatic exigencies of social order, and the critical quest of truth for its own sake, within his own life and experience.'[37] The theologizing of Christological and Trinitarian faith presupposes – quite simply – living in Christ and in the Trinitarian mystery, living in the Spirit.

Ricoeur attributes the philosopher's unease with the notion of revelation to a suspicion of intellectual heteronomy; and much of his treatment of revelation in terms of 'poetics' is designed to elaborate and defend the idea of 'non-heteronomous dependence'.[38] We speak because we are called, invited

---

[36] *Summa Theologiae* I.xiii.8; God is *nomen operationis* in the sense that the name is 'ascribed' on the basis of the universal activity of providential oversight. 'God' *means* the context of all that is experienced and understood as actively good towards us; it does not therefore give us an essential definition, an account of 'what it is to be God'.

[37] *Theology on Dover Beach* (London: DLT, 1979), p. 103.

[38] Ricoeur, *op. cit.*, pp. 115–17.

and authorized to speak, we speak what we have been *given*, out of our new 'belonging', and this is a 'dependent' kind of utterance, a responsive speech. But it is not a dictated or determined utterance: revelation is addressed not so much to a will called upon to submit as to an imagination called upon to 'open itself'.[39] The integrity of theological utterance, then, does not lie in its correspondence to given structures of thought, its falling into line with an authoritative communication, but in the reality of its rootedness, its belonging, in the new world constituted in the revelatory event or process. If anything, Ricoeur's concentration on the revelatory *text* still suggests something of an imbalance, giving insufficient weight to the revelatory character of interpretation itself. God 'speaks' in the response as in the primary utterance: there is a dimension of 'givenness', generative power, and the discovered new world in the work of the imagination opening itself.

So God's revealing of himself in this fashion does indeed point us to the sort of God with whom we have to do: our final and comprehensive 'context of meaning' is both creative initiation and creative response. We cannot simply define God – and therefore the redeemed or godlike consciousness – as the absence of dependence. But if we are going to develop a Trinitarian theology on this sort of basis, the meaning of 'non-heteronomous dependence' will need some further precision and clarification in relation to the Christian 'foundational' story itself. Christian belief involves us in a form of life and reflection which assumes in all sorts of ways that liberty and dependence are not mutually exclusive.[40] Indeed, the argument of this paper is meant to suggest that the actual conduct of Christian theology, in its movement between Word and Spirit, confession and debate, image and negation, embodies just this principle. So we come back to the question of how this is learned; we turn to our generative events, to Jesus, to ask why the community of *Jesus* is the kind of community in which issues of liberty and dependence are worth discussing. We listen to the gospel itself from this perspective, attending to the way in which gospel narrative interweaves the themes of liberty and dependence. And the belief that the Spirit is at work in any constructive puzzlement about why certain kinds of debate arise in the Church is some encouragement in this enterprise.

---

[39] Ibid., p. 117.
[40] See the reflections of Dorothee Sölle on this theme in 'Paternalistic Religion as Experienced by Women', *God as Father* (*Concilium* 143, Edinburgh, 1981), ed. J. B. Metz and E. Schillebeeckx, pp. 69–74.

Chapter Ten

TRINITY AND ONTOLOGY

I

Donald MacKinnon's writings from about the mid-1960s onwards, at least, return regularly not simply to the fundamental theme of 'realism *versus* idealism', but to the treatment of this issue by G. E. Moore in a classical essay on 'External and Internal Relations'.[1] This, along with certain other writings by Moore and Russell in their assault on idealism,[2] sets the terms of the problem for MacKinnon; and it is important to remember this when, as is sometimes the case, the words 'realism' and 'idealism' seem to become impossibly loose in their scope. Behind all the discussion of the question of fundamental ontology in MacKinnon's maturest work stands a set of rigorous arguments in logical theory, in the light of which this work requires to be understood; and without this perspective the heart of Mackinnon's theological achievement remains opaque.

Moore's target is primarily Bradley's contention that every relation in which a specific term is involved enters into the being of that term, so as to be intrinsic to it. Moore's first clarification (pp. 281–2) is to note that, strictly speaking, it is 'relational *properties*' that are in question, not relations – i.e., Bradley's claim is one about relations to particular and distinct terms that are truly predicated of another single term ('*A* is the father of *B*', not '*A* is a father' only). The claim then amounts to saying, 'Without the relational property *p*, *A* would not necessarily be *A*' (p. 284); not-*p* entails that the

---

[1] *Philosophical Studies* (London, 1922), pp. 276–309. This is referred to in *ACS, PM, IR* and *RI* (see Abbreviations at the end of this paper). I have generally restricted myself in this paper to those of MacKinnon's works published after 1965.

[2] E.g., Moore's 'The Refutation of Idealism', *Philosophical Studies*, pp. 1–30, and ch. 5 of Bertrand Russell, *My Philosophical Development* (London, 1959), quoting at length (pp. 55–61) from a 1907 paper dealing largely with the logic of relations.

subject of p is qualitatively and numerically different from A. But there are clearly relational properties of which this cannot hold (a materially discrete or discernible part in a composite whole, for instance, may or may not possess the relational property of being part of the whole; it would not necessarily be numerically different if it did not): thus it *may* follow that if x is not p, it is not A, but there is no necessity, no *deducibility* of not-A from not-p. There is, Moore proposes (p. 291), no *entailment* of not-A by not-p, no logical relation, that is, comparable to the deducibility of 'B is less than A' from 'A is greater than B'.

If not-p always and necessarily entailed not-A, every true proposition would entail every other true proposition. ($p.q$) would be analytic of p; with the unpalatable consequence that every *false* proposition would entail every other proposition, true and false (p. 285). This is manifestly absurd, and there are obvious examples of conjunctions of true propositions neither of which can in any accessible sense be deduced from the other (pp. 300–1, 304–5). Relational properties thus cannot all be internal in the sense of belonging necessarily to their terms: some are, but some are not and cannot be. Even if we allow (p. 309) that a relational property entails some quality in the term that makes it capable of having that property, such a quality does not entail the property. Thus – though Moore does not so express it – there are contingently true propositions not deducible from others.[3] To know the truth of p does not mean knowing the whole scheme of true propositions; there are things we *come* to know, so that a certain attitude to the timebound nature of our knowing is involved here. If A is not necessarily p, A must be knowable as changing, as 'entering into' relations and ceasing to be involved in them. Granted what has been said about the *conditions* in A for p, it is not true that A is made to be A by p; and this is what is meant by asserting the existence of *external relations* – not, crudely, the chance juxtaposition of intact atomic subjects, but simply the fact that there are some non-constitutive relational properties.

If there really are 'external relations', Bradleian idealism must be fatally confused; its flaw lies in the assimilation of all relations between true propositions to entailment, which is (to say the least) counter-intuitive. At best, this assimilation is a kind of eschatological myth; at worst, it is simply a muddle about the language we actually speak. Of this demonstration of the flaw in such an epistemology, MacKinnon writes: 'What Moore establishes in this paper is something about the world . . . a fact of a peculiar order; indeed, one is hard put to it at first . . . to say clearly what sort of fact it is.'[4]

---

[3]   Compare *SC*, p. 287.
[4]   *ACS*, p. 99.

I am not sure that it is helpful or intelligible to speak of 'a' fact here; if Moore is right, what we actually have is something more like a definition of what facts are, a grammatical stipulation, or (lest that be thought to sell the pass again) an ontological framework. If p and q can, independently of each other, be known to be true, they are known to be *contingently* true; $(f)x$ does not have to be so. The functional variable does not shift according to a necessary law-governed pattern. x is now this, now that, and what it is cannot be predicted as if it were the end of a mathematical operation of a certain kind.

But this means also that there is one distinction that is somehow onto-logically positive: that between the constant and the variable terms of prop-ositions, between the processes of change and that which changes (without which, of course, we could have no notion of change at all).[5] 'The concept of the thing is the concept of the way in which various sorts of event are organisable or constructible', as MacKinnon puts it in an essay published in 1972:[6] we cannot do without the notion of self-continuous subjects in talk-ing about the world, since there is no other way, it seems, of making sense of the flux of perceptions. But even that is a profoundly misleading way of putting it, suggesting that there might *first* be perceptions of something like 'events', which we subsequently carve up into things. We should need to revise and intensify MacKinnon's 1972 phraseology to do justice to what he is attempting to say: the concept of the thing is what is presupposed in the very concept of a perceived world.[7] The world could not show itself in our thought and language as an intelligible, utterable, discussable continuum did we not know 'first' (the word should not be taken with chronological liter-alness) what a thing was.

Here we are in very deep waters indeed. MacKinnon rightly repudiates the 'crudities of the picture-theory of the proposition',[8] and regards straight-forward logical atomism as mythological.[9] It sounds from much of his writing as though it is in fact impossible to give a satisfactory account of what a thing *is*; we are certainly not being invited to see the world as div-ided into discrete lumps answering to nouns in our language. Correspond-ence is not a scrutable relation between words and things, but something more like a controlling *image* for our understanding of understanding.[10] 'I

---

[5]   *ACS*, p. 101.
[6]   *SC*, p. 287.
[7]   This is clearly implied in *ACS*, p. 114.
[8]   *RI*, p. 154.
[9]   *IR*, p. 142.
[10]   As suggested in *IR*, pp. 142 and 145–6, and *RI*, p. 154.

suspect that the emphasis on the ontological irreducibility of the thing, the self-continuous subject, actually represents a kind of 'negative metaphysics'. If the truth of $(f)a$ and the truth of $(f)x$ can be independently known, we can at least know that a and x are neither of them part of the definition of the other. We cannot but treat them as subjects of their distinct histories, even though neither is real *apart* from those histories:[11] there is no Lockean substrate to be excavated. But if this is how we speak and are constrained to speak, we also know, from the reciprocal non-entailment of p and q, that we recognize as true what *comes to be true* and whose coming to be true is not predictable; and if it is not predictable, it is nonsense to say – in extreme idealist fashion – that it is 'made to be true' by the knowing mind. The unpredictable is, necessarily, that whose truth is a matter of question and puzzlement (we *come* to know it), to which understanding must adjust:[12] it is what changes the very scope of the knowing mind. We may not be able to give a clear answer to the question. 'How are objects of experience possible?' but we must ask it in order at least to register the fact that our speech is marked by the pressure of 'experiential constants', place, date, continuity of subject, causal agency.[13] 'If these constants are expressive of the form of the world, they are so expressive as realizing the inescapable limits of our understanding.'[14] The idealist temptation is to foreclose the issues raised in this remark by treating its unavoidable anthropocentrism ('*our* understanding') as a solution rather than a problem[15] – i.e., by turning the notion of 'inescapable limits of understanding' into a theoretical prohibition on considering what understanding actually understands, and ultimately into a denial that this latter consideration has any meaning.

Some of the difficulty and unclarity in all this is, I think, due to the fact that MacKinnon tends to elide various kinds of anti-realism, producing an implicit portmanteau scheme which no one philosopher has held or could logically hold. There are several targets for his polemic that need to be distinguished. As we have seen, the first and perhaps most basic of these is the doctrine Moore sets out to refute, that there are no propositions that are contingently true; the rejection of this implies the primitivity of discrete subjects ('things') in our language, and MacKinnon thus turns to attack the idea of the reducibility of things to events or event-clusters. He is wary of

[11]   *SC*, pp. 284–8, *ACS*, pp. 103–5.
[12]   *IR*, p. 146.
[13]   *IR*, pp. 140–1.
[14]   *IR*, p. 140.
[15]   *IR*, pp. 149–50.

the pitfalls of crude atomism, yet insists that the 'constants' of our speech are not arbitrary; and this leads him to reject the suggestion that all we know is how our language works. But the rejection of arbitrariness in the sense of non-determination by extra-linguistic reality involves him equally in dismissing the idea that what can and shall be thought, known or spoken is up to us, is our 'creation', resting on our 'decision'.[16] This last point is both the weakest and in some respects the most important in MacKinnon's polemical outline of realism – weakest because least related to any serious idealist views and involving him in what seems a rather contentious, even distorting, account of Wittgenstein on the foundation of mathematics, most significant because it brings out the *moral* force of the first and strongest part of the polemic, the assertion of the reality of external relations. One could perhaps represent this by saying: if the world is not a system of necessary interconnections, and if knowledge is therefore genuinely historical,[17] coming to know what comes to be true, then the will can have no finally determinative role in our relation to the world. To suppose that it can is not only a lie, but a destructive (and self-destructive) lie. Logically, the universality of internal relations and the primacy of the will as a 'world-causing' reality have nothing to do with each other, but for the practical reason both may serve to secure the ego a kind of invulnerability from interruption,[18] challenge, resistance; both may reinforce the idea that the hidden, immutable essence of subjectivity is limitlessness, and that there can be no genuinely diminishing injuries to the subject, no real defeats. The indeterminate depths of selfhood abide.

We are back with what earlier I called a 'negative metaphysics'. Filling it out, without destroying its negative character, is a programme of daunting proportions which MacKinnon himself only hints at, and which is beyond the compass of this essay. One or two things, though, might be said, in a kind of parenthesis, at this juncture. First of all, it is important to keep in sight the possibility that the 'correspondence' metaphor might be edged away from its focal position without thereby sacrificing the concerns of realism. If we are prepared to jettison picture-theories of propositions, the correspondence we can speak of becomes a far more elusive thing: it is not the cor-

---

[16] E.g., *IR*, p. 143 (on Wittgenstein), *RI*, pp. 156–7.

[17] Compare the remarks on knowledge and *learning* in Rowan Williams, 'Trinity and Revelation' [ch. 9 above, especially 131–2].

[18] On 'truth as interruption', compare Eberhard Jüngel, 'The Truth of Life: Observations on Truth as the Interruption of the Continuity of Life', in Richard McKinney, ed., *Creation, Christ and Culture: Studies in Honour of T. F. Torrance* (Edinburgh, 1976), pp. 231–6.

respondence of photograph to scenery or physiognomy, nor yet that of, say, a chemical formula to a specific chemical reaction in the laboratory. Is it, then, more like the *appropriateness* of a move in chess? The exhibiting of a proper and conventionalized but not totally determined skill in responding to what is presented? This sails very near the pragmatist wind, but cannot be accused of covert voluntarism, at least. If picture-theories must go, are we left with any option but something like this: a realism which 'shows itself' in the halts and paradoxes, shifts and self-corrections of language itself as a material and historical reality? Following on from this: MacKinnon certainly hints that the concept of a 'thing' is analogical, but does not fully tease out the implications of this. There have been those who suggest that if the idea of self-continuous substance is analogical, the prime analogate is the concept of human subjectivity. But lest this should turn into an appeal to the justly unpopular notion of separable (disembodiable) selves, we must insist that what is in question is the self as embodied agent. If language expresses irreducible discontinuities, this has something to do with the fact that what we ordinarily count as consciousness involves assuming the difference between our bodily presence and what acts upon it or resists it. To be conscious is to be 'placed' in respect of bodily limits. It is also to be (at least potentially) a speaker, defining oneself in saying 'I' and presenting – in response to the address of what is materially other (including words) – the construct of a self-continuous subject. The intertwining factors of body and speech *oblige* us to be in the world as individual subjects: that is how we speak, think, and so are. And it is on the basis of this that we are able to learn to give names, to acquire the skill of identifying 'things'. Regular patterns of interaction between body and other can only be formulated in the language of 'things' if the body is first located as 'addressed' and required to organize or present itself in response, so that there is a constant in respect of which patterns can be established as regular.

This is no more than an attempt (indebted in some ways to von Balthasar's metaphysical sketch in *Herrlichkeit*;[19] less obviously, to some of the recent work of Fergus Kerr,[20] and with a cautious glance in the direction of Lacan) to indicate how MacKinnon's central concerns about the avoidance of the mythology of the knowing self's illimitability might be pursued and discussed further, once realism is detached a little more from atomism and

---

[19] *Herrlichkeit. Eine Theologische Ästhetik. III. 1. Im Raum der Metaphysik. II. Neuzeit*, 2nd edn (Einsiedeln, 1965), pp. 943–83.

[20] I have in mind particularly the sequence of articles on the soul in *New Blackfriars*, 64 (1983), pp. 76–85, 124–35, 188–98, 225–34.

picture-theories. It is meant to allow (i) that the sentient individual is more than a 'logical construction out of events'[21] without involving us in speculative fancy about naked individual subjects existing prior to relation and perception; (ii) that while there is no way in which the individual is graspable without seeing that it is constituted in and by the material fact of bodily limit and the relation of being – as I have put it – 'addressed', and formed as a speaker in and by the linguistic community, this does not and cannot mean the kind of relational determinism in all aspects of its particular history that Moore repudiates;[22] (iii) that the concept of a thing is indeed indispensable, primitive, but is ultimately dependent on the condition of continuous perception – or, in plain English, things exist as continuing subjects of change because speakers do. The fact that (iii) depends on a particular analysis of the material-linguistic conditions of perception itself may rescue it from the charge of vulgar Berkleianism.

This has been a laborious prologue to the consideration of strictly theological issues; but MacKinnon's own insistence that theology cannot neglect the questions of ontology makes such a preliminary exploration necessary. It will be clear that I have some misgivings about MacKinnon's residual tenderness towards an 'atomist' realism and about the degree to which varieties of idealism are – I think – too hastily assimilated to voluntarism; and I have tried to see whether MacKinnon's concerns can be preserved in a reconstruction that gives more ground than he would to strategies associated with constructivist and coherentist accounts of truth – to the idea of 'reality without reference'.[23] However, the determination to demythologize a free, triumphant, endlessly resourceful, sovereign willing self remains focally important: MacKinnon's *moral* interest in realism is one of his most valuable contributions to the whole of this tangled debate, and I share his conviction that it is a crucial dimension for our philosophizing and theologizing. We must turn next, then, to what exactly is involved in this moral interest, and to its theological import.

II

If the world is our creation, or even if the world is masterable as a system of necessities, the idea of irreparable and uncontrollable *loss* ceases to make

[21] SC, pp. 284–5.
[22] SC, pp. 287–8.
[23] The title of an influential and important study by Donald Davidson, reprinted in *Inquiries into Truth and Interpretation* (Oxford, 1984), pp. 215–25.

sense: there are no tragedies. But in brute fact, human disaster does not submit itself to a calculus of perceivable necessities in this or any imaginable world (Ivan's challenge to Alyosha about torturing a single child to secure the happiness of the world is perhaps the starkest of familiar expressions of this).[24] All explanation of suffering is an attempt to forget it *as* suffering, and so a quest for untruthfulness; and it is precisely this kind of untruthfulness that is served (in MacKinnon's eyes) by anti-realism. It is pointless to ask whether the moral failure of anti-realism leads us to seek for a logical crit- ique, or whether its logical muddles help to make it a moral delinquency to hold it: chickens and eggs. Both the moral and the logical criticisms of anti- realism involve a certain appeal to the counter-intuitive character of the idea of the world as a necessary system; and, for MacKinnon, the most important aspect of such an appeal is that it reminds us that we do speak of and experi- ence tragic loss, senseless, inexplicable, unjustifiable, unassimilable pain. 'People change and smile, but the agony abides.' The resolution of the sheer resistant particularity of suffering, past and present,[25] into comfortable teleological patterns is bound to blunt the edge of particularity, and so to lie; and this lying resolution contains that kind of failure in attention that is itself a moral deficiency, a fearful self-protection. It is just this that fuels the fantasy that we can choose how the world and myself shall be.

MacKinnon's Gifford Lectures[26] return more than once to the Kantian principle of the primacy of the practical reason; and it is in a very clearly Kantian way that the transition from these observations about the unassimilably particular to theology is realized. The world is such − *is*, independently of our choice and our fabrication − that we cannot think away particulars into comprehensive explanatory systems; the world is such that attention to par- ticularity is demanded of us. If we are to speak of God, can we do so in a way that does not amount to another evasion of the world? There is a way of talking about God that simply projects on to him what we cannot achieve − a systematic vision of the world as a necessarily inter-related whole. Trust in such a God is merely deferred confidence in the possibility of exhaustive explanation and justification; and deferred confidence of this sort is open to exactly the same moral and logical objection as any other confidence in syst- emic necessity of this kind in the world. A God whose essential function is to negate the 'otherness' and discontinuity of historical experience, and so to provide for us an ideal *locus standi*, a perspective transcending or reconciling

---

[24]   *The Brothers Karamazov*, vol. 5, ch. 4 ('Rebellion').
[25]   See, for example, *IncT*, pp. 90–3.
[26]   *PM*; see especially ch. 5.

discontinuity into system, is clearly an idol, and an incoherent one at that: if he is the negation of the reciprocal negations or exclusions of worldly subjects, either he is the completion of the process of historical dialectic (in which case he cannot strictly provide a *locus standi* outside it for us *now*, as there is no alternative to living through that dialectic); or else he is simply a further object, of a rather unusual kind, standing in opposition to the rest of the objects that there are (in which case there is no ultimate overcoming of discontinuity). These are familiar cruces in monist ontologies, from Plotinus and Iamblichus to Hegel, Marx and beyond.

Apart from this threatened incoherence, though, there is also the fact that no content can be given to the concept of such a God, let alone to the 'explanation' he is meant to provide – except that a Hegelian might reply that the 'content' is the whole rational process of the universe. However, even if such a form of theism were capable of intelligible statement and defence, it would hardly be compatible with the Christian doctrine of God as loving and active 'in his own right', irrespective of there being a world. Between God and the world is a relation which approaches the limit of 'sheer externality',[27] in that God is in no sense *made to be* what he is by the sum total of worldly fact. The Christian problem then becomes one of elucidating the sense in which God *is* related to the world, most particularly in Jesus Christ. If God is neither a quasi-Hegelian organizing principle, nor an abstract postulate, nor yet an agent among other agents, what *is* to be said of him?

Christian practice begins to answer that question by repeating the story of Jesus: what is to be said of God is that Jesus of Nazareth was born, ministered in such and such a way, died in such and such a way, and was raised from death. This is an odd statement, in that it treats the narrative of a human being as predicated of a substance or subject which is God; and all sorts of qualifications must at once be introduced in order to avoid the obvious pitfall of failing to allow that we are, after all, speaking of a human individual.[28] But what is being claimed is that the substantiality, the 'subjecthood', the continuous identity of this individual is so related to the substantiality of God that it cannot be grasped in its full reality without allusion to God as *constitutively* significant for it: this human individual's relation to God is 'internal to the term assumed', so that the humanity of Jesus as independent of its assumption by God is abstract or 'impersonal' (anhypostatic)[29] – a feature

[27] *RI*, p. 161, *PC*, p. 157.
[28] The dangers are spelt out in *PC*, pp. 149–53.
[29] *PC*, pp. 149–50, 153.

of classical Christology normally so misunderstood and distorted in contemporary discussion that MacKinnon's presentation of it must itself be accorded something of a classical status.

God is what is constitutive of the particular identity of Jesus; that is what can be said of him, and it is what the *homoousion* of Nicaea endeavoured to say. If we say less than this, the identity of Jesus becomes external to God and so 'parabolic' in its significance: it is one determinate thing pointing to another. Jesus is 'like' God in certain respects, and presumably not in others, which licenses us to leave out of account in our theology what in the story of Jesus is held on some prior grounds to be unassimilable for language about God. Thus we are swiftly brought back to the question of the authority by which we may say anything at all of God. Christ as parable relieves us of Christ as paradox; and it pushes back towards the purely negative characterization of God once more, as that which is not involved in the world's discontinuities. MacKinnon's repeated insistence that we attend to the *tragic* in the narrative of Jesus[30] belongs with this rejection of parabolic status for this narrative: only that to which the *homoousion* points can hold before us the full human particularity of Jesus, and so prevent us from yet another variety of fantasy and avoidance of the truth. For Jesus to have been a temporal individual at all is for him to have changed and learned and made decisions whose full consequences he did not control; for him to have been *responsible*, as all adult persons are, for the injuring and diminution (even if it was also the self-injuring and self-diminution) of others. His innocence or sinlessness becomes a dauntingly complex matter if it is not to be taken as a complete alienation from the realities of temporal existence. It must be something compatible with the experience of what we would have to call 'moral limit':[31] MacKinnon speaks of an 'historically achieved innocence',[32] implying that sinlessness can only be a judgement passed on the *entirety* of a life in which the inevitable damage done by human beings to each other has not sealed up the possibility of compassionate and creative relationship (even to those most deeply injured: what could one say here of the relation between the figure of Jesus and post-Holocaust Judaism, as perceived by modern Jewish writers? Does this give a hint of what the content of 'sinlessness' might be?).

---

[30] See *IT passim* and especially pp. 96–8, *IncT*, p. 104, *ARH*, pp. 65–6, the short piece on 'Theology and Tragedy' in *SA*, pp. 41–51, and several of the earlier articles. The recurrent themes are the responsibility of Jesus for the damnation of Judas, and the connection between the events of redemption and the history of Christian anti-Semitism.

[31] See the fine essay by D. Z. Phillips, 'Some Limits to Moral Endeavour', in *Through a Darkening Glass: Philosophy, Literature, and Cultural Change* (Oxford, 1982), pp. 30–50.

[32] *IncT*, p. 97.

If, then, we are serious about the constitutive character of God's relation to Jesus, we are saying that we speak and cannot but speak of God in the context of *limit* – the limits of particularity, of bodiliness and mortality, of moral capacity, of creatureliness. For Jesus is also a creature who prays to God, someone addressing a Father in heaven; and what is more, he is shown to us – in Gethsemane and in the Johannine farewell discourses – as interpreting, at starkly painful cost, the final 'limit' of his approaching torture and death as the moment, the 'hour', in which the act of the Father in and through himself is to be accomplished.[33] The otherness, the final unmasterable otherness of the world present to all of us as our approaching death, is for Jesus inseparable from the otherness to him of God. So the paradoxes are sharpened: if we affirm that God's relation to Jesus makes Jesus to be what he is, we move on inexorably to saying that God constitutes in Jesus a life which is – so to speak – paradigmatically *creaturely*, distanced from God. The God who is the ground and form of Jesus's particular history is also the God to whom Jesus calls through the mortal darkness of Gethsemane and Calvary. The God present *in* Jesus is present *to* Jesus in the enduring of his comfortless death: sheer externality.

It is this that compels us to the trinitarian enterprise; not to find a resolution for all this, but to continue with the question of what is to be said of God, to find a language for the proclaiming of Christ that does not break down into nonsense or presage retreat into abstract theism (God as ideal negation). In the conclusion of his 1976 essay on 'The Relation of the Doctrines of the Incarnation and the Trinity',[34] MacKinnon writes: 'If we suppose that in the theology of the Trinity an *analogia personarum* can be complemented by an analogy of *limits* (in the pregnant sense of the Greek *peras*), it may go some way towards grounding within the eternal the essentially human element of temporality, the sense of inescapable limitation.' If we are to speak of God in terms of Jesus, we must say that in God there is that which makes possible the identity-in-difference – indeed, identity in distance or in absence – of Jesus and who or what he calls Father: something approaching the 'externality' of creator and creation, yet decisively not that, but a mutually constitutive presence, an internal relation of terms. What is to be said of God must be 'expressive of a total spontaneity and absolute mutual response'.[35] Creation in its 'externality' to God and its 'externality' within

---

[33] *ARH*, pp. 63–4, *SC*, p. 290, *PC*, pp. 158–60, etc.

[34] *IncT*, p. 104.

[35] *IncT*, p. 104; compare *ARH*, p. 68, and the remarks in *SP*, p. 85, on the 'contingency' of the proposition that the Father raises the Son – given that this is a profoundly unsatisfactory word, 'necessity', MacKinnon insists, is no better.

itself can be so because the life of the creator is what it unchangingly is in a relation we only perceive as something teasingly and disturbingly like self-negation; but *not* that.

This is, I think, what MacKinnon means by saying,[36] in the wake of von Balthasar, that the presence of God in Christ is a 'putting at risk' of the unity of the divine life. I do not believe that MacKinnon is flirting here with any kind of residual Valentinian mythology – the fall of Sophia – or with any of the less intelligent and intelligible versions of process thought. The point is surely this: we cannot say what God is in himself; all we have is the narrative of God with us.[37] And that is a narrative of a 'journey into a far country' (to borrow Barth's powerful image,[38] itself of normative importance to MacKinnon), a story of God's Son as a creature and a mortal and defeated creature: the unity of God and his Son in this story is not, in the actual detail, moment by moment, of the story, desert temptation, Gethsemane, dereliction, realized for us as an unshakeable, already achieved thing. It emerges at last, when Christ goes to his Father risen and glorified, as the issue of a temporal process, with all its ambiguity, the uncontrolledness of its effects ('moral limit' again), the precariousness of its growth. That is what temporal process *is* for us. In other words, it is a story of 'risk'; and only at Easter are we able to say, 'he comes *from* God, just as he goes *to* God', and to see in the contingent fact of the resurrection – the *limited* events of the finding of an empty tomb and a scatter of bewildering encounters – that which is not contingent, the life of God as Father and Son together.[39] We cannot start from this end-point in the sense of treating it as the given framework for making complete and satisfying sense of the angular, specific and untidy narrative of ministry and Cross, because the sense of *this* ending emerges only from the telling of *this* story. Bultmann's kerygma, 'The crucified is risen', stops short of that decisive key to speaking about *God* offered in the proclamation that 'The risen one – the exalted Lord, the heavenly and eternal Son – is the crucified.'

We have, then, no concrete language for the unity of God but this story of risk and consummation, of unity forged through absence and death between God as source (Father) and the created life of Jesus of Nazareth (as

[36] *IncT*, pp. 101–2; compare *ARH*, p. 67, *PC*, pp. 157–8, and MacKinnon's introduction to Hans Urs von Balthasar, *Engagement with God* (London, 1975).
[37] For a particularly lucid exposition of this, see Herbert McCabe, 'The Involvement of God', *New Blackfriars*, 66 (1985), pp. 464–76.
[38] Karl Barth, *Church Dogmatics*, IV.1, section 59.1.
[39] See, for example, *SP*, pp. 75–9, 81–3.

Son). We are left with only the most austere account of God's life as such: that it must be what makes this possible. Even if we say, for instance, that this establishes God as free to be what he is even in dialogue and difference, to be himself in the other, we are no further forward, except insofar as we have thereby done away with the idea of God as an individual all of whose relations to what is not himself are in the crudest sense external to the other term of the relation as much as to himself, the relation of one atomic individual to others – an idea hard to reconcile with any serious doctrine of creation as well as with any theology of grace as divine indwelling or 'information'.

We do not avoid the pressure of the negative by speaking of God in trinitarian terms; but this apophaticism is at least not merely abstract, not a matter of articulating God's life solely as the opposite of temporal *altérité*. As MacKinnon fully allows, negative theology of this sort is an indispensable element in the whole enterprise, so that we should not delude ourselves that God's difference is merely that of one thing from another: we need to put down those formal markers (immutable, impassible, omnipotent, etc.) as a way of insisting that we cannot write a biography of God. As has already been said, his history is Jesus. If anthropomorphism is always perilously close in the kind of trinitarian pluralism which the life of Jesus seems to enjoin upon us,[40] it is still finally deflected by the recognition that the 'essential' or 'immanent' Trinity can finally be characterized only as that which makes this life (and death and resurrection) possible and intelligible. Without reference to the immanent Trinity, we are liable to idolatrous 'trivialization of the divine';[41] but MacKinnon is well aware that there can be a trivialization no less disastrous and idolatrous in a kind of mythological pluralism, projecting on to God the limits of created identities with no sense of *metabasis eis allo genos* in our speech.

It could be said, perhaps, that in this perspective what is wrong with an Hegelian view of the Trinity is that it projects the 'achieved' character of Christ's union with the Father as enacted in history on to eternity (and so destroys the proper contingency and unresolved or tragic limitedness of that and every history). And – although MacKinnon can write appreciatively of Moltmann[42] – it is clear that the same kind of projection is at work in the kind of pluralist doctrine that gives to the *historical* encounter of Jesus with

---

[40]   *IncT*, p. 103.

[41]   *IncT*, p. 100.

[42]   *IncT*, p. 105. The parallels would be worth exploring in more detail, as would the important divergences. It is perhaps surprising that MacKinnon has never undertaken a fuller discussion of Moltmann.

the God of Israel a constitutive role in the life of the Trinity as such. God would not be God were he not the God who is such as to be the ground and 'form' of this encounter; but this is not the same as to say that God would not be God were it not for a set of contingent events in the first century of our era. Both Hegel's and Moltmann's trinitarian models are controlled by the desire to take history seriously, to bridge the gap between a remote eternity and the concrete temporal world; but they end in evasions of the temporal – Hegel by generalizing Good Friday into a necessary moment in the universal dialectic, Moltmann by weakening the force of the recognition that Jesus' suffering is humanly inflicted, through his concentration on the cross as the Father's giving-up of the Son, a transaction in a mythical rather than historical space.

These two models, so apparently – and in many ways really – close to MacKinnon's, fail because they reverse the *ordo cognoscendi* of revelation. We do not begin with the trinitarian God and ask how he can be such, but with the world of particulars, cross, empty tomb, forgiven and believing apostles, asking, 'How can this be?' Hence MacKinnon's image of 'transcription':[43] what we first know is the reality we subsequently come to know as derivative, transposed from what is prior. Kenosis is defined as the common form of Jesus' earthly life (as service, acceptance, authority in and through dependence) and the life of God (as gift or commitment to an other and the simultaneous imaging and returning of that act). The self-abnegation of Jesus in its specific form of active and transfiguring acceptance of the world's limit is not at all a mere paradigm for conscienceless obedience or resignation;[44] it is what puts to us the question of how God can be if this is how he is historically. Thus the abiding importance of the language of self-emptying is salvaged without recourse to the clumsy Apollinarian mythologies of some of those writers associated with 'kenotic theories' of the Incarnation.[45]

The trinitarian theology thus sketched by MacKinnon represents an im-

---

[43]   *IncT*, p. 104.
[44]   The whole question of the ethics of obedience is one that has long preoccupied MacKinnon; see, for example, the essay on 'Moral Objections' in *Objections to Christian Belief*, by D. M. MacKinnon, H. A. Williams, A. R. Vidler and J. S. Bezzant (London, 1963), and 'Authority and Freedom in the Church', *SA*, pp. 52–61. Both show signs of bitter hostility to any conception of obedience that relieves people of the risk and responsibility of choice.
[45]   The Apollinarian risk is certainly present in Gore. More recently, David Brown's skilful apologia for pluralist trinitarianism and kenotic Christology (*The Divine Trinity*: London, 1985) fails to avoid the pitfall of treating the Incarnation as an episode in the history of a divine subject, though it is not clear that he is guilty of a simple confusion between the Word and the psyche of Jesus of Nazareth.

pressively balanced 'retrieval' of a number of classical themes; but its greatest significance lies, I believe, in the thorough integration of trinitarian language with the over-riding concern for a truthful moral vision. The connections may not be at once obvious, but there is in fact a close link in this scheme between the evasion of the tragic and the denial of the relational character of God. However, we need also to note that MacKinnon's account of the tragic and of its reinterpretation in the language of Trinity and Incarnation has aroused some suspicion lately. In the final section of this paper, I propose to look briefly at these suspicions and to attempt a response based on indications offered in MacKinnon's own writing.

III

The problem is said to be this:[46] that any emphasis on the acceptance and interpretative transformation of moral or spiritual defeat is dangerously open to an ideological use that amounts to a commendation of passivity. What is absent from the 'tragic' orientation is a proper seriousness about the imperative to transformative *action*, and thus to protest: as Marx understood, interpretation is not enough. The Christian commitment is to a world of reconstructed relationships, not to a venture merely of 'reading' or 're-reading' the world. This is a weighty charge, and it must be allowed to possess some degree of plausibility. Christ as an exemplar of unresisting suffering is undoubtedly an ambivalent symbol; even Christ as the enactment of divine *solidarity* in suffering can be distorted in similar ways. And if – as MacKinnon many times insists – divine solidarity is a shocking and unmerciful judgement upon human and specially ecclesiastical power relations, what does this judgement *change*, other than ways of seeing and speaking? How shall we avoid being left with moralistic recommendations to abjure earthly power?

One point that needs making at once is that the tragic *by definition* deals with human limit; that is, with what is not to be changed. There is pain in the world that is, so to speak, non-negotiable. The suffering that *has* happened and cannot be made not to have happened (the irreversibility of time) is, in spite of various kinds of vacuous, insulting and brutal rhetoric, religious and political, unchangeably there for us. And there is present suffering, terminal illness or irreversible brain damage or what you will, that is equally, as

---

[46]   See Philip West, 'Christology as "Ideology"', *Theology*, 88 (1985), pp. 428–36, for a strong statement of this case.

a matter of bald fact, beyond us to change.[47] There can be a paralysing obsession with the tragic, but there can also be an attempt to evade the limits of
time and particularity through an attempt to bypass or rationalize pain and
death. Lionel Trilling's remarkable and underrated novel, *The Middle of the
Journey*, memorably shows us a man, recovering from a near-fatal illness,
who realizes that his devoted and courageous socialist friends see him and his
experience as a threat: death is reactionary. And this dread is shown in the
novel to be as destructive and untruthful as the tragedy-soaked rhetoric of
Gifford Maxim, the hypnotically eloquent ex-Communist and apprentice
neo-conservative.

In the *Guardian* of 10 February 1986, the playwright Howard Barker offered '49 asides for a tragic theatre'. Among these theses were the following:

> Ideology is the outcome of pain . . .
> Tragedy liberates language from banality. It restores the power of expres-
> sion to the people.
> Tragedy is not about reconciliation. Consequently it is the art form for our
> time.
> Tragedy resists the trivialization of experience, which is the project of the
> authoritarian regime . . .
> In the endless drizzle of false collectivity, tragedy restores pain to the indi-
> vidual.
> You emerge from tragedy equipped against lies. After the musical, you are
> anyone's fool . . .
> . . . Only tragedy makes justice its preoccupation.

It would be impertinent to gloss these remarks, except to point out that
the tragic here is not simply the order of the world that must be accepted
(tragedy is not accident, says Barker): it is *one's own* appropriation of the
limits of possibility, in protest against a polity and a culture that lure us to
sink our truthful perceptions in a collective, mythologized identity that can
shut its eyes to limits (and so can talk of mass annihilation without pain).

No one acts without perceiving something. And if that is so, the disjunction between interpretation and transformation becomes less absolute. If interpretation is not an explanatory reduction, but the gradual formation of a
'world' in which realities can be seen and endured without illusion, it is not

[47]   West's article appears in the same issue of *Theology* as Margaret Spufford's 'The Reality of
Suffering and the Love of God' (pp. 441–6), which offers a profound and moving reflection on
suffering that we *cannot* change.

alien to the only kinds of transformation that matter, transformations of what is actually present, without prior distortion or trivialization. Tragic theatre forms such a world, and so is a point of reference over against claims to final resolutions of our condition. But we need to take the question further: interpretation does not happen because an individual or individuals invent a set of symbols. The possible world of truthful perception depends on what has been concretely *made* possible, however precariously and impermanently, for actual persons in communication with each other. How do you learn to confront the fact, say, of racism in British society? Not by information, not by words. They produce the kind of pain we cannot handle, and we take refuge in ideological denial of the facts of power in Britain. To confront both the suffering of the victims of racism and my own *de facto* involvement in and responsibility for this, without fantasizing and self-lacerating guilt, requires specific encounter and the possibility of its continuance; not reconciliation, but a kind of commitment without evasion. The 'reading' of our situation in certain terms rests on existing small-scale transformations – and also, of course, assists in the creation of further transformation.

Tragedy is capable of being lived with and articulated because – once again – of the particular, the narratively specific, out of which certain kinds of new language grow. So, to return to the strictly theological frame of reference, if we see the cross as the identification of God with the limits of time, and learn from this a different reading of the temporal world, this 'seeing' of the cross, and through it of the world, is concretely made possible through the existence of 'reconstructed relationships' – not an internal shift of attitudes but the coming into being of a community with distinctive forms of self-definition. This is relatively seldom explored in MacKinnon's work; and this near-silence helps to explain why it is possible to suspect his scheme of stressing interpretation at the expense of change. But it is also related to another near-silence: in common with so many contemporary writers on the Trinity, he has little to say of the Holy Spirit. The Spirit as that which forms or sustains the new world of perception through the constant recreation of the Church as it is judged by its foundational charter in the paschal event[48] is the condition of the Christian reading of the cross; once this is granted, the essential unity of interpretation and historical, public transformation is theologically grounded.

Putting it another way: trinitarian reflection begins in the recognition that the encounter of Jesus with the God of Israel 'transcribes' the encounter that

---

[48] See the essay on 'Parable and Sacrament', *Explorations in Theology*, pp. 166–81, on the focusing of this judgement in the Eucharist.

is intrinsic to the life of God, but it does not finish there. God is constitutive of the identity of Jesus; God is also constitutive, in a different sense, of the process of the Church continually coming to judgement – the encounter of believers with the encounter of Father and Son. God is 'other to himself' or 'himself in the other' not only in the difference of Father and Son, but in that 'second difference' (borrowing the term from John Milbank's admirable recent essay)[49] that enables the communication of the *Gestalt* of Jesus' life in the Church. Not only Jesus' distance from the Father, but our distance, our critical 'absence', from Jesus is included in the eternal movement of God in and to himself. Without this, we should indeed be able to do no more than look at Jesus as exemplar, with the ideological risks that implies, making the life of God once again undialectically external in its realization to our present history.

If, then, we extend MacKinnon's methodology in this way to secure a serious doctrine of the Spirit as the divine condition for truthful 'coming to judgement' in the Church's life, some of the doubts raised about ideological ambivalence can be turned aside. The encounter of the Spirit with Christ is potentially an encounter with our own complicity in the cross, and so with the crosses of our own making in the present and past; it should, then, if it is what it claims to be, form a central strand in Christian protest and the articulation of such protest in transforming *action*. But it must also hold us to penitence, the acknowledgement that our present possibilities are shaped by our past, that limit remains inescapable; and so it can save us from facile and shallow utopianism, which so readily spills over into authoritarian expression. MacKinnon's relentless insistence on attention to the costliness of historical action[50] and the unconsoled nature of historical pain remains the most disturbing and important lesson he has to teach – when all the necessary qualifications or reservations have been raised. 'when society is officially Philistine,' writes Barker (and he is not making a preciously aesthetic judgement, but speaking of moral insensibility), 'the complexity of tragedy becomes a source of resistance.' 'Complexity as a source of resistance' is no bad summary of MacKinnon's theological project; what he has done is to help us see that the need for resistance, so passionately spoken for by Barker (and a good many more), ultimately looks to a theology that can deploy, publicly and critically, its central, classical doctrinal resources of trinitarian and

---

[49] 'The Second Difference: For a Trinitarianism Without Reserve', *Modern Theology*, 2 (1986), pp. 213–34.
[50] On the question of cost, see 'Lenin and Theology', *Explorations in Theology*, pp. 11–29, among other more fragmentary discussions.

incarnational language in a time of false and would-be painless consciousness. Can we do this? If not, and if MacKinnon is right, there is no point in
pretending to be theologians at all.

Abbreviations

ACS   'Aristotle's Conception of Substance', in Renford Bambrough, ed., *New Essays on Plato and Aristotle* (London, 1965), pp. 97–119

SA   *The Stripping of the Altars* (London, 1969)

SP   'The Problem of the "System of Projection" Appropriate to Christian Theological Statements' (1969), reprinted in *Explorations in Theology* (London, 1979), pp. 70–89

ARH   'Absolute and Relative in History: A Theological Reflection on the Centenary of Lenin's Birth' (1971), reprinted in *Explorations in Theology*, pp. 55–69

SC   ' "Substance" in Christology: A Cross-Bench View', in S. W. Sykes and J. P. Clayton, eds, *Christ, Faith and History: Cambridge Studies in Christology* (Cambridge, 1972), pp. 279–300

PM   *The Problem of Metaphysics* (Cambridge, 1974)

IT   'Some Notes on the Irreversibility of Time' (1975), reprinted in *Explorations in Theology*, pp. 90–8

IR   'Idealism and Realism: An Old Controversy Renewed' (1976), reprinted in *Explorations in Theology*, pp. 138–50

IncT   'The Relation of the Doctrines of the Incarnation and the Trinity', in Richard McKinney, ed., *Creation, Christ and Culture: Studies in Honour of T. F. Torrance* (Edinburgh, 1976), pp. 92–107

RI   'The Conflict between Realism and Idealism' (1977), reprinted in *Explorations in Theology*, pp. 151–65

PC   'Prolegomena to Christology', *Journal of Theological Studies*, 33 (1982), pp. 146–60

Chapter Eleven

TRINITY AND PLURALISM

'The mystery of the Trinity is the ultimate foundation for pluralism.'[1] Raimundo Panikkar's essay on 'The Jordan, the Tiber, and the Ganges' is essentially a study in Trinitarian theology, the kind of Trinitarian theology elaborated in his remarkable book on *The Trinity and the Religious Experience of Man*; as such it represents a quite different variety of religious pluralism from that shown in the rest of the book in which the essay appears. For Panikkar, the Trinitarian structure is that of a source, inexhaustibly generative and *always* generative, from which arises form and determination, 'being' in the sense of what can be concretely perceived and engaged with; that form itself is never exhausted, never limited by this or that specific realization, but is constantly being realized in the flux of active life that equally springs out from the source of all. Between form, 'logos', and life, 'spirit', there is unceasing interaction. The source of all does not and cannot exhaust itself simply in producing shape and structure; it also produces that which dissolves and re-forms all structures in endless and undetermined movement, in such a way that form itself is not absolutized but always turned back towards the primal reality of the source.

This is a very inadequate summary of Panikkar's book, one of the best and least read meditations on the Trinity in our century. It affirms that God, as the foundation of reality as such *and* of history, cannot be thought except in some such terms. There is the God of whom nothing at all can be said except that this is what of its nature *begins* the process of all reality. There is the God who, as foundation of the ordered relations of the world, is the ground of all intelligibility. Between these first and second terms, there is a relation we can only think of metaphorically as comparable to self-knowledge – because

---

[1] Raimundo Panikkar, 'The Jordan, the Tiber, and the Ganges: Three Kairological Moments of Christic Self-Consciousness', in *The Myth of Christian Uniqueness*, ed. J. Hick and P. Knitter (Maryknoll, NY, 1987; London, 1988), pp. 89–116, esp. p. 110.

there is no substantive difference between source and form, they are not two *things*, but two moments *in* one unbroken act.[2] And there is the God who animates a world of change – ordered relations in a kaleidoscopic movement whereby they constantly shift and adjust within the continuing framework of some sort of harmony. God as the context of the world we actually experience requires this structure, and, Panikkar argues, this becomes even more clear if we try to understand the patterns of *religious* experience. If we are to avoid the conclusion that these patterns are simply unconnected, or that they should be reduced to a single form underlying their differences, or that one strand alone is valid or authentic, we need an account of God that grounds them *in* their plurality and so demonstrates their unity in diversity. The Trinity thus appears as a comprehensive model for making sense of human spirituality. Only such a 'pluralist' doctrine of God can allow for the equal validity of finding God as the fundamental and indescribable ground of all, as a partner in personal dialogue, and as the energy of one's own deepest selfhood – and only such a doctrine can present these elements as united with each other, requiring each other to make full human sense.

It is on this basis that Panikkar proceeds in his more recent essay. Particularly important is the relation between the second and third terms of the Trinitarian pattern: 'Being as such . . . does not need to be reduced to consciousness. . . . The Spirit is freedom, the freedom of Being to be what it is. And this is, a priori as it were, unforeseeable by the Logos. The Logos accompanies Being; it does not precede it; it does not predict what Being is. It tells only what Being is. But the *is* of Being is free.[3] Logos, in other words, intelligible structure, is not something containing or surpassing concrete life; the reality of existence is not to be defined as what intelligence can master by grasping structures. Logos is there for the sake of life, not vice versa.[4] And if Logos does not exhaust being, a unified theory of religion is not going to be possible; neither traditional Christian exclusivist *nor* the ordinary variety of liberal pluralism can be defended. The actual lived plurality of religious life may be understood through certain unifying themes or images, but these do not constitute theories of the essence of religion or definitions of some single intelligible form to which all diverse historical religions unknowingly aspire.

---

[2]   Raimundo Panikkar, *The Trinity and the Religious Experience of Man: Icon – Person – Mystery* (London and New York, 1973), pp. 47–8. It is worth comparing this with the discussion of the different roles of Word and Spirit suggested in the theology of Russian Orthodox writer Vladimir Lossky. See Vladimir Lossky, *The Mystical Theology of the Eastern Church* (London, 1957), chs 7 and 8.
[3]   Panikkar, 'The Jordan, the Tiber, and the Ganges', pp. 109–10.
[4]   Ibid., p. 103.

To affirm the plurality of religions in the way Panikkar does is actually the opposite of being a relativist and holding that all religious positions are so conditioned by their context that they are equally valid and equally invalid. That would be to take up a position outside all historical stand points and real traditions, and Panikkar in effect denies that this can be done. He is himself entirely committed to believing certain things about the way reality is – that is, he is committed to an *ontology*. And the heart of this ontology could be summarized by saying that *differences matter*. The variety of the world's forms as experienced by human minds does not conceal an absolute oneness to which perceptible difference is completely irrelevant. If there is a unifying structure, it does not exist and cannot be seen independently of the actual movement and development of differentiation, the story of life-forms growing and changing. In human terms, this is to say that, from the standpoint of history, we cannot articulate in a theory the meaning or pattern of history.

Hence Panikkar's plea for a reflection that is 'concrete and universal' rather than 'particular and general'.[5] Each concrete reality in some sense represents the whole and is indispensable as representing the whole in *this* way, not another; the universal is the entire field of concrete reality insofar as it centres upon a single point that cannot itself be abstracted or represented. In contrast, the kind of thinking represented by 'particular' and 'general' looks on the one hand to *isolated* phenomena and on the other to abstract, reduced structures. Paraphrasing Panikkar, we might say that a concrete reality is a form taken by a universal process of reality or action or energy, a form stable enough to set up that resonance we call recognition and knowledge, a form whose specific character cannot, however, be reduced to a final and closed pattern that we might register and file away, since it is what it is *only* in virtue of the entire, still moving, and therefore unknowable, flow of universal interaction. We cannot plot all the relations in which it stands, and therefore, although we may respond to it accurately or truthfully, we may also be surprised by it and mistaken about it. Thought and thing are moments in one process, but there is a necessary tension between them if we really wish to be truthful; that is, to see each concrete moment embedded in a whole pattern which comes to *this* particular point of complexity *here*.[6] The individual reality or situation is like a single chord abstracted from a symphony: it can be looked at in itself, but only with rather boring results, since what it

---

5   Ibid., p. 107.
6   Compare the vision being set out in the remarkable work of the physicist David Bohm, *Wholeness and the Implicate Order* (London, 1980), esp. ch. 3. This work provides a different kind of theoretical underpinning for the kind of account Panikkar wants to give of a relational universe.

is there and then is determined by the symphony. What it is *is* the symphony at that juncture.

Thus there is no perspective outside plurality, but no legitimacy either in *stopping* with unorganized plurality. In and from our concrete situation we must struggle for understanding, for seeing the movement of which our situation is a moment. This does not mean abandoning our situation, but looking harder at its history, its defining relationships, to see if we may catch a glimpse of a broader picture. Panikkar argues that Christian language and perception – looking from the specifically Christian position – sees the unity of things in terms of 'christic universal vision'[7] or the 'christic fact'.[8] The different phenomena and different perspectives of Christian history all turn around this: Christians may, for various historical reasons, understand their calling as *faith*, commitment to and conversion to what the event of Jesus concretely enacts; or they may see their calling as *belief*, commitment to an institution and its mythical cosmology; or they may be concerned with *confidence* in the general human future as capable of displaying what is shown in Christ, confidence 'that Christianity simply incarnates the primordial and original traditions of humankind'.[9] This third style of Christian understanding, which Panikkar calls Christianness, as opposed to Christianity and Christendom, is what we are bound to work at in our present circumstances, when a particular global awareness has been forced upon us; it does not completely negate the other two dimensions. What it means, though, is that being Christian now is going to be more a matter of living out a distinctive witness to the possibility of human community than of 'preoccupation with self-identity' at the public and corporate level.[10] The Christian does not ask how he or she knows that the Christian religion is exclusively and universally true; he or she simply works on the basis of the 'christic' vision for the human good, engaging with adherents of other traditions without anxiety, defensiveness or proselytism, claiming neither an 'exclusivist' perspective invalidating others nor an 'inclusivist' absorption of other perspectives into his or her own, nor yet a 'pluralist' meta-theory, locating all traditions on a single map and relativizing their concrete life.

Panikkar is clearly an uncomfortable ally for the more familiar 'pluralist' case. He is not interested in the essence of religion as something that might in principle be tracked down and isolated, nor is he content with amiable

---

[7] Panikkar, 'The Jordan, the Tiber, and the Ganges', p. 92.
[8] Ibid., pp. 97–8.
[9] Ibid., p. 102.
[10] Ibid.

mutual toleration. The model he proposes, however, is difficult to grasp, and looks, at first sight, doubtfully consistent. I believe that it does, in fact, possess a real consistency and plausibility, but needs some specific clarifications precisely in the area of its fundamental Trinitarian orientation. And insofar as Panikkar's understanding of the Trinity acts as a check to certain kinds of ambitious theorizing, it has a great deal to say to the enterprise of systematic theology itself.

Panikkar makes it clear, here and elsewhere, that the Christian preoccupation with history is, in his view, a rather ambiguous affair. A Christian theology of history has all too often in recent centuries allied itself with a Western doctrine of linear progress, which has functioned as an enemy of native cultures and world-views in the non-Western world. Indeed, the current American interest in the notion of the 'end of history' – the triumph of consumer capitalism as the ultimate determining force in the fate of national communities – simply reflects the culmination of a particular sort of historical thinking: there is one decisive human story and only one, the story of European and North Atlantic markets. And this is recognizably a secular version of salvation history, the vision of a unifying thread through time, leading to a moment of decisive meaning and real presence. In criticizing a history-dominated religious scheme, Panikkar is criticizing this oppressive model of how the world is, in the name of a 'radical cultural pluralism.

But, granted the need for such an attack, is it still worth raising the historical question in another way? Understanding any religious system ought to entail understanding *how it came to be*, the process of its 'production'. Having some notion of this does not give us a complete and reductive explanation of how the system operates, but it shows us how words acquire their use and import. Panikkar is inclined in all his writing to take for granted the developed structure of Trinitarian theology, without too much direct consideration of how this pattern of speaking about God actually came to be (his treatment of it in *The Trinity and the Religious Experience of Man* is quite heavily marked by Augustinian and scholastic formulations, and sketchy on origins). I want to suggest that an examination of this might actually assist the over-all coherence of Panikkar's argument and might indeed fill out the content of his third category of Christian existence, Christianness, in a way that shows it to be not simply a contradiction of the other two. This involves asking how exactly the relation of Logos and Spirit is spelled out in the *events* of Christian origins.

The language of the first Christian theologians, Paul and John above all, assumes that *Christ* is a word that has come to mark out the shape of the potential future of all human beings, while remaining at the same time the designation of a specific person. The event of Jesus' life, death and resurrection is not (or not only) an external model to be imitated. The important thing about it is that it has created a different sort of human community; professing commitment to Jesus as Lord connects us not only to Jesus but to one another in a new way. This connection is, specifically, a matter of building up one another into the liberty and power appropriate to a child of God, the liberty which was supremely and consistently at work in Jesus. Thus each believer is, *through* the agency of other believers, growing into a 'Christ-shaped future', in the sense that his or her possibilities are defined with reference to Jesus. We may have the same freedom, the same direct intimacy with God, the same commission of healing and restoration. We are to be the tangible presence of Christ in the world – a 'body' that like other bodies is a system of co-operative movement among subsystems. Thus, differences in gift, temperament, and a sense of one's own possibilities are indispensable for the functioning *as one* of the community; the fullness of Christ's presence *is*, in history, the entire ensemble of Christian stories.

This is simply to paraphrase I Corinthians 12. The point for our present purposes is that the social reality of early Christianity – at least as idealized by Paul – was of a wholly collaborative process, aimed at creating 'analogues' of Jesus, persons whose life-patterns might be understood as belonging together because all are related to the style of praying and the sense of a mission of restoration and re-creation for God's people associated with the story of Jesus. The climax of that story – the 'covenant sacrifice' of the cross and the reconstitution by the resurrection of the disciples' fellowship – serves as the ground for the existence of a new people of the covenant (a people existing because of God's promise to be their ally), a new unit in which the process of the shared creation of free persons, adult children of God, could go forward. The creative act of God in all this can only be articulated in terms of two quite irreducible moments: the establishing in the life of Jesus of a unifying point of reference, and the necessarily unfinished ensemble of human stories drawn together and given shape in relation to Jesus. This means that the actual concrete meaning of logos in the world, the pattern decisively and transformingly embodied in Jesus, could only be seen and realized through the entire process of the history to which the event of Jesus gives rise, with all its fluidity and unpredictability. To speak in this context of history as theologically important is precisely *not* to think of a unitary movement in history that can be reduced to a conceptual scheme.

So the relation between Jesus and Christian believers is the basis on which there comes to be built up a particular vision of God's nature and action.

There is the single authoritative form of human flourishing, liberty before God and full response to God, the Logos made flesh in Jesus; we speak of Jesus' existence as a divine act from first to last because it is recognized as having a potential for bringing together the whole of the world we know in a new unity and intelligibility. This potential is realized in a way that is always historically incomplete – so that the unity and intelligibility can never be seized as a single object to a single mind. It can only be hoped and worked for, as lives are touched and changed, moving into the likeness of Jesus' freedom before God, and that movement of manifold change, the endless variety of imitations of Christ, is where we recognize the divine action as *Spirit* – the same divine action as establishes the form of the incarnate Logos, but working now to realize that form in a diversity as wide as the diversity of the human race itself. Thus, in theological terms, human history is the story of the discovery or realization of Jesus Christ in the faces of all women and men. The fullness of Christ is always *to be* discovered, never there already in a conceptual pattern that explains and predicts everything; it is the fullness of *Christ* that is to be discovered, a unity that holds together around this one story.[11]

This is, I think, what Panikkar implicitly assumes in his distinction between Logos and Spirit. The conviction that 'Being . . . does not need to be reduced to consciousness' can be less abstractly expressed in speaking of the endless, unpredictable imitation of Jesus of Nazareth in the stories of human beings. It is part of Panikkar's considerable genius to take the twofold Logos–Spirit pattern thus established and to see it as a legitimation for the creative interaction between traditions of faith for which he wants to allow. My point so far has simply been to note that this Logos–Spirit relation takes shape in a particular historical process and social practice; without this reference to the importance of the material and temporal differences among persons, and the historically distinct focus of the events of Jesus' story, the unity–plurality balance so crucial to Panikkar would be in danger of collapse. We might have a plurality that existed only on the surface of things, a set of arbitrary and intrinsically insignificant variations on a single theme that could be perfectly well stated without any of them. We might, on the other hand, have a unity that was purely theoretical, existing only at the level of the synthesizing consciousness. With regard to the inter-faith encounter, as Panikkar understands it, we might have either an imperialistic Christian claim to *theoretical* finality, providing an unchallengeable set of explanations, locat-

---

[11]   Compare R. Williams, 'The Unity of Christian Truth', *New Blackfriars*, vol. 70, no. 824 (1989), pp. 85–95 [ch. 2 above].

ing every phenomenon on a single map, or else a merely tolerant pluralism, with different traditions drifting in and out of co-operation on the basis of a vague conviction that all were, more or less, about the same thing. Panikkar's ideal of a genuinely interactive pluralism is the product of a particular option concerning God, which rules out these alternatives.

The goal of any specific moment of inter-faith encounter is thus – presumably – to find a way of working together towards a mode of human co-operation, mutual challenge and mutual nurture, which does not involve the triumph of one theory or one institution or one culture, but which is in some way unified by relation to that form of human liberty and maturity before God made concrete in Jesus. To put it slightly differently, and perhaps more traditionally, the Christian goal in engaging with other traditions is the formation of children of God after the likeness of Christ. For Panikkar, this formation may already be under way in other traditions; if we ask what then is the point of specifically Christian witness, the answer might well be that explicit Christianness, to use Panikkar's favoured term, is a catalyst for drawing together these processes of formation in a way that is self-aware, critical, and actively concerned about sustaining common human action. Witness to the 'christic fact' as an integrating reality proposes to the world of faiths the possibility of a kind of critical human norm that can be used in the struggle against what limits or crushes humanity.

This is to put words into Panikkar's mouth. But I think it is a necessary development of his insights. Panikkar's pluralism is not limitless. (Is there any pluralism that is?) It involves resistance to the homogenization of human beings – *cultural* resistance, in other words, and *political* resistance, to the forces in our world that make for the reduction of persons and personal communities to units in large-scale, determined processes, resistance to the power of the universal market or the omnipotent state.[12] Such resistance is, as we have seen, grounded for the Christian in a vision of the necessary and irreducible reciprocity between Logos and Spirit, and thus grounded in a model of the relation between Christ and his Body. Because of this *specific* ground, learned in this particular social and historical way, the Christian will naturally argue that this brings to light what is otherwise not recognized or 'thematized' in other contexts (that is, not named and explored in its own right, not articulated as a goal). The Christian face to face with other traditions thus comes with queries as well as affirmations, queries shaped by the

---

[12]   The alliance between the interests of market and state is a question discussed by political 'pluralists'; see especially Paul Hirst, 'Associational Socialism in a Pluralist State', *Journal of Law and Society*, vol. 15, no. 1 (1988), pp. 139–50, esp. 140–1.

conviction that the stature of the fullness of Christ is what defines the most comprehensive future for humankind; shaped too by the form of its basic story, which is about the conflict between God and a particular kind of corrupt politicization of faith by the religiously powerful.[13] The Christian Church ought to carry in its language and practice a deep suspicion of the alliances between hierarchies in faith-communities and hierarchies in absolutist political administrations — Caiaphas and Pilate, and their many more recent analogues. It hardly needs saying that the Church is monumentally forgetful of this; yet in continuing to celebrate the resurrection of a condemned man — not something that figures all that largely in Panikkar's account[14] — it preserves at least some clear ground on which this suspicion may continue to take root.

So it may be true to say, as does Panikkar,[15] that the contemporary Christianness, which has moved beyond both Christendom and Christianity, is more at home with the discovery that Christianity's supposedly specific doctrines 'are humanity's common good and that Christianity simply incarnates the primordial and original traditions of humankind'; but if this is to be more than a sentimental appeal to natural religion beyond the constraints and corruptions of human tradition, it must involve the capacity to challenge current versions, secular and religious, of 'humanity's common good' in the name of its own central and *historically* distinctive Trinitarian insight. To emphasize historicality here is only to note that, even if the Trinitarian schema can be shown to cope with and to ground the most pervasive concerns of human spirituality, it takes its concrete meaning from a particular process of learning in community. The *Christian* goal in interfaith encounter is to invite the world of faiths to find here, in the narrative and practice of Jesus and his community, that which anchors and connects their human hopefulness — not necessarily in the form of 'fulfilling their aspirations' or 'perfecting their highest ideals', but as something which might unify a whole diverse range of struggles for human integrity without denying or 'colonizing' their own history and expression. This is not all that easy to express theoretically, though the work of other writers with Indian and Sri Lankan connections has given a good deal of focus to how the process advances practically. The late Bishop Laksham Wickremesinghe, in an essay

---

[13]   Recent New Testament scholarship has frequently emphasized the significance in this connection of Jesus' conflict with the Temple authorities in Jerusalem as representing the fusion of oppressive religious, political and economic power.

[14]   See, for instance, the rather sketchy treatment of the reasons for Jesus' death in Panikkar, *The Trinity and the Religious Experience of Man*, p. 20.

[15]   Panikkar, 'The Jordan, the Tiber, and the Ganges', p. 102.

written in 1977,[16] wrote of a 'Christ-centered reciprocity with other religionists', in which the Christian tradition acts as an interpretative catalyst, drawing out or underscoring what it is in other traditions that is analogous to its own goal of common work for the kingdom in the Body of Christ.

This means, of course, that a Buddhist engaged with other religious traditions would have comparable goals: he or she would want to propose a model of unity and co-operation centred upon the Eightfold Path and would search for points of analogy in the language of partners in dialogue. Panikkar's pluralism entails that there can be no single goal for *the* inter-faith dialogue. As soon as you begin to give expression to any such ideal, you are stepping outside the perspective of an actual *participant* in dialogue, who has, as such, a specific point of view. If Panikkar is right, those involved in dialogue will have the goals appropriate to their own traditions as a starting-point. More than that, it will be some aspect of their own traditions that both validates the notion of dialogue or co-operation itself and determines the direction in which they wish it to go. Inter-faith dialogue is not a discussion about how best to reach a target that is independently defined, nor is it about collaborating in a self-evidently good and constructive activity. Certainly the process of engagement will change the participants: Christian and Buddhist alike will learn something of their own heritage that would otherwise be obscure by seeing it as analogous to an initially 'alien' theme. It may be possible to learn about the characteristic pathologies of religious language and practice also in such an encounter, and so to return to our native tradition with freshly critical eyes.

But, supposing one partner in the conversation decides that his or her particular starting-point is essentially a symbolic variant on the other partner's position, or that both are variants of something more fundamental, the character of the encounter would have changed, and one's reasons for carrying on with it would be quite radically different. They would no longer be grounded in whatever feature of the native tradition had initially stimulated the engagement, whatever feature had given justification for the hope that a stranger's commitments might turn out to be familiar after all. In Panikkar's terms, the dialogue would no longer rest on the conviction that reality itself was grounded in an absolute source acting both as Logos and as Spirit; it would cease, that is, to be pluralist in the sense Panikkar wants to give to that word, and, by abstracting to some underlying structure separable from the

---

[16] Laksham Wickremesinghe, 'Christianity in a Context of Other Faiths', in *Today's Church and Today's World* (preparatory articles for the 1978 Lambeth Conference) (London, 1977), pp. 79–87, esp. pp. 82–4.

historical particularity, the imagery and practices of *this* social group, it runs the risk of precisely the intellectualism Panikkar wants at all costs to avoid.

If Panikkar is right in seeing Trinitarian Christianity as the proper foundation for an inter-religious engagement that is neither vacuous nor imperialist, the doctrines of Christian credal orthodoxy are not, as is regularly supposed, insuperable obstacles to dialogue; the incarnation of the Logos is not the ultimate assertion of privilege and exclusivity, but the centre of that network of relations (implicit and explicit) in which a new humanity is to be created. This network has its symbolic form in the Christian Church, but its life is not identical with the institutional reality of the Church. In Rahner's words, 'Christianity as such demands no *particular concrete* future'[17] – though this is an unhappily ambiguous formulation. Christianity as such imposes no single institutional project or future in its engagement with other traditions, but its concrete future must be conceived in terms of Christlike humanity, humanity delivered from a slavish submission to an alien divine power and participating in the creative work of God. It engages in dialogue and encounter to discover itself more truthfully, to put to other traditions the question that arises from its own foundational story, and to propose a focus for common human hope and action. Beyond that, on Panikkar's account, we cannot go. We do not, as Christians, set the goal of including the entire human race in a single religious institution, nor do we claim that we possess all authentic religious insight – the 'totality of meaning', to pick up a phrase used to good polemical effect by Jacques Pohier.[18] And this is a problem only if we *expect* – as Christians, as religious people of other traditions, as philosophers – to be able to provide a theoretical programme and explanations for the unifying of the human world. If there is such a unification possible – as Christians and others believe – it is attained only in the variety and unpredictability of specific human encounter, and so can only now be a matter of hope; though this is hope nourished by the conviction that the story of Jesus and the Church, of Logos and Spirit manifest in the world, affords us a truthful vision of how God is – not exhaustive, not exclusive, but truthful. And the practical thrust of this truthfulness is its grounding of a hopeful and creative pluralism, its affirmation of the irreducible importance of history, of human difference and human converse.

Panikkar's stance is paradoxical, at first sight. It involves a clear commitment to a distinctive vision of what unifies reality, and a clear option about the

---

[17] Quoted by Gavin D'Costa, 'Karl Rahner's Anonymous Christian – a Reappraisal', *Modern Theology*, vol. 1, no. 2 (1985), pp. 131–48, esp. p. 145.
[18] See Jacques Pohier, *God: In Fragments* (London, 1985).

nature of God; but the more deeply we enter into that vision, the more we are able to see it as the ground for a non-exclusive dialogue with other visions. Panikkar goes a long way to establishing his claim that he offers something other than either classical 'inclusivism' or conventional liberal pluralism, and I believe that he, almost alone among the authors of *The Myth of Christian Uniqueness*, provides guidelines for an authentic *theology* of inter-religious engagement. The two reservations I should want to enter have to do with the need to keep in view the specific process of discovery whereby the Trinitarian, Logos–Spirit pattern is brought to light, and with the *critical* responsibility of Christian witness (even in the unstructured form of 'Christianness') towards the traditions it encounters. I take for granted that such a critical responsibility should be mutual in any authentic dialogue. And the paradoxical nature of this approach may be more apparent than real. If the object of dialogue is the discovery of how the Christian can intelligibly and constructively unite with the Buddhist or Muslim in the construction of the community of God's children, rather than arriving at an agreed statement, a religious meta-theory, or (worst of all) a single institution with a single administrative hierarchy, there is no contradiction in a 'Trinitarian pluralism'.

And it is perhaps here that Panikkar makes his most substantial contribution to the Christian enterprise itself. Trinitarian theology becomes not so much an attempt to say the last word about the divine nature as a prohibition against would-be final accounts of divine nature and action. To the extent that the relation of Spirit to Logos is still being realized in our history, we cannot ever, while history lasts, say precisely all that is to be said about Logos. What we know, if we claim to be Christians, is as much as anything a set of negations. We know that the divine is not simply a pervasive source and ground, incapable of being imaged, but we know that the historical form of Jesus, in which we see creation turning on its pivot, does not exhaust the divine. We know that the unification of all things through Christ is not a matter of a single explanatory scheme being manifested to us, but of the variousness of human lives being drawn into creative and saving relation to the divine and to each other. We know that the divine is not simply the promptings of 'interiority', religious sensibility, in us, but is called to account by the critical memory and presence of Jesus' human identity. At each point, we are urged *away* from what looks like a straightforward positive affirmation standing alone.

This is very finely expressed by Nicholas Lash in his suggestion that Trinitarian doctrine is the grammar, the structure, of the Christian 'school of discipleship'.[19] It instructs about how God is to be known. God can be

---

[19]   Nicholas Lash, 'Considering the Trinity', *Modern Theology*, vol. 2, no. 3 (1986), pp. 183–96.

encountered as sheer creativity, the generative power in things, but this perception must be tested and in a sense denied by the awareness of waste,
cruelty or disorder in the immediate context of the universe. However, that
denial is itself brought into question by the creative newness of Christ, the
Word spoken from the middle of cruelty and disorder to call together a
community living in shared hope. Here again, though, there is a testing
to be faced: we can fix our attention on the achieved form of Christ as
something essentially in the past and conceive our faith-commitment primarily as loyalty to this past. We must be taught to find God in the present
tension between tradition and unforeseen possibilities. Thus the doctrine of
the Trinity provides 'a pattern of self-correction for each of the three prin-
cipal modes of our propensity to *freeze* the form of relation into an object or
possessed description of the nature of God'.[20] What is more, this endlessly
self-corrective movement is most readily compatible with a view of the
Christian mission as 'making a difference'[21] – providing a parable of how
human history might be lived in opposition to what seem to be the powerful
and successful trends in the world's story, so that power and success are
never allowed to go without challenge. The Trinitarian insight is, at the very
least, part of what prevents Christian witness finally and irrevocably turning
into the mirror image of the monolithic empires of 'the world'. Christianity
has often been totalitarian or near-totalitarian in its history, but has not ever
settled down for good and all in such a pattern; in spite of all, there remains
an obstinately mobile and questioning force within its fundamental language.

Lash and Panikkar both suggest that commitment to the Trinitarian creed
(and, I should want to add, an understanding of how that creed came to be
affirmed) is a precondition for doing what Christians should do, making the
contribution they alone can make to the world of faiths and the world in
general. Being Christian is being involved in witness to and work for a comprehensive human community because of what has happened to specific
human beings and their relationships in connection with the ministry, cross
and resurrection of Jesus – those happenings which have been held to force
upon us the reconstructed vision of God as source and Logos and Spirit (*icon,
person* and *mystery*, in the terms Panikkar employs in *The Trinity and the
Religious Experience of Man*). Being Christian, if it means acting for these goals
and for these reasons, is believing the doctrine of the Trinity to be true, and
true in a way that converts and heals the human world. It is not to claim a

---

[20] Nicholas Lash, *Easter in Ordinary: Reflections on Human Experience and the Knowledge of God*
(Charlottesville, VA: University of Virginia Press; London, 1988), p. 271.
[21] Ibid., p. 284.

totality of truth about God or about the human world, or even a monopoly of the means of bringing divine absolution or grace to men and women. The Christian says, 'Our religious history shows us that God is *thus*: a God who can only be known and witnessed comprehensively in a human form of life in which Logos and Spirit are held in balance with each other. This is the form of human being for which we work, and of which the Church is the sign and focus. What it *will* finally be is not something theory will tell us, but something only discoverable in the expanding circles of encounter with what is not the Church.' This not only enables but impels dialogue, and, more significantly, practical work together; it also recognizes the inescapability of conflict, even judgement, when there are different perceptions of the nature of human unity at work. In Britain we saw such conflicts emerging over the Salman Rushdie affair in the late 1980s, an episode that has obliged many Christians *and* secularists to think a good deal harder about the *positive* foundations, and the limits, of pluralism in society. Panikkar's Trinitarian concern and his focus on Christianness as the most significant category in the present context allow for a fully self-critical account of witness and even mission, and for a proper priority to be given to 'redeemed sociality' as the heart of this (even though his own account of Christianness is not by any means free of the risk of a 'privatization of Christian identity',[22] and needs, I believe, a much sharper critique than he offers of the privileged status of 'inner experience'). In showing how a certain kind of practical pluralism can be unconditionally faithful to the gospel, and in warning us away from the lust for religious Grand Theory, Panikkar does an exceptional service to authentic engagement between traditions *in* their particularity, in a way not to be found among programmatic relativists.

---

[22] Panikkar, 'The Jordan, the Tiber, and the Ganges', p. 107. The expression 'redeemed sociality' I owe to Daniel W. Hardy, 'Created and Redeemed Sociality', in *On Being the Church: Essays on the Christian Community*, ed. Daniel W. Hardy and Colin F. Gunton (Edinburgh, 1989), pp. 21–47.

Part Four

MAKING SIGNS

Chapter Twelve

BETWEEN THE CHERUBIM: THE EMPTY TOMB AND THE EMPTY THRONE

This paper is a meditation on images, their connections and their failures. Arguing *from* iconography or patterns of imagery is always dangerous. We can't expect to establish anything very definite from simply noticing convergences in this sort of area, and I am not setting out to *prove* anything in this essay. But convergences can at least suggest paths in to a subject that arguments cannot, and, in an area where arguments – historical, philosophical, dogmatic – can be inconclusive or bitter or both, there is something to be said for coming at the issue another way.

Of course this risks being evasive or self-indulgent. I take it that this is the complaint of Professor Maurice Wiles, when he describes an earlier venture by the present writer as possibly 'shirking' confrontation with the questions of historical evidence or conceptual coherence.[1] I hope this need not be the case. As far as the historical question goes, it is clear that the scholarly analysis of the resurrection narratives, in and out of the canon, has not yielded a single and compelling resolution to the numerous difficulties that the texts pose.

To take two recent examples, the estimates of the historicity of the traditions of Jesus' burial by Crossan[2] and Lüdemann[3] are dramatically at vari-

---

[1] Maurice Wiles, 'A Naked Pillar of Rock', in *Resurrection. Essays in Honour of Leslie Houlden*, eds Stephen Barton and Graham Stanton (London: SPCK, 1994), pp. 116–27, particularly pp. 122–3.

[2] John Dominic Crossan, *The Historical Jesus. The Life of a Mediterranean Jewish Peasant* (Edinburgh: T. & T. Clark, 1991), particularly pp. 391–4 and ch. 15 *passim*.

[3] Gerd Lüdemann, *The Resurrection of Jesus. History, Experience, Theology* (London: SCM, 1994), pp. 44–5.

ance: Lüdemann allowing a definite historical substratum to the record of a burial by Joseph of Arimathea; Crossan dismissing the entire tradition on the assumption of anonymous burial in a common grave. Likewise, the two disagree strongly over how the tradition of the women at the tomb is to be assessed – a politically sensitive question these days. Lüdemann regards the women as latecomers to the resurrection proclamation, Crossan seeing the Magdalene tradition as competing on a fairly even footing with other stories, and, like them, functioning as ammunition in a set of struggles for authority in the primitive communities. Elisabeth Schüssler Fiorenza, in her recent essay in feminist Christology,[4] would go further in maintaining that the empty tomb tradition, that is, the tradition of a primitive resurrection proclamation by women, may be more primitive than the apparition stories, which are clearly designed to 'authorize' the male leaders of the community. Those familiar with film and fiction will recognize the dramatically effective use to which something like this last view can be put if they recall the reconstruction of the resurrection in *Jesus of Montreal*, and the account of Mary Magdalene's experience in Anita Mason's exceptional novel, *The Illusionist*.[5]

Nor have we yet a clear consensus about the actual genre of (at least) the canonical resurrection narratives. The attempt to find parallels in the Hellenistic novel seems to have been abandoned; reference to *Chaereas and Callirhoë*, with its striking episode of the unexpected discovery of an empty tomb, seems less interesting when we know (what some who have discussed the parallels seem not to know) that the work is from the second Christian century.[6] Alsup's suggestion that we look to stories of angelic manifestation in the Old Testament for analogues is a good and, I think, sound one. But, while it helps provide a rhetorical and narrative hinterland for the recognition stories (Luke 24, John 20 in particular), it does not take us very far with the origins of the tomb tradition itself.[7]

---

[4] Elisabeth Schüssler Fiorenza, *Jesus: Miriam's Child, Sophia's Prophet. Critical Issues in Feminist Christology* (London: SCM, 1995), pp. 119–28; see below for some further discussion of this proposal.

[5] London: Abacus, 1983, pp. 143–5.

[6] The allusion is made by E. Schillebeeckx, *Jesus. An Experiment in Christology* (London: Collins, 1979), p. 341, in the context of a discussion of alleged genres of 'rapture' stories involving the absence of a corpse. The whole account of such a supposed genre or family of genres is badly flawed, and the text of Chariton's novel has nothing at all to do with 'rapture' (the episode is about grave-robbery). Unfortunately, Pheme Perkins repeats the reference in her generally admirable and comprehensive *Resurrection. New Testament Witness and Contemporary Reflection* (London: Geoffrey Chapman, 1984), p. 150.

[7] J. E. Alsup, *The Post-Resurrection Appearance Stories of the Gospel Tradition. A History-of-Tradition Analysis* (London: SPCK, 1975).

Now, given this situation in the scholarly world, we have a number of options. It is possible, of course, to decide that one or other reconstruction on the market is the correct one – this is the historian's privilege, and the historian knows that such a decision is vulnerable – as vulnerable in this case as, for example (to turn to a field where I have a little more competence), the decision that the two letters of Bishop Alexander of Alexandria about the beginnings of the Arian crisis in the early fourth century have been put in the wrong order by most twentieth-century scholars (I think they have, but I have not managed to convince the majority of experts in the period . . .). Here one takes a position, knowing that it is contestable, willing to provide a reasonable amount of back-up, but acknowledging that judgements will simply vary. This is fine for the historian; and for someone who has no particular investment in the resurrection narratives, the option for Lüdemann or Crossan (say) as regards Joseph of Arimathea need not be more charged than my options about the correspondence of Bishop Alexander. But, of course, these narratives have a life of their own outside the study – in liturgy, piety and, indeed, theological construction.

Quite a lot of readers will not want to leave the matter where the historian would. So we could say that the need is to work at the historical material until it becomes clear that there is only one historical judgement that could sensibly or responsibly be made: thus the resurrection becomes a matter of accessible *public* truth, something anyone could in principle know, even if some were just obstinate in refusing to see what was under their noses. Pannenberg's is the name most often associated with this,[8] though in a less sophisticated form it remains the staple of a lot of apologetic writing on the subject by Christians. This strategy has at least two risks, though. By assuming a historical conclusion, it will always be suspect on purely methodological grounds to the uncommitted student: there *must* be a question about the method of a scholar who really does know what she is looking for, who really does know what is to be proved (at all costs); and the identification of belief in the resurrection with acceptance of a set of demonstrable historical facts raises the difficult issue of how 'the resurrection' is being defined. Notoriously, the demonstration of the emptiness of the tomb as a matter of history does not entail the veracity of subsequent visions, missionary commissions, or whatever.

It is possible simply to leave the historical questions unresolved and to settle for a proclamation of the resurrection that regards them as essentially

---

[8] Classically laid out in W. Pannenberg, *Jesus – God and Man* (London: SCM, 1968), particularly pp. 98–106.

irrelevant. In some sense or other, the work of Jesus is not concluded; the crucified is announced and identified as the risen one, 'risen into the *kerygma*', in the memorable phrase that summarized Bultmann's approach to this.[9] But even here, in what seems to be a bold and clear resolution to the problems of understanding and responding to the scriptural texts, we cannot avoid noticing that there is an implicit option buried in the overt one: if the tomb was empty, there is no substantive theological conclusion to be drawn from that. Whatever we find to say about the resurrection, it will not include anything that depends on the non-availability of Jesus' corpse. This option is not, therefore, quite as agnostic as it looks. It will effectively be claiming that what is vital to Christian discourse about the resurrection can be stated exclusively in terms of what happens to the minds and hearts of believers when proclamation is made that the victim of the crucifixion is the one through whom God continues to act and speak. And, while this is near the centre of what we must say theologically about the resurrection, it leaves us with the conclusion that the narrative form of the New Testament proclamation is pretty incidental to the substance of the proclamation itself. There may be theological as well as literary-theoretical queries worth raising here, if that is indeed what is being suggested.

So I return to the starting-point of this reflection. Is there anything in the structure, the patterning of the stories, which might bring us in to the substance of resurrection belief by a different route? My title indicates one such possibility. The angels at the tomb in John's gospel are seated one at the head and the other at the feet of the grave slab. As commentators like Barrett have noted, this is a distinctive addition to the picture given in the other gospels, and, as with other deliberate Johannine narrative expansions, we can reasonably ask what it is doing here.[10] Iconographically, it recalls, of course, the mercy-seat of the ark, flanked by the cherubim.[11] What I want to propose is that – whether or not this is what John had in mind, which would be practically impossible to settle one way or the other – this at least focuses for us the possibility of seeing the empty tomb narratives as saying something about the character of divine presence or action that badly needs saying if we are not to mistake the whole direction of the gospel witness to the resurrection.

[9]   For a fine summary of Bultmann's perspective, see Gareth Jones, *Bultmann. Towards a Critical Theology* (Cambridge: Polity Press/Blackwell, 1991), pp. 51–62.
[10]   C. K. Barrett, *The Gospel According to St John* (London: SPCK, 1956), p. 469.
[11]   This is noted by Westcott, *The Gospel According to St John* (London: John Murray, 1882), p. 291, but is not discussed by most more recent exegetes.

For the cherubim flanking the ark define a space where God would be if God were anywhere (the God of Judah is *the one who* sits between the cherubim or even 'dwells' between the cherubim); but there is no image between the cherubim. If you want to see the God of Judah, this is where he is and is not: to 'see' him is to look into the gap between the holy images. What is tangible and accessible, what can be carried in procession or taken to war as a palladium is not the image of God but the throne of God, the place where he is not. Whatever the historical origins of the iconography of the ark of the covenant, by the time of the composition of our canonical texts it is clear that YHWH is not capable of being represented definitively or indeed at all except as the one who is invisibly enthroned on the *kapporeth* of the ark. And if John does mean us to catch an allusion here, we must suppose that it is to this non-representable, non-possessible dimension of the paradoxical manifestation of God to God's people; it may even connect with the stories of non-recognition which John and his editor or continuator in the final chapter of the gospel as we have it clearly find so fertile a ground for narrative meditation. But whatever was in the evangelist's mind, the space between the angels is no bad metaphor for a number of features of the tomb tradition that should concentrate our minds theologically.

If we read the resurrection narratives as having to do with the Jewish proscription of idolatry, in a new and distinctive key, not only the empty tomb tradition, but the very confusion and historical uncertainty surrounding it may be of theological import, insofar as both the narrative and the nest of critical questions around it make *closure* so difficult. The stories themselves are about difficulty, unexpected outcomes, silences, errors, about what is not readily accessible or readily understood. We have a variety of stories, not easily reconcilable as regards location or timing or *dramatis personae*, stories which, while they appear to presuppose a background of prophetic anticipation are in fact about laborious recognition, as often as not, the gradual convergence of experience and pre-existing language in a way that inexorably changes the register of the language. In short, it is not a straightforward matter to say what the gospels understand by the resurrection of Jesus; but this seems to have something to do with the fact that the Christian communities of the last quarter of the first Christian century didn't find it all that straightforward either.

The stories as we have them are, as we might now say, ideologically under-determined; we cannot display the ways in which they are controlled by specific theological interests, though we can, as already indicated, identify with reasonable clarity some of the interests at work (there is no point in disputing the manifest truth that the stories in the gospels and in I Corinthians reflect struggles for authoritative status in the communities). The texts are *shaped* by such concerns; but we cannot decisively show how the narrative genre of the tomb tradition in particular is fully *determined* by the political agenda, or even how all the narrative particulars in the various vision stories (particularly the motif of non-recognition) can be anchored in these interests.

This indeterminacy in the resurrection stories is one way of saying what the content of the stories is meant to convey: that Jesus of Nazareth who was crucified is not confined in the past, and that this non-confinement is more than just some sort of survival in the minds or memories of Christian believers. Belief in the resurrection, in Christian scripture and Christian theology, affirms that the action of God in and through the acts of the human subject Jesus continues to be associated with Jesus after his death and to be accessible through his human identity.

What exactly this means is immensely complex, once we start trying to spell it out. It means at least that in the community stemming from that first community of the friends of Jesus, those who had received his announcement of the Kingdom that was available to outcasts and sinners, God continues to do what was done in Jesus' ministry, that is, to re-form a people whose corporate calling was to show the world at large what was the scope and resource of divine love. Yet to say only that would leave us with the risk of identifying the actions of God with the acts of the community, which becomes a dangerous and potentially nonsensical and blasphemous claim when the community's history and administration is so manifestly vulnerable to distortion and betrayal.

Once again, the resurrection narratives themselves insist that the risen Jesus is not grasped, owned or perfectly obeyed by his friends. The Church continues to *attend* to Jesus to discover what it is to be; and it is this attention that constitutes the heart of the oddity and difficulty of resurrection belief. It is not meditation on the teaching of the founder – this can be of much significance, but it hardly exhausts what Christian scripture means by relation with the living Jesus, and it was clearly of variable significance in the early communities, given the uneven state of recollections of Jesus' teaching and the evident freedom taken for granted by the evangelists in re-ordering or re-working the traditions of Jesus' words. It is not reflection on the inspiring example of a hero; of course, it is common to appeal to the example of Jesus as innocent and non-retaliating victim, but this is not the same as the appeal to a continuing and determinative presence that qualifies the believer's relation to God in certain focal respects. And, although visionary encounter with the glorified Lord had a very important role in the life of the early communities, notably and visibly in something like the Johannine Apocalypse as a guarantee of the authority of the teacher, it is clear that this is debatable territory. It should not be identified as the common ground that might hold together communities as diverse as those addressed by Paul and John.

Jesus is 'in heaven' until the last days; that is one way of putting it. In his earthly life he initiates a re-drawing of the boundaries of God's people in such a way that response to his invitation becomes decisive for the relation of persons to God. Response to him remains decisive in just this way (even if, as in Matthew 25, people do not know that it is he to whom they are responding); so that, at the end of time, what is uncovered is the history of the world as a history of response to or rejection of what Jesus offers. He remains 'there' as the point of reference, God's standard of judgement.

Jesus is active as bestower of the 'spirit' that enables us to relate to God as he did; he is the cause of the fact that we can pray as we do (as he did). But he is not the cause of this in the sense of an increasingly remote historical origin; we do not simply continue his practice. Attention to or openness to his presence (faith?) makes possible the receiving of new kinds of prayer and awareness of, or confidence in, God as a *gift*.

Jesus is active in the corporate life of the Church; what he gives to human beings, he gives in significant part through the mediation of the common life, which is itself his 'body', his material presence in the world, though it does not exhaust his identity or activity. To be incorporated into the community by its initiation rite is to become a 'bearer' of what Jesus has to give to other believers, to be entrusted with his renewing or creating agency by means of a ritual setting-aside of 'ordinary' identity. What is distinctive is that this ritual change of identity is not confined to the ritual context, but continues in the practical interactions of the common life. And the further ritual of the 'Lord's Supper' dramatizes all this; the concrete food and drink of the meal is interpreted as the material presence of Jesus, and the conduct, the 'style', of the meal, so Paul argues, is supposed to display the character of the community as itself the body, the material thereness, of Jesus (and when it fails to do this, the community comes under severe, even annihilating, judgement).

We could go on, summarizing and synthesizing the ways in which Christian scripture evokes the idea of continuing personal presence on the part of Jesus. The claim is certainly not that Jesus survived death, or even that he *will* survive indefinitely; it is that he continues to give shape and definition to the act of God initiated in the history of Israel and in his ministry. He is, so to speak, 'held' in the divine action, his identity and human priorities as proclaimer of a Kingdom for the hopeless and impure and materially or morally destitute becoming the channel for God's work of reconciliation. What God did in the ministry is what God still is doing. The medieval image of God the Father holding in his arms the cross on which Jesus hangs, displaying him to the onlooker, captures something of this. God's act continues to 'display' Jesus as the form of the divine agency in the renewal of God's people and the universalizing of their calling. We could perhaps express this by saying that the continuity of Jesus' identity as 'other' rests on the action of God, not on the minds of human beings. That Jesus is alive is not a function of the excellent human memory of the Christian community, its profound closeness to the God of Jesus or its vivid evocation of a deceased founder.

The belief that Jesus is alive in any of the senses outlined above amounts to claiming that his 'story' is not over; the narrative of what Jesus did is not a completed thing, as the author of the Fourth Gospel characteristically reminds us in saying that the whole world could not contain the full record of the acts of Jesus. Thus, controversy in the earliest Church is not, typically, about the 'ownership' and the correct transmission and interpretation of a foundational narrative and set of teachings, but about access to the 'spirit' of Jesus — a far more annoyingly nebulous and irresoluble kind of conflict, as Christian history amply shows — which is no doubt why debates over the sacred text do emerge by the third and fourth Christian centuries as the central form of theological debate.

There is, it seems, an unavoidable untidiness in Christian talk about authority and authorization, in that the foundational texts display a haziness of focus as to the priority of any one claimant among the witnesses of the risen Jesus, and, even more strikingly, what some scholars have seen as a quite deliberate polemic against such claims, in the shape of the original ending of Mark's gospel. This, it is argued, is not to be read as an apologetic explanation of why the empty tomb story did not circulate sooner, but as a conscious splitting-off of the reality of the resurrection from the competing claims of visionaries (whose diverse chronologies are reflected in the awkward juxtaposition in I Corinthians 15 of what look like rival accounts privileging Cephas and James respectively). What belief in the resurrection affirms is something other than the authority of witnesses. The risen Jesus is not, for Mark, available for work in the negotiating of the Church's business, and the empty tomb (combined, of course, with Mark's radical scepticism about the wisdom or insight of the Twelve) serves to keep empty the seat of ultimate authority in the Church. In the terms of my governing metaphor, the empty tomb is precisely an empty throne or *cathedra*.

Elisabeth Schüssler Fiorenza's recent treatment of the question offers a similar reading, though it works with a rather undialectical opposition of absence and presence in the stories, and slips rapidly into what might be an over-reductive identification of the Risen One with those involved in the struggle for justice.[12] She argues that, while it is difficult, perhaps impossible, to settle as a matter of historical certainty or even probability whether the story of the women at the tomb or the predominantly male tradition of apparitions came first, it is theologically enlightening to look at the whole question of the significance of the resurrection through a 'privileged' reading of the tomb tradition. This narrative affirms that death, pain and injustice are where God is *not*, at least not in the sense that the experience of these things automatically carries divine meanings (Schüssler Fiorenza here pursues her consistent critique of what she sees as the Christian sacralizing of pain and passivity). It also honours the 'honouring' of the victims of oppression on the part of the faithful women at the cross and the grave; and, above all, it announces that the Risen One is 'going before' into Galilee, into the place where the practice of the new order of God's *basileia* has been initiated.

> The empty tomb does not signify absence but presence: it announces the Resurrected One's presence on the road ahead, in a particular space of struggle and recognition such as Galilee. The Resurrected One is present in the 'little ones', in the struggles for survival of those impoverished, hungry, imprisoned, tortured and killed, in the wretched of the earth . . . Jesus is going ahead – not going away.[13]

The contrast is between a Risen One who is present both in the suffering and in those working against injustice for the sake of the Kingdom, and a Risen Lord who has removed himself to heaven, where he may be 'seen' by the privileged and the spiritually gifted. In the latter context, the concrete outrage of crucifixion is increasingly obscured by the treatment of Jesus' sufferings as religiously necessary, and so in a sense removed from their proper setting in a political struggle. To engage properly with Schüssler Fiorenza's passionate critique of a *theologia crucis* would take up far more space than we have here, though I should have to say that I think it suffers from the pressure to construct an 'ideal type' of what she calls 'kyriarchal' theology (theology preoccupied with domination and its legitimacy). But there is a point of substance in her argument as a whole.

The resurrection belief, as laid out in Christian scripture, is ideologically

---

[12] Schüssler Fiorenza, *op. cit.*, pp. 125–8.
[13] Ibid., p. 126.

messy. It incorporates major tensions between presence and absence, legitimations and subversions. The empty tomb *is* – and here, I think, Schüssler Fiorenza smoothes out the surface a little – an absence, in the sense that the Risen One is not there for the legitimation of any particular programme. Even the crucially important themes of the identification of God with the powerless and oppressed and the 'honouring' of love and solidarity offered to them do not exhaust what the narrative says, in the sense that the absence at the tomb prevents the risen Jesus becoming simply a heavily freighted code for the needs and dignities of the oppressed. This is an equation that would rob the figure of the Risen One of its 'freedom' to judge and transform, to speak, even in the context of the struggle for the sake of God's *basileia*, for God rather than human enterprise and aspiration. And the 'presence' of the Risen One, even as ascended to heaven and active through visionaries or prophets, is, as I have suggested, a presence other than that of a foundational tradition, other than the beginnings of a succession of leadership, because it ascribes to the Risen One in heaven something like agency and liberty, over against the community and its leaders. This may be obscured and distorted, even in our earliest materials; but it is seldom so straightforwardly a tool of institutional legitimation as a reading of Schüssler Fiorenza might suggest. Reading the apparition stories and the tomb stories together can be one effective way of preserving or highlighting the elements of absence and subversion contained in the tomb stories and allowing them to shape our reading of the apparitions. Once again, Luke 24 and John 21 seem to be working on just this frontier of indeterminacy and destabilization of any simple appeal to legitimating visions.

What I have been proposing is that the empty tomb tradition is, theologically speaking, part of the Church's resource in resisting the temptation to 'absorb' Jesus into itself, and thus part of what its confession of the divinity of Jesus amounts to in spiritual and political practice. Jesus is not the possession of the community, not even as 'raised into the kerygma', because he is alive, beyond qualification or risk, he 'lives to God'. The freedom of Jesus to act, however we unpack that deceptively simple statement, is not exhausted by what the community is doing or thinking – which allows us to say that Jesus' role for the community continues, vitally, to be that of judge, and that those who are charged with speaking authoritatively for or in the community stand in a very peculiar and paradoxical place. The distance from the community that is built into their role has to be something other than a claim to share the kind of distance that exists between the risen Jesus and the community. They remain under the judgement of the Risen One, along with the rest of the community, and their task is to direct attention away from themselves to Jesus, to reinforce the community's awareness of living under Jesus' judgement. The point at which they claim to foreclose the judgement of the risen Jesus is the point at which they occlude the reality of the continuing life or freedom of Jesus. Their rationale is to remind the community of the danger of swallowing Jesus up in its own life and practice; but they have to be aware themselves of the enormous risk of identifying their own 'difference' from the rest of the community with the difference of God. Ideally, the fact that ordained ministry operates with sacramental symbols designed to emphasize the presence of Jesus in his own proper difference ought to be a safeguard against the rampant ideologizing of clerical power. To say that this is not always how it has worked is an understatement of epic dimensions.[14]

The tomb tradition, then, should be the ground of certain kinds of questions put by the Church to itself, especially as regards its attitudes to institutional authority. Just as the focus of Israel's religious integrity in the canonical period was an empty throne, a deliberate repudiation of a graspable image, an absence reflected in the strange formulation of the divine name in Exodus 3, so for the community of the Christian covenant there is a fundamental ungraspability about the source of whatever power or liberty is at work in the community, a quality most easily comparable to that of a contemporary personal other. To vary the metaphor, the silence with which Mark's gospel ends indicates that the speaker of the gospel and the subject of the gospel as a narration is not himself *silenced*. It is not just a homiletic point to say that the 'missing ending' of Mark's text is the response of the reader or community of readers rather than a textual lacuna of some sort.[15] The narrative of Jesus is not finished, therefore not in any sense controlled, even by supposedly 'authorized' tellers of the story; his agency continues, now inseparable from the narrative of God's dealings with God's people, and so his story cannot be simply and decisively told.

The telling of the story of his life and death is, as in Mark above all, but also in the other gospels in varying degree, a process designed to bring the believer to the point of recognition that this is not a life exhausted in any text or ensemble of texts, in any performance or ensemble of performances. Jesus remains subject of his history. What 'controls' what can be said of Jesus is the

---

[14] I have attempted some discussion of this in 'Women and the Ministry: A Case for Theological Seriousness', in Monica Furlong, *Feminine in the Church* (London: SPCK, 1984), pp. 11–27.

[15] Cf. N. T. Wright, *The New Testament and the People of God* (London: SPCK, 1992), pp. 140–3 for a comparable picture applied to the Christian scriptures as a whole.

record of his own historical and political practice, in life and death – his historical acts and sufferings, which specify the kind of thing it makes sense to say of him (proscribing, for example, any discourse about Jesus that leaves him identified with uncriticized power, systemic exclusion, resentment or violence); not just anything may be said of Jesus, but the determination of that 'not just anything' does not lie with a Church into which the life of Jesus has been absorbed without remainder. In this sense, the empty tomb serves to mark in the Church's reflection the unfinished business of the historical Jesus: he is not a dead founder, but neither is he a heavenly Lord whose power and very identity is untrammelled by any record of historical acts and sufferings. The problematic space in which this 'neither/nor' has to work is what the tomb tradition protects.

In short, I should want to claim that the story of the empty tomb is not in fact incidental or secondary in the exposition of what the resurrection means theologically. The form of New Testament proclamation, the *mélange* of stories about the empty tomb, about 'authorizing' apparitions and about misrecognitions and epiphanies in the experience of unnamed or ambiguous figures (Magdalene, the disciples going to Emmaus), is bound up with the substance. Without these narratives, the Church is left with a problem as to how it will avoid making belief in the resurrection simply a belief in its own capacities, making present the Christ who is 'going ahead', not where he has been laid.

But, it will be asked, does this mean that I think belief in the empty tomb as an historical fact is essential to belief in the resurrection? Actually, yes. But this is a deeply unfashionable conclusion, and immediately runs into the problem of the immense variety of possible conclusions as to the tomb tradition from the point of view of historical and critical enquiry; it may seem to be limiting in advance what such enquiry may turn up. I don't think there is any short cut here; as I have already indicated, I am not happy with either an apologetic colonizing of historical study or a theologically dictated indifference to history. The underlying issue is whether what is so unsatisfactorily called dogmatic theology has any identity or integrity of its own. If the answer to that is yes, if there is a proper and disciplined mode of reflection on the 'grammar' of the assertions of Christian faith, it is open to the theologian *as* theologian to say that there are identifiable moral and spiritual issues for the Church involved in what is said about the character of the resurrection of Jesus, and that a rendering of that belief in primarily 'internalized' terms brings grave difficulties. The empty throne, the space between the cherubim, is filled by identifying Jesus with a dead teacher or a living memory – with a human construct or the object of human mental activity, rather than with the aniconic and paradoxical 'presence' of the God of the covenant.

The catch is that all this would be just as true if we were able confidently to point to a demonstrable historical miracle, a phenomenon that would give us a clearer grasp of what the risen identity is like (i.e. like a resuscitated physical body). To affirm the theological significance, indeed cruciality, of the tomb tradition obliges us to say that the continuing life or presence or agency of Jesus of Nazareth is *material* in the sense that it is not a matter of mental operations on the part of believers. That materiality is associated with the historical realities of community and sacraments and transfigured persons, but it is not completely exhausted in these, nor can the scriptural accounts be translated without remainder into talk about these things. But a speculative confidence about what more is to be said, any pretence at a quasi-scientific discussion of the character of the risen body, takes us back again to a strategy for filling the gap between the cherubim. Is it so intolerable a conclusion for theology that it has to admit what it cannot say here? I believe this is only evasive if it refuses to map out the ways in which the tomb narratives work towards a salutary theological critique of the community of faith. If that is an uncomfortable task, picking a path between 'conservative fundamentalism and liberal existentialism', well, then it is an uncomfortable task.[16]

Dogmatics cannot solve an historical question; the orthodoxies of modern scholarship are correct, and to deny this is to deny the proper integrity of scholarship itself. But where scholarship returns again and again to an historical aporia, the theologian may be pardoned for taking this as matter for reflection. If the issues remain genuinely open, theology may well consider, as suggested earlier, that the indeterminacy of scholarly analysis may be interwoven with the indeterminacy of the various narratives themselves. They do not fall tidily into familiar genres; they do not easily present themselves as fulfilments of prior expectation. (It is worth noting the sharp contrast between the numerous references to fulfilment of prophecy in both infancy and passion narratives and the total absence of such formulae in all the resurrection stories; there are references to the fulfilment of Jesus' prophecies and general appeals, as in I Corinthians 15, to the fulfilment of the scriptures, but no correlation of specific incidents as in the other contexts.) They are painfully untidy stories, reflecting sometimes all too plainly the various political interests at work in the formulation of the tradition, yet containing more than those interests can manage. The central image of the gospel narratives is

---

[16] Cf. Christopher Morse, *Not Every Spirit. A Dogmatics of Christian Disbelief* (Valley Forge, PA: Trinity Press, 1994), p. 159.

not any one apparition but the image of an absence, an image of the failure of images, which is also an absence that confirms the reality of a creative liberty, an agency not sealed and closed, but still obstinately engaged with a material environment and an historical process. Perhaps we really cannot say much more; not least because, to turn once more to Anita Mason's novel, 'There is a kind of truth which, when it is said, becomes untrue'. The theologian's job may be less the speaking of truth, in a context such as this, than the patient diagnosis of untruths, and the reminding of the community where its attention belongs.

Chapter Thirteen

THE NATURE OF A SACRAMENT

Sacraments are perhaps harder to understand the more we isolate them as a set (let alone a pair) of unique actions prescribed by Jesus as guaranteed and effective signs of the new covenant. We are apt to feel something arbitrary about this; or else, in terms of the language of devotion, we may come to stress the way a sacrament demonstrates God's unconditional power. How remarkable and unheard-of that bread should turn into flesh, that water should wash away sins! How doubly remarkable that the power to effect this should be mediated through frail earthen vessels (clergy)! and so forth. There is in fact very little ground for all this, even in the most conservative strands of Catholic theology; and what I hope to do in these pages is very briefly to sketch out an approach that may help to avoid the risks of an emphasis on what sounds like arbitrary divine power by returning to and exploring St Thomas Aquinas's admirably and typically simple observation that what makes sacraments distinct is what they are *for*, the activity in which they are caught up, which is making human beings holy.[1] To put it another way, what makes the Christian sacraments unique is not so much something inherent in the doing of them, some 'specialness' in the action, but the uniqueness of Jesus Christ in his dying and rising.

1. In order to grasp fully what is implied in this, we need to bear in mind some basic elements in the Christian understanding of human nature. It is a matter of brute fact that being human is irreducibly bound up with language and culture, and so with 'transformative action', changing the environment. In a sense, all animals do this, and we talk of analogues to culture and society, even language, among bees and weaver-birds; there is action, the making of new things. But, what there is not is *history*, deliberate and dateable innova-

---

[1] *Summa Theologiae* III.lx.2c and ad 1.

tions in practices over and above what is functionally necessary, a story of the development of theme and convention in the doing of things, as if the mere getting a job done were not enough. In the human world, the performing of a task regularly calls out a response in the form of another way of doing it, 'commenting' on the first, as it were, engaging and extending it, depending on it, yet challenging it. For good or ill, our practices move forward, in a kind of gratuitous exploration or refinement; we have a cultural story to tell, which bees do not. No Wren or Hawksmoor or Mies van der Rohe interrupts the steady practice of constructing honeycombs or ant-hills. The human modification and transformation of the environment has no simple functional determination, and so no obvious 'natural' limit – beyond what we are bitterly discovering about the limits of the environment itself as a resource.

Human doing and making has a 'conversational' dimension in its calling forth unceasing response and reflection in the form of further doing. Can you imagine a situation in which it could be said: 'We have now discovered how to cook a meal, bring up a child, build a house, plan a taxation system, bury the dead', so that there would be no comment possible, no engagement with what has been done except to imitate it? The world in and on which we work is constantly augmented by what is said and done. Cornelius Ernst was right in saying that we are involved in a 'process or praxis by which the world to which man belongs becomes the world which belongs to man';[2] but the world that is thus all the time being brought into the circle of human meaningfulness does not stand still. Each effort to make the world 'belong' to us, to make sense, puts a fresh question; each organizing or explanatory strategy becomes itself a new puzzle or code, in need of imaginative 'reading' and re-ordering. In a paradoxical yet quite familiar way, human beings are, in one and the same activity, looking for *and* creating meaning: patterns of order, schemes of communication in which the confusing experience of life in the world to which we belong (and to which we did not choose to belong) is drawn into language, into the ever-extending web of sharing perception, experience, selfhood itself, that constitutes human being as human.

In spite of various naive theories about things and their names, we are in a world in which things are not allowed to stay still. The 'stable' bits of definitions, by which we assure ourselves that we are doing broadly the same thing as last time, are not the whole of speech, nor even its most important dimension. We talk things into new connections and so cause their boundaries to become vaguer: what at first might seem to be labelled objects and

[2]   Cornelius Ernst, *Multiple Echo* (Darton, Longman & Todd, 1979), pp. 55, 75.

no more themselves come to be meaningful; they point us to other things, other situations, they become part of what we say. And what we do with a 'thing' thus activated to point to something else becomes part of what the next speaker-agent has to work on. We are not, in short, lumps of stuff in a museum of lumps of stuff; we are not even very clever animals successfully performing necessary functions by devising regular practices involving lumps of stuff. Over and above what we need for survival, we work on our world in what seems an insatiable desire for new perception and new possibilities of action. All of which is perhaps only another way of saying that we are con-scious of living in time, with memory and hope – not just as individual psychological possessions, but as part of the structure of language and under-standing as such, part of that human belonging that makes us the sort of beings we are.

All that I have said so far can apply pretty generally to human acts, not least to science and technology. So far from being – as we might simple-mindedly suppose – a matter of seeking to fulfil neatly defined needs, the technological enterprise itself creates new needs. Only rather belatedly have we realized that this, too, is a practice engaged in the gratuitous, exploratory re-making of the world; so that at last we realize that we are in large measure choosing our needs, and are delivered from supposing that they are natural and uncontro-versial (and without moral cost). But this picture of human being as bound up in the tumultuous and self-challenging project of re-working the world is most obviously linked with art. We do things that have some kind of extran-eous goal, some specification by need, even though we gratuitously modify goal or need in the history of doing them; more strangely, though, we do things and make things that have no point beyond themselves. They are purely exploratory of the capacities of language and meaning in the material world, exercises in the creation of beautiful, excellent or novel *form*.

In what is surely the best account in English this century of sacramental theology, David Jones argued that art was an essentially religious activity (art here including technology, but supremely visible in the gratuity of sheer form-making in itself). Looking back to the cave-painters of Lascaux, Jones insists on the fact that, from the earliest appearings of homo sapiens (and beyond, for that matter: the Neanderthals buried their dead with ritual), the human being has freely and gratuitously reflected on and enlarged his and her existence in producing significant (communicative) shape. And: 'it is on account of the anthropic sign-making that we first suspect that anthropos has some part in a without-endness'.[3] We make signs, and make ourselves through

[3] David Jones, 'Art and Sacrament', in *Epoch and Arist* (Faber, 1959), p. 156.

signs, and because that project has no necessary termination (think of the absurdity of claiming to be concluding the last conversation, writing the last poem, playing the C minor Cello Suite for the last time . . .), it becomes itself, Jones argues, a sign, something claiming to be 'read', questioned and answered – a sign (for the believer) of human anchorage in an unlimited working, an unconditional power of innovation: all art is 'a sign of the form-making activities universally predicated of the Logos. It is then the form-making which is also a sign-making that causes man's art to be bound to God's'.[4] The very existence of this kind of life, a questing through the making, dissolving, superseding and re-making of form, with the loss and re-creation of selfhood and relation that is implied in this, puts to us the question of the context that would finally make sense of the effort to make sense: a first word in the conversation, a first making of communicative form; the creative Word of God.

Be that as it may, Jones is wholly right in saying that humanity without the making of sign and form is nothing, and in going on to maintain that this is really a recognition of the fact that we are bodily. So far from signs (including language itself) being a regretable necessity in view of our minds being sadly muffled up in bodies, they are intrinsic to our actual thinking and living as bodies. 'We are committed to body and by the same token we are committed to Art, so to sign and sacrament'.[5] There is, incidentally, much illumination to be got on this point from Fergus Kerr's brilliant and lucid book, *Theology after Wittgenstein*[6] and Aquinas is again in the background, asserting as he does when discussing the question of whether a sacrament must always be a thing perceptible to the senses that it is natural for human beings to know ideal structures and spiritual matters only through sense-objects.[7] St Thomas here, in fact, makes in passing a point of some interest: a sign is the means of coming to the knowledge of someone or something other than ourselves; the work of God for our salvation is 'spiritual' – i.e. it is not itself an item, an object that can be isolated in our world, it is supremely alien to the everyday world, yet not in any way an identifiable reality in competition with it; so it can only be shown or signified materially. What I think St Thomas is saying is that if we try to signify God and his work by resorting to abstract expressions, talking about minds and ideas in a vacuum, we dangerously forget what *we* are (flesh and blood, timebound),

---

[4]   Ibid., p. 160.
[5]   Ibid., p. 165.
[6]   Blackwell, 1986.
[7]   *Summa Theologiae* III.lx.4c.

and create a phantom world of pseudo-objects alongside our own familiar one. But the 'otherness' of God is not like that; it is more radical. And it is only by speaking and engaging with the material world in a particular way that we come to express truly and respond properly to the real otherness of God. Wittgenstein's much-quoted remark that 'the human body is the best picture of the human soul'[8] says the same kind of thing, as does the dictum quoted by Patrick White as an epigraph to his novel, *The Vivisector.* 'There is another world, but it is the same as this one.'

So far, then: being human, being bodily and being a user of 'signs' are inseparable. We reflect on ourselves and 'answer' our individual and social past by doing things and making things, re-ordering what the past and present world has given us into a new statement of meaning, self-interpretation and world-interpretation. I think that, if we are trying to map out the context within which sacramental practice makes human sense, we should begin there rather than with some general principle of the world as 'naturally' sacramental or epiphanic: a pot-pourri of Jung, Teilhard de Chardin and a certain kind of anthropology, sometimes invoked as a prelude to sacramental theology, will run the risk of obscuring the fact that signs and symbols are *made* – even if in response to some sense that the world itself is charged with glory. The difficulty, recognized by Ernst,[9] is to hold on to the conviction that sign-making is a material and historical practice, without making it seem like an arbitrary imposing of form on passive stuff 'out there'; and to counter this we need, of course, the kind of philosophical framework which reminds us that the world is never neutral and passive in a simple sense, but already, primitively, known and thought in signs (in language and meaningful action). Symbolic forms are not just lying around, nor are they thought up as arbitrary glosses on straightforward experience of the world; they are what we live through as humans – as beings capable of recalling and re-moulding what is given us, taking it forward and so re-moulding ourselves, the horizons of our understanding and our hope.

2. The history of particular communities becomes, in this perspective, a history of sign-making – in that it is a record of how communities 'make sense' of themselves in the words and practices they evolve. Quite apart from the rather banal sense in which this is true in the whole spectrum of any genuinely *social* life, there are particular 'signs' in which the identity of the specific group is stated, reflected on and communicated, tacitly or explicitly;

---

8   *Philosophical Investigations*, p. 178.
9   *Multiple Echo*, p. 55.

not only public ceremonial, the ritual of the law or the armed forces, but, more importantly, the manner and ethos of a culture, local ways of doing things, that are themselves deepened and sustained by specific corporate celebration. Thus, if we look at ancient Israel, we see how signs operated for a community which believed that it owed its origins solely to the initiative and promise of God. The whole life of Israel was, through the Torah, increasingly organized as something that would be appropriate to a nation resting on God's covenant. The code of Deuteronomy assumes that the contemporary Israelite is 'contemporary' with those who came out of Egypt and wandered in the desert (e.g. Deuteronomy 29.14–15), so that all its injunctions are made under this rubric: the liberating act of God requires faithfulness answering to the divine faithfulness; acts performed under the divine law are 'significant' of the God who brought the slaves out of Egypt. The integral keeping of the divine commands is linked (e.g. Deuteronomy 10) to the unique privilege of Israel, the fact that sets them apart from the 'nations', the fact that they are brought together solely by the free choice of God. To maintain this peculiar status is to honour and to express the freedom of God: the 'name' of God will be present, not only in the central shrine but in the life of the whole nation (cf. Deuteronomy 28.9–10). The same themes reappear in Leviticus, especially in the 'holiness' regulations of chapters 19 to 26: the separateness of the people of Israel, and the separations between holy and profane enforced within the nation in the realms of food and sexuality are explained by reference to the absolute untouchable holiness of God. God's nature is expressed in the life of his people. Furthermore, in all the variegated documents of the Torah, all this is anchored in the great festivals when Israel returns to the formative events of Exodus and desert wandering, to *become again* the people whom God chooses; festivals whose origins were probably agrarian are transformed into historical recollection so as to serve the distinctive vocation of Israel.

Here is a very pervasive and organized 'sacramentality', a sign–making consciously extended to an enormous range of activities. The sense Israel seeks to make of its life is bound to the conviction that for it to be there at all is miraculously surprising, the work of God: so its enacted reflection, in the forms of its speech and practice, is meant to 're-work' its world in order to show the face of the holy and liberating God. This is, of course, part of what makes it possible for the covenantal faith to survive the destruction not only of the Temple but of the priesthood: the daily observation of Torah is sacramental to such a vivid degree that it can almost dispense with the cultic – I say 'almost', because Judaism without its festivals would hardly be imaginable, even when those festivals are turned into 'lay' celebrations, without sacrificial and clerical ritual. As sign-makers in their observance of the Law, the whole of Israel is a priestly people. And, in much later Judaism, the Hasidic tradition was to interpret the life and acts of the righteous person, in the very smallest details of daily life, as an unveiling of the Shekinah, the glory of God's presence, which is hidden in all things.

In this way, then, we can further concentrate the focus of this discussion. Human beings in general are makers of signs, each of us is a 'self-seeking hunter of forms' (Geoffrey Hill's phrase in 'Pavana Dolorosa', the fifth of his sonnet-sequence *Lachrimae*), and communities like individuals seek the utterance of their 'selfhood' in the making and re-making of forms. In the history that stands behind – and within – the Christian revelation, we see a people signifying, 'intending', a belief in their creation *as* a people by the hand of God, and making social and ritual signs to embody the nature of the God who has so acted. And in this light, we can look afresh at what is done in and by the Israelite Jesus of Nazareth.

It is clear that the tradition of his deeds and words is heavily influenced by the sense that he was a sign-maker of a disturbingly revolutionary kind. He worked – we are led to understand – on the assumption that a time of crisis had begun in which the people of God would be both summoned to judge-ment and restored under God's kingship so as to become a people bound to God in unprecedented closeness. The covenanted faithfulness of God would once and for all overcome and cast out the unfaithfulness of the people. Thus Jesus acts for a community that does not yet exist, the Kingdom of God: he chooses rabbis and judges for the twelve tribes of the future, he heals and forgives, he takes authority to bring the outcasts of Israel into this new world by sharing their tables. His strange isolation, the suspicion and incomprehension he meets, have to do with the fact that his acts are signs of a form of human life yet to be realized and standing at odds with the political and cultic status quo. The 'sense' he is making is entirely rooted in the fun-damental Jewish conviction that God is the God who, by his free commit-ment, brings a people into being; yet the 'people' in whose name he acts, whose forms and signs he constructs in his healing and fellowship, both is and is not identical with the Israel that now exists.

This paradox is most evident in the last of the 'signs' of the kingdom which he performs, the unexpected variation on the passover theme in which he announces a new covenant sealed in his forthcoming death. The Last Supper is not a simple, primitive fellowship meal; as far back as we can go in the tradition about Jesus, it is seen as 'intending', meaning, the event that finally sets Jesus and his followers apart from the continuities of Israel and makes the beginnings of a new definition of God's people. Maundy Thursday *means* Good Friday and Easter, the sealing of the new and everlasting covenant. In the costly gift of his chosen and beloved to the risk of rejection and death, God uncovers the scope of his commitment in a way that alters the whole quality of human trust and commitment to him: he creates *faith*. And he creates a community of faith called, exactly as Israel is called, to show his nature in their life by following out the logic of Torah itself. Every act must speak of God, but not in such a way as to suggest a satisfying of divine demands, an *adequacy* of response to God's creative act. What we do is now to be a sign, above all, of a gift given for the deepening of solidarity – or, in Paul's language, ethics is about 'the building up of the body of Christ'. If our acts with one another speak of mutual gift and given-ness, they are signs of the radical self-gift which initiates the Church.

So, it is readily intelligible that the most characteristic (i.e. self-identifying) acts of the Church from its beginnings should be the signs of the paschal event. Baptism is already, in the tradition about Jesus, something that stands not only for commission and empowerment, but for the specific commission to die at the hands of the powerful of this earth, to realize God's power through the gift of one's own life to him (Mark 10.38–39, cf. Luke 12.50), so that the washing of the convert becomes an identification with this death, this gift and this empowering. The supper draws us into the event of the covenant's sealing, placing us with the unfaithful disciples at table whose unfaithfulness is to be both judged and set aside by God – for the supper is also celebrated as the meal shared with the risen Jesus.

Jesus, baptized, tempted, forgiving and healing, offering himself as the means of a new covenant, is himself 'sacrament': it is his identity that is set before us as a sign, the form of a new people of God. Just as the whole life of Israel is meant as a sign of God, showing God by showing God-with-his-people, showing how life moulds itself under his pressure, so the life (and death) of Jesus is a sign of God, showing how a human biography formed by God looks. What leads us to say that Jesus's life is sacramental in a uniquely exhaustive way is that this life not only points to God but is the medium of divine action for judgement and renewal. Its determination by the future, God's kingdom, means in practice an authoritative and creative freedom, whose effects slowly break the mould of the existing Israel, so that the life of God's people under law can now be read as a sign not only of God but of the *new* work of God in Jesus and the Church (cf. Aquinas[10]); here – so the New Testament claims – is what the sacramentality of the Law *means*, an ultimate intimacy between God and his people, a radicalizing and consummation

---

[10]   *Summa Theologiae* III.lx.2 ad 2.

(and therefore revolutionary modification) of the covenant bond. What Torah was, Christ is; and what *Israel* was, Christ is. He is the sign both of the active pressure and creative grace of God, a new 'law', and also of obedience, love and gift as the shape of a possible community, a new Israel. He proclaims the imperatives of the kingdom, realizes them in his life and death, and so begins to make the possible community actual in the post-Easter experience of his followers. He is thus an effective sign, a converting sign. Every sign, every reflective, exploratory and declaratory form-creating act, has effect, of course, as we have seen; new forms generate more. But the effect of Jesus' life and death is, so believers have held, unprecedentedly comprehensive: by offering and effecting forgiveness, and forming a community around this reality, human relationships and potentialities are set free from the paralysing and self-intensifying consequences of hostility and aggression to each other and to ourselves, from the lethal symbiosis of violence and guilt. There is a 'new creation'; so that this sign, the identity of Jesus, is of fundamental significance. Even more than the passover of the first covenant, the signifying of his life and death presents the gracious liberty of the creator and exposes us to the action of that liberty in us.

From the outside, the signs of the covenant in the Church can be neutrally described. They are intelligible as parts of a ritual process whose context and structure have been admirably and thoroughly detailed by anthropologists like Turner or Leach. In still more general terms – the terms with which this discussion began – they belong with the whole complex of human sign-making. And, as suggested, it is not the fact of doing sacramental things that is special, humanly or religiously, but what the Church signifies in doing these things – the new covenant and new creation in the life, death and raising of Jesus. In these acts the Church 'makes sense' of itself, as other groups may do, and as individuals do; but its 'sense' is seen as dependent on the creative act of God in Christ. Hence the problems theology has over sorting out the relation between divine and human action in the sacraments, the weary controversies over baptismal regeneration and eucharistic sacrifice. It is perhaps because we are so generally inept at recognizing that the meaning of our acts and relations rests, moment by moment, on God's creative grace that we so readily end up in bad-tempered confrontations of a singularly unproductive sort over 'what we do' and 'what he does' in the sacraments – as if (thinking back to St Thomas once again) the purely spiritual and divine could be thought of as something side by side with the material and human. No, the sacraments are performed, in obedience to Jesus Christ, by those already caught up in God's work, those who have received and live by God's promise: their acts in opening themselves to the converting sign of Jesus himself are the modes of receiving, not independent assaults on God by alienated, distant creatures.

Our signs are created by what Christ creates – his own self as a gift of God. 'He placed himself in the order of signs', to quote that dictum of de la Taille which so haunted David Jones,[11] not only, however, on Maundy Thursday but in the entire formation of his life as bearer of the Kingdom. And Jesus Christ's formation of his life and death, as something to be present in the language and practice of his followers, is of such an order that Christians hold it to be the direct utterance of the uncreated God, the presence to us of the first of signs, the Logos, called by St Bonaventura the 'art of the Father', *ars Patris*. Derivatively, then, but really, the Church's sacramental action is the Father's art, not our unaided reflection on human existence, nor even our attempt to render present an absent divine act or a distant promise; they are the drawing of believers into the life of the kingdom of God. All our discussions of regeneration and sacrifice, eucharistic presence, indelible character or whatever suffer to the extent that they fail to take proper account of this utter dependence of our sign-making on that of God in Christ.

3. In conclusion, taking up a point more than once hinted at in these pages: the primary concern should be for sacramental actions rather than an attempt to focus on 'sacralized' objects. There is a perfectly respectable theology (which I accept) of devotion to the consecrated eucharistic elements; but to concentrate on the presence of Christ in this way in some near-total abstraction from the context of the eucharistic action is to court the distortions we began by noting – the isolation of sacrament as a sign of the divine power's capacity to produce a miraculous 'thing'. It is parallel to the strangeness of doing Christology as if the Incarnation could be isolated from the words and work of Christ as a miraculous epiphany of divine power in conjoining two alien realities. Wonder at the *admirabile commercium* of divinity and humanity or flesh and bread should not be allowed to result in a sort of theological immobilizing of a sacred object: the sign that is Christ and the signs of Christ equally are God in act. The Reformers were right in their insistence that theology and devotion must never treat God as passive, but always respond to him as active; and in this insistence they are loyal to the Catholic insight of Aquinas quoted earlier, as well as to the New Testament.

When the Anglican Articles bluntly declare that the doctrine of transubstantiation 'overthroweth the nature of a Sacrament'[12] their hostility is intel-

---

[11]   *Epoch and Artist*, p. 179.
[12]   Article XXVIII.

ligible against the background of a devotional practice that seemed to 'immobilize' Christ in this sort of way. But there is a deeper objection also. Signs are signs of what they are not: they are transformations of the world by re-ordering it, not destroying it, so that the tension of 'otherness' remains, itself part of the fluid and dynamic nature of sign-making. The object relocated and worked at in the process of making sense does not disappear in the process: it is still itself in its new context, and that new context may spill over into the context of similar objects. 'My love is like a red, red rose' not only elaborates my understanding of my love, it changes my perception of roses, touches them with the 'meaning' of a human beauty. All bread and all wine are shadowed with their eucharistic use. This would not be so if the sacramental matter ceased to be itself. What the Reformers worried over was the suggestion that the sacramental bread and wine were diminished in respect of their worldly reality in order to make room for the supernatural, so destroying the oneness-in-otherness of a sign, 'the nature of a sacrament'. Whether that is at all a fair account of what St Thomas understood by transubstantiation is open to doubt (he is careful to deny[13] that there is an 'annihilation' of the substance of the elements); indeed, his remarks, quoted above, about the need for material signs, show something of the same concerns as those of the Reformers. We do not encounter God in the displacement of the world we live in, the suspension of our bodily and historical nature. There is indeed a sense in which we meet God in emptiness and silence, in the void of Good Friday and Holy Saturday, in the darkening of sense and spirit in prayer; but we should not allow the weighty and important language of 'God at work in our nothingness' to deceive us into thinking that Good Friday is not history or that the soul in the night of contemplation ceases to be bound up in its material creaturehood. God acts in emptiness by bringing resurrection and transforming union, not by lifting us to 'another world'.

'There is another world, but it is the same as this one'. All sign-making is the action of hope, the hope that this world may become other and that its experienced fragmentariness can be worked into sense. The sacramental action of the believer is, at one level, a working into sense like any other; the difference is that this 'working' is done to open to us the sense already made by God as creator and redeemer. The hope of the world becoming other is anchored, in the Christian sacraments, by the conviction that all human significant action arises from the primordial action, the art and sign, of a God committed to drawing our lives into the order of healing and communion,

---

[13] *Summa Theologiae* III.lxxv.3.

who brings all things gratuitously into existence, and, no less gratuitously, renews them and saves them from vacuity and decay. He makes the world, in Christ, to be his 'sign' a form of living and acting that embodies his nature and purpose. Christian sign-making – in the whole of the community's discipleship as in ritual acts – is a working in and with that creative energy. The world is made so as to be everlastingly re-made to God's glory, and of that sure hope our sacraments speak. The material history of creation is not waste, no person or transaction, public or private, can finally fall out of God's purpose, God's 'sense' for the world – which is, as the sacraments themselves intimate, not explanation or justification but eternal renewal, transfiguration.

Chapter Fourteen

SACRAMENTS OF THE NEW SOCIETY

I

The Christian sacraments are not just epiphanies of the sacred; or rather, the *way* in which they are epiphanies of the sacred is by their re-ordering of the words and images used to think or experience social life. Without at this stage introducing any specifically theological language, we can say that a Christian community involved in activities it calls 'sacramental' is a community *describing* itself in a way that is importantly at odds with other sorts of description (secular or functional ones).

More precisely, the sacramental action itself traces a transition from one sort of reality to another: first it describes a pre-sacramental state, a secular or profane condition now imagined, for ritual purposes, in the light of and in the terms of the transformation that is to be enacted; it tells us that where we habitually are is not, after all, a neutral place but a place of loss or need. It then requires us to set aside this damaged or needy condition, this flawed identity, so that in dispossessing ourselves of it we are able to become possessed of a different identity, given in the rite, not constructed by negotiation and co-operation like other kinds of social identity. The rite requires us *not* to belong any more to the categories we thought we belonged in, so that a distinctive kind of new belonging can be realized. When this transition takes place, the presence and the power of the sacred is believed to be at work. I shall not try to discuss how far you can usefully employ the term 'sacrament' outside the Christian framework; but diverse religious traditions certainly recognize corporate actions designed to reconstruct or radicalize a common identity, above all in sacrifice and festival.

Christianity is distinct in the non-seasonal frequency of its ritual celebrations, and in the way in which its two commonest sacramental actions recapitulate aspects of a single story, the paschal narrative of Jesus' death and resurrection; and that may suggest that the themes of transition and transformation are more insistently present in Christian language than in some other traditions. While theologians have sometimes rather loosely talked about the sacramental 'principle' in Christianity as an affirmation of some inherent capacity in material things to bear divine meanings, the actual shape and rhetoric of sacramental *actions* says more about how such meanings emerge from a process of estrangement, surrender and re-creation than we might expect if we begin only from the rather bland appeal to the natural sacredness of things that occasionally underpins sacramental theology.

II

That, I know, is an alarmingly abstract beginning. What I hope to do in what follows is to trace how these ideas operate concretely in baptism and the eucharist, so as to see more clearly what the society is that is imagined and, according to the believer, realized in these actions. Details of ceremony and formula, of course, vary greatly, but clearly comparable patterns are present across confessional frontiers, if only because the central *actions* with water, bread and wine are invariable. To begin with baptism: the 1662 Book of Common Prayer begins its baptismal liturgy with particular sharpness, telling us that all are born in sin, and that the gift looked for in baptism is something 'which by nature [the child to be baptized] cannot have'; and it proceeds to rehearse stories of transition and rescue – Noah and his family, 'the children of Israel thy people'. The apparently neutral condition of the infant is thus redescribed as one of danger or unfreedom, liability to divine 'wrath'; what is necessary is incorporation into the society that is within the ark, where it becomes possible to be 'rooted in charity'. Prayers are said for the 'death' of the child's existing human identity and the distorted affects that go with it, and God is petitioned to number the child among his chosen. After the immersion or affusion, the child is said to be 'grafted into the body of Christ's Church', and prayer is further made that the child may share Christ's resurrection as it has already, symbolically, shared his death. In conclusion, the duties of the baptized are spelled out, reiterating the theme of death and resurrection: what is symbolically done here, the putting to death of 'corrupt affections', is to be renewed daily in concrete behaviour.

What ought to strike us is how both the kinds of belonging evoked here – the condition of sin, belonging with Adam, and the new life of belonging in or with Christ – are not *elective* matters, not things over which the subject has any control. First there is the unsought and unwelcome solidarity of being in danger, then the 'grafting' into a new reality. The danger is associated with misdirected 'affections', which we could almost render as malfunctioning instinct and desire – we want, are drawn by, are moved by, what will kill us; so that, by contrast, the new life is implicitly associated with new attractions, a new sensibility. We are first drawn by objects that fill gaps in our self-construction, so that what we desire is repletion, which is immobilization, a kind of death. We must receive the grace to want the endlessness of God. But unlike the developments of sensibility or desire in our ordinary conscious life, this has nothing to do with being *educated* into new perception: there is a gift bestowed (though its exact nature is not spelled out) which orients us in a certain way, and what must follow is a discipline to ensure we do not lose sight of it.

What the gift might be is a notable site of contention in theology, as it happens, but it is (at least) evoked, if not comprehensively defined, by the use of words like 'regeneration' and 'adoption'. The only thing in the language of the rite that looks like an elective move, a matter of choice or policy, is the decision to bring the child to baptism in the first place. This is described as a 'charitable work' which God 'favourably alloweth', but it is itself only a response to the scriptural promise of Christ to receive and bless children; and the reference to charity here points us back to the *givenness* of the bonds between those grafted into Christ and 'rooted in charity'. In short, we look in vain, in the course of this liturgy, for an autonomous subject choosing its companions. The subject coming to baptism is not only a subject incapable of choice, an infant, it is also enmeshed in unchosen relations and subject to irresistible and destructive compulsions; in the course of the rite, it is symbolically stripped of all this and given a new context and new associates, new goals and (implicitly at least) new desires. Everything about the rite seems to push *choice* to the margin.

III

Now I know and you know that the 1662 Book of Common Prayer is a document very heavily charged with polemic, and with many apparently innocent phrases that in fact are carefully designed to say or not say certain things. The Baptismal Order has to balance a whole set of not easily compatible theological constraints, and what it takes for granted is controversial to most modern ears. We do not like constructing the 'danger' of the unbaptized in terms of divine wrath, and we are a bit more uneasy than our forebears were about the obliteration or displacement of personal commitment in a rite whose New Testament roots seem to be a good deal more interested in moments of choice. I shall not try to solve any of these tangles, or to pronounce on the (typical) tightrope walking between Calvinism and Catholicism evidenced in this particular text; I want only to draw out a little further the picture of ourselves that the rite suggests, and to note how that picture might affect our social imagination. For beyond the particular character and contour of this one rite, heavily conditioned by its historical setting, there are features of the rite itself, in its universal outlines and imagery, that press the same questions on us. If *this* is the nature of the transition between secular identity and sociality and Christian identity and sociality, what do we have to think, as Christians, about social identities?

The first point I would like to make is that the rite leaves no space for an identity constructed by the will starting from scratch. Whether or not we are comfortable with the way the Book of Common Prayer dismantles the illusory neutrality of 'just' being born as a member of the human race, the baptismal event necessarily reminds us that we are born into a context we did not choose, and our options are already limited for us. We cannot choose our company – obviously not, as infants, but as adults too – since the solidarity of the secular world continues to distort our perceptions and taste even when we *think* we are choosing.

The second point is that what constitutes our belonging together, morally and spiritually, is our corporate relation to God. That is to say that what unites us with other human beings is not common culture or negotiated terms of co-operation or common aims, but something *external* to human community itself, the regard of God upon us. In the Book of Common Prayer's terms (which are actually the terms of the majority of Christians, historically speaking), we are either bound together by being 'seen' by God as distant, as strangers, or bound together in a common assurance that we are received, affirmed, adopted. The status of other subjects, morally and spiritually, is wholly beyond our determination – though, in Christian tradition, not wholly beyond our knowledge: a very ambiguous element in all this, since a quick reading of the difference between baptized and unbaptized would lead to a very sharp exclusivism. What softens and 'unsettles' such exclusiveness is the constant possibility of transition and the essential independence of this transition from any human corporate policy. We may find it odd that sixteenth-century Spanish theologians had to argue about whether the native peoples of the Americas were human (and so able to be converted to the Catholic faith), but, as they and their compatriots well knew, there was an immediate political linkage between being capable of receiving baptism and the capacity to be a 'citizen'.[1] To be even potentially the object of affirming regard and adoption makes certain policies such as systematic enslavement of one group by another a good deal more problematic. Subsequent history shows how easily even grave theological tensions can be lived with, if the price is right; but we need to remember that the appropriateness of baptizing slaves was still being questioned in British colonies in the eighteenth century; some at least dimly saw the dangerous connections here.

The baptismal perspective, in insisting that we are caught up in solidarities we have not chosen, is an admittedly uncomfortable partner for the post-Enlightenment social thinker. It gives disappointingly little ground for developing a discourse of human rights or claims, since it sidesteps the whole milieu of the tribunal in which I can enforce what is owing to me: in the baptismal perspective, we confront something we cannot 'plead' with. The decisions have already been taken. Yet *if* – and it is an enormous if – we are quite serious about the radical difference of God or the radical liberty of God, the consequent picture of human status is perhaps still more challenging than the conventional construction of 'rights'. Not only is a fundamental equality established by the indiscriminate regard of God, but, still more significantly, a fundamental compatibility and interdependence in human goals when rightly perceived. In that God's affirming regard is given to the subject specifically as a member of a community, the implication is that, within that community, what is good or desirable for each is consistent with what is good and desirable for all others.

The new desires that replace the 'corrupt affections' of pre-baptismal humanity must therefore be desires free from competitive patterns or rivalry; as Augustine put it in his treatise on the Trinity, our wanting of the good and our loving of the just is, in the communion of faith, a desire for the same good to be in all.[2] It is a love of love itself, desiring that all should realize the same self-forgetful longing for the good of the other. This may not be a discourse of 'rights' in the modern sense, but it offers something that such a discourse often fails to deliver, a sense of the interlocking of different kinds of good or welfare. There cannot be a human good for one person or group that necessarily excludes the good of another person or group. The passage from talking of rights to talk of a common good in which I recognize the

---

[1] See 'On the American Indians', in F. de Vitoria, *Political Writings* (Cambridge: Cambridge University Press, 1991), pp. 231–92; A. Pagden, *Spanish Imperialism and the Political Imagination* (New Haven: Yale University Press, 1990); A. Pagden, *European Encounters with the New World* (New Haven: Yale University Press, 1993).
[2] Augustine, *De trin.* VIII. vi–vii; *Works* VII, Nicene and Post-Nicence Fathers (Edinburgh: T. & T. Clark, 1873), pp. 211–17.

unity of my desire with the desire of all is enabled by what baptism, sacramentally understood, speaks of: a divine reality with which claim and negotiation are impossible. In this light, critical questions become possible about our actual desires and how far they remain in essence competitive or exclusive – how far, that is, the symbolic death and dispossession is consciously realized, how far the givenness of new desires is appropriated or understood.

Hegel, writing about baptism, captures the tensions here:[3] the new identity of the baptized self is 'implicit spirit, which must become explicit'; this process may entail, subjectively, a 'real, infinite anguish', but the fact of the Church's existence declares that, at the level of the community, at the level of speech and understanding, the battle has been won. The reality of the common life in which spirit recognizes itself in the life and welfare of the other has already been established in the foundational events of the Church, and does not *depend* on any group or individual in later history successfully realizing it at any particular time. Or, in more conventionally theological language, baptism, most fundamentally, announces the givenness, once and for all, of the new humanity in Christ.

IV

It is this same pivotal conviction of the givenness of the new world that constitutes the sacrament of the Lord's Supper as socially disturbing in a comparable way. Here again, sometimes more obviously, sometimes more subtly, we are dealing with narratives or dramas of transition. The eucharist recollects an event already complex, already 'doubled' – the Last Supper interpreted as a sign of Jesus' death and its effects, or, from the other end, the death of Jesus metaphorized as a breaking and sharing of bread. The central transition here, as in baptism, is a death, a death here presented as a passage (once again) into new solidarities: the wine poured out as a sign of the shedding of blood is the mark of a *covenant* being made, on the analogy of God's covenant with Israel. The movement, then, is towards a declared commitment on God's part, sealed or assured by Jesus' death.

If we follow here the same interpretative lines we used earlier, the conclusion is that the 'pre-sacramental' state is one in which God's commitment is not assured, or not perceptible to us as certain. The profane or secular con-

---

[3]   G. W. F. Hegel, *Lectures on the Philosophy of Religion*. One volume edition; The Lectures of 1827, ed. P. C. Hodgson (Berkeley: University of California Press, 1988), p. 477, no. 231.

dition from which we start is one of uncertainty: we are shown ourselves initially as those who are unable to trust the faithfulness of God. Put this alongside the fact that all eucharistic liturgies in the mainstream of Western Christian tradition begin with some sort of penitential acknowledgement, and the further conclusion suggests itself that our sins have something to do with the fundamental condition of untrustfulness. Some rites – notably the much maligned Communion Order of 1662, but also, in a very different idiom, the Byzantine liturgy – heighten the tension by returning at significant moments to the rhetoric of penitence and unworthiness, up to the very moment of communion. It seems that until we have actually received the tokens of the covenant we remain locked in sin, in the hostility to God and each other that flows from lack of assurance in God. When we physically receive the pledge of that assurance, we become 'covenanted' ourselves to God and each other (the Book of Common Prayer speaks of our being thus made 'living members' of a 'holy fellowship'). The divine initiative of promise creates a *bonded* community, a 'faithful people' (to quote 1662 again).

But this transition depends on a transition at another level. The material elements of bread and wine are to be made holy by the prayer that associates them with the flesh and blood of Jesus. Whatever the particular theology of eucharistic presence in a tradition, there is invariably a setting-aside of the elements and a narrative recalling Jesus' self-identification with the bread and wine as 'representative' bits of the created order, a convention whose origins go back to some of the earliest eucharistic texts and eucharistic theologies we have: Irenaeus, in the second Christian century, can refer to them as 'first fruits', as if they were a sort of harvest thanksgiving offering,[4] and the resonance of this with the imagery of Christ as 'first fruits' from the dead (I Cor. 15.20) is obvious. The harvest of the natural order becomes the harvest of God's action: Christ as the first visible sign of God's new order is shown under the form of the first signs of fruition or fulfilment in the inanimate creation. The identification itself establishes a continuity (a fidelity) in what God does in the natural order and in history. The transition, the symbolic transformation of the bread and wine, uncovers a deeper unity between radically different orders.

Not simply a natural or obvious unity, however: it is effected or uncovered by a particular act, a particular word in the history of revelation. Jesus 'passes over' into the symbolic forms by his own word and gesture, a transition into the vulnerable and inactive forms of the inanimate world. By

---

[4] Irenaeus, *Adversus Haereses* IV. xvii–xviii; *The Writings* V:I, Ante-Nicene Christian Library (Edinburgh: T. & T. Clark, 1868), p. 430.

resigning himself into the signs of food and drink, putting himself into the hands of other agents, he signifies his forthcoming helplessness and death. He announces his death by 'signing' himself as a thing, to be handled and consumed. This *further* level of transition is the most basic and the most disturbing here: the passage into the community of those who trust God's faithfulness is effected by God in Christ passing from action into passion; the act of new creation is an act of utter withdrawal. Death is the beginning of the new order, and this divine dispossession points back to questions about the very nature of the creative act itself, as more like renunciation than dominance.

Jesus giving himself over into the hands of the disciples anticipates his own *being given over*, his betrayal. The classical liturgies follow Paul in I Cor. 11 in explicitly locating the action 'in the same night that he was betrayed'; and in thus bringing the betrayal within the symbolic scope of the action of taking and breaking bread, the text finally brings into focus the way in which the rite overall embodies the making of a covenant. God's act in Jesus fore-stalls the betrayal, provides in advance for it: Jesus binds himself to vulner-ability before he is bound (literally) by human violence. Thus, those who are at table with him, who include those who will betray, desert and repudiate him, are, if you like, frustrated as betrayers, their job is done for them by their victim. By his surrender 'into' the passive forms of food and drink he makes void and powerless the impending betrayal, and, more, makes the betrayers his guests and debtors, making with them the promise of divine fidelity, the covenant, that cannot be negated by their unfaithfulness. The relinquishing of power in the face of the impending violence of desertion and denial paradoxically allows the Jesus of this narrative to shape and struc-ture the situation, to determine the identity (as guests, as recipients of an unfailing divine hospitality) of the other agents in the story. And so the sequence of transitions finally effects the transformation of the recipients of the bread and wine from betrayers to guests, whose future betrayals are already encompassed in the covenanted welcome enacted by Jesus. The eucharistic ritual narrative thus condenses into itself the longer and more diffuse historical sequence of passion and resurrection – the betrayal fol-lowed by divine vindication and the return of Jesus as host at the table (as in Luke 24 and John 21). What is thus laid out as a sequence, the discovery of the dependability of God's acceptance on the far side of the most decisive human rejection, is, in the action of the Last Supper, anticipated in a single gesture, the gesture in which Jesus identifies himself with the 'passive' stuff of the material creation.

So the overall movement from untrustfulness to covenant faith is sustained and explicated in a whole series of interlocking transitions, of which, as I said earlier, some are dramatically obvious (the consecration of the elements, and their actual consumption), some less so, but equally insistent and important. As with baptism, the symbolic end-point is the community created and bound together by an external assurance, something not evolved or negotiated, something that precedes and outlives particular fractures and failures (betrayal, denial). The most intimate may be a traitor; the most rebellious is already invited as a guest. There is no need to labour the point that the eucharist is at least the climax of Jesus' extending of and accepting of hospitality in relation to the marginal or disreputable in the course of his ministry: the offer of the assurance of God's favour is there inseparable from the acceptance of a specific welcome, the agreement to sit down at table with Jesus. The covenant is, in practice, the guarantee of hospitality. The other becomes the object of love and trust because 'invited' by God, and so, in some sense, trusted by God. God's promise to be faithful, even in advance of betrayal, points towards a community whose bonds are capable of surviving betrayal, and which thus can have no place for reprisal, for violent response to betrayal and breakage, or for pre-emptive action to secure against betrayal. There is no promise that people will not be unfaithful and untrustful towards each other, but there is an assurance that the new humanity does not depend on constant goodwill and successful effort to survive: its roots are deeper. If it is, properly, defenceless, that is because it does not need defending and *cannot* be defended by means that deny its basic assurances (again a theme familiar in Augustine, as in the final book of the *City of God*).[5]

V

Into this pattern too comes an insight about materiality, about our physical environment. The material creation itself can appear as the sign of a divine renunciation: the processes of the world have their integrity, their difference from God, and God's purpose is effected in this difference, not in unilateral divine control, just as the saving work of Christ comes to completion in a renunciation, a surrender of control. This puts at least some questions against an instrumentalist view of material objects. Simone Weil's remarkable imagery about the world of 'dead' matter as the active incarnation of God because it represents the supreme integrity of divine self-effacement as the

[5] Augustine, *De civ. Dei* XXII. vi; *City of God*, ed. D. Knowles, trans. H. Bettenson (Harmondsworth: Penguin, 1972), p. 1088.

only way in which divine love can be received by us without idolatry and distortion, is pertinent here: 'He emptied himself of his divinity by becoming man, then of his humanity by becoming a corpse (bread and wine), matter.'[6]

The objects of the world, seen in the perspective of the eucharist, cannot be proper material for the defence of one ego or group-ego against another, cannot properly be tools of power, because they are signs of a creativity working by the renunciation of control, and signs of the possibility of communion, covenanted trust and the recognition of shared need and shared hope.

There is, then, in sacramental practice, something that does indeed reflect on how we see matter in general; but it is not, I think, a 'sacramental principle' enabling us to recognize divine *presence* in all things. It is more that the divine presence is apprehended by seeing in all things their difference, their particularity, their 'not-God-ness', since we have learned what the divine action is in the renunciation of Christ, his giving himself into inanimate form. And so we can rightly learn to be theologically and morally wary of an anthropocentrism that denies difference or integrity to the material environment, that sees matter always as 'raw' material, the building-blocks of something we are to determine. Matter serves human meanings, and we cannot be so 'deeply Green' as to say that the world must be left untouched by human meanings and human practices; but it is not there simply *to* serve human meanings. The eucharist hints at the paradox that material things carry their fullest meaning for human minds and bodies – the meaning of God's grace and of the common life thus formed – when they are the medium of *gift*, not instruments of control or objects for accumulation. If I may quote words written some years ago: 'in spite of a proper caution about speaking too loosely of the elements as "offered" to God in the Eucharist, we still need to say that the moment of *relinquishing what is ours* is crucial in the eucharistic process.'[7]

VI

What the eucharist thus intimates about matter is that it is itself transfigured into significance in the most comprehensive way when it is dealt with in such a way as to show not dominance but attention or respect, the with-

---

[6] S. Weil, *The Notebooks*, trans. A. Willis (London: Routledge & Kegan Paul, 1956), p. 283.
[7] R. Williams, *Resurrection* (London: Darton, Longman & Todd, 1982), p. 111.

drawal of the controlling ego; and this has some obvious implications for a religious aesthetic as well as a religious economics. But is also pinpoints what is generally difficult and challenging in a sacramental theology of the kind sketched here. Sacramental practice seems to speak most clearly of loss, dependence and interdependence, solidarities we do not choose: none of them themes that are particularly welcome or audible in the social world we currently inhabit as secular subjects. We are told, in effect, that the failure to see ourselves and find ourselves in one or another kind of corporateness is a failure in truthfulness that is profoundly risky. Our liberty to choose and define our goals as individuals or as limited groups with common interest is set alongside the vision of a society in which almost the only thing we can know about the good we are to seek is that it is no one's possession, the triumph of no party's interests. The search for my or our good becomes the search for a good that does not violently dispossess any other – and this not on the basis of rights whose balance must be adjudicated, but because of a conviction that the creative regard calling and sustaining myself is precisely what sustains all. And what makes this something different when an imposed collectivism is the fact that it is appropriated by no force but by trust, by the recognition of the hidden unities of human interest: our own transition, our own 'passover', into the need of the other, wherever and whoever the other may be.

Jean Vanier, in one of his meditations on the experience of the L'Arche communities, observes that being alongside the 'handicapped' frightens the supposedly 'normal' or 'able' person because it obliges them to recognize, sooner or later, the poverty and vulnerability they have in common with those regarded as subnormal; so much more than mere objects of the compassion or benevolence of the competent, the decision-makers.[8] Beyond such fright or disorientation lies the difficult knowledge that I *need* the good, the healing, of the 'handicapped' for my good, as they do my good, my wholeness; and the dignity of being free to give to another is part of what a working Christian community can uncover in those who are marginal, useless or embarrassing to the secular imagination. And a French philosopher associated with L'Arche has added that the common life in such a context obliges us to re-define the whole idea of autonomy: it is not the self's ability to select and freely execute its goals, but the skill of knowing whose aid and companionship you need and the freedom to depend on that.

This is unmistakably an outworking of the sacramental vision. The recog-

---

[8]   See, for example, *The Broken Body* (London: Darton, Longman & Todd, 1988); and also *Community and Growth* (London: Darton, Longman & Todd, 1989).

nition of a shared poverty may sound an evasion of some harsh social questions, but what it essentially points to is the challenge of how there might be
a social order in which the disadvantaged and even the criminal could *trust*
that the common resources of a society would work for their good, and in
which those who, at any given moment, enjoyed advantage or power would
be obliged to examine how their position could be aligned with the given
fact of common and mutual need, how they would act so as to release others
to become 'givers' to them. Now this is not a social *programme* and the sacramental life of the Church does not exist to inspire political attempts to im-
prove society. But the sacraments faithfully performed hold up a mirror to
other forms of sociality and say that these are at risk and under judgement.
The Church declares, symbolically if all too seldom in its own social concreteness, that there is a form of common human life that 'means' or communicates the meanings of God, and it is a form of life in which unchosen
solidarities are more significant than 'elective affinities', and the status of an
invited or desired guest is accessible to all. Because of the assured trust-
worthiness of God, the possibility of a society characterized by fidelity can
be imagined, a society in which mutual commitment consistently judges and
limits sectional acquisitiveness.

It is this capacity to imagine a 'faithful people' that seems to me the most
significant irritant offered by sacramental practice to the contemporary social
scene. One of the most ill-diagnosed features of the present crisis in capitalist
society (fast being exported to aspiring capitalist societies elsewhere) is the
decline of *trust*. Privation today brings cynicism in its wake: there is little
reason for anyone to believe that others are dependable, that resources work
for the common good. If this is a fundamental perception or experience of
the social order, it becomes practically impossible to 'socialize' people who
see their world like this – the young or the old, marginal or suspect communities of any kind, those in prison, the disabled. This invites an adversarial
relation to those institutions felt to have *betrayed* the disadvantaged, directly
or indirectly (why are schools in impoverished areas regular targets for ar-
son?). We can easily misunderstand the much-discussed problem of a so-
called 'culture of dependency' among the disadvantaged. It is not, surely,
that the ideal of collective welfare as such is disabling: welfarism *becomes*
disabling when society is such that recipients or clients of social and health
services are frozen in the attitude of suppliants, never becoming fellow-agents
with those administering aid. They need but are not needed. It is not surprising, in such circumstances, that a discourse of rights *and* claims becomes
more and more strident and – often – uncritical, unexamined.

As will be clear, I do not think myself that this addresses the underlying problem, which is the sense, in the United Kingdom as elsewhere in the North Atlantic world, that there are no social bonds that cannot be re-negotiated in the interest of those already advantaged, and thus that there is no ground or precious little possibility of any investment in construction and collaborative action, inside or outside classical political and social institu-tions. It has been said of our educational flounderings in recent years that the problem arises from the fact that we have no notion of what it is we want to 'induct' young people into in terms of a form of common life; and at present the very possibility of common life in this sense, a practice oriented towards a non-sectional, inter-dependent set of goods, seems remote and theoretical.

I have tried in this essay to outline some aspects of the logic of Christian sacramental action in baptism and eucharist so as to bring out what they assume about social identities. Insofar as they raise for us questions about unities of interest beyond our choosing and our control and about the foun-dations of social trust or fidelity, they should disturb us a good deal. There is little enough symbolic therapy (if I may coin a term) in our societies to reinforce a sense of common need or dependence, and a contingency and vulnerability we share as finite agents. All the more important, then, to resist anything that trivializes or shrinks the symbolic range of our sacramental practice – baptism as essentially a mark of individual confession, the eucharist as a celebration of achieved local human fellowship. They are too important as reminders, to believers and non-believers, of the need to put to death corrupt attachments to a false anthropology. Let them still speak of naked-ness, death, danger, materiality and stubborn promise.

Part Five

LIVING THE MYSTERY

Chapter Fifteen

INCARNATION AND THE RENEWAL OF COMMUNITY

A century ago, the idea was rapidly gaining ground that, if the Church of England had anything to contribute to the spectrum of human society, let alone the spectrum of the Christian churches, it lay in a dual theological principle, underpinning the Church's practice and theory: a principle that could be described as incarnational and sacramentalist. God had become human and thereby shown that human nature could carry the divine glory; God had raised the *whole* of human nature and therefore every man and woman to new dignity, by opening to all a share in the fellowship of Christ's body; the human God had established, as abiding tokens of his presence, material acts and objects, bread, wine and water, and so declared all material existence to be potentially charged with the life of God. In the hands of F. D. Maurice, this added up to a powerful polemic against the Church's withdrawal from the public square: the Incarnation manifested Christ as the head of all humanity, in whom all people in their social and familiar relations were 'included'. The state and the family were already, in some sense, in the Church, because they belonged to the 'Kingdom of Christ' (the title of one of Maurice's most substantial works). The natural relationships of human beings are re-established on firm foundations by God's assumption of human nature; and so getting these relationships right, allowing them to achieve proper fruition and mutual balance, is a matter of clear theological significance. The Church as a distinct institution is provisional, existing until the natural order of human society has been fully penetrated by the saving presence of God. Because the Church reveals that the roots of human relation in family, society and nation lie in the purpose of God, the relational, trinitarian God, a vision emerges of how these forms of relation can be welded together in harmony. All must work towards the same end, no form of relationship can claim absolute right or prerogative over others; the goal is 'liberty', though of a rather elusive and indefinable kind – liberty, it seems, to reflect the social harmony of the Trinity, liberation from the bondage of egotism.

Incarnation here is the bridge between human and divine society, the revelation of how human community is rooted in the communal existence of Father, Son and Holy Spirit. The logic needs a little teasing out, but it will bear examination. A divine person, constituted by the completely reciprocal and selfless relations of God as Trinity, comes to act and live as a human person; thus, where this person is concerned, there is possible a different level, a different depth of human relation than would be the case with any other. As we are reconstituted by relationship with Christ, our capacity for relation with each other is naturally changed as well. All our relationships with each other thus acquire new dimensions; all may be open to the totality of divine relation. The 'point' of the Incarnation is above all the establishing of human communion by showing what the ultimate foundation of common life is, and actively drawing us – with all the forms of common life we are already involved in and which define our existence – into the common life of God. The Church, therefore, is not a 'special' system of human relations, but the place where the rationale of all other relations is made plain and their deepening and securing made possible.

Something like this was the theology that animated not only Maurice but Gore and Scott Holland, Westcott and Stewart Headlam and Conrad Noel; nearer our own time the prophets and apostles of the Parish Communion movement – A. G. Hebert particularly – kept the flame alive. The refusal to draw a firm boundary between sacred and secular became the great theme of the 1960s: Bonhoeffer's prison letters were brought into a rather surprising alliance with the Maurician tradition so as to affirm the holiness of the everyday. There was a theological nexus uniting industrial mission with offertory processions, a new concern to connect the eucharistic celebration with some sort of perceivable human togetherness (coffee at the back of the church, exchanging the peace), and a consequent sense that the eucharist was the proper and natural thing to do at any corporate Christian event. Essentially, despite all the silly misrepresentations that clutter up our present squabbles, the theology of the 1960s was rooted in a whole set of deeply traditional assumptions about doctrine; it would have made no sense at all without the underlying notion (often, of course, quite deeply buried) that the history of Jesus formed what I've called a bridge between human and divine society: some kind of Kenotic Christology (enabling a strong doctrine of the identity of Jesus' human a subjectivity with the person of the divine Word), and a markedly pluralist or 'social' doctrine of the Trinity seemed almost self-evident. And the Hellenic, Platonizing side of some of the great nineteenth-century thinkers bore fruit in a renewed enthusiasm for Eastern Christianity and a certain embarrassment about what was usually thought of as 'Latin' or 'Augustinian' individualism.

Most of this is still with us, if in rather muted ways. The Church of England's Alternative Service Book of 1980 enshrines some of this theology, particularly in the eucharistic order and the rite of matrimony (an eloquent statement of continuity between divine and human relation); concern with tangible marks of human fellowship at the eucharist is still intense in many quarters; the Board for Social Responsibility often continues to assume that its working parties will be doing theological reflection on what people are already doing; the recent surge of interest in 'creation theology' has brought some very Maurician themes back into focus; and, last but not least, public debate about the Incarnation suggests that the identification of Jesus as human subject with the second person of the Trinity is still ardently held. I suspect that Moltmann's *The Crucified God* (1974) was the single most influential book of 'technical' theology for clergy and interested lay people in the 1970s, and it is a book quite pervaded by such an identification. As a theology of *solidarity*, it sharpened the edges of Maurician Anglicanism quite a bit, yet remained within a strangely similar framework: human forms of relatedness are to be judged yet also transfigured by the solidarity of God with human beings. Moltmann's later work, *The Trinity and the Kingdom of God* (1981), explicitly took up the work of some of the Anglican Christian Socialists and their heirs. On the ecumenical front, the adoption of Eastern Orthodox theologies like Lossky and Zizioulas has ensured that the 'bridge between human and divine society' is still a decisive basis for thinking about the Church; ARCIC's use of *Koinonia* as a key category owes something to the same background.

However, there have in fact been deeply damaging criticisms made of what I shall call the incarnationalist consensus; these have not made much impact on our public rhetoric as a church, but they have led a good many theologians in the Church to move with more caution, to admit that they are less clear than their predecessors about the Incarnation and its social consequences. I want to look at the two main kinds of criticism around, and attempt to assess their seriousness; and then to see whether the consensus can survive – and, if not, what there might still be to say about Christ and society.

First of all, the incarnationalist consensus has been exposed, directly and indirectly, to *political* criticism. Maurice's picture (and, to a lesser extent, that of later writers in the Christian Social Union circle) assumes that the Incarnation is a crown and consummation for a world whose patterns of relation are not *fundamentally* askew. Family and nation, in particular, are of themselves good patterns of sociality, needing only the context of incarnational theology to save them from idolatry and set them on a firm base. But the secular analyst of ideology may object: if you say that the social forms of family and nation are good, but waiting for the seal of Christian completion, precisely *what* forms are you talking about? These are very basic categories of human belonging, the inescapable systems into which we are born: we cannot have no kin, no nation, no shared history, however little we know or care about it. Granted; but at any given point in history, families and nations will be organizing themselves in particular, contingent ways. History tells us that these social units do not have a single, natural, timeless structure; to appeal to such a supposed structure is always to select, prefer (there may be reasons for this, but that's not the point here), not to utter what everyone always knows.

Thus, to say in 1889 or 1999 that family and nation are essentially good, and that their goodness and fruitfulness are indicated and fulfilled in connection with the trinitarian relations of God to God, mediated to us in the Incarnation, can be tantamount to saying that family and nation here and now are the (necessary?) underpinning of Christian identity, and thus to giving massive religious sanction to these institutions more or less as they are. In other words, the doctrine of the Incarnation has come to be functional to a particular social order; and this entails that a criticism of that order in family and society will involve a criticism of the doctrine, and the decay of the social pattern will make the doctrine less believable.

Is this fair to the 'incarnationalist consensus'? Partly; in the terms outlined, it does indeed lay itself open to the charge of sacralizing what already exists, assuming the givenness of the present order, and underplaying the role both of historical chance and of human creativity in social life, including the actual concrete forms of family and national life. It moves with rather suspicious quickness from the observation that there are sorts of belonging that we don't and can't choose to the uncomfortable implication that our relation to these contexts is basically 'contemplative', a penetration by theological understanding into their essential structure in the mind and will of God. It gives us very little *theological* ground for asking awkward questions about the social realities of belonging, let alone for suggesting that there is a rather fundamental Christian vocation of *not* belonging, in families, nations, patriarchal 'organic' states. And this points to the second area of criticism, to the deep theological problem raised by the incarnationalist consensus: it can encourage a marked degree of *abstraction* from the story of God incarnate.

The life, death and resurrection of Jesus are not an epiphany, a simple showing of God, a moment in which the world's history is touched and changed.
There is a specific *shape* to the story: it is part of a history marked by a strong
dimension of conflict. The gospels make it harshly clear that belonging with
Jesus upsets other kinds of belonging – of family, of status, even of membership of the children of Abraham. Jesus on the cross is consciously portrayed
as isolated, condemned by the political and religious communities to which,
in one sense, he belonged. An incarnational theology has to deal with the
question passed by the cross: it is not enough to say *Christus Consummator*, in
the face of a story of discontinuity and costly separation.

And this is equally the story of early Christianity. It claimed to do for
Jewish faith and history what Maurice believed the gospel did for the natural
orders of social being, yet found itself bitterly at odds with the synagogue,
incapable of saying what it had to say in the terms of historical Jewish faith
alone. The Church becomes something different from Israel, and soon, of
course, generates the poisonous legacy of hatred and contempt for Israel that
has shadowed its entire history. The Church is equally unassimilable in the
Roman Empire: it subverts the family by encouraging the vocation of the
homeless celibate teacher (male or female); and even when it makes an uneasy truce with patriarchal domesticity, it is still at odds with a political order
that lays claim to religious sanction. Christ was followed by the wandering
teachers of the earliest days of Christianity by martyrs and confessors, by
communities whose links across the frontiers of empire could be a source of
political danger (as late as the 320s a bishop could be executed by a pagan
administration because he was suspected of having contacts in the Christian
kingdom of Armenia, at a time when border warfare was impending). Christians were universally accused of bad citizenship because of their unwillingness to do military or civic duty in a state whose officers represented a 'divine'
monarch. They were suspected of fantastic outrages precisely because of not
taking family and empire for granted: if they questioned these things – so the
pious citizen reasoned – no wonder if they practised incest and killed and ate
children!

We seem to be rather a long way from the gospel that sets a seal on the
natural forms of corporate life: Christian forms of relationship here stand *over
against* other kinds, with little sense that they reveal the inner structure or
rationale of these latter. 'Natural' systems of relation, family belonging, membership of a 'race' or nation, provide the metaphors for the relations of Christians to each other and to their God; but this is less to do with some vision of
natural analogies than with a claim to establish the *true* relationships of which
existing systems are a distorted reflection. It is only gradually that this is

domesticated in such a way as to suggest that the analogy legitimates, rather than overthrowing, the existing order. Jesus, in Matthew's gospel, orders his followers to call no-one 'Father' except God, just as he insists that family relationships are superseded by relations between himself and those who hear and obey God's word; but by the time of writing of the letter to the Ephesians, the Father is the one from whom all fatherhoods take their name – which implies a kind of continuity, and may (though not necessarily) carry the implication that relation to human fathers ought to mirror our relation to the heavenly Father, an implication with rather ambivalent further consequences. The subsequent history of ethical reflection in the early churches shows the tensions arising over the interpretation of statements like this.

The point is that Christian beginnings give at best a limited support to the 'incarnationalist' model. There is certainly a pull towards the idea that Christian faith makes people better members of family and society, a trend visible in the Pastoral Epistles and in second-century apologetic; but it does not succeed in itself giving a rationale for the existence of that distinct human network of relations called the Church, existing as something which is neither family nor nation nor *imperium*. It is this that should prompt us to look harder at 'incarnationalism' in the forms I outlined earlier; and to ask, ultimately, whether the incarnationalism of this particular tradition actually undermines the doctrine on which it rests, by obscuring for us the logic of that doctrine and the process whereby it found articulation.

So I shall try to begin somewhere else, by asking a little about that process. The Christian movement, as far back as we can trace it, is a *missionary* movement: that is, it works on the assumption that it has something to say that is communicable beyond its present boundaries and is humanly attractive or compelling across these boundaries. It assumes that it has the capacity and the obligation to seek to persuade persons from all imaginable human backgrounds that it is decisively relevant to their humanity, that it can deliver from whatever bondage women and men may happen to live under. Its relevance to all *depends* on its difference from existing patterns of human relation and power: if it 'fulfils' anything, it is a buried capacity for communion between human beings as such – as flesh and spirit, as mortal, sinful and walled-off from each other, in need of a relation God alone can provide. The Church is authorized to bring people into this unconstrained relation with God and each other through its participation in the authority of Jesus raised from the dead: the Risen One who is Lord of the Church is the one rejected by the existing patterns of human corporate life, dying alone, so that his new life beyond death 'belongs' to none of those patterns. Just as, in his ministry, Jesus establishes community in his own right and on his own authority with those outside the values and the validations of kindred and nation, those who are not 'family' and not a 'people', so, decisively, as risen from the dead, he is the one who empowers the community to make a new people, a new kindred, out of those who do not belong in Israel by birth, as well as those such as Jesus met in his lifetime who had put themselves out of Israel by failure or unfaithfulness. The Church, in other words, proclaims and struggles to realize a 'belonging together' of persons in community in virtue of nothing but a shared belonging with or to the risen Jesus.

To ascribe to Jesus, in his ministry and in his risen existence, the authority to re-make the frontiers of human belonging is already to raise the question of the source and nature of that authority. For both Jew and Gentile, the setting of the boundaries of a community was divine work: for the Jew because Israel was a people gathered and defined by the summons of God in the covenant tradition; for the Gentile because gods provided the sanctions of law and custom in the Greek city, and a divine monarch sanctioned the unity and cohesion of the *imperium Romanum.* Jesus stands as a potential rival to both; though his own unswerving relatedness, obedience, answerability, to the God of Israel held back most Christians from wholly disowning the Jewish past. But there should be no doubt that, as the defining focus of a new people, a new citizenship, a new kingdom, Jesus functions as a divine figure. And perhaps at a more lastingly significant level – he functions not simply as a god but as *the God of Jewish scripture* in two respects: he creates a people by *covenant* (as in the ancient and widespread tradition of the Last Supper), and by a summons that makes something radically *new.* In giving to the outcast, the powerless, the freedom to take their part in renewing the world and setting aside the existing tyranny of faceless powers and human betrayals, God brings life out of emptiness, reality out of nothing: Jesus Christ, as the bodily presence of that summons, the concrete medium for that gift to be given, is the presence in our world of the absolute creative resource of God, God's capacity to make the difference between something and nothing. God has chosen things low and contemptible, mere nothings, to overthrow the existing order (I Cor. 1.28); Jesus, reaching out to those who are nothing, is the tangible form of God's creative choosing.

In short, the question of Jesus' status arises out of his role in the formation of a human community different from what we ordinarily think of as 'natural' communities, a community whose limits are at the same time the ultimate natural 'limits' – 'the ends of the earth'. *The world we inhabit* is the potential scope of the community that is created by relation to Jesus. It is, you might say, a social vision that shapes the doctrine of the Incarnation, in the first instance, not the reverse; or rather, it is the social *fact* of a community with no foreordained boundaries. As Paul argues in II Cor. 5, what now decides our awareness of and attitude to another human being is no longer what he or she is by race or kin; all human beings are in principle cut off from their identity in these terms and seen a fresh as related to Jesus. When that relation is realized, 'there is a new world' (15–17); and what is it that can constitute a world by relation to itself but God, who must therefore be acknowledged to be 'in Christ reconciling the world to himself'. Nowhere in the NT is the logic of the confession of Christ's oneness with God on the basis of the new creation so fully and clearly set out as here.

The 'incarnational consensus' is right to say that (as I put it earlier) 'as we are reconstituted by relationship with Christ, our capacity for relationship with others is . . . changed as well'; but this is not in the sense that our existing relations acquire an extra 'depth' or a clearer legitimacy. The NT suggests rather that relatedness to Christ establishes relations that are *sui generis* with other human beings – relations which have something of the sheer givenness of family connection (i.e. we don't choose them according to private preference and convenience), yet which are based on no 'natural' substrate except common humanity, common creatureliness, common pos-session of that image which is the potential for growth into the likeness of Christ. What those relations are like we learn once more from the most theologically charged pages of the NT, in Paul and the Fourth Gospel.

It is not simply that relations of 'love' are established; that would tell us very little. Far more important is Paul's conviction, very fully elaborated in the closing chapters of Romans and underlying the discussion of the Body in I Cor., that the relation of Christians to each other is one of building up: we are engaged, in Christ, in *constructing* each other's humanity, bringing one another into the inheritance of power and liberty whose form is defined by Jesus. And that form, as Paul makes equally clear, is precisely the power that gives authority and assurance to others and the freedom that sets others free. There is a quite proper circularity to the ethics of the Christian community: I am called to use the authority given me by Christ (by Christ's *giving away* of power conceived as control and security) so as to nurture that authority in others, so that they may give it away in turn – to me and to others. So in John 13 what Jesus gives (service) is to be the currency of exchange between believers: to grow into Jesus' 'Lordship' (his freedom from all other powers) is to become able to wash one another's feet, that is, to welcome them as a guest at the same table. These relations are not those by which 'this world' defines itself; and, for John, the re-enactment by Christians of the service of Christ provokes hatred and conflict. The systems of this world cannot con-tain or control the rival 'world' established by Christ in which the fundamental form of relation is the mutual construction of persons in the likeness of Jesus.

So Christology exists because of the reconstruction of community – that reconstruction which carries with it the vision of a human belonging more comprehensive than any existing form of human connectedness, race, kindred or *imperium*. By presenting itself as a new *world*, Christianity finds itself in its early years often in sharp conflict with family, synagogue and kingdom; but not as another society competing for a position alongside them. Maurice and his heirs were right to be suspicious of an undue interest in the Church as a distinctive *institution* among others. The Church claims to show the human world as such what is possible for it in relation to God – not through the adding of ecclesiastical activities to others, and not through the sacralizing of existing communal forms, but by witnessing to the possibility of a common life sustained by God's creative breaking of existing frontiers and showing that creative authority in the pattern of relation already described, the building up of Christ-like persons. The Church's good news is that human community is possible; the Church's challenge is in its insistence that this possibility is realized only in that giving away of power in order to nurture authority in others that is learned in the giving away of God in Jesus, and its further insistence that the relations constituting Christ's Body neither compete with nor vindicate others, but simply stand in their own right as the context which relativizes all others.

So it seems as though, for us to grasp that the event of Jesus is the act of God, the Church must first understand its distinctiveness and separateness – not from the human race but from all communities and kinships whose limits fall short of the human race. The Church's primitive and angular separateness, the Church as envisaged in the gospels and as it existed in many areas of the early Christian world, is meant to be a protest on behalf of a unified world, the world that holds together in and because of Jesus Christ. This paradox is a hard one to live out. It suggests, certainly, that if we are to keep on learning about Christ, then at the very least the Church needs practices, conventions and life-patterns that keep alive the distinctiveness of the Body: the prosaic historical witness of the religious life, with its affirmation that discipleship may over-ride the family, the witness of those committed visibly to peace between peoples, the active interchange of mission between churches in diverse cultures. These things are more necessary than ever in a church historically prone to see itself as a national institution. To use the heavily loaded language common in these discussions; a church which does not at least possess certain features of a 'sect' cannot act as an agent of transformation. If there is a case for the Church's establishment it must be cast in terms of the Church's witness to a community without boundaries other than Christ – not the Church's guardianship of the Christian character of a nation (which so easily becomes the Church's endorsement of the *de facto* structures and constraints of the life of a sovereign state). The legal establishment of a church *might* be a state's witness to the reality of goals beyond its own, even of a state's acknowledgement of being answerable to the community of human beings as such; though it must be said both that legal establishment in a sovereign state such as ours (having no concept of *limited* sovereignty) begs a good many questions, and that it is doubtful whether such a situation could speak of unrestricted human community when it will inevitably be seen as privileging one of a number of religious groupings within the state. A Gore Lecture by Professor Donald MacKinnon more than twenty years ago dilated on the inescapable tension between 'Kenosis and Establishment'. I'm not sure that anything very much has changed.

A brief note may be in order here, prompted by the word 'kenosis'. I noted earlier that the 'incarnationalist consensus' made much of the continuity between the second person of the Trinity and the subjectivity of Jesus, and, in more recent years, of the solidarity of God with human suffering guaranteed by this continuity. The picture that emerges from early Christian belief as I have been trying to 'read it' is slightly different. The divinity of Jesus is what we recognize in finding in him the creative newness of God: his life and death and resurrection *as a whole* effect the new creation. Thus that life and death and resurrection are in a highly distinctive sense the act and the speech of God. Because they create by renunciation, by giving away, we learn to see God's creative act as in itself a giving away, a letting go; and because the giving away of Jesus is itself a response to the giving God whom Jesus calls *Abba*, we learn that God's act includes both a giving and a responding, that God's life is itself in movement and in relation with itself. The ground is prepared for a doctrine of God as Trinity. Jesus is the fleshly and historical form of God's act of giving in its responsive dimension – God's answer to God, the embodiment of God's own joy in God. 'Kenosis', renunciation, is the way of Jesus in his historical life, opening to us the vision of how God always is; but it is not the *process* which links divinity to humanity, it is not what God must undergo to become human. This is why I confess to being cautious about moving too rapidly to a doctrine of God having human experiences 'through' Jesus. It is true to say that because of Jesus there is a change in our relation to other suffering human beings: if the community of the new creation depends upon the building up of each by all and all by each, the pain and frustration of any human beings is mine. It is true to say that because of Jesus we recognize God's action as essentially

directed towards healing, restoration, pity and renewal; it is not inappropri-
ate to speak of God's act and life engaged or involved at the depths of human
pain. But it seems to me not clear that we should conclude that God, by
suffering as direct subject the human sufferings of Jesus, becomes more profoundly involved in human pain of all kinds than he would otherwise be.
On the contrary, God's loving involvement is *there already*: what happens in
Jesus is that we are drawn into a community in which our engagement in the
fate of human beings acquires something of the same exposure and
unconditionality as God's.

Identifying Jesus and the second person of the Trinity as if they were two
comparable individuals now recognized as the same in different 'phases' is
not what early Christianity (or medieval, for that matter) meant by recognizing the divinity of Christ; to hold that it is so is to invite serious problems.
How can the *specific* agony of Jesus be God's doorway into all human suffering without losing its historical distinctness? How can the identifying of
Jesus with God's Word avoid presenting the human Jesus as a static icon of
the divine rather than the embodiment of God's act to create a moving and
expanding network of saving relationship (the feminist objection to some
supposedly traditional Christologies is rooted in this anxiety)? Can we make
sense of God literally turning into a portion of the world? These and other
objections to the 'consensus' doctrine of the Incarnation, including many of
those raised by Anglo-Saxon theological liberals in the late 1970s especially,
should give us pause. But part of my intention is to suggest that a better
understanding of the origin and logic of incarnational doctrine is able to
meet the difficulties of both feminist and radical, and to point a way forward
to a fuller integration of our doctrine of Christ and our commitment to the
Church's mission in creation.

To return, then, to this latter question: does all this mean that the only
authentic Christian witness is separation, monastic or sectarian? The New
Testament already has to face something like this question as, in the writings
of the second generation, we begin to find the rationale for a Christian
family life remarkably like that of the best of Roman morality and a general
insistence on good order and a public good name. By the time of Augustine's *City of God*, there is a complex theory of belonging in a cosmic order
that includes the family and the empire. But it is Augustine's model – surprisingly, perhaps – which gives us some hints about a way forward, as we
shall see. If the Church exists, as it does, at an angle to the forms of human
association we treat as natural, the temptation is to seek to ignore or abolish
these forms: to treat people as if they were not deeply and permanently
moulded by their natural and unchosen belonging, to a family or a language

group or a political system. But this is manifestly damaging and illusory. The Jesus of the gospels is not a human cipher and does not speak to human ciphers; any attempt to pretend otherwise simply means that it is not the whole or the real person who is brought before God. The persons who are involved in the community of the Kingdom are not 'new creations' in the sense of having all their relationships and affiliations cancelled. The question thus becomes how existing patterns of belonging can collaborate with the patterns of the new community, if at all, how the goals and priorities of these existing patterns are to be brought together with the constructive work of the Kingdom, the Body.

The pattern of the Body, and the universal scope of Christian mission, immediately suggest certain clear criteria. There are forms of human belonging which, when affirmed and endorsed as they are, when treated as normative or final, are manifestly at odds with the Kingdom: if belonging to such a community means deliberately internalizing its estimate of itself, the Christian is bound to say that anyone so involved needs to find a way of distancing themselves. Like Bonhoeffer in the Third Reich, such a person may discover that, though they cannot forget the sheer fact of belonging to a nation, their most important Christian service to that nation may be resistance, active or passive – a calling of their community to account in the name of a wider human fellowship, possible and partly actual through Christ. This example is almost a cliché; but it serves to sharpen the contour of the issues here. Any racial group or language group or sovereign state whose policy or programme it is to pursue its interest at the direct cost of others has no claim on the Christian's loyalty in itself. Loyalty is to be given to the associations of human belonging to the extent that they equip their members for life in the Body, for the creative formation of persons by the receiving and giving away of Christ's authority in the community. With Augustine, we can rightly speak of the city of God as rejoicing in and making use of secular peace and order to the extent that it nurtures (quite unconsciously, it may be) the vision of the horizons of God's commonwealth; though we might have – in an idolatrous and hard-hearted century – more to say about what it means *not* to co-operate with a secular order systematically crushing the liberty of other groups or its own citizens.

The question the Church is authorized to ask of any human association is whether it is making it more or less difficult for people to grow into a maturity in which they are free to give to one another and nourish one another, free enough to know that they have the capacity to be involved in re-creating persons. That maturity is made substantively possible in encounter with the giving God incarnate in Christ; but the empirical human possibilities of growing in it are to a great extent shaped, even if not fully determined, by what we already belong to, and how. So the Church does not either affirm or deny 'the state' in the abstract: it asks what kind of humanity this or that state fosters – what degree of power in its citizens, what level of mutual care, what vision that is more than local, what scepticism about claims to absolute sovereignty and the right to absolute security. The Church does not either affirm or deny 'the nation' in the abstract: it asks whether or not people living with this or that corporate history, common language and culture, are capable of seeing it as a thread in a larger tapestry, or whether it is understood as something whose purity and survival are worth any price in blood and misery. And – a thought uncongenial, I know, to many British Christians – the Church does not either affirm or deny 'the family' in the abstract: it asks about the structures of material and psychological control in this or that family, about how the various patterns of family relation fail or succeed in creating creators of mutual relationship. It is a dangerous mythology, to which the Church readily falls victim, to talk glibly about the family. Historically, the Church has blessed the faithful sexual union of man and woman as an effective sign of God; but it has not formally absolutized any structure of kinship or model of authority in the family – however much in practice it has endorsed patriarchy as 'natural' – and it *has* blessed and theologized the life of single adults in religious community.

So it will not do simply to think of the Church uncovering the rationale of natural human associations. The Church, I suggest, judges and interacts with all these, and in some circumstances gives thanks for them just as in others it questions or resists them. But *as* Church it cannot easily generalize; *as* Church, it is that form of human association that claims to ground the possibility of unrestricted community and shared and co-operative freedom among people; and that is its concern. It is here, in the acknowledgement of the Church's *specific* and *constructive* vocation, that the 'incarnationalist consensus' has been weakest. It perceived that the Church was not simply an interest group, with distinct skills and virtues running in parallel to those of other groups – and to turn to Maurice or Westcott from the ecclesiastical controversies of the nineteenth century can certainly restore a damaged sense of reality – but it concluded that *therefore* the Church was a dimension, a moment, a presence within the group life of human beings. I have argued that the truth is otherwise: that the relations of human beings in the Body of Christ, relations dependent simply on a shared commitment to and promise to be with the risen Jesus, provide the context and the critique for other systems, the irritant that can prevent the human world from simply settling down with mutually exclusive and competing tribalisms. This is the conviction on which the confession of Jesus as God-with-us initially rests; and I believe that the doctrine of the Incarnation is recovered and revitalized so often as we recover our authority as a *Christian* community to challenge and resist what holds back *human* community – and that the doctrine looks redundant or impenetrable only when we have lost that vision. We owe so much to the great figures of the 'consensus', not least the plain sense of the theological weight of social issues; but I wonder if their doctrine would have been clearer if they had been able to re-imagine the Church in a more prophetic mould – and if their constructive engagement in society would have been deeper and harder if they had let themselves be more *surprised* at the incarnate God. Christology after all, like thought itself, should begin (and end) in wonder.

Chapter Sixteen

INTERIORITY AND EPIPHANY: A READING IN NEW TESTAMENT ETHICS

I

Common to a good deal of contemporary philosophical reflection on human identity is the conviction that we are systematically misled, even corrupted, by a picture of the human agent as divided into an outside and an inside – a 'true self', hidden, buried, to be excavated by one or another kind of therapy, ranging from the intellectual therapy of the post-Cartesian tradition (the modern 'philosophy of mind', the epistemological struggle) to the psychological therapy of another 'analytic' tradition, the tradition inaugurated by Freud and still flourishing in various serious and more popular forms. Modern ethics and theology alike have been haunted by a presence usually called the *authentic* self: an agent whose motivation is transparent, devoid of self-deception and of socially conditioned role playing. As a therapeutic fiction, this is a construct of great power and usefulness. I suspect, though, that it is also a fiction that is intellectually shaky and, in the last analysis, morally problematic. It plays with the idea that my deepest, most significant or serious 'interest' is something given and something unique; it brackets the difficult issue of how we are to think through our human situation as embodying a common task, in which the sacredness of the authentic self's account of its own interest is not the beginning and the end of moral discourse.

'No depth exists in subject until it is created. No *a priori* identity awaits us . . . Inwardness is a process of becoming, a work, the labour of the negative. The self is not a substance one unearths by peeling away layers until one gets to the core, but an integrity one struggles to bring into existence.[1] This sharp formulation by a contemporary American philosopher who attempts to bring Hegel, Heidegger, Marx and Freud into fruitful conversation concentrates our thinking very effectively. For if there is no pre-existent 'inwardness', where is the 'real' self to be found or made but in the world of exchange – language and interaction. More particularly, this statement of the question makes it clear that the self as self-conscious is the product of *time*. We tend to conceive interiority in terms of space – outer and inner, husk and kernel; what if our 'inner life' were better spoken of in terms of extension in time? the time it takes to understand?[2] My sense of the 'hiddenness' of another self is something I develop in the ordinary difficulty of conversation and negotiation. I don't follow; I don't know how to respond in such a way that what I want can be made clear and achieved. Conversation and negotiation are of their nature unpredictable, 'unscripted'; their outcome is not determined. Thus I develop the sense of the other speaker/agent as *obscure* to me: their motivation or reasoning is not transparent, not open to my full knowledge, but always waiting to be drawn out and clarified. In this process I develop correspondingly the sense of myself as obscure: I must explain myself if I am to attain what I want, and as I try to bring to speech what is of significance to me in such a way as to make it accessible to another, I discover that I am far from sure what it is that I can say. I become difficult to myself, aware of the gap between presentation and whatever else it is that is active in my acting. It is not surprising that I embody these things in the picture of one hidden self confronting another, both hampered by the inadequacy of language or shared conventions – with the result that we can then fall into the trap of supposing that there could be a self-presence without difficulty, a real or truthful apprehension of myself and another agent or agents, freed from the distorting effects of our imperfect linguistic or social tools.

In other words, we assimilate the difficulty of mutual understanding between two agents to the difficulty of two people speaking a different language; somewhere there are better tools, a speech in which we are more properly or honestly at home. But in fact the difficulty is not that experi-

[1]   Walter A. Davis, *Inwardness and Existence. Subjectivity in/and Hegel, Heidegger, Marx, and Freud* (University of Wisconsin Press, 1989), p. 105.
[2]   See Rowan Williams, 'The Suspicion of Suspicion: Wittgenstein and Bonhoeffer', in Richard H. Bell (ed.), *The Grammar of the Heart. New Essays in Moral Philosophy and Theology* (San Francisco: Harper, 1988), pp. 36–53, especially pp. 48–9.

enced by two speakers, one or both of whom are working in an unfamiliar or problematic medium. The exchanges of conversation and negotiation *are* the essence of what is going on, not unsatisfactory translations of a more fundamental script. The difficulty is inherent in what is being done, and could not be removed by a more adaptable or familiar medium. Difficulty and what goes with it, the awareness of possible error (in how I hear and how I am heard) form the stuff of my awareness of what we commonly call the 'interior' life, mine and the other's. It thus becomes abundantly clear that my interiority is a construct that emerges through the labour of exchange – which is not to say that it is a reducible, secondary, epiphenomenal matter. Quite the contrary: what is lost in this analysis is not the ideal of a truthful self-perception but the myth of a truthful perception that can be uncovered by the re-description of the self's linguistic and social performance as the swaddling-clothes of a hidden and given reality – which, of course, divorced from the reality of performance, becomes formal to the point of emptiness.

The 'for-myself' and the 'for-another' of awareness and speech are thus not separable. Even when I try to formulate or picture my 'real' self, what I am in effect doing is imagining an ideal other, an ideal interlocutor and observer, a listener to whom I am making perfect sense. The danger, of course, is that this imagined other, the perfect listener, blocks out the actual, less perfect, less sympathetic hearers with whom I am actually and temporally doing business, so that my self-perception remains firmly under my own control. The proper logic of this recognition that my self-knowledge emerges from converse and exchange enjoins a consistent scepticism about claims to have arrived at a final transparency to myself. If it is converse that gives me a self to know, the continuance of converse means that I have never done with knowing. I do not cease to be *vulnerable* to other accounts of myself, to the pressure to revise what I say of myself at those points where I have to recognize a breakdown in the movement of exchange, the delay and obscurity that drives me back to ask, 'What *did* I mean?' The point at which I cease to ask or even understand such a challenge is, arguably, the beginning of mental sickness, the index of a pathology. And this vulnerability must also extend to my account of my own interest or 'good': I cannot assume that my good or my destiny is specified by the mysterious interior reality that is imagined to underlie the surface activities of language and negotiation. I shall discover what is good for me, I shall discover how to construe and articulate my interest, just as I construe everything else about my self-perception – in the processes of encounter and exchange, not in the excavation of a buried inner agenda.

II

This is the point at which substantive conflict seems to arise. Say that we are indeed in the process of constructing the inner life and the integrity that is believed to go with it in the processes of conversation or negotiation: this cannot deliver a vision of anything like a *common* good in itself. To discover what is good for me in the process of converse may well in the first instance mean discovering the need for resistance, the need to *deny* that my interest is specified for me by some other in a unilateral way. That there is an adversarial moment in the construction of the self and its knowledge of itself is, of course, the insight that fuels Hegel's entire discussion of the Lord and the Bondsman;[3] and in the complex political situation of our century, it some-times appears to be the dominant motif in the discovery or appropriation of selfhood: I discover who or what I am by the discovery of myself as victim, stripped of my 'true' identity by some other. My interest must be articulated by denial and revolt, by a distancing from the other's definition of the linguistic field. Hence what we might call the 'separatist moment' in all twentieth-century liberationist movements, racial, gender-based and so on. I/ we am/are not what you have taught us to be and to believe; to be what *we* truly are, we must reject *your* account of reality and overturn what it privileges (European rationality, pale pigmentation, masculine bias in language, hetero-sexual coupling). Current debate about 'political correctness' in the United States and elsewhere is often clouded by a twofold misunderstanding (curable, perhaps, by the digestion of more Hegel): on the one hand, the separatist moment is absolutized in an insistence that self-definition, defini-tion 'from within', is the most fundamental moral need in a situation of manifest and continuing inequity; on the other hand, objectors fail to see the significance of the recognition entailed here that language and negotiation are about *power*, and that the bestowal of power on the powerless requires the most unsparing interrogation of the processes by which groups, persons and interests are in fact, historically and socially, defined. The former ends up in the crudest kind of mythology about self-realization on the basis of some mysterious inner essence, unpolluted by converse; the latter remains at a resolutely pre-reflective (and so essentially pre-political) stage of awareness. Both sides of the debate, insofar as they fall into one or other of these atti-tudes, explicitly or implicitly, assume there is no *difficulty*, to use the word yet again, about the discovery of interest, and no continuing agenda to lead

---

[3]   *Phenomenology*, 133–50.

us into questioning about *common* interest. They remain at the level of adversarial definition: interest is secured at the expense of another.

The problem to be faced and overcome, then, is one about how we move beyond rivalry; how we are to arrive at ethics properly so called, instead of a battleground between competing interests (I take it that ethics is nothing if not a discipline for evaluating and judging local or individual claims to know the good in the light of accounts of the good that are not purely local or individual). This leads us back to reflection on the processes of self-discovery already sketched in this essay. We learn how to 'speak' ourselves, how to 'utter' ourselves, in conversation, in the presence of an interlocutor. To imagine an ideal interlocutor, what I earlier called the perfect listener, the presence to which I am wholly transparent or to whom I make sense, is to imagine a presence with which I do *not* in the ordinary sense 'negotiate'; the capacity of the other for attention, an attention complete enough to assure me of unconditioned space or time to develop and discover what I am to be, is in such an ideal case not shadowed at all by the other's own particular agenda, by another set of interests comparable to mine. Yet to spell it out in these terms is to display the character of this ideal interlocutor as a fantasy. On the one hand, my language and self-presentation only acquire identity in the *contentions* of exchange with another, in a set of particular and historical encounters with those elements in the world of personal transactions that deny my illusions of control, my passion for 'scripting' the language used around me; I become a self only in the self-dispossession of discovering that there are things I cannot acquire, goals I cannot attain. On the other hand, to absolutize contention is to remain trapped in a stage of consciousness where the other is always liable to be apprehended as a threat or a rival. Thus I do not emerge into selfhood without concrete otherness; I do not discover my humanity in the absence of frustration, the resistance of the world to my will (if I can even be said to have a 'will' in the absence of the linguistic specificity that is developed in negotiation). But I do not recognize the convergence of my interest and the other's without a move beyond opposition and negotiation. In the crude terms of recent social debates, it is in a measure true that we do not grow without competition; but competition without mutual recognition and mutual need is barbarous and self-destructive.

The other who is concrete yet not a partner in negotiation, not engaged in a process of mutual 'adjustment', seems, then, to be what we look for and perhaps presuppose in the search for a way into ethical discourse. The concreteness of the other cannot be sacrificed; the ideal listener will not do, since this figure has no 'resistance', and is, ultimately, only at the service of my development; and an other purely instrumental to my specification finally collapses back into the chaos of my undifferentiated existence, into pre-consciousness rather than a conscious self-appropriation.[4] A concrete other of this kind would have to be apprehended as other *equally* to my own project and interest *and* to any specific other subject in the field of negotiation; neither competing with me for moral space, nor endorsing or protecting my moral space over against other subjects. In this sense, we can say that it must be articulated as that to which I and others are commonly answerable; it is what makes sense of me as a moral subject (i.e., as a subject not determined by my private calculation of my interest or good), and is therefore what I appeal to in making sense of my positions or policies. But, precisely because it is what makes sense of me in this way, questioning and re-shaping my would-be private or partisan account of what is good for me, it is more than a static principle of legitimation for what I happen to decide. If I appeal to it in the struggle of negotiation, I do so in the acknowledgement that I as well as the other will be exposed to its challenge, and liable to be changed by it. Further, I can accept this situation as something other than simply the triumph of another will over mine in the battle for moral space, since this non-competitive other remains other as well to the specific 'rival' subject that confronts me at any given moment. The appeal either of myself or of a specific historical other to this presence with which neither of us can negotiate provides a ground for discourse about our human negotiation that is not immediately trapped in rivalry: a common discourse before a common other, to which I and the other are alike vulnerable or responsible.

If we can and do presuppose something like this in trying to formulate a moral discourse at all, that is, a discourse not determined by the tribalism of competing accounts of the good, a discourse of shared self-criticism, what exactly is it that we are talking about? We could say, as a good many would, that this is a necessary fiction if we are to find a Kantian 'tribunal' for the settling of moral dispute.[5] But as soon as the appeal to common answerability is defined as an instrumental construction, we are in danger of returning to our starting-point: *really* human interests are conflictual, but it is more convenient to pretend otherwise, since social harmony is desirable. However, on

---

[4]   This would be my central criticism of 'non-realist' accounts of theological discourse, in particular the work of Don Cupitt; see, for example, his *Creation Out of Nothing* (SCM Press, 1990), *What is a Story?* (SCM Press, 1992), etc.

[5]   See Kant's First Critique, ch. 1, section 2 of 'Transcendental Doctrine of Method' on this idea of the universal tribunal; cf. my own discussion of this in 'Doctrinal Criticism: Some Questions', Sarah Coakley and David Pailin (eds), *The Making and Remaking of Christian Doctrine. Essays in Honour of Maurice Wiles* (Oxford University Press, 1993), pp. 239–64, esp. pp. 258ff.

such an account, it is desirable, presumably, because it is in *my* interest. I don't like being disturbed. And I assume that others have a similar distaste for being disturbed, and will to that extent co-operate in realizing my desire. This passive and minimal version of the foundations of law remains vastly popular in the liberal North Atlantic milieu, and – before it is too readily criticized – it must be said that there are worse accounts. The trouble with it is that it is inadequate to *adjudicate* anything, or to assist in the negotiation of conscientious matters rooted in a coherent moral world-view: hence the chaos of 'liberal' responses to the presence of Islam in the West; hence the violent bitterness that characterizes the debate over abortion and the law, especially in the USA. The classical theological principle that what is just for me is bound up with what is just for my neighbour, and that my desire, if it is to be genuinely for a good beyond the private and local, must be a desire for the good of my neighbour[6] is not necessarily capable of being stated in the terms of mutual non-disturbance. A fictive or abstract account of shared answerability takes it for granted that what we first learn as human subjects is *private* desire, and that this remains a fundamental: the social ideal is to discover a means of securing maximal realization of private desires, under a 'contractual' arrangement whereby certain of them are sacrificed so as not to interfere too severely with the private policies and goals of other individuals. We are, in fact, back with the priority of the private, of the inner life. This account of the situation is as problematic philosophically as it is practically.

If we are *not*, then, talking about a notional or contractual tribunal, must we be talking about the apprehension of an 'absolute' presence, a transcendent interlocutor? The temptation is to give a rapid 'yes' to this question, without noticing that this would still leave us with the problem of how the moral world is concretely learned. It is, notoriously, not enough to appeal to universal moral intuitions, an innate code; the supposed deliverances of anything like this are at best trivial, and fail to offer any method other than a majority vote for settling moral conflict. If we are serious about the material and temporal character of learning selfhood, we have to ask about the material and temporal processes whereby a sense and a practice of common answerability might be intelligibly generated. How might I or we historically be educated in a relation with something I cannot negotiate with?

One of the earliest attempts to give some moral substance to a notion of common human interest appears in Stoicism and Cynicism. The precise social background out of which these philosophical movements developed is

---

[6] Cf. Augustine, *De trinitate* VIII (esp. vi.9) on the connection between love of the good and love of justice (since loving the good means desiring that the good be present in all subjects).

difficult to analyse, but one can at least say that they both have something to do with disillusion about the possibilities of the conventional classical ethics of public life. In a period of endemic warfare between Greek states, there was much to be said for developing a foundation for ethics independent of the traditional civic context. Cynicism has its alleged origins in the fourth century BCE, and Stoicism enters its first major period of evolution in the century following, when the rise and disintegration of Alexander's empire had still further weakened the old civic patterns of virtue and raised the awkward questions of cosmopolitanism.[7] The idea of the human being (or at least the *free* human being) as a 'citizen of the universe'[8] initiates a tradition of reflection on the unity of kinship of human agents, and consequently a kind of egalitarianism (a *kind* of egalitarianism, since the theoretical allowance of equality is not in practice or, often, in theory, extended to slaves). The fundamental unifying factor is wisdom or the capacity to be taught it, and this wisdom is defined as living according to 'nature'. The difficulties of this were already being extensively discussed in antiquity:[9] philosophers had noticed that appeal to 'nature' was an unhelpful move when it came to specifics, and the critics of Stoicism in particular were unhappy with a double list of possible actions, those performed according to nature and those wholly indifferent, for which there could be no fully reasonable grounds. Both Stoics and Cynics also seemed to go no further with their universalism and egalitarianism than a strong commendation of attitudes to be shared by the non-civic community of the wise; they remained figures deliberately marginal to the public sphere.

Such a summary is, of course, a simplification of complex history, social and intellectual; but it is worth pondering in the light of the comparisons frequently drawn in recent New Testament scholarship between the recorded preaching of Jesus and the Cynic tradition.[10] It is easy, perhaps, to assimilate too glibly the universalism of Stoic or Cynic to the universalism of the Christian Church, without considering the difference between an ethic of shared attitudes among a fraternity of the wise and a specific social struc-

---

[7]   Diogenes, the 'patriarch' of Cynicism, flourished in the middle of the fourth century BCE, and was thus contemporary with Alexander; Zeno established the Stoa at the end of the same century.

[8]   Diogenes, as reported by Diogenes Laertius 6.63; see John M. Rist, *Stoic Philosophy* (Cambridge University Press, 1969), p. 59, for a good discussion of the meaning of this phrase.

[9]   Rist, *op. cit.*, pp. 62–3, 68–80.

[10]   See especially F. Gerald Downing, *Christ and the Cynics: Jesus and Other Radical Preachers in First-Century Tradition* (Sheffield Academic Press, 1988); John Dominic Crossan, *The Historical Jesus. The Life of a Mediterranean Jewish Peasant* (San Francisco: Harper, 1990), esp. pp. 72–88.

ture existing alongside the ordinary civic systems of the Roman Empire, in a perennially uncomfortable relation with them for several centuries. My point is that the earlier question of how a non-tribal ethic might be historically learned can be answered at one level by adducing the radical universalism of Stoic or Cynic; these ideas enter the moral vocabulary partly in reaction to a situation of moral scepticism in the context of a reshaping of social boundaries. But the ideas themselves have no clear embodying structures. To the extent that the Christian Church is an embodying structure for an ethic of shared accountability and common interest, it needs closer examination in this connection. In the next part of this essay, I shall be suggesting that the narrative (not simply the recorded teaching) of Jesus functions in such a way that it mediates historically the meaning of a non-negotiable and therefore non-competitive presence 'before' which ethical discourse is conducted; and that, when conducted systematically in that light, the character of ethical discourse itself is significantly affected.

III

There are two aspects of the narrative of Jesus that immediately establish the centrality of a 'non-competitive other' in the construction of an ethic capable of dealing with common interest or common good. The first and most evident is what the gospels present as Jesus' offer of access to God for all, including – and perhaps especially – those who could have no claim of moral or spiritual privilege. The God of Jesus is the God who sends rain on the just and the unjust; and this entails a community of God's people *not* defined by their prior satisfactory behaviour. It is what J. D. Crossan, in his important, if controversial, study of *The Historical Jesus*[11] refers to as an 'unbrokered' society – that is, one that does not rely for its workings upon control by some privileged class of the means of access to power or acceptability. In proclaiming, in action as well as words, that the welcome of God is like an invitation to a meal with no social rationale, no ritual for ranking guests and marking their various levels of wealth or importance, Jesus 'makes . . . no appropriate distinctions and discriminations. He has no honor. He has no shame.'[12] In consequence, the God of the gospels ceases to function as

---

[11]   See n. 10; this book is a valuable essay in comparative anthropology, and makes a strong case for the affinities of Jesus with Cynic teaching. It is weakest in its highly speculative reconstructions of the history of the gospel tradition, especially the passion narratives.
[12]   Crossan, *op. cit.*, p. 262.

guarantor of a particular set of conditions for access to the holy and the transformative. This is a God who resists being used ideologically, or used as a criterion for the exclusion of the unsatisfactory and alien. To turn to a rather different intellectual milieu from that of recent New Testament scholarship, we may recall René Girard's observation: 'The Gospels deprive God of his most essential role in primitive religions – that of polarizing everything mankind does not succeed in mastering, particularly in relationships between individuals.'[13] Girard goes on to offer a reading of the parable of the talents in terms that make this 'deprivation' clear:

> The servant who is content to bury the talent that was entrusted to him, instead of making it bear interest, also has the most frightening picture of his master. He sees in him a demanding overseer who 'reaps where he has not sown.' What happens to this servant is, in the last analysis, in exact conformity with his expectations, with the image he has constructed of his master. It does not derive from the fact that the master is really like the servant's conception of him (here the text of Luke is the most suggestive), but from the fact that men make their own destinies and become less capable of breaking away from the mimetic obstacle the more they allow themselves to be fascinated by it.[14]

In their different idioms, both Crossan and Girard are, I believe, saying that the proclamation of Jesus makes concrete the presence of a non-competitive other: God is not to be approached through skilled intermediaries who will see to it that God's 'interest' is safeguarded in a transaction that, by giving privilege to us, may compromise the divine position. And, if God is conceived as needing to be conciliated so that violent reaction may be averted, as in the mind of the unprofitable servant in the parable, God is still within the competitive framework; God has a 'good', an interest, that is vulnerable. Whereas, if God's reaction can never be determined by a supposed threat to the divine interest, God's action and mine do not and cannot occupy the same moral and practical space, and are never in rivalry.

God's action is never, in this picture, *reactive*: it is always, we could say, *prior* to human activity, and as such 'gracious' – that is, undetermined by what we do. This in turn changes how I am to see my activity: what it can

---

[13] René Girard, *Things Hidden From the Foundation of the World* (Athlone Press, 1987), p. 185.
[14] Ibid., p. 189. The term 'mimetic obstacle' refers to the way in which a desired object possessed by another subject occasions frustration; the possessor has what I want, and is therefore what I want to be like, what I desire to imitate, but his/her possession of what I want is not only the occasion but the obstacle of my desire.

never be is any kind of bartering for a favourable or advantageous position *vis-à-vis* the universe and its maker. That God is never threatened by finite action entails that there is a level at which my own being is not capable of being threatened. It is simply established by God's determination as creator – that is, by God's will for what is authentically other to the divine being to exist. My behaviour does not have to be a defensive strategy in the face of what is radically and irreducibly other, because the radicality of that otherness is precisely what establishes my freedom from the necessity to negotiate with it. There is no question here of saving the interest of diverse parties to a transaction. The traditional theological commitments to the timelessness of God, or at least God's non-participation in the same scheme of temporality as ours, and to the doctrine of creation from nothing are very far from being abstract and speculative matters for the believer, examples of the philosophical 'corruption' of theological reflection. They are ways of safeguarding the fundamental point of the proclamation of Jesus, that God's acts are undetermined by ours, and that therefore we can never and need never succeed in establishing our position in the universe.

If this is how we are to understand the nature and activity of the Christian God, and if, consequently, no failure or defeat within the human world can ultimately determine our standing before God, one further consequence is a change in how we understand our being-in-time. God's difference from our temporality leaves us with a time that can be seen as *given*, as an opportunity for growth or healing, since no disaster is finally and decisively destructive. The theological assurance about the future that is proclaimed in Christian discourse has to be read in this light. It is not a conviction that there is or must be a happy ending to any particular human story; this would be to make trivial (and often almost blasphemous) the doctrine of divine providence. Rather it is an assurance that time is always there for restoration; that we are never rendered incapable of action and passion, creating and being created, by any event. To be the object of God's non-historical regard is to be assured not only of a *status*, but also of an *involvement*: we are always 'addressed'. That is to say, our time can be apprehended by us as a question, or a challenge, as something to be filled. To sense my future as being a question to me is to sense that what I can receive, digest and react to is not yet settled or finished. What God's regard, as pronounced by Jesus, establishes is my presence as an agent, experiencing and 'processing' experience. I continue to be a self in process of being made, being formed in relation and transaction.

Here, then, is one way in which the gospel announced by Jesus, in separating out our action from the business of establishing a position in the universe, might be said to liberate ethics. What we are to say in evaluation of our behaviour is not to be determined, or even shadowed, by considerations of how this or that action succeeds in securing the place and interest of a particular subject or group *vis-à-vis* its environment. This vision of a convergent human good thus appears almost as a kind of by-product of the proclamation of indiscriminate divine welcome. If there is no anxiety of rivalry in our ethical reflection, no anxiety about the possible ultimate extinction of our interest in the presence of God, it follows that every *perceived* conflict of human interest represents a challenge to work, to negotiate. This can sound as though all conflicts are simply matters of error, and require better explication in order to be resolved; but such a utopian piece of ethical intellectualism would overlook the way in which (as outlined earlier) 'real' or 'true' interest is itself only formed in the process of engagement, interaction. It is true that consciousness repeatedly mistakes itself, its nature and its good; but this is an error corrigible only within action and interaction that modifies the consciousness and changes its position.[15] But, as suggested in the first part of this essay, a commitment to what might be called, in a rather Hegelian phrase, the *labour* of ethics can emerge only as the social world is freed from the assumption of basic and non-negotiable collisions of human interest. To put it another way, the self is free to *grow* ethically (that is, to assimilate what is strange, to be formed into intelligibility) only when it is not under obligation to defend itself above all else – or to *create* itself, to carve out its place in a potentially hostile environment.

Theology has formalized the teaching of Jesus on the 'non-competitive difference' of God and God's indiscriminate welcome in terms of justifying grace; we are reckoned to have a right to be, by God's free determination. My basic argument has been that ethics is only going to *be* ethics if it assumes something like justification. However, if all we can say is that Jesus introduces into our discourse about the good a fruitful new idea, we are in danger of returning the whole discussion to abstractness. I turn finally then to the second aspect of the narrative of Jesus, to what lies beyond not only his recorded teaching but also his practice of hospitality and absolution. The practice of Jesus in his ministry is bound up with the formation of a community in which the acceptance and welcome of God is not negotiated into being, not 'brokered' by an intermediary or a system of administered conditions. As such, it might be simply an historical experiment,

---

[15] This is brought out very finely in the work of Gillian Rose on Hegel; see particularly *Hegel Contra Sociology* (Athlone Press, 1981); and *Judaism and Modernity* (Blackwell, 1993), especially the Introduction.

leaving an inspiring example. That it has *not* been understood in such terms is significant. From the beginnings of Christian discourse, the community around Jesus in his ministry – the community of disciples and of others, including those who have received from him healing or absolution[16] – was held to be continuously present, so that to join the community was to become 'contemporary' with Jesus (this is what is taken for granted in numerous sayings, especially in the Matthaean tradition, such as Mt 18.20 and 28.20). How is it that the 'unbrokered kingdom' becomes more than an historical project dependent on the physical presence of Jesus, or the direct 'personal' inspiration of Jesus?

The narrative elucidates this by recording that the historical *failure* of the mission of Jesus, conceived as a call for the renewal of Israel in certain radical ways, is overridden. Jesus proclaims the indefeasible and indiscriminate and indestructible regard of God for all, regardless of merit and achievement; yet he falls foul of the religious and political authorities and is executed. But to proclaim that he has been raised from death is to say that both the proclamation and the practice of Jesus cannot be brought to an end by an authority, even one that has the power of life and death. What Jesus does is, in theological language, owned and vindicated by God as *God's* proclamation and practice; as such, it is not ultimately vulnerable to history, in the sense that its continuance is never at the mercy of human will or the institutions of the world. Put another way, Jesus' action becomes recognizable as divine action when it is shown to be something that endures beyond the strongest rejection. Jesus remains as the focus of the new community, not as a memory but as a living presence. While this last formulation needs a great deal more elucidation, it expresses the sense in the first Christian documents of belonging to a community of interactive fellowship with Jesus, rather than a community founded by a figure in the past. The precise form of his ministry continues, in healing and absolution, in the introduction into new forms of prayer and intimacy with God, in the activity of extending the limits of God's people beyond the limits of the legally satisfactory. Gradually but inexorably, the practice of Jesus' continuing ministry in the community extends also beyond the boundaries of the ethnically and historically acceptable members of God's people – to the non-Jewish world. As I have argued elsewhere, this extension to the non-Jewish world is a major factor in the development of classical Christology, in that it carries the assumption that Jesus is 'free' to be heard and received throughout the human world, and to

---

[16] This is how Mary Magdalene is introduced in Lk 8.2, as one of a number of female followers alongside the Twelve, distinguished as those who have been healed by Jesus.

re-define the perceived will of God in respect of God's people by universalizing
the scope of God's call.[17]

The resurrection of Jesus can thus be read as the way in which God's
indefeasible commitment to welcoming the human creation and constructing communion among diverse human beings appears as an historical phenomenon, as the *temporal* persistence of the action and the gospel of Jesus.
That Jesus cannot be described, in Christian terms, as a *past* figure only means
that what he is and does endures – through his own literal and material
presence and so through all the ways in which who and what he is is obscured, betrayed or apparently historically defeated in the life of the Christian community as in the life of the entire human world. The theological
idea of the indestructible regard of God, with all its implications for the
possibility of reconciled community, is capable of being perceived and learned
as an historical matter through the perdurance of Jesus' life in the life of the
community and as the continuing source of *judgement* to which the community looks. We are not talking about an *identity* of Jesus and community; if
we were, the distinctiveness of the claim that Jesus remains *active* in the
community would be lost; his action would simply be initiating the activity
of the community. The doctrine of the resurrection is, among other things,
an attempt to distinguish between the emergence of the new community
as an historical fact and the continuance of Jesus' activity in calling and forming the community. This latter is, of course, not available for historical inspection in the same way; but the early Church, in associating the resurrection
with the empty tomb, insisted that the perdurance of the practice and proclamation of Jesus was not reducible to 'internal' shifts in the collective consciousness of the Church. This matter remains, I believe, problematic wherever
the theology of Jesus' resurrection fails to separate out the changes in the
Church's mind from the action of God in respect to the person of Jesus. The
question of the empty tomb is not theologically indifferent.

What I have been attempting so far is not a natural theology, a digging-
out of a conceptual space into which theological claims can be inserted. It
simply seeks to identify a practical as well as conceptual problem in our
world, a problem about the foundations of a non-tribal, non-competitive
ethic, in such a way as to suggest that the Christian theology of justification,
grounded in the narrative of Jesus' ministry, passion and resurrection, provides a structure and vocabulary for discussing this problem. Is it then an
essay in apologetics? In a sense, yes. The claims made by classical Christian

---

[17]   Cf. Rowan Williams, *Mission and Christology. The J. C. Jones Memorial Lecture 1994* (Church
Missionary Society Welsh Council, 1994).

theology for the universal pertinence of the proclamation of Jesus, the claims to a decisive authority in shaping the human world, can only be given flesh by trying to see if, in fact, the narrative of Jesus *can* offer resources for an ethic and an anthropology with some ability to liberate us from the manifestly self-destructive spirals of human interaction. It is only in the unceasing and manifold generation of such attempts at seeing the world in the light of the gospel narrative that Christian theology can make *concrete* sense of its own convictions – not by winning a succession of arguments that 'prove' the inadequacy of secularism, but in displaying at least the confidence that our theological discourse has the ability to promise human transformation.

IV

Thus a Christian theological statement has to be – at least – an invitation into a world of possible readings of the world in terms of the gospel, and possible responses to the given narrative of Jesus; not a provider of occult information, but, to borrow a famous phrase from Eliot on the metaphysical poets, a modification of sensibility. This in turn implies that the criteria for theological coherence and adequacy are going to be quite complex: general considerations of how hypotheses may be given plausibility by argument are not going to be obviously the best tools, nor will arguments about the explanatory force of doctrinal formulae (as making sense of odd phenomena) best address the significant issues.[18] We must ask about how we test a theology's force or comprehensiveness in consolidating a distinctive and resourceful perspective on the diverse narratives of human agents; we must consider whether a particular theological idiom or construct strengthens the sense of an integral fullness of perception and discernment in respect of human agency, whether it shrinks or extends the fundamental conviction about the transforming pertinence of Jesus' narrative and identity to all human situations. In the rest of this essay, I propose to look at aspects of the theological style of two elements in Christian scripture which are often supposed to be problematically diverse: the primary Pauline literature along with the disputedly

---

[18] Cf. the essay cited above, n. 5; also Bruce D. Marshall, 'Absorbing the World: Christianity and the Universe of Truths', in Bruce D. Marshall (ed.), *Theology and Dialogue. Essays in Conversation with George Lindbeck* (University of Notre Dame Press, 1990), pp. 69–102, on the 'assimilative power' of theological utterance and Christian discourse in general as a (long-term) criterion of adequacy and truthfulness.

Pauline letter to the Ephesians; and the gospel of Matthew. My aim will be to underline how Pauline and Matthaean theology alike approach what we might call ethics and spirituality by a twofold strategy, drawing out how Christian behaviour is to be interpreted in terms of the *manifestation* of God through Jesus Christ, and at the same time making it plain that this manifestation is not restricted to *successful performance*: the comprehensiveness of the structuring vision emerges in the way in which failure, recognized and accepted as such, entails a 'dispossession' that itself mirrors the divine gift as narrated in the history of Jesus. Only (I suggest) when we can trace this dual, ironic strategy can we properly assess the theological import of Paul (and deutero-Paul?) and Matthew, in relation to what we have already traced in the Jesus tradition at its most basic level.

Paul first: for him, being co-opted into the divinely chosen community, being in Christ, is inseparable from co-option into the divine action; and this action is not only God's active pursuit of reconciliation with the world, but also God's self-revelation. The Christian life is, from one perspective, the repetition or recapitulation of the act and the narrative of God, primarily but not exclusively in the incarnate Christ: this we could draw out of, for example, the meditation in II Cor. about the ministry of reconciliation (II Cor. 5.11ff.). We find many other passages in the Pauline corpus where the imitation of God in Christ is a central theme. We are not to consider our own interests above those of others, for Christ did not so consider himself (Rom. 15.2–3); rather, we are to welcome or accept each other as Christ has accepted us (15.7). We are to give generously to each other – Christ became poor for our sake, and made others rich by that voluntary poverty (II Cor. 8.9). We are to offer our lives as a sacrifice to the Father, as Christ did (Eph. 5.1), and to follow the pattern of self-emptying or non-grasping embodied in Christ, pre-incarnate and incarnate (Phil 2.1–11). And so on: but the argument does not stop simply with an appeal to what Jesus has done. It is significant that such passages repeatedly move towards a further level of 'grounding' the appeal when they go on to speak of 'glory' as the goal or product of certain sorts of action. This is particularly clear in Rom. 15: the mutual forbearance of believers, their acceptance of each other, issues in God being glorified – not simply through the voice of the community's praise, though that is a significant part of the meaning of Rom. 15.6, but also surely through the manifestation of the character of God that is involved. If we accept each other 'for the glory of God' (15.7), this is part of a display of God's self-consistency (15.8), which issues finally in the joy and gratitude of the non-Jewish world. That is to say, Gentiles don't rejoice only because they are granted a spectacular privilege, but also because the glory of God is made plain to them. Indeed, the gift is inseparable from the delight: here as elsewhere, 'the glory of God' functions as a rationale for certain styles of action (e.g. I Cor. 10.31, II Cor. 4.15, 8.19). Generosity, mercy and welcome are imperatives for the Christian because they are a participation in the divine activity; but they are also imperative because they show God's glory and invite or attract human beings to 'give glory' to God – that is, to reflect back to God what God is. Giving glory is practically identical with rejoicing – rejoicing 'in' God, being glad that God is God, not merely that God is well-disposed towards us.

Thus, the imperative changes it character: we are to act in such a way that the nature of God becomes visible, in the way it was visible in the life and death of Jesus. The further rationale for acting so as to manifest the nature of God is ultimately that the nature of God is that which provokes joy, *delectatio*. The point of the whole history of divine action which our acts imperfectly recapitulate is that there should be cause for rejoicing. This, I believe, is the sense in which Paul's ethic carries the dimension of 'contemplative fruition': our final purpose is to enjoy seeing something of what God eternally is. II Cor. 9 puts this very plainly in recommending financial generosity so that there may be an overflow of thanksgiving to God (9.11–14): the beneficiaries of the Church's generosity do not rejoice simply because their needs are met, but because it makes plain the divine and fundamental character of gift itself; because God has become manifest. Or, to put it in more tendentious terms, the Pauline ethic has a powerfully *aesthetic* foundation: delight in the beauty of God is the goal of our action, what we minister to each other and to the human world at large. In some passages, like Rom. 15 and II Cor. 9, Paul even seems less interested in the receiving of God's mercy by the Gentiles than in the fact that bestowal of this mercy calls forth praise – presumably not exclusively from believers.

If this is correct, then the writer to the Ephesians is closer to a central Pauline theme than he is sometimes assumed to be. Ephesians makes much of the manifestation of God's long hidden purposes, God's longing to exhibit the full range and depth of the divine liberty to give and recreate (1.5ff., 12, 2.7, 3.10–12, 16–21). God does what God does so that the divine glory may be known, praised and enjoyed – and I take the three words to be necessarily interlinked. I should want to add that the believer's knowing is 'intellectual', in the scholastic sense in which intellect is itself a participation in the reality understood, so that the mind's reception of what God is believed to have done becomes another channel for the divine reality to manifest itself. The Christian's thinking is a vehicle of 'glory', an occasion for praise and thanksgiving.

Ephesians uses very freely the language of 'mystery' to describe what is shown in Christ, in the preaching of Christ and in the living of the believing life; the word is more frequent in this epistle than anywhere else in the Christian scriptures. It is, as I have indicated, connected with the idea of God revealing hidden purposes. But it is actually in the undoubtedly Pauline literature that one finds a use of the word that links it more clearly to the themes we have just been considering. Paul, in I Cor. 4.1, famously refers to himself as a 'steward' of God's mystery, the person who handles or administers or conserves the narrative of the divine purpose. The usage, however, follows immediately upon a sharp polemical discussion of the divisive issue in Corinth concerning the authority and status of the various missionaries: Paul's conclusion is that the preacher of the gospel is bound to point away from himself of herself, to divert attention from any simply individual skill, power or fluency. The preacher is not there to impose a personal philosophy, but to introduce people to the fullness of God's work in Jesus; this is accomplished when preachers put themselves at the disposal of the hearers. 'All things are yours', says Paul: through the preacher's self-deliverance into the hands of the hearers, the hearers are 'delivered' into the possession of Christ and thus into divine ownership (or, better perhaps, divine 'owning', divine acknowledgement of responsibility for us). This is what leads on immediately to the image of the apostle as *oikonomos* of the divine mystery. The apostle's stewarding role becomes manifest, it seems, when the apostle is *dispossessed* of individual power or expertise, the kind of power that comes from the successful deployment of rhetoric. The divine purpose, as Paul is constantly repeating in these early chapters of I Cor., is realized in the vulnerability and awkwardness of the human voice proclaiming it.

Could we then go a step further, admittedly beyond the explicit words of Paul, to suggest that the mystery that is the purpose of God is in some way rooted in a perception of God as naturally self-dispossessing or self-giving? There is kind of convergence between the idea of a *practice* of generosity as sharing in and making visible the character of the generous or welcoming God, and the experience of an 'anti-rhetoric' of human inarticulacy and unskilledness in verbalizing the nature and purposes of God. The practice of the ethical life by believers is a communicative strategy, a discourse of some sort; and equally the speech of believers is an ethical matter, morally and spiritually suspect when it is too fluent, too evidently grounded in the supposedly superior quality of the speaker. A form of religious persuasion that insists upon its right to possess or control its own outcome, whether by appeal to status or privilege (in Paul's terms, especially the status of ethnic and/or legal 'purity') or by insistence upon its own excellent performance fails to communicate its intended matter, which is the action and nature of God. If the substance of the gospel has to do with God's giving up possession or control – in Paul's language, the Father giving up or giving over the Son to the cross, or Christ giving up his 'wealth', security, life for the sake of human beings – then the speech appropriate to this must renounce certain kinds of claims and strategies. This is why (a point we must face candidly) Paul's correspondence is characterized by a sense of moral danger: Paul himself is walking the tightrope of Christian persuassion with something less than total success as far as the renunciation of possession and control are concerned. He can be bullying and manipulative, even in the very passages where he most plainly articulates his own ethic of preaching. Perhaps this is why generations of Paul's readers, including those who framed the liturgical offices for the feast of his conversion, have found the agonized contradictions of II Cor. 11–12 very close to the heart of his theology and ethics; as if here he is recognizing that his very failure to observe his own prescriptions for the rhetoric of the gospel is turned to persuasion by its recognition of its own failure and folly. 'When I am weak, them I am strong': not only the 'weakness' of stumbling language or confused argument, but the scandal of the self-acknowledged moral crassness of Paul's appeal to authority and experience.

What follows or might follow from this is the problematic agenda of Christian theology for some centuries after Paul. In the first place, the idea of a self-dispossessing witness being transparent to a self-dispossessing God, the idea (to borrow a significant insight from the *Contra Arianos* of Athanasius) of a God whose essential life is the generation of difference that is still conceivable as communion or continuity, is built into the slowly evolving model of God as Trinity. To say that Paul, or any writer in the corpus of Christian scripture, simply enunciates a 'trinitarian ethic' is, of course, anachronistic and over-simple. But it is always worth asking what it is that the language of Christian scripture *prompts*, makes thinkable, gestures towards. At this level, it is not nonsense to suggest, I believe, that a trinitarian structure for discourse about the eternal life of God offers the fullest explication of Paul's moral rhetoric. But secondly, there is a particularly sharp (perhaps rather distinctively Protestant?) paradox implied if this is pursued in reading Paul. The self-forgetting of God, God's putting the divine life 'at the disposal' of what is not God, becomes manifest precisely in the acknowledged inadequacy, the fractured and failed character, or all Christian rhetoric, whether in word or in deed. What in the created order mirrors the giving-away of God is not simply the practice of concrete generosity – which remains of focal importance, of course – but the practice of penitent irony about the misapprehensions of the life and speech of faith. If I may here pick up a notion I have very briefly touched on elsewhere, we understand the truth of Christian God in the very apprehension of our own *misapprehensions*;[19] our spiritual conformation to the life of the trinitarian God involves, among a good many other things, a scepticism, both relentless and unanxious, about all claims to successful performance in our life and our discourse.

Matthew and Paul have regularly been represented as – at best – tensive, if not contradictory poles in Christian ethical discourse.[20] Matthew is interested in Jesus as a second Moses, Paul is interested in a new creation to which the law, even in intensified or interiorized form, is marginal. But the Matthaean ethic is in fact as concerned as the Pauline to avoid an ideal of the self-construction of the righteous agent by successful performance. There are *appropriate* kinds of performance, but what is constitutive of fundamental identities is a relation with God that is shaped not by the pursuit of consistent moral policies but by that puzzling mix of disposition and circumstance sketched in the Beatitudes. The commendatory rhetoric converges surprisingly closely at certain points: ethics is about manifestation. The Sermon, when it appeals to the correlation between human and divine forgiveness (Mt 6.14–15), when it exhorts the believer to a perfection consisting in indiscriminate love (5.43–48), when it implicitly grounds the constants of human generosity or responsiveness in divine willingness to give, faintly imaged in human dispositions (7.7–11), nudges us in precisely the same direction as Paul: Christian virtue is there to display a reality that will cause thanksgiving and delight, that will cause people to give glory to the Father (5.16).

What is more, the external situations in which 'perfection' is to be realized are almost all circumstances of discomfort or disadvantage. Christian 'excellence' is in significant part a matter of how we are to deal with our powerlessness or dispossession, just as the conditions listed in the Beatitudes are conditions of vulnerability or conditions metaphorized as vulnerability ('hunger and thirst' in the cause of justice).[21] We'd better notice carefully what this does and doesn't say. These is no commendation of passivity as such, no simple advice to the systemically powerless that they accept their lot: the counsels are being given to people who have expectations of exercis-

---

[19] See Rowan Williams, 'Between Politics and Metaphysics: Reflections in the Wake of Gillian Rose', *Modern Theology* 11.1 (1995), pp. 3–22, esp. 11–12, 17–18.
[20] A significant recent exception is Dan O. Via, Jr, *Self-Deception and Wholeness in Paul and Matthew* (Fortress, 1990). This book converges at several points with my argument here, and I am glad to acknowledge my debt to it.
[21] See Via, *op. cit.*, pp. 112–27 on the Beatitudes as presenting the dialectical character of a present blessedness conceived in terms of present 'emptiness'.

ing power but are placed in circumstances where they lose it or have it undermined. When I am injured, I have the means of possible redress; I have power to restore the balance that has been upset (I can retaliate, I can go to court or whatever.). But I also have, as a believer, the freedom to alter the terms of the relation: I can decline to see it as a challenge to equalize the score, and opt to display positively the sovereign liberty of God not to retaliate or defend an interest. In other words, I can either attempt to close off my vulnerability or I can so work with it as to show the character of God. If we come to the Sermon looking either for an ethic of passive obedience to external authority or an ethic of resistance and liberation as conceived in our own age, we shall be disappointed. Matthew's Jesus is a more teasing character than either model would suggest; and the Sermon ought to be read with great patience and nuance before we try to derive a political ethic of the right or the left from it. But more of this later.

So the substance of the Sermon seems to direct us, as does Paul, towards the focal point of a renunciation of certain kinds of defence of safety as itself an imaging of the divine character suitable for provoking gratitude or glorification directed towards God. This may be reinforced if we look, secondly, at the rhetoric of 'inwardness' that appears as a unifying theme in much of the Sermon. Our contemporary intellectual climate, as we noted at the beginning of this essay, has taught us to be wary of interiority – the privileging of motive, the search for authority or integrity or authenticity in an 'inner' identity unsullied by the body or history, the essentialism in various doctrines of human nature that arises from a preoccupation with the hidden and true 'centre of the self'. Nietzsche's denunciations of Christian moral discourse frequently return to this point, to the poisoning of the wells of human life by encouraging scepticism about appearances. The Sermon has, it seems, a lot to answer for, if this is its progeny.

Well, yes, it does; we have to grant the ways in which a rhetoric of inferiority which Christianity has consistently fostered has had philosophical and moral and cultural consequences that have been corrupting. But if we jump to hasty conclusions here, we shall have missed something of the Matthaean ethic; it is not developed with the conscious and extravagant irony of Paul, but it suggests its own ironies. Matthew does indeed take it for granted that integrity belongs in an inner realm and that it is not to be constructed or construed in terms of patterns of action alone. But if he privileges truth in the inward parts, it is not, as in most of the more modern varieties of discussing interiority, so as to allow the inner to be *deployed*. If the interior is the place of truth, it can *never* be deployed; you cannot use it to win arguments, to ground anything about your or anyone's identity, to establish sincerity of good intentions. The inner life, in this context, cannot be *spoken*; it silences moral defence and debate. If you do what you do to be seen by human eyes, you have your reward; your moral 'audience' is the Father *en tō kruptō*, the one whose habitat is secret places. Because of the Father's secrecy, the divine judgement, the only one actually of any truthfulness or final import, remains beyond anyone's power of utterance. It is not an *esoteric* truth – which is what the appeal to interiority has so regularly become – but an inaccessible truth. In short, the appeal to the inner world is another strategy of disempowerment for the Christian moral agent.

Hence, of course, the injunctions about not judging. There is no secure access to the inner life of another, and if you judge by external standards, you may expect to be open yourself to equally shallow and unmerciful judgement. When Matthew's Jesus uses the word 'hypocrite', as he so freely does in the Sermon, we must not think immediately of disjunction between inner and outer, of a problem about *sincerity*, but of the moral or spiritual weakness of someone who expects to be judged on external performance: in ch. 6, 'hypocrites' are not necessarily people who don't mean what they do, or who are trying to conceal inner unfaithfulness; they are simply (as the Greek word implies) 'actors', agents who consciously construct themselves in the process of performance. The word's negative resonance of deceit or simulation arises from the fact that, if selves cannot really be so constructed, the self that is evolved in patterns of behaviour is some way false. The 'hypocrite' has not learned that the self is not a sort of possessed object, to be refined or matured by conscious practice; the 'hypocrite' has to recognize the uncomfortable truth that the self's standing, the self's adequacy or excellence or attunement to God ('blessedness'), is out of the agent's control.[22] Matthew foreshadows here the later Christian paradoxes explored in Gregory of Nyssa and Augustine, paradoxes concerning the systematically unknowable character of the self. But he has given this theme a more clearly defined moral edge by linking it with the proscription of judgement or, more exactly, of offering oneself for judgement by humanly perceptible criteria.

Of course Matthew's general rhetoric in the gospel is liberally strewn with judgement and with hostility towards the outsider, the non-believer, the unconverted Jew; this is a still darker aspect of the legacy of the first gospel. This should not, however, lead us to a simple rejection of the ethic of the Sermon, or even a accusation of 'hypocrisy' in the modern sense. Matthew, like Paul, is exploring an area of moral danger, and the riskiness of the discourse is exhibited, as with Paul, though less self-consciously, in the failures

---

[22]   Ibid., pp. 92–8, on hypocrisy as self-deceit.

of consistency. The challenge is still audible: can the moral agent relinquish the centrality of an image of herself or himself *as* moral agent? So long as we are, so to speak, polishing the image of the agent, what our actions show is a successful will; the *meaning* of the actions terminates in the will's success. If we let go that image, the meaning of what is done is grounded in God, the act shows more than the life of the agent: it shows the character of the creator. But to get to that point, the discipline that the agent has to undergo is attention not to performance but to an interiority that is not to be possessed. It is visible and judgeable only by God. So that, finally, for Matthew, Christian excellence is what it is for Paul: the manifestation of the divine reality in such a way as to provoke thanksgiving and delight. Externally focused morality is unacceptable not because it encourages insincerity, but because it is in grave danger of always terminating in itself, in the successful will, not in the life of the creator. And successful wills do not provoke contemplative joy, on the whole.

V

In the last part of this reflection, I want to look rather sketchily at the sorts of moral practice and moral critique that might emerge from these considerations. Scepticism, penitence irony about performance, the dissolution of the solid moral self built up by good actions – all of this could issue in a morality that is profoundly individualized, incapable of thematizing ethical questions or of providing a critical edge to the believer's engagement with the wider culture. A sophisticated Protestantism in particular lends itself to some such style, and its literary heritage would be interesting to explore, across a spectrum ranging from John Updike to Antonia Byatt or Iris Murdoch. There are times, too, when this kind of moral scepticism (i.e. scepticism about the attainability, but not the reality, of virtue) is a welcome relief from the deafening new rhetoric of common virtue secured by the balancing of rights and the reparation made for offence. This is a proper concern in reflecting on the conditions of justice, but a poor substitute for the discourse of virtue. Whatever the attractions of this sceptical and reticent ethic, it is not finally a fruitful basis for ethical talk, to the extent that it concentrates upon the realm in which no negotiation takes place, no public risk, no common policies; and it certainly represents only a sliver of the moral world of the writers we have been looking at. I want to propose three elements of the ethic outlined here that might have bearing on the contemporary language of public or common moral practice and speech.

(i) The sceptical or reticent principle, in the context of Christian scripture as a whole, is the negative side of a positive insight. The controlling question of much, if not most, of our New Testament is about who belongs among the community of the friends of God, formerly identified exclusively with the people of Israel. Paul and the evangelists build on the clearly remembered practice of Jesus, for whom the friends of God are those who are content to accept the assurance of Jesus that their willingness to trust God's word through him is the sole basis of belonging with God's people. To hear and accept that word is not to perform a task (there is no satisfactory answer to the rich man's question as Matthew records it, 'What good *deed* must I do to have eternal life?'), but to enter into the sharing of Jesus' company, forswearing any other kind of *claim* to God's favour than the assurance given by God of an unearned and prior favour freely offered. Virtue in this new community of the friends of God thus comes to be bound up with the steady critique of all practices that reinstate or try to reinstate claims on the love of God grounded in achievement. Positively, this casts light on the way in which Paul, especially in Rom. and I Cor., treats ethics, questions of specific behaviour, as governed by the principle or 'edification': good acts are those that build up the Body of Christ. Virtue thus rests upon the fundamental process of curing the delusion that I have an interest or good that I alone can understand, specify and realize. It is essentially to do with the definition of an interest that is both mine and the other's, since what we most basically share is the assurance of being equally valued or welcomed by God. What I think I possess is there to be given for the sake of that newly envisioned common interest. When Paul deplores 'boasting', as he so frequently does, it is to undermine the nonsense of any language about claims within the Christian community.

Christian ethics thus suggests a nuanced approach to some of those issues of justice or reparation touched on earlier. On the one hand: the Church has or should have a quite disproportionate interest in how mechanisms of exclusion work in human societies, in what sort of things are deployed so as to make claims that allow this person or group in and shut that one out. Christian 'bias to the poor' is not simply a doctrine that God likes poor people better than others, and that is all there is to it. It is, rather, a persistent critical concern about how claims to do with security and legitimation are made, both in and out of the Church. It is a 'bias' in the sense that the Christian begins with a non-negotiable commitment to basic egalitarianism.

On the other hand: Christian ethics can never be happy with a model of justice that is solely or even primarily reparative. The good or interest of the excluded matters not in itself but as the indispensable and unique contribution it constitutes to the good of all. The language of 'rights' is an important *dialectical* moment in ethical discourse, but becomes sterile when it is divorced from a proper conception of the human good that has to be worked on in conversation with others. In this sense, strange as it may seem to put it thus, Christian ethics is relentlessly political, because it cannot be adequately expressed in terms of atomized rights invested in individuals or groups, but looks beyond to the kind of community in which free interaction for the sake of each other is made possible. That means adjustment and listening; it means politics.

(ii) When ethics ceases to be about securing claims, it is free to rethink itself as something like the reading of a particular language; that is to say, it can concern itself with what acts mean or communicate, not what they contribute to a tally of successful performances and whatever results may accrue from that, nor how acts correspond to a scale of rightness and wrongness constructed in the abstract. The crucial question that has to be asked in the Christian moral evaluation of act or character is, does it speak of the God whose nature is self-dispossession for the sake of the life of the other? of the commitment and dependability of the divine action towards the creation? of the divine relinquishment of 'interest' and claim as embodied in the life and death of Jesus? These are not, I think, issues that leave us with an individualized or uncritical ethic. They are matters capable of being raised in the context of sexual ethics as much as the ethics of business or international relations. And it may be that something like this is rather badly needed as the discourses of Christian ethics polarize increasingly between legalism based on the injunctions of the text and a vacuous experientialism, appealing to precisely the wrong sort of interiority for its criteria. It might allow us to recognize that the actions of Christians are constantly called upon to manifest God so that God may be glorified, and yet are enacted in a world where circumstances oblige us to choose between more and less damaging (and therefore, in respect of God, more and less opaque) options; where this happens, where the tragic dimension of the moral world impinges, what gives glory is – if we have been reading Paul (and even Matthew) correctly – the candid acknowledgement of powerlessness, in grief, not in complacency, because this in its way models the divine dispossession.

(iii) Finally, let me be allowed one more use of that annoying word, 'paradox'. The kind of interiority that seems to be evoked in the Sermon on the Mount points not to an undervaluing but to a revaluing of the *bodily* agent in our ethical thinking: a paradox. If the interiority in question is the 'secret place' where God lives, then, as we have seen, it is not a higher and better sphere of performance: motive and intention cannot be elevated above practice or treated as sources of authority or legitimation. The challenge is to move entirely out of the performance-oriented world. External achievement does not secure status, but neither does intensity, sincerity, or good will. The inner sphere belongs to God's judgement and is not available. What *is* available is action: judged not according to how it serves to secure a position before God and others, but according to its fidelity to the character of God, its 'epiphanic' depth. This allows us to pick up the sound Aristotelean point that doing worthy acts is a way of becoming a worthy person, in the sense that options may be evaluated by their possible transparency to God, not by their presumed correspondence to a hidden good (or otherwise) will: the inner may well follow the outer, as far as the actual processes of transformation go. But the basic point remains: of course, I cannot *become* a worthy person in any sense that would presume to make me worthy *of* God's regard. But attention to the degree to which my choices might be read as open or not open to God's glory might help to free me from the tyranny of both motivation and achievement. If this at all recalls Luther's notion in chapter 27 of *The Liberty of the Christian* that the believer, like Christ, acts in charity because a given (not attained) reality is simply expressing itself in his or her life, that is no accident. If it also recalls Eliot's transcription of the Gita on detachment from 'action and the fruits of action', doing what corresponds to truth and wisdom for its own sake, not because of a clear calculation of results, that is no accident either.[23]

[23] Sections 1 to 3 of this paper have appeared as *Ethik und Rechtfertigung* in *Rechtfertigung und Erfahrung*, ed. M. Beintker, E. Maurer, H. Stoevesandt and H. G. Ulrich (Gütersloh, 1995), pp. 311–27. Much of the remainder was prepared as a response to the then unpublished manuscript of Ellen Charry's *By the Renewing of Your Minds. The Salutarity of Christian Doctrine* (New York, 1997), discussed at a symposium in March 1995 at the Divinity School of Duke University on ethics and the New Testament. I must acknowledge my great indebtedness to Professor Charry for insights contributory to the present essay.

Chapter Seventeen

RESURRECTION AND PEACE: MORE ON NEW TESTAMENT ETHICS

There is a New Testament passage used rather too frequently in the Week of Prayer for Christian Unity and on other occasions when we are being urged to be conciliatory to each other – the verses in Ephesians 2 about Christ as our peace.

> Gentiles and Jews, he has made the two one, and in his own body of flesh and blood has broken down the enmity which stood like a dividing wall between them; for he annulled the law with its rules and regulations, so as to create out of the two a single new humanity in himself, thereby making peace . . . So he came and proclaimed the good news: peace to you who were far off, and peace to those near by; for through him we both alike have access to the Father in the one Spirit. (Eph. 2.14–18)

The words are echoed in Colossians (1.20): 'Through him God chose to reconcile the whole universe to himself, making peace through the shedding of his blood upon the cross' – though here the 'peace' in question is primarily a new relation with God rather than a new relation with each other. In any case, what is clear is that there is one important strand in the New Testament, associated with Paul and his reflections on the effects of Jesus' death, that sees the result of the cross as a drawing together of the human world, an overcoming of hostility: because of the death of Jesus, God and the world are no longer strangers to each other, and thus too the world is not divided into communities that are for ever strange to one another. Peace is practically identical with the condition of the new universe, the wholeness that now exists where before there were only fragments of human reality at odds with each other. The further implication that this wholeness does not stop with the human world only, but involves some kind of renewal of human relations with the rest of the universe is not explored, nor is it now our primary theme; but we should keep it in view as we reflect on the consequences of this in the immediate human context.

What is often missed in the reading of the Ephesians passage, though, especially in contexts where its use is a bit sentimental and unreflective ('reconciliation' is such a seductively comfortable word, fatally close to 'consensus' in common usage) is that the writer of the epistle associates the new possibility of a world of non-strangers with the annulment of the Law and of the sense of an *exclusive* covenant between God and God's people. The human starting-point for the writer is that there is a community that has received promises and commitments from God on the one hand, and a sort of shapeless human conglomerate on the other – not really a 'people' at all, not possessed of a firm corporate identity. There is Israel, which has a clear source for its sense of itself, and there is the 'non-community' of the Gentiles, who have no name of their own, and no sense of a future that is distinctively theirs, no awareness of a security in promise. But the problem which forms the subtext of these words is that the security of Israel has become ambiguous: the Law and the covenant are matters of gift; but because they are expressed in terms of clear and identifiable demands, it is possible to think that, as a recipient of this gift, you gain some kind of secure control over your identity. How do we know who we are? In doing what is required of us, in performing a set of measurable duties that will define in unmistakable terms a secure belonging, an image of 'rightness', a place in the universe. The moral or spiritual risk in this comes in at this point: what *we* do establishes us in the world. It is the distinctive practices of this group as distinct from others that guarantees our life to be meaningful – not passive, anonymous, vulnerable to circumstances. So, to recast the original polarity, we have a set of people who are actively constructing meanings by actions that they are assured are right and approved, and another set who are incapable of so acting: they are at the mercy of their own momentary states of body or mind ('we . . . obeyed the promptings of our own instincts and notions' – Eph. 2.3).

The writer to the Ephesians claims that *both* these conditions are to be put behind, that they are locked in a demonic symbiosis of hostility. The life that defines itself confidently in its ordered doing, *and* the life that steps aside from the painful question of meanings and continuities together form a pathology of the human world. They are the roots of violence and mutual rejection between people; they are both challenged and transformed in encounter with the crucified Jesus, and the 'peace' that we may hope for as a result of the act of God in the death of Jesus is something that stands against each of them alike.

But how does this symbiosis work? On the one hand, the idea of a life that defines itself by successful performance commonly involves the presence of unsuccessful performance as something to measure itself against, define itself against. I or we can *know* what it is to be successful performers because we have a clear picture of what it is to lack this success, provided by the lives and experiences of others; and the energy that fuels the pursuit of good performance is supplied by an anxiety generated by the familiar prospect of failure. The Pharisee in the gospel parable thanks God for his virtue, as he should, but it is given added public definition by the presence of someone who lacks virtue, who has no claim in the company of the good performers. Performance demands such a public measure, demands therefore that there be failures. And the failure is both necessary to the culture of success, and threatening to it: we need to have it there, yet it is also something that is capable of making inroads upon us and weakening or spoiling our own clarity. The result is that we defend the 'territory' of success with great energy and commitment; the Other, the 'failure', is both enemy and ally, a necessary enemy who supports and confirms the project of succeeding, in an oblique or negative way, the shadow that picks out the sharp contours for us.

On the other hand, the life that steps out of the whole business of patterns, meanings, intelligible wholes, carries with it the assumption that there is such a thing as a natural independent selfhood buried in each of us, a spiritual essence whose liberty is infringed by the insulting limits of time and language and other realities, by death and the body and all that is not consciously chosen by this immaterial ego. It works with no less intensive a model of competition for limited space than the order and success model, though its language about this is more muted. In presupposing that we are answerable only to an 'inner truth' of instinct or the claims of the moment, this perspective risks obliterating any awareness of belonging in a context that has not been chosen or invented, and so also risks losing the knowledge of that characteristically human tension that has to do with learning creativity through engagement with the limits of the world and other subjects. Those limits are seen primarily as negative, as menacing. There is a lack of sense that there might be a work to be shared, a future that can be corporate as well as individual, and so too a lack of resources to deal with necessary loss or postponement – an impatience with time. Yet here too, energy is commonly generated by protest or refusal, by the active battle to avoid being formed by a context, belonging to or with others; a curious kind of activity designed to protect the idea of responsiveness to the sheer process of the moment, of the inner motion.

Of course, what I have been trying to describe is not precisely what the writer of Ephesians had in mind in talking about Jews and Gentiles! But once we start asking why the making of peace should have something to do with the removal of both law and lawlessness, we are bound to look at the wider questions of what these apparently simple religious disjunctions are saying about the divisions in human self-perception, individual and collective. Just as in Romans Paul sees law and lawlessness at work in a single self, so here we are dealing with more than a distinction between two visibly different groups of human beings. This is actually fairly clear if you look at the curious fact that the writer is both addressing Gentiles, those who are simply ethnically non-Jewish, as if they were distinct from him, and speaking of a 'we' who share the Gentile condition. The mention of outward or 'fleshly' identification as Jew or Gentile in v. 11 is a caution to those who believe the distinctions being discussed are primarily those between empirical groups. So, between the lawkeeper and the lawless is a gulf of enmity that is not simply ethnic or cultural prejudice. The careful ambiguity over 'we' and 'you' urges towards a recognition that the conflict and the violence are bound up with the world of human self-interpretation and social construction overall. This is a world, then, in which there is no peace because it seeks for clarity and self-identification in ways that are necessarily fragmenting and destructive. The active world-shaping impulse, creating order by the imposition of patterns and regularities, requires in practice the contrast of disorder or failure to achieve its own definition; it looks for and when necessary creates its opposite, generating images of disorder, rebellion, irrationality, projected on to others and attacked. The 'freedom' of the life of passion, the organization of life around gratification, is intrinsically incapable of producing a properly social sense at all (witness the erosion of community sense in the wake of advanced capitalism), yet can foster a picture of human living together that is rigid and oppressive in its very resistance to the possibility of a shared future for which it is necessary to reflect, plan or sacrifice. In deferring or refusing the problem of common human language, shared meanings, it also refuses to question its own conflicts, imbalances and exclusions. Law and lawlessness equally issue in an acceptance, tacit or admitted, of strife as humanly necessary; both work with the assumption that the world is irreducibly a place of victory or defeat, in which it is unthinkable that there should be a common future. The two models of human practice have a hidden alliance; and to look at actual human societies is to see generally a fusion of these two impulses – just as to look at individual human beings is to see the interweaving of the hunger for order and the hunger for fulfilment beyond external control.

What these ideal fictions of human life together both insist upon is, ultimately, that human identity is for humans to *control* – either in the overt form of the construction of successful human performances, or, more subtly, in the enacting of the desires of a given and unconstrained selfhood. Both therefore have two denials in common: they resist the vision of a universe in which reasoned control or liberated desire is not ultimate – in other words they resist the idea of a *belonging* that cannot be dictated or constructed by the human self (personal or social); and they have no room for the awareness of *gift* in the relation of humanity to its total environment. If we are to explore further what might be involved in seeing peace as the overcoming of the polarity of law and lawlessness in the building of another sort of humanity, it seems that peace has something to do with the creation of this dual awareness, of belonging and gift. In the rest of what I have to say, I shall turn to the question I am meant to be addressing, of how this kind of peace is rooted in or conditioned by the event of Easter, on which the confession of Christian trust rests.

The life of Jesus – insofar as it can be characterized in a few brief phrases – has to do with proclaiming and enacting a disturbing truth: that achievement in the terms of a religious ordering of things is not of itself decisive in forming the reaction of God to the human world, and that what *is* decisive is a commitment of trust in God's compassion that shows itself in costly and painful letting go of the obsessions of the self – both the obsessive search for the perfectly satisfying performance and the obsessive search for the perfectly unconstrained experience. Indeed, these two apparently antithetical urges are shown to have an uncomfortable amount in common: the unprincipled rich man, the unreflectively vindictive servant, the person who unquestioningly indulges aggressive or lustful fantasy are close kin to the accumulator of religious merit. They have not learned to lose what they believe to be crucial to their identity, they work in different but recognizably related modes of acquisitiveness. To all such, the word of judgement is addressed: the person who faces and acknowledges inner contradiction, failure, the breakdown of performance and the emptiness of gratification, is the person who is capable of hearing and answering the invitation to loss and trust.

The invitation is in practice an invitation to accept the 'hospitality' of Jesus himself – often literally as well as figuratively. And so it is that the challenge of this invitation is put at its baldest and most alien when Jesus himself *fails*. His actions and words are sufficiently inflammatory, sufficiently a relativizing of the existing forms of political and religious sense, that the administrators of political and religious power, the governing elite of priestly aristocrats and the occupying forces of Rome, combine to bring about his death; and he is left to die alone and despairing, because his failure is too difficult and strange to continue with. The incipient 'new Israel' of the Twelve is scattered as Jesus is taken to his execution. The Twelve have hoped for a gratification of longings for power – the fire of judgement from heaven for their enemies, the positions of influence and authority in the new age (what Jesus himself calls the 'Gentiles' or 'the nations', modes of governance in Mark 10). They have looked for a restoration of God's people that will involve fuller and better answers to the problem of what performance is required of them (Peter's famous question about how often he must forgive). Jesus in yielding to his failure, his appalling mortality, finally refuses these projections – as if only *by* this failure of all that has been fantasized and longed for can he at last 'say' what is to be said; as if the silence of his dying is the only rhetoric for his gospel. In this sense, the cross is the end of both 'law' and 'lawlessness' as defined already; the roots of human enmity are here brought to nothing.

But: to be able to *say* this depends upon a transformation of self-perception. The writer to the Ephesians rightly speaks of the central event as the shedding of Jesus' blood; this is what provokes the final crisis for trust in Jesus. In the aftermath of the cross, the friends of Jesus are left stripped both of their inherited identities (they have become marginal in the world of public law-keeping) and of the confused and embryonic new identities they had begun to learn in the company of Jesus. The inadequacy and weakness of those new selves are exposed as they find they cannot survive his failure and dereliction. Any identity, any reality they now have will have to be entirely gift, new creation; not generated from their effort or reflection or even their conscious desire. To be able to speak at all about the cross as a moment where meaning is given is to speak from the gift of new perception. Jesus has taken his friends beyond the normal bounds of law and lawlessness, and they have found that beyond those bounds they cannot survive in their own resource; the loss that threatens is too sharp and humiliating to be borne. So life beyond law and lawlessness must be the life of God's gift, the assurance that failure and loss do not mean final destruction or emptiness. Meaning, promise, the future, the possibility of continuing to live in freedom and in the resource to love – all these are 'held' in the being of God, which is communicated to us as mercy, absolution. 'Because I live, you will live' (John 14.1).

These constipated and abstract words are an attempt to say what I think the New Testament documents conceive to be the nature of 'resurrection' life. I have tried to set out elsewhere at greater length the ways in which I believe the actual narratives of the resurrection of Jesus work to show the centrality of forgiveness, restoration and gift in the apprehension by the apostles of the risenness of Jesus, and am here assuming such a reading of the stories, and of some of the reflection on resurrection to be found elsewhere than in the narratives. The essential point is that resurrection is the transaction in human beings that brings about the sense of a selfhood given not achieved – as well as an event that bridges the history of Jesus and the history of the Church; or rather, it is this latter in that it is the former. Otherwise it would simply be a rather exceptional 'paranormal' occurrence, whose historicity or non-historicity could be debated in isolation from the creation of commu-nity involved. The resurrection of Jesus may be (as I for one believe) at least the empty tomb, but it is most importantly the overcoming of the loss, the death-of-identity, in the experience of those who had followed and then abandoned Jesus, and the proclamation to his executioners of hope or salva-tion through their victim. Resurrection, the new life from a moral and ma-terial nothing, is judgement upon the attempt to construct a system of action and understanding so impregnable that it cannot live with prophetic criti-cism, and judgement too upon our sentimental assumption that we can sus-tain newness of life beyond the regularities of 'law' independently of relation to a 'giving' reality, a point of personal love and affirmation. Peter's promise of fidelity even to prison and death is harshly exposed as this kind of illusion; he becomes capable of that sort of witness when he has discovered the ex-treme vulnerability of his emotional commitment, and discovered beyond that a continuing vocation, discovered that he is still trusted.

These things are said in the New Testament in an individual register, and are most readily comprehensible to us perhaps in terms of the stories of particular persons. But in fact they have to do no less with our societies. To look at our own nation at the moment is to see, in some important respects, the kind of tension I have been trying to explore. We have a public rhetoric in which repentance, provisionality, openness to judgement, the acknow-ledgement of failure, are all apparently unthinkable. And we see also a 'hu-manist' opposition, a conglomerate of alternative patterns of human living together, sceptical of the possibilities of social organization and law as we know them, sharply and accurately critical of the self-serving processes of political power (exercised by left or right), yet apparently stuck in a perma-nent minority position, without the means to establish and sustain their vision for a society at large, rather than just a self-selecting sub-culture. The failures and divisions of this amorphous 'opposition' are a major source of that temptation to cynicism that regularly overtakes anyone not hypnotized by the claims of organization for success; and this is something the peace movement has to confront with particular urgency, committed as it is to the kind of change that can only be effective on a more than personal level, yet so often finding its supreme moments in the intensity of experience offered by a sub-culture type of group (I suppose that this tension is especially painfully focused in and around Greenham and all that it stands for).

Our social experience (there is nothing very original or profound in noting it) suffers from the non-communication between competing ways of constructing human identity: an ideology of achievement that punishes failure, and a utopian hope of justice and reconciliation that is consistently vulnerable to its own failure to transform more than the interpersonal, and thus tempted to reinterpret failure as success (the classic reaction of the left after an election defeat, the reiterated insistence on the felt warmth of companionship at a peace demonstration that fails to touch public opinion . . .). Both styles of living find strangeness in speaking of what lies beyond failure as gift or trust or entrustment; which is to say that both have difficulties with the idea of a creative forgiveness. Law can allow for reparation, lawlessness can sidestep the issue of accountability, of a life that is morally connected within itself, and so can devolve the idea of failure onto fate, the operation of processes we are not answerable for. But a vision that can hold to the reality of personal and corporate tragedy, the possibility of betrayal and inadequacy unleashing powerfully destructive processes, *and* also continue to affirm that our individual resources, even the sum of our individual resources, are not the only resources for life or renewal in the world – this is a vision that may keep us from the urge to 'master' our identity in the world, whether by the orientation towards performance and satisfaction of 'law' or by the orientation towards immediacy and transparency – transparency of acts to passions, transparency of persons to each other, transparency of social order to personal claim – of utopian opposition, personal and political.

This is not to say (God forbid!) that the gospel of the resurrection, as represented by the practice of the Church, offers a quick solution to the tensions of our social life. Indeed, once you have put the tensions in the sort of way I have suggested, you can see that the Church itself is divided by exactly the same polarity, urged into the same 'solutions' by way of law and by way of experiential utopianism. The Church is itself unsure of how to handle forgiveness, reducing it to the possibility of reparation or drowning it in a rhetoric of a forgiving and forgetting God, so that the notion of offence itself evaporates, and there is no real injury to be healed by mercy. However, this is to be expected if the Christian community remains an historical human community; these are, quite simply, part of what it is to be being whose identity is in process of formation rather than unproblematically given in a non-historical 'nature'. What is different in the community of belief is the story told of its origins in a paradigmatic discovering of a gift over and above the attempts of human beings to settle by human resources the question of their truth or reality, a gift we can variously call absolution, conversion, transformation (even, for one ancient and reputable Christian tradition, deification), but which is firmly anchored in the unique and particular narrative of betrayal, cross and resurrection. The community exists in distinctive, perceptible shape because of this, its self-identifying actions in the sacraments are celebrations of what is given in this. Christian language states that failure is both real and not final, and so offers the possibility of a corporate or individual self-perception that can cope with honesty about the past and thus imagine a future in which all of that past can be held together; but the discovery of such a possibility depends not on ingenuity and effort, nor on a release of 'natural' energy from the depths of pre-existent selfhood, but on the contingency of someone's history, or rather of the histories of a whole nexus of persons and forces in conflict around the figure of Jesus.

What the gospel of the resurrection has to say about peace, then, seems to me to be most clearly audible if we grasp that the resurrection promise has something to do with the roots of our mistrust and violence in our unwillingness or inability to receive our human identity from God as a gift, at every juncture in our experience. This means being able to leave behind the fantasy of a decisively successful performance as a human being, or a human society: building into my projects and hopes a provisionality that acknowledges the possibility of defeat and thus the possibility of repentance. It means leaving behind no less the fantasy of life in untrammelled immediacy of experience and expression, or life in transparent companionship with those like myself: building into my sense of myself the unavoidability of conflict, the lack of resolution in any effort to transform the human world, the reality of moral and spiritual error, limitation and exhaustion. These are fantasies that have a lot to do with where and how 'enmity' begins. Not to recognize our creatureliness, our incapacity to master all the conditions under which we are becoming what we shall become, is close to the heart of our unfreedom, since this refusal binds us to pervasive struggle. We need, as I have said, to take on the reality and inevitability of conflict; our error is often to see this as a kind of metaphysical statement about the inevitability of mutual exclusion and strife, rather than about the ways in which we are formed in the hard tasks of responding to the resistance, the otherness of the world (people and things), and in the accepting of our inability to guarantee ourselves or anyone an untroubled passage through it. The assumption that strife is an absolute 'given' in the world grows from the conviction that we possess a territory to be safeguarded, whether of law-based achievement or naturally given essential selfhood. The gospel of the resurrection proposes that 'possession' is precisely the wrong, the corrupt and corrupting, metaphor for our finding place in the world. What we 'possess' must go; we must learn to be what we receive from God in the vulnerability of living *in* (not above) the world of change and chance.

It must be said again that this is not a claim to be able to point to some realization of 'resurrection' life; it is certainly not a blueprint for 'reform'. It is that by which we may judge all our efforts at life together, and that which prevents us from giving up on the hope of non-destructive human living – a hope that has nothing at all to do with our ability to realize it for ourselves. Let me quote some words of Peter Selby (from a talk given at Leeds during a 'teaching week' at the University in 1985):

> Christianity has to start with confronting the notion of our self-understanding that is produced by an ideology of victory and defeat; and to confront that, of course, means to re-evaluate all our defeats . . . [T]hey no longer have to be forgotten, they no longer have to be your enemies, but can in fact become the building blocks from which you make a new future. Life under that kind of promise is what Christianity is all about, and the processes which it offers people – prayer, worship, meditation – are about the possibility of getting in touch with your own defeats and putting those defeats in touch with the defeat of Jesus, in order that, like his life, your life can become part of the new and better future which is promised to us . . . Your self-understanding and mine, corrupted as they are by our involvement in the processes and the ideologies of victory and defeat, have to be turned round so that we come to see them alongside the defeat of Jesus as the world's ultimate friend, so that the world is befriended by its defeat, and not by victory achieved at the expense of other people's defeat.

We began with the Epistle to the Ephesians on the overcoming of enmity, and noted too the language of Colossians about peace being made with God. If the foregoing pages make sense, and if we follow Peter Selby's powerful characterization of what is fundamental in Christianity, it is clear that the enmity we know in the world is grounded in our urgency to forget defeat, because it speaks to us of what we have not successfully controlled. When we can shed this enmity towards our failures, we have taken a step towards the end of enmity between people. And the discovery of this possibility is the discovery of the friendship of God. How do we 'make friends' with defeat? As Peter Selby proposes, we do so by setting it alongside the defeat of Jesus, in the knowledge that that defeat is absorbed in life – the knowledge of the resurrection gospel. God in Jesus is the friend of the world, shown to be so by the fact that Jesus' death in desertion is not the end of God's promise of absolution and renewal through his life and action. For God, no defeat is final, and that is the ground for *our* trust that no defeat is final. It is, then, possible to stop fearing defeat as if it meant the dissolution of all possible reality for us; it is possible to look at other human beings and understand that they too face the traps of fear, that they share a vulnerability with us that they are incapable of admitting. If we can find, in the light of the gospel, a language for us and for them to *communicate* this common vulnerability, we shall have realized the 'new humanity' that is in Jesus. We shall have accepted the impotence of our fantasies of control; or, as you might say, we shall have repented and believed the gospel.

Chapter Eighteen

'NOBODY KNOWS WHO I AM TILL THE JUDGEMENT MORNING'

Trevor Huddleston's name stands in the forefront of the names of those who have understood that the experience of racial struggle in Africa, and especially in South Africa, is not something different in kind from what goes on in the 'advanced' societies of the West: so much is clear from his work and witness in the UK, as Bishop of Stepney, and as an active and activating presence in so many anti-racist movements for nearly twenty years. It is appropriate, then, to celebrate such a man by attempting a sketch of what it is that unites the various forms of racial injustice, and what exactly it is that the Christian Church's reflection has to bring to bear on what is becoming a more, not less, critical situation in our own society and in the world at large. This means attempting a definition of 'racism' and beginning the task of theological critique. It may be thought that this is both too elementary and too ambitious a project – too elementary because we know what racism means, and it is a waste of time to devote more words to it (rather than getting on with practical responses); too ambitious because it requires a degree of historical and sociological expertise, personal engagement, and innovative theological power that few people – certainly not white academics at Oxford – possess. None the less, the effort seems to be worthwhile, however inadequate its results. I am aware both of a continuing confusion about the word 'racism' itself, and of a rather uncertain quality to some of our theological responses – as if the appeal to a liberal sense of human equality would do the job for us; if this chapter can suggest a few clarifications in both these areas, it will not have been wasted.

I

It is still common enough in Britain to assume that 'racism' is essentially a word that refers to *attitudes*. If we hear statements like 'Britain is a profoundly racist society' or 'the Church is a racist institution', we are inclined ('we' being a large part of the white population – and even the black population – of the United Kingdom) to be baffled or angered. It sounds as if someone is accusing the nation or the Church of racial prejudice, of disliking or despising black people; and it is reasonable enough, in many cases, to reply that we do *not* have such attitudes, that we do not consider black people inferior or treat them differently. This *may* be a self-deceiving response, but it is not always so; and a person in Cornwall or Cumbria or Norfolk may genuinely not know what could possibly be meant by being told that she or he lives in a 'racist' environment. The sense in which it is true that they do so needs careful statement.

Two things compound confusion here, I believe. One is the common radical elision of 'racism' and 'Fascism', manifest in the names of several anti-racist pressure groups, as if racism were simply a function of a particular kind of authoritarian politics, classically represented by the Third Reich and its allies. Several points need to be made about this. German (not Italian) Fascism did indeed rest upon a commitment to the superiority and glorious historical destiny of a particular variety of Caucasian peoples; but if it is suggested that racism entails commitments like this, it is manifest nonsense to say that ours is a racist environment. The running together of racism and Fascism as a single compound iniquity is – you might say – a subtle device of the devil to prevent us grasping the *real* dangers of these phenomena. If we suppose that racism *is* the crude mythology of the *Herrenvolk*, and if we suppose that Fascism *is* the overt and brutal suppression of non-Caucasians, we are dangerously narrowing our political imagination, making ourselves less capable of seeing and understanding racism in the structures of societies, and Fascism in a pervasive and often elusive trend towards centralized authority, the disenfranchizing (effectually if not openly) of a working population, and the militarization of a national economy. Of course, there are neo-Nazi groups around, which need to be resisted strenuously; the fact that ours is a society that tolerates them, and that our police forces in some areas can give every appearance of lukewarmness in enforcing the law against them, is scandalous. But that is where the heart of the racist problem lies – in those who *know* they are not 'Nazis', but are culpably unaware of the nature of their society as a whole. If racism were simply a problem about the

National Front, it would be a good deal easier; as it is, the glib identification of racism and Fascism provides an excellent alibi for the powers that be, because it is so obviously absurd. 'If *this* is racism, of course we're not guilty of it.'

Racism, then, is not the same as overt supremacist ideology. But here the second confusing factor comes into play. Racism is not overt, so it must be hidden; it must be buried deep in our consciousness, needing to be excavated by suitable means. Part of this is rooted in a familiar kind of liberal self-punishment: my good will alone does not secure change, and so perhaps it is impure and in need of challenge and refinement. The popularity of 'racism awareness' as a theme for training events inside and outside the churches, and the development of a whole philosophy of concealed racism, reflect this sort of response. It is not wholly to be dismissed, thought it has come in for some fierce criticism from writers both black and white:[1] there are, for most of us, areas of unexamined prejudice and fear that are none the worse for being looked at. But what is there here beyond the inducement of further white guilt exposing itself to further black anger? If 'racism awareness' suggests that the solution lies in improved consciousness of one's own imprisonment in negative attitudes, it risks making the whole issue private, or even seeing it as primarily a question about white people's minds rather than black people's lives.

To a lesser degree, the same thing holds for the pouring of energy into campaigns for the sanitizing of children's reading. There is no doubt that, *given certain cultural circumstances*, a book such as *Little Black Sambo* will reinforce models of black people as alien, mildly comic, or mildly alarming. But since reading is and ought to be – for adults as well as children – an experience in which acceptable and unacceptable images and proposals crowd upon us together, there is never any real possibility of wholly 'safe' literature. There are circumstances in which we ought to be *very* wary of exposing children to certain images; but if we are really interested not in preserving a child's supposedly innocent awareness but in an effective change of relations in society at large, a degree of sceptical detachment about the literature issue will probably do no harm. The banning of a 'racist' book in an area – a country – in which black people are systematically disadvantaged is not go-

---

[1] For a particularly savage attack, see A. Sivanandan, 'RAT [Racism Awareness Training] and the Degradation of Black Struggle', *Race and Class* 26:4 (1985), pp. 1–33. On some of the cultural difficulties involved in 'selling' white middle-class techniques of group work to the black community, David Moore has some barbed remarks in 'Liberty to the Captives', in *Voices from the Urban Wilderness*, ed. P. Barnett (Bristol, 1984), p. 36.

ing to get us very far (any more than a ban on alcohol advertising at Christ-mas would reduce the menace of drunken driving in a context in which seasonal alcohol abuse is taken for granted). The priorities should be (and happily often are) the reinforcement in newly written literature of the nor-mality of racial pluralism, and, still more, education in understanding a social history and a social practice which has built racial disadvantage into itself (part of which will, of course, involve the explanation of how literary and narrative and pictorial stereotypes are created).

If these confusions – racism as overt supremacist ideology and racism as secret sin – are set aside or at least put in context, how are we to define the term? The World Council of Churches produced in 1975 a brief report on a consultation dealing with 'Racism in Theology and Theology against Racism', in which they suggested seven marks of the presence of racism;[2] these provide an unusually clear picture of what we are talking about.

Racism is present whenever persons, even before they are born, because of their race, are assigned to a group severely limited in their freedom of movement, their choice of work, their places of residence and so on.

Racism is present whenever groups of people, because of their race, are de-nied effective participation in the political process, and so are compelled (often by force) to obey the edicts of governments which they were allowed to have no part in choosing.

Racism is present whenever racial groups within a nation are excluded from the normal channels available for gaining economic power, through denial of educational opportunities and entry into occupational groups.

Racism is present whenever the policies of a nation-state ensure benefits for that nation from the labour of racial groups (migrant or otherwise), while at the same time denying to such groups commensurate participation in the affairs of the nation-state.

Racism is present whenever the identity of persons is denigrated through stereotyping of racial and ethnic groups in text books, cinema, mass media, interpersonal relations and other ways.

Racism is present whenever people are denied equal protection of the law, because of race, and when constituted authorities of the state use their powers to protect the interests of the dominant group at the expense of the powerless.

Racism is present whenever groups or nations continue to profit from re-gional and global structures that are historically related to racist presupposi-tions and actions.

---

[2] *Racism in Theology. Theology against Racism. Report of a Consultation* (Geneva, 1975), pp. 3–4. For further discussion of the definition of racism, see the entry on the word in F. Ellis Cashmore (ed.), *A Dictionary of Race and Ethnic Relations* (London, 1984), pp. 225–9.

Racism is here presented with exemplary lucidity and comprehensiveness for what it is, an issue about power, decision, and definition. As Ann Dummett points out, in what is still one of the best available studies of racism in the UK, it is in this respect closely akin to other sorts of disadvantage, 'one kind of injustice among many. The very poor in England are insulted for their poverty, bullied by officials, exhaustively interrogated before they can get free school meals or a clothing allowance for their children, placed under intolerable strains and then told they are inadequate when the strains are too much for them';[3] though racism compounds the injustice by assuming the right to tell people (including British citizens) where they can live, the right to deport those deemed undesirable. And it is a simpler matter to identify the victim because of accent or skin colour. But the oppression of the poor and the oppression of the ethnically distinct have in common one central feature picked out by Ann Dummett at the very beginning of her book:[4] the oppressor makes the claim to *tell you who you are*, irrespective of your intention, will, preference, performance. Only certain people have the right to construct an identity for themselves; others have their roles scripted for them. Although all human beings are liable to be drawn into the fantasy lives of others, individual and collective, racism and, in a rather different way, class injustice allow fantasy to be acted out in reality: with these people we really can impose the roles we fantasize because we have the political or economic power to determine the options of the powerless and, in some measure, the very *self*-perception of the powerless. Many of the Victorian poor adopted the images offered them by the wealthy, as even the barest acquaintance with nineteenth-century fiction will show. Many of the disadvantaged in our present society will at some level do the same, accepting the social estimate of their own worthlessness – if not overtly, then in forms of behaviour that express 'worthlessness', violence or extreme passivity or the abuse of the body by alcohol and other drugs. And there are still sections of black communities willing to accept white definition into their own imagining of their humanity.

All the signs of racism identified in the WCC document take for granted this same fundamental privation, the taking away of a right to determine the

---

[3]   Ann Dummett, *A Portrait of English Racism* (London, 1973), 2nd edn (CARAF Publications, 1984), p. 150. On the interrelation of race and class dominance, see Philip Mason, *Patterns of Dominance* (Oxford, 1970).

[4]   Dummett, *op. cit.*, pp. 55–8. A recent work which pinpoints the 'intentional' factors in various forms of disadvantage – i.e. the processes of creating roles for the disadvantaged, over and above the economic elements involved in these structures – is Arthur Brittan and Mary Maynard, *Sexism, Racism and Oppression* (Oxford, 1984); see esp. pp. 214–17.

conditions and possibilities for a specific variety of human living, of the freedom to define oneself, as person or as community, of the freedom to contribute as one wishes and needs to the *public* life, the shared conflict and
conversation that shapes the wider community of a state. Ann Dummett
comments on the 'Black Power' phenomenon of the late 1960s and 1970s
that it makes one central statement: 'I shall tell you what I am. Black Power
can mean a hundred different things, but it is always supported by this basic
significance.'[5] This statement has commonly been interpreted as implying an
unrealistic and destructive separatism: white critics are quick to say that the
aspiration to say 'what I am' independently of other communities and persons is a sign of infantile disorder, neurosis, and to talk of 'black racism'. But
this is a giveaway. White domination has been built on the assumption that
whites may say what they are independently of the needs and *reality* of other
groups, who are built into white self-definition. The refusal of that definition is not a bid for an unreal autonomy – though it may need and use
violently separatist rhetoric, and some, black as well as white, may be de-
ceived by that rhetoric – but a necessary move in challenging one human
group's existing practice of 'saying what they are' in just the infantile and
disordered way they are so eager to condemn. And if 'black racism' unquestionably exists, as a matter of structural oppression or discrimination
exercised between black groupings, it is *not* to be confused with 'black consciousness' or 'Black Power' movements in their hostility to white culture.

　　If a dominant culture (linguistic, ethnic, sexual) does in fact work by assuming the right of definition, it is hardly surprising if the reaction is, 'We
don't need you to tell us what we are'. Certain kinds of separatism are
necessary to highlight the reality of a difference that has been overridden by
the powerful conscripting the powerless into their story. From being a domesticated curiosity, whose strangeness or otherness is defused by absorption,
functionalized by the dominant group, the disadvantaged group must become *real* strangers, with a life manifestly *not* like that of their former masters.
They must acquire or re-acquire a kind of shared secret, a distinct human
'dialect' bound up with a distinct group life. Oppressed groups have often
done this even in the midst of their very oppression – secret languages, covert religious rituals, a subterranean scheme of authority relations within the
group. Liberation has something to do with the presenting and owning
in public of this reality of shared life behind and beyond the roles defined
by the power-holders; and this means an accentuation, not an erosion, of

---

[5] Dummett, *op. cit.*, p. 57. A helpful guide to the evolution of black consciousness movements is offered by Chris Mullard, *Race, Power and Resistance* (London, 1985).

difference – which is why racial justice and racial equality do not begin with 'treating everyone alike'.

The liberal assumption that 'treating everyone alike' is the answer rests on a view of human nature which is deeply problematic. It assumes that there is a basic 'inner' humanity, beyond flesh and skin pigmentation and history and conflict, which is the same for all people. But human existence is precisely life that is lived in speech and relation, and so in history: what we share as humans is not a human 'essence' outside history, but a common involvement in the limits and relativities of history. The only humanity we have is one that is bound up in difference, in the encounter of physical and linguistic strangers. Of course there is a sense in which we are all *biologically* the same; but the whole point is that properly human life is not confined to biology, to the level of 'species-being', as it has been called. It is unavoidably 'cultural', making and re-making its context, and so unavoidably diverse. When great stress is laid upon our oneness 'under the skin', there is always the risk of rendering that as 'this stranger is really the same as *me*' – which subtly reinforces the dominant group's assumption of the right to define. The norm is where I or we stand. This risk is one reason for looking very hard at the goal of 'treating everyone alike'. It represents the worthy and correct commitment to avoid discrimination that overtly disadvantages or distances the stranger; but it can fail to see the prior need to allow them to *be* strangers.

But the liberal's anxieties have some point. Careless talk about proper distances, allowing the independence of another's story and perspective, and so on can be costly, for at least two reasons. The 'licensing' of difference, even the practices of positive discrimination, on the part of a dominant group will fail to move things forward if it is simply a concession that does not alter the basic realities of power in the 'public spaces' shared by dominant and subordinate groups. Or, in plain English, the dominant group's own possibilities have to be affected by this process if there is to be real change. Otherwise, you have the situation classically exemplified in the black 'homelands' of Southern Africa: grants by the dominant group to sustain a fictionally distinct economy, with special opportunities for aspiring black entrepreneurs in their 'own' setting – and a regressive interest in picturesque tribal tradition for its own sake. Nothing substantial has changed.[6] This leads on to the second point. It is actually impossible in any imaginable future world that human groupings should be able to pursue their goals in total mutual in-

---

[6] See e.g. David Sheppard, *Built as a City: God and the Urban World Today*, 2nd edn (London, 1985), p. 188, on the dangers of replicating white patterns of inequality within the black communities.

dependence: 'separate development', by whatever name, is a fantasy in a world of interlocking economy (and ecological crisis). The challenge then is how human beings unashamed of their difference and strangeness are to work with the constraints of this environment – how are they (to use a fashionable term) to discover a common 'human project'? The liberal rightly sees that a world of encapsulated group identities pursuing self-defined goals is a ludicrous and dangerous idea, and insists on some kind of assumption that the human race can acknowledge a shared context and a shared goal – and that at once implies, if it is taken seriously, an effort towards shared 'power' in the world; which in turn involves certain groups facing the potential diminution of the power they actually have.

These remarks are not original or profound: they reflect what has been variously acknowledged by the Brandt Report and explored imaginatively by writers like Schumacher and Capra. However much these explorations may be Utopian dreams, I think it is important that any discussion of racism should carry the recognition that the problem of power and its sharing is a global one. The issue of racism and the combating of racism in this country and its churches, the problems (so wearyingly routine sometimes to those practically involved, black and white) of educational justice, serious attention to even the most elusive forms of disadvantage, vigilance about the methods and assumptions of law enforcement – all this is part of what even the least Utopian must see as the facing of a world-wide crisis about the distribution of power. That it *is* a crisis should be clear enough once we start thinking about the chaotic economies of poorer nations, at the mercy of markets elsewhere, the alarming pressures of drought and famine in Africa, in countries without (or denied) the resources to deal with them, and the way in which East–West conflicts poison and intensify the wars of the Third World (not least through the atrocity of the arms trade). If South Africa dramatizes in its internal life the racial conflict elsewhere, its external relations with Mozambique equally sharply crystallize the far wider problem of First World – Third World relations in all these aspects. Defining racism ought to introduce us to the larger task of defining this human crisis overall.

II

The Christian response to these issues can appear banal. The issue of racism is not much illuminated by the bald statement that all human beings are equally in the image of God and so deserving of 'equal treatment'. The belief in equality before God co-existed happily for centuries with all kinds of practical injustice (slavery, the oppression of women, and so on). It is probably right to see *theories* of racial inequality as a product of the post-Renaissance period, as new relations with 'subject peoples' required rationalization — a rationalization commonly provided in the new language of 'primitive' and 'civilized' peoples, further compounded by theories of physiognomically conditioned differences in levels of intelligence, evolving in the heyday of scientific expansionist confidence in the nineteenth century. The problem, in other words, is not directly with the Christian view of human nature. It is how to prevent that view turning into an impotent abstraction in the face of the development of new power relations and the obstinacy of old ones. And this will involve an attempt to theologize in a way that does not seek to avoid the particularities of human history and yet can act as a point of judgement and hope within that history.

Christianity should have no quarrel — quite the contrary — with what has been said about the unavoidably cultural character of human beings. The Christian faith is, after all, a network of communal relations before it is a theology, and it claims insight into the truth of the universe only by way of engagement in a specific ethnic history (that of the Jewish people) and in the new 'nation' or 'race' of those who come to be in Christ. It is, as is so often pointed out, concrete and narrative in its account of itself and its origins. It is not that we *begin* with a belief in human equality and then try to work it out (or not, as the case may be), but that the inner logic of life shared with others in relation to Jesus of Nazareth pushes the community outwards to 'the ends of the earth' — with all the implications that has for a vision of the common goal or project of the human world as such. *All* may now be invited to share the hope of and the work for the Kingdom; all may find their humanity defined afresh in this project. All therefore can be delivered from the claims to finality of the definitions given them by their social and political context — as Paul suggests in I Cor. 1.26. Those without tangible status are given standing by God, who thereby demonstrates *his* freedom from the social order and the relations it takes for granted. It may be too that those with *anomalous* status in society, those whose actual influence cannot be recognized fully in the terms of the dominant pattern (the freed slave, the independent business woman), are drawn in to such a group.[7] In any case, the point is that the society of the Church in its origins creates considerable tension with the society around because it will not take for granted (even if

[7]   See, for discussion of these and other possibilities, J. H. Elliott, *A Home for the Homeless* (Philadelphia and London, 1981), and Wayne Meeks, *The First Urban Christians* (New Haven and London, 1983).

it will not often challenge head-on) the finality and authority of the socially prevailing accounts of status and power.

The more Christianity ceases to be a distinctive communal life to which adult persons choose to commit themselves, the more this tension is eroded. The more 'natural' it is to be a Christian, the more Christianity will be assimilated to what seems 'natural' in society – a process already visible within the New Testament itself, in the fairly well-established churches to which the letters to Timothy and Titus belong. There is little point in longing romantically for the rediscovery of a purely 'sect-like' Christianity, because that would be to ignore the historical inevitability of second-generation problems, the transmission of belief through upbringing rather than preaching, and so on. But we can ask at least what this definition of human beings in relation to the Kingdom actually means, what it is that gives the Church *some* continuing point of reference beyond what either it or the society around it takes unreflectively for granted. In what is left of this chapter, I want to point to two aspects of Christian language that may represent something of this abiding point of reference, and may shed some light on the problems we have been looking at in the first part.

(*a*) For Paul, the Church as 'body' is a system of *interdependence*: no one part can be reduced to a function of another (defined in terms of another) and no part can claim to subsist in its own right (I Cor. 12). And this is not simply a static observation on the underlying structure of the community, but acts as a principle of judgement and direction in its life. In I Cor., Paul is chiefly concerned with relativizing the claims of the charismatics; but earlier, in I Cor. 10, as in Rom. 14, he deploys it also against those who assume the right to set standards of behaviour in disputed matters. There are those who are persuaded (rightly, Paul thinks) that food regulations are of no significance; but such people may see their 'right' to eat anything as a kind of status-conferral, carrying with it the power to prescribe to others the abandonment of their traditions. This is as bad as the tyranny of (presumably Jewish-Christian) conservatives, and is a fertile seed-bed for resentment and division. Paul sharply reminds the anti-traditionalists that Christ died for the Jewish-Christian conservative too (Rom. 14.15), and directs all to the central principle of 'building up' (Rom. 14.19, I Cor. 10.23). Action in the Church must be regulated not by abstract rule but by the goal of reinforcing and affirming the other believer in such a way that the community overall is affirmed and strengthened and moved on towards the Kingdom. In other words, my act must be a *gift* for the deepening and strengthening of another's faith (and I must be open to receive such a gift likewise); it cannot ever be a

manifestation of my status or 'liberty' or 'maturity' as a thing in itself. Paul
makes it generally clear in word and practice that one's action can at times be
a gift in the form of a challenge (Gal. 2.11ff.): because it is a particular *kind* of
community that is being built up, there are divergences that cannot be toler-
ated – such as the exclusive and rigorist policy of some of the very Jewish
Christians Paul elsewhere defends. Compromise here is *collusion* with what is
actually destructive of the other person and of the whole group's integrity.

On the one hand, then, it is foolish and destructive to sneer at the forms of
devotion others cling to, however 'weakly' or irrationally. If you want this
to change, you must not assume *you* have the right to decide for change, but
should ask, 'How can I come to be *trusted* by the other in such a way that we
can both be changed?' On the other hand, it is equally foolish and destructive to say, 'I will tolerate this or that assertion of right and status, whatever
the cost to those victimized and bruised by it.' That leaves no real opening
for change – repentance – at all. Both perspectives take it wholly for granted
that change, constant conversion, is central for the Christian community,
and that no one group has the right to define unilaterally for others what this
is going to mean. There is no alternative to the work of mutual trust – which
already implies a certain relinquishing of power. The hope is for a shared and
reciprocal *empowering* for growth towards the Kingdom.

This is something like the insight of the desert father who said, 'Our life
and our death is with our neighbour'.[8] It is not without each other that we
move towards the Kingdom; so that Christian history ought to be the story
of continuing and demanding engagement with strangers, abandoning the
right to decide who they are. We shall none of us know who we are without
each other – which may mean we shan't know who we are until Judgement
Day. In the words of the spiritual movingly quoted by Sandra Wilson at the
end of a lecture on 'A Black Theology of Liberation', 'Oh nobody knows
who I am / Till the judgement morning'.[9] And this should also be related to
the great wound and humiliation in Paul's own experience, the growing rift
between the Church and the Jews. In Rom. 11, he turns on the Gentile
Christians with passion: they think Israel has been rejected to make room for
them, but in fact their welcome into God's people is only an episode in the
greater history of God's reclaiming of all who have been his own. There will
be no Gentile salvation without the ultimate reconciliation with the Jews:

---

[8]   Attributed to St Antony the Great; B. Ward (trans.), *The Sayings of the Desert Fathers* (London, 1975), p. 2.
[9]   *Anglicans and Racism: The Balsall Heath Consultation, 1986* (Board for Social Responsibility,
1986), p. 15.

'not without each other', once again. The Church's alienation from the Jews is precisely the kind of separation that is necessary for a final unity that is more than trivial. And in the perspective of our own century, these are notions with a sobering immediacy. The Christian must say, 'not without the Jewish victims of the death-camps' – not knowing what imaginable future would find us a common language with them. But it is more important to look unknowingly to such a future than to devise hasty Christian theologies of (definitions of?) the Jewish experience in this century, and to recognize that the Church remains incomplete and in some ways deprived of a fully truthful language for God so long as this wound is open.

That is a matter needing constantly more thought and prayer; but it is not wholly immaterial to what we should say about racism, power and faith. We have seen a picture of the Church in its beginnings as a community challenging both externally and internally the idea of persons being 'told who they are' by the possessors of a certain kind of status. We are all to find who we are in the light of God in Jesus, and that finding *is* the process of living in a community struggling to discover means of mutual empowering and affirming, in the conviction that we shall not live or flourish if we consider any person or group dispensable, or merely functional for our own self-definition. And behind the life of such a community stands the event – and the *power* – by which it lives. To understand the Church, we must look at what generates it.

(*b*) Christian scripture (which includes Jewish scripture and is conditioned by it) answers the question of what God it is that Christians worship by relating the stories of communities: this is what a human group that believes itself to be brought into being by God looks like: from this group, you may learn what 'God' means, in its behaviour, its hymns and myths, laws and chronicles, in its social conflicts and resolutions. Above all, you may learn what 'God' means in the ministry and execution of Jesus, and in the re-creation of a faithful community in his name at Easter; you may learn God in this breakage and healing in the story of the community of God's people, 'the tribes of Yahweh',[10] as it becomes the beginning of a community for all nations.

The point is that the pattern of the Christian story shows a God who lets himself be spoken of – defined – in terms of the relation between him and creatures, in terms of the human history he sets in motion and shapes. He

---

[10]   The title of Norman Gottwald's important study of the meaning of God for ancient Israel in terms of the pattern of their social life (London, 1979).

chooses to be the God of Israel and of Jesus Christ, chooses not to exist
without his creation: he does not merely establish an order other than himself, but engages with it in such a way that we do not and cannot speak of
him only as a remote cause, but must 'define' him in and through the lives
that struggle to respond to his pressure and presence. Humanity is defined by
him; but, for us, God is defined by humanity also – never completely or
adequately, because the relation is always a restless and growing one. Yet the
most basic point of reference for the Christian believer, which justifies and
establishes this possibility and regulates what *kind* of humanity it is that 'carries' the definition of God, is the crucified and glorified human identity of
Jesus. Whatever else is to be said, whatever further shifts and developments
our language about God undergoes, this at least remains: God is not to be
spoken of without humanity, but that humanity is centred not upon a generalized definition of the human, but on Jesus Christ.

In other words, the relations that exist *within* the Church, of mutual gift
and reciprocal definition, are founded upon the fact that the Christian God
reveals himself, becomes utterable, in a mortal human history. God, so to
speak, risks himself in the form of vulnerable humanity – because a particular
human life, Jesus, is given to him freely to be a sign and a word. The pattern
of mutual definition, the *admirabile commercium* of classical theology, is the
ground of the Church's speech and action, so that within its life it seeks to
renounce just that kind of unilateral and invulnerable power that God re-
nounces in the history he shares with us as the God of Israel and as Christ.
God does not impose his definition and meaning by clear and absolute words
of relevation, but perfects his speech to us in and through the contingencies
of Israel's and Jesus's history. While in retrospect we may see a logic, even a
necessity, in the whole story, it is at each *particular* point a matter of human
liberty and risk.

These theological refinements may seem to be a long way from our starting-point; but they may provide a firm basis for a theological critique of
racism to the extent that they spell out the nature of Christianity's attitude to
power. We are not talking about a repudiation of the whole notion of power,
as a hasty reading of the tradition might suggest, but about how the creative
and transfiguring power of God actually is seen in our world. God's power
'tells us who we are' only in the risk and reciprocity of God's life with us in
Christ, as God displays his identity in the terms of human freedom and
human vulnerability. That is the power by which the whole world is given
newness of life, humanity itself is given new definition. And because it is *that*
kind of power, refusing to functionalize and enslave what it works with, the
process of preaching a transfiguring gospel must take place in a community

that resists the idea that one human group can ever have licence to define another in terms of its own needs or goals or fantasies. All must be free to find that ultimate self-definition in the encounter with a God who does not use us as tools for his gratification but shares a world of risk and contingency with us to bring us to our fullest liberty in relation with him and each other.

We have seen that this cannot be without conflict and rupture, or without cost to those who claim the power of definition without noticing that this is what they are doing (and yes; it must be said again that the very enterprise of writing as a white academic about racism runs this risk). The Church has been slow to see how and where it is itself trapped in 'telling people who they are'; it is gradually getting used at least to the *idea* that its institution and decision-makers must learn a new tentativeness in listening to those they have assumed they understood – those they have assumed were 'contained' in the categories they work with. But the concrete redefinition of power – as enabling the stranger to be heard, deciding that the stranger has a gift and a challenge that can change you – limps very slowly, in the Church's listening to the voice of women and homosexuals as much as blacks. We are still desperately ill equipped to do what, with daily increasing urgency, presses to be done: to offer our world an effective, a converting, judgement upon a whole culture of exploitative control – the human crisis mentioned earlier in this paper. And we are ill equipped partly because we have so imperfectly heard this judgement as it is passed upon *us* as a Church. What a Church genuinely converted in this respect *can* offer, in judgement and in promise, to the world is something we can, thank God, glimpse in the effect of the lives of those who, like Trevor Huddleston, have responded with integrity to what the Christian gospel has to say about true and false power, who have so let God, and God alone, 'tell them who they are' in Christ that they are free to free others for that encounter. Such lives show us something of what it might be to grow *together* in discovery and definition 'Till the Judgement morning'.

INDEX

Compiled by Meg Davies (Registered
Indexer, Society of Indexers)

CPSIA information can be obtained
at www.ICGtesting.com
Printed in the USA
JSHW050302300722
28628JS00005B/122